Playing Doctor

Playing

Joseph Turow

NEW YORK / OXFORD

Doctor

Television, Storytelling, and Medical Power

OXFORD UNIVERSITY PRESS / 1989

Oxford University Press

Oxford   New York   Toronto
Delhi   Bombay   Calcutta   Madras   Karachi
Petaling Jaya   Singapore   Hong Kong   Tokyo
Nairobi   Dar es Salaam   Cape Town
Melbourne   Auckland

and associated companies in
Berlin   Ibadan

Copyright © 1989 by Joseph Turow

Published by Oxford University Press, Inc.,
200 Madison Avenue, New York, New York 10016

Oxford is a registered trademark of Oxford University Press

Library of Congress Cataloging-in-Publication Data
Turow, Joseph.
Playing doctor.
Bibliography: p.   Includes index.
1. Medicine in television.   2. Medicine—Public
opinion.   3. Physicians—Public opinion.   4. Medicine—
United States—Societies, etc.   I. Title.
PN1992.8.M43T8   1988   306'.46   88-9849
ISBN 0-19-504490-8 (alk. paper)

1 2 3 4 5 6 7 8 9

Printed in the United States of America
on acid-free paper

For Jonathan, Marissa, and Rebecca

Acknowledgments

Writing *Playing Doctor* meant telling stories about storytelling. I couldn't learn those stories without the help of people who were quite generous with their time and their memories.

Thanks are due to Gerald Abrams, Harry Ackerman, George Andros, M.D., Marvin Antonowky, William Asher, Lew Ayres, Larry Balmaggia, Ed Begley, Jr., Douglas Benton, Buzz Berger, William Blinn, John Block, Josh Brand, Bert Briller, Don Brinkley, James Brolin, Dorothy Brown, Joseph Campanella, Robert Claver, Calvin Clements, Joe Cohn, Jackie Cooper, Tia Dankowki, R.N., Michael Dann, Jerry Davis, Larraine Day, Howard Dimsdale, Walter Dishell, M.D., Robert Easton, Vince Edwards, John Falsey, Mike Farrell, Norman Felton, John Furia, Stephen Furst, Lou Gallo, Larry Gelbart, Jack Ging, James Goldstone, Elliot Gould, Perry Grant, Abby Greshler, Robert Halmi, Eugene Hoffman, M.D., William House, M.D., Chris Hutson, R.N., Jerry Isenberg, Bettye Ackerman Jaffe, Jay Kahn, M.D., Norman Katkov, Joel Katz, Sheldon Keller, and Dennis Koenig.

Thanks also go to Michael Kozoll, Barbara Krause, R.N., Thomas Kurzy, Perry Lafferty, Arthur Lewis, Norman Lloyd, Jerry McNeeley, Howie Mandell, Abby Mann, Randy Mantooth, Lawrence Marks, John Masius, Bernard McEveety, Burt Metcalf, John Mitchell, Christopher Morgan, James Moser, Marvin Moss, E. Jack Neuman, David Newman, David O'Connell, Bernie Orenstein, Barry Oringer, Bruce Paltrow, Matthew Rapf, Robert Reed, Gene Reynolds, Clinton Roath, M.D., Joel Rogosin, Sam Rolfe, Victor Rosen, M.D., Wilton Schiller, Beth Hill Shafer, Lou Shaw, Hannah Shearer, Max Shulman, Charles Siebert, Andy Siegel, Sterling Silliphant, Elliot Silverstein, Martin Starger, Andy Stein, Thomas Stern, M.D., Susan Sullivan, E. W. Swackhamer, Brandon Tartikoff, Jerry Thorpe, Robert Van Scoyk, Elena Verdugo, David Victor, John Whelpley, Shimon Wincelberg, Robert Wood, Robert Young, M.D., Michael Zinberg, and Randy Zisk.

A number of individuals and organizations helped me with the resources and the time to work on this book. I am grateful to National Endowment for the Humanities for supporting an important segment of this research. Purdue University and, later, the University of Pennsylvania also helped by funding portions of the research and writing. The Communication Studies Program at UCLA pitched in by hiring me to teach a summer course as a visiting professor while I was conducting many of the interviews. UCLA's Paul Rosenthal, Paul Von Blum, Kathy Montgomery, Jeff Cole, and Mardi Gregory were kind to share ideas and contacts with me while I was in the formative stages of the project.

There were others who helped at critical times, Susan Grant, Ann Livingston, and Helen Banks, my research assistants, involved themselves wholeheartedly in the search for articles about doctor shows in the popular and trade press. Leslie Slocum, head of the Television Information Office Library, helped make my work there enjoyable and efficient. Marsha Siefert, my editor, offered many insightful suggestions and comments about the manuscript as it moved toward completion. So did George Gerbner and Karen Tombrello. The people at *TV Guide* were wonderful about allowing me to choose photos from their collection for use in the book.

Sandra Dijkstra, my agent, was right to steer me to Oxford University Press. At Oxford, Stephanie Sakson-Ford was a helpful copyeditor and Rachel Toor coordinated the many activities needed to get the book out on time.

My wife, Judy, has followed all of this from beginning to end. Her genuine enthusiasm for the project has mixed with good critical insight, an ability to help me place the whole thing into perspective, and remarkable patience. I thank her most of all.

Philadelphia   J.T.
April 1988

Contents

Introduction

John Whelpley, head writer for the *Trapper John, M.D.* television series, was working furiously to finish the modifications in tandem with the shooting schedule. The final shooting script, a two-parter titled "Game of Hearts," was dated July 12, 1985. Whelpley intended to create a story that would call special attention to the series as it started its seventh year on CBS's Sunday night lineup.

To kick off the season, he and the show's producers had decided on a two-parter with two parallel subplots. One would be a love story centering on Gonzo Gates, Trapper's younger colleague. The other would be an artificial heart implantation, a headline-making operation that Trapper John, a cardiovascular surgeon, would perform. Whelpley had been partial to emphasizing the love story, but it was the implant that quickly became the center of attention for the production company.

True to the program's storytelling style, Whelpley's dramatic strategy for the operation was to focus on the physician, not the patient. He emphasized the pressures facing Trapper as he carries out the experimental procedure on Jack Dearborne, a longtime friend whose age and arteriosclerosis make him ineligible for a transplant.

The surgeon angrily repudiates his cost-conscious hospital administrator's concern that the process will be prohibitively expensive ("Don't put a price on the patient's head"), and finally bullies her into going along with him. Trapper then throws himself into the battle against death. He jousts with an inquisitive press as he gets increasingly worried when blood clots begin to overtake his patient. In the end, the patient dies despite Trapper's valiant effort.

At least, that's how Whelpley and the producers intended it to end. *Trapper John's* permanent M.D.-advisor, Walter Dishell, had not voiced any objections to the patient's fate. Indeed, blood clots, strokes, and death were unfortunate norms among the actual artificial heart patients of the day. But when the producers sent the script to Dr. Robert Jarvik, the surgeon who created the plastic implant and pioneered its use, they received a startling surprise. He suggested firmly that the patient ought not die. In fact, he expressed strong reservations about the patient even getting a blood clot.

In a phone conversation with executive producer Don Brinkley, Jarvik argued that Whelpley's script, however accurate in terms of the past, was inaccurate with regard to the present and future. He insisted that progress on the artificial heart was happening too fast to shape a scenario according to even the most recent news stories. What was left unsaid, but what Brinkley and the creative staff well understood, was that an unsuccessful heart implant in prime time could damage public relations for Jarvik and Symbion, his stock corporation responsible for developing the heart. Conversely, a successful implant on CBS's Sunday night schedule could be a boon to the image of the heart and its corporate sponsor.

Jarvik, though, held leverage of his own. The producers' reason for sending him the script was not just to get his reading on the accuracy of the material that Whelpley had researched. They were hoping that Jarvik and Symbion would agree to supply equipment and lend expertise to create the aura of realism necessary to the episode. With that in mind, Brinkley accepted the surgeon's invitation to have *Trapper John*'s technical advisor, Chris Hutson, visit Symbion's headquarters in Utah for further discussions.

In Utah, Hutson, a registered nurse, was given the full-court public relations treatment. She came back to Stage 5 at Twentieth Century Fox exuberant about the artificial heart's possibilities and about how Jarvik could help the episode. Symbion had lent her two artificial hearts for use in the program. They had sent along several detailed photographs to use in setting up surgical scenes. They even offered to ship, at their expense, a heart driver machine so that Jack Dearborne's room would look absolutely realistic. Based on what she had seen in Utah, Hutson argued that having Dearborne live would not be stretching reality very far. And, she added, "if we don't play ball with Symbion, we won't get the advice and equipment that we need to make the show realistic."

The script was quickly reshaped. Out went Trapper's discourse on Dearborne's ineligibility for a donor heart because of arteriosclerosis and age. Jarvik had suggested, and recent news reports agreed, that surgeons were beginning to see the artificial heart as a temporary life support device until a donor heart could be found. The strong possibility of blood clotting was eliminated, and the implications of the patient's stroke were toned down. The new ending implied that Jack Dearborne had come through Trapper's anguished "game of hearts" mentally able and likely to live substantially longer.

Whelpley made the changes somewhat wearily, but philosophically. He knew that some dramatic power in the romantic subplot was being lost to the glitz of the heart implant. He noted that some of the most emotional scenes in both subplots had to be cut from the script in favor of action and technology. But he also knew very well, he said, that television is a collective activity. In a medical story, in any TV tale, a writer or a production company has only limited power. The storytelling process is shaped from within and from without the television industry.

Telling stories on television is, above all, a game of power. Whether the program is tender or tough, whether it is aimed at children or adults, whether it is pronounced high-class or trash by the very people who create it, the power game is still the same.

One need only sit in the offices of TV producers; walk through the lots and cavernous sound stages of Los Angeles's great movie-making studios; watch the actors, writers, directors, casting directors, consultants, network executives, production crews, and public relations personnel move through the day. Doing that, one feels the competitive tension in the talk, sees it in the pace of work. Many of the people involved will exult in the excitement, the challenge, and the pay. But more than a few will also admit to agreeing with a casting director who confided that "it's a fear business."

That stands to reason, since the stakes can be very high. Television storytelling is an industrial activity that costs billions, makes millions, and reaches large segments of the American population. For many who are involved in it, it is a craft that can lead to fame and good living. Others, especially people who represent interests outside the production firms and networks, approach it primarily as a route to social influence. They see television as a canvas with images that might be sketched to fit one or another organization's interest.

It is not unusual for the two approaches to intertwine or collide. The struggle that results when they do either or both can have important reverberations for the TV industry and the rest of society.

My purpose in this book is to understand what happens when parties with different interests grapple over the creation of television entertainment. In particular, my aim is to explore the way powerful forces within an American institution try to guide TV's fictional images of their institution. The institution in this case is medicine. The focus is on the prime-time doctor show, a program tradition that spans the history of commercial network television in the United States and has its roots in other media before that.

The actual story of the TV industry's relationship with the medical system begins in Chapter 1. The point of this introduction is to show how the story connects with enduring issues that people have raised about mass media and social power. In the next several pages I will sketch a general framework through which forces that affect television might be understood. And I will suggest how this tale of playing doctor can help answer important questions that have generally been neglected by media researchers.

Institutions (e.g., medicine, law, education) are loosely knit sets of organizations (hospitals, bar associations, teacher unions) that hold authority over fundamental aspects of social life. The organizations that make up institutions must compete with one another and with organizations outside the institution for resources—money, people, supplies, permission, prestige, and information—if they are to survive and grow. These key resources are not distributed randomly through an organization's environment. Rather, they are often under the control of particular organizations.

That control equals power. Power is the ability of an "actor"—an organization or individual—to use its resources (people, money, etc.) to affect activities in its environment.[1] Clearly, certain actors control more resources, and more influential resources, than do others. Relatively "mainstream" organizations typically hold the most power within an institution. They are organizations that draw their resources from the wealthiest elements of society—governments, elites, huge segments of the population. In the medical system, for example, the American Medical Association, the American Academy of Pediatrics, and the American Hospital Association are solidly part of the mainstream. By contrast, faith healers and witch doctors—and, to choose a more controversial example, midwives—are examples of medical groups that typically must find support outside of society's mainstream.

In any society, telling stories about an institution is a way of sharing ideas about how the institution works. In the United States, commercial network television is the most shared storyteller. Not only is television available to 98 percent of America's households, the TV set is turned on a good part of the time—over six hours a day, on average. Most people who watch television tend to watch one of the three major commercial networks, ABC, CBS, and NBC. In fact, during "prime time," the evening hours when viewing is at a peak, nearly one of every two American homes is likely to be tuned to network TV.

Prime-time fiction is especially compelling as a vehicle for portraying rules of the game. With an intensity that newscasts cannot match, TV fiction brings millions of viewers behind the scenes to outline vividly acceptable forms of behavior by the organizations that make up an institution. Not all viewers interpret these portrayals in the same way. Many may judge them as "the way it is," or the way it should be, for others if not for them. Still other people feel discontent. They may want to place their versions of the world on TV, to call attention to the organizations they champion and to gain legitimacy for their cause.

Whatever the reaction, though, there will likely be agreement that television treats certain areas of the institution as more legitimate than others. The portrayals may lead viewers to act publicly as if TV's approach is the norm, even if they don't believe in it. The portrayals may also highlight certain institutional issues and concerns for viewers while turning them away from other issues and concerns.

The result is that TV fiction can have a major effect on the perception of, and the clout of, an institution in society. A key task of research on television fiction should be to investigate how portrayals of institutions get established, reinforced, and changed. Surprisingly, that hasn't been done. My focus here on the way the television industry portrays the medical institution is aimed at making the connection between TV and social power more concrete and observable than it typically seems.

I would also like to be able to use my findings to predict how the television industry relates to institutions other than medicine—education and the military, for example. That means thinking about the larger meaning of the activities that will be explored here. A way to start is to examine how control over resources affects the power which an organization from outside the television industry has over its representation on TV.

One approach says that there is a straight line between outside control over resources and control over images. People who take this position stress that commercial television gets its most important resources (money, authority, personnel, services) from the heart of the modern capitalist system, the giant advertisers and the ad agencies. Because these nodes of power are tied into other mainstream segments of society, it is unlikely that network television executives would risk offending the major, established organizations within any American institution. The result, so the argument goes, is that network television stifles debate about institutions and, instead, continually reflects the visions and goals of society's power structure.[2]

This position becomes especially compelling when one considers the *benefits* that flow to the TV production firms when they cultivate good relationships with powerful organizations. Communication researcher Oscar Gandy notes that government and corporate agencies often offer TV storytellers a gamut of resources, including free advice and equipment, that lower the cost of producing programs. He argues that this ability to offer attractive "subsidies" gives wealthy parties the ability to shape media portrayals to their liking.[3] As Gandy points out, these considerations are likely to move storytelling away from being a place where anti-establishment ideas can get a hearing.

As persuasive as this position may seem, though, it is incomplete. It is true that the Jarvik story that began this book shows how a powerful organization can use its resources to guide content. Incidents of direct one-way leverage can and do occur. The sociology of organizations suggests, though, that the exercise of organizational (and institutional) power is likely to be more complex and embroiled than that.[4]

For one thing, executives in production organizations may realize that demands from within and without the industry create conflicting, often incompatible, pressures on them.[5] Each constituency might offer valuable resources, but may, in turn, demand the creation of images that dissatisfy the other constituency. The reason production firms survive despite the tensions is that the suppliers need them as much as they need the suppliers. Producers, after all, can provide those organizations with an important resource—access to large audiences. With this clout, production executives can encourage compromises among the parties that will allow the program creators some independence.

To be more specific, consider the complex pressures from inside the TV industry that TV producers must weigh against outside pressures.[6]

It is a fact of television life that the most decisive demands on firms that create fiction for American television come not from the institutions being depicted but from the television industry itself. Three commercial networks, ABC, CBS, and NBC, pay for the shows. They get their money—eight and a half billion dollars in 1986[7]—by proving to the satisfaction of the advertising industry that they can lure huge audiences who have the cash and inclination to buy a wide range of consumer goods. The do-or-die criterion for the success of the programs is therefore their ability to get high ratings for their networks.

The most direct test of a production firm's utility to a network is not whether it will portray the establishment respectfully. It is whether the firm can create popular material on time and on budget. The combination of requirements is nerve-racking, so to reduce at least some of the enormous tensions involved, network and production personnel have adopted a number of interrelated routines for choosing and arranging the bulk of TV fare.

One important routine for reducing risks involves the use of formulas. A formula consists of plot types, character types, and locales (a police station, a hospital) that have a reputation for success in television.[8] TV storytellers are convinced that, by combining these predictable elements in somewhat different ways, their chances for a successful crop of stories are increased compared with having to generate these anew for each program. They are also convinced that formulas work best through the basic building block of prime-time TV, the series.

A series is a collection of stories that have the same characters moving through them. Consensus in Hollywood holds that some kinds of formulas work better than others in series over time. For example, people agree that a "franchise show" is a dependable kind of drama series. This is a program where the main character has a legitimate reason to get involved with other people's lives week after week. Many TV executies feel that franchise shows with professional busybodies—lawyers, police, physicians—make more dependable series heroes than protagonists in other occupations. It is an approach that goes far toward explaining the dominance of these professions in prime-time programming.

In addition to relying on comfortable formulas and series types, the people involved in creating the shows have developed specific guidelines for producing, mounting, programming, and airing their programs in order to cope with the enormous tensions of Hollywood. These guidelines have political implications. Over the years, they have shaped the way TV tells stories about lawyers, doctors, teachers, soldiers, and other professionals. Leaders of institutions in which these professionals work therefore have strong reasons for trying to ensure that the guidelines fit their liking.

But here is precisely where conflicts might develop between production executives and institutional leaders. Many of the former's routines come about because of requirements within the TV industry. Yet the portrayals that result from those routines might not coincide with depictions that the latter would favor.

Conflicts may take place even if the institution's leaders historically had a strong say about those portrayals. The reason is that they may feel the portrayals no longer suit their needs. Sparks may also fly when program creators try to update their settings, plots, and characterizations for contemporary audiences without consulting leaders from the area of life they are depicting. The storytellers may feel that they know how to insert changes into formularized plots so as not to disturb the most important routines that lower their risk. But the people they are portraying may not like the result.

They may also not like watching criticism of themselves on the home tube. The storytellers, on the other hand, may insist that being controversial is important for grabbing and holding viewers. As a result, they may be attracted to certain criticisms of the institution's establishment, or they may be interested in depicting certain fringe sectors of the institution in a positive light.

Of course, when production firms and networks allow creators to hurl barbs against the establishment they take the risk that a gored organization will carry out political and economic revenge against them and their advertisers. Still, taking that chance every now and then has its benefits. Social criticism can lend a morale-boosting aura of moral mission to storytelling. It can give the personnel involved a sense of creative independence. Not least important, the TV industry can enhance its own credibility with its audience by revealing the faults of powerful people and organizations in the society. The message that "we're on your side" can go far toward cultivating a loyal following for the show and the advertisers.

It seems clear, then, that television creators work under systems of creativity and constraint that encourage continuity with the establishment as well as deviation from it. The result of the complex cross-organizational headaches would seem to be mixed: TV's creations are not platforms for the democratic presentation of a wide gamut of ideologies. But neither are TV's programs mere channels that transmit the established powers' versions of their world through prime-time stories.

The odds are that the relationship between storytellers and mainstream institutional professionals will be symbiotic—a pattern of "you scratch my back, I'll scratch yours" interactions that is built on a common attitude toward the society's hierarchies and privileges. But the chances are also that the symbiotic relationship will be threaded with strong tensions that will force ongoing conflict between the creators and the various parties involved.

Some of the conflicts might even spill over into other media (newspapers and magazines, for example), as each organization jockeys to frame public understandings of the portrayals and the conflicts in ways that benefit it. Overall, the relationships will probably be so complex that often the parties involved will not have fully controlled, predicted, or perhaps even wanted, the particular portrayals that finally emerge.

What is needed now is a study to put these expectations to the test. We need to ask fundamental questions about the portrayals of institutions on TV.

How do the portrayals develop? What causes them to change over time? How much leeway do creators have in depicting an institution and its controversies? What happens when the demands which storytellers get from the networks and advertisers conflict with demands they get from people who work in the institution? What happens when certain groups challenge the influence of other groups on the storytelling process? What role do other media play in the decisionmaking chain? And, ultimately, to what extent do all these activities enrich or impoverish Americans' conceptions of their institutions?

Television's doctor shows are a good place to start this exploration. In doctor shows, physicians and their work represent the medical institution. They bring viewers behind the scenes to rehearse lessons on whom society should care for, why, where, and how. As a result, doctor shows potentially ignite a range of deep tensions between television's creators, who tell stories with their own industry's demands in mind, and medical professionals, who would likely view TV programs about themselves with primary concern for their own public images.

The point applies to more than just a handful of scattered TV presentations that include doctors. It reaches to the heart of a prime-time storytelling tradition that spans the history of American network television. Fifty-five drama and comedy series centering around physicians have aired on one of the three major U.S. networks since the start of commercial TV in the late 1940s. From the days of *Ben Casey* and *Dr. Kildare* through *M*A*S*H* and the contemporary *Trapper John, M.D., St. Elsewhere, Buck James,* and *Heartbeat*, television's doctor shows have reached tens of millions of people almost every year. *M*A*S*H* remains one of the most popular off-network programs in syndication. And *Marcus Welby, Quincy, Medical Center, The Lazarus Syndrome, Nurse, Trapper John, The Bold Ones, Ben Casey,* and *Emergency!* continue to make their weekly rounds on local stations and cable systems throughout the country.

There is, in addition, a special reason to explore the development of the doctor-show formula. The medical world today has changed fundamentally from the way it was when Dr. Kildare first walked prime-time hospital corridors. Of course, the techniques and technologies of health care are vastly different. More significant, many of the basic assumptions and structures that guided medicine before World War II and in the two decades since have been challenged dramatically by lawmakers, government bureaucrats, hospital administrators, and insurance company executives.

Around the turn of the 1970s, these and other public and private policymakers took steps to slow what they saw as an alarming rate of increase in the nation's health care costs. To cap the upward spiral of medical spending, they forced enormous changes in the makeup and philosophy of the nation's health care delivery systems. The developments have already altered basic relationships between physicians, patients, hospitals, insurance companies, and employers—and there are more changes to come. It is not surprising that the situation has instigated concern and perhaps confusion among members of the public.

Tracking doctor shows historically provides an opportunity to examine how their creators related to these critical developments in medicine. More generally, it provides a look at whether, and how, a struggle for influence over television's version of an institution's (i.e., medicine's) reality changes over the years.

My investigation demanded a variety of methods. To follow the actions of the people and organizations who developed the doctor-show formula, I interviewed many of the producers, writers, directors, actors, network executives, and medical consultants who worked on the programs over the years. To learn about the public ideas Americans shared about the shows during four decades, I examined almost forty years of American newspaper and magazine articles. To refresh my memory about the programs themselves, I watched many of them and read scripts of others.

Much of my viewing took place at the Motion Picture and Television Archive at the University of California, Los Angeles. Universal Pictures Television and MTM Enterprises allowed me to view series and TV movies in their studios. I found other shows at the Museum of Broadcasting in New York. The Television Script Archive at the Annenberg School of Communications, University of Pennsylvania, was a valuable place to read scripts of programs that I was unable to view in the archives or studios, or on TV.

I turned to the *Reader's Guide to Periodical Literature, Index Medicus,*

Business Periodicals Index, the New York Times Index, and the last three and a half decades of Variety and TV Guide for magazine and newspaper articles on medicine and television. In addition, I found a gold mine of newspaper clippings and network press releases in the files of the Television Information Office Library.

Contacting people to interview began by plugging into the relatively small network of producers who have worked on network TV's fifty-five prime-time doctor series. Fortunately, the doctor show is young enough that many of its creators are still alive. Most were generous with their time and encouragement. Their stories led me to the somewhat larger web of people who were influential in the creation of most of the medical series and TV movies that have aired on the home tube. These people, too, were typically helpful, though a number of individuals declined to be interviewed. No one requested anonymity, but four did ask that certain comments not be associated with their names. I interviewed 109 people in all.

From all that has been said to this point, it should not come as a surprise that the shaping of medicine's images in doctor shows has been a complex, argumentative process. On both sides, the following chapters make up a tale of respect and coercion, victory and frustration, adulation of the doctor-show formula and attempts to escape from it. Hollywood's approach to the formula hardened over the years so that even the medical establishment that helped create it would today have a difficult time changing key images, if it seriously wanted to. The result is a disconcerting conclusion about the model of contemporary medicine that TV creators have been casting up: under the guise of increased realism, doctor shows of the 1980s have actually been giving viewers less entry into the medical scene than they did thirty years before.

To understand all this—how it happened, why, and with what implications for social power—we have to go back to the flashpoint in the development of the doctor show, the historical moment when the formula began to jell. We have to go back to the mid-1930s.

Playing Doctor

1

"Internes Can't Take Money"

> We are told that writing is mechanical, but now and then a story is written from the heart, to make its mark upon the minds of men.
>
> "Internes Can't Take Money," by Max Brand, is one of those stories.
>
> Brand, whose real name is Frederick Faust, conceived this story of internes who are not allowed to receive fees for operations, while he was lying on a hospital cot recovering from a serious operation.
>
> He was grateful to those men in white who had served him and other patients—so he wrote the tale of one of them to go down in history.[1]

The story about the 1936 film's conception is only partly true, exaggerated by the Paramount Pictures publicity department to titillate the public's romantic inclinations. The publicists were right about one thing, though: Here was a man in white who would go down in history. For *Internes Can't Take Money* was the first rumble in an avalanche of Doctor Kildare offerings that would cover the American media for the next forty years. Kildare inspired fifteen films, seven books, several magazine short stories, a radio series, two television series (one network, one syndicated), a few public controversies, and an uncounted number of toys, lunchboxes, and shirts. The young doctor and his activities also inspired the basic approach that network television producers were to take toward a small army of fictional physicians who followed him. The beginnings of Doctor Kildare point to the roots of the formula. So while theatrical movies are not the focus of this book, it does seem appropriate to start an examination of TV physicians by inquiring into the birth of the one who set the mold.

Kildare in the Context of His Time

Just forty years before *Internes Can't Take Money* was made, near the turn of the twentieth century, it would have been inconceivable that a young physician could become a popular culture hero. Before the twentieth century, medicine was a sometimes near-subsistence occupation whose practitioners had to fight fiercely for legitimacy with a spectrum of other contenders for control over human health. One reason was that physicians often didn't do any good, and too often did terrific harm.

At the turn of the 1800s, doctors had not progressed all that much beyond their counterparts of the Middle Ages, who had practiced with the aid of philosophy, myth, and prayer. The early nineteenth century saw physicians in the U.S. and elsewhere employing a "therapeutic" system that had no basis in any real understanding of the human body and was not really therapy. Devised by the famous Philadelphia doctor Benjamin Rush, it came from the belief that there was only one disease in the world. According to social historian Paul Starr,

> The one disease was "morbid excitement induced by capillary excitement," and it had but one remedy. This was to deplete the body by letting blood with the lancet and emptying out the stomach and bowels with the use of powerful emetics and cathartics. These stringent therapies were to be used with courage. Patients could be bled until unconscious and given heavy doses of the cathartic calomel (mercury chloride) until they salivated.[2]

"Heroic therapy" of this kind dominated American medical practice in the first decades of the nineteenth century. Not only was it painful, it was deadly. Bloodletting could weaken a sick person even more, and calomel—which was used on anything from the plague to teething pains—was a slow-acting poison that eroded the gums, teeth, and jaw. One contemporary observer wryly described heroic medicine as "one of those great discoveries which are made from time to time for the depopulation of the earth."[3]

The areas allied to medicine were no better. Surgeons—at the time considered doctors' helpers—had the status of being one step above barbers. Their handiwork often led to severe infections and death. Hospitals, too, were danger zones. During the Revolutionary War, Benjamin Rush called them "the sinks of human life," places where the poor and the homeless went to die. The description applied well into the nineteenth century. Trained nursing was virtually unknown. Hospital nurses were often forced laborers taken from the local almshouse or penitentiary.[4]

It isn't hard to understand, then, why a great many nineteenth-century Americans cringed at the thought of asking help from a physician. "Regular" doctors looked on in chagrin as millions of people eschewed them in favor of patent medicine vendors, who promoted sometimes harmful elixers for self-medication. Millions also turned to relatively benign forms of healing—Thompsonianism, the Hygienic Movement, Eclecticism, Homeopathy. While not necessarily more effective than "regular medicine," these approaches at least had the benefit of not leaving the living patient permanently scarred and pained.

As a result, physicians often found it difficult to make money. Many founded schools with the aim of supplementing their office work with the training of new doctors, who paid them directly for the training. Actually, calling these medical mills schools is to dignify them tremendously. Large numbers were unclean, ill-equipped buildings or flats that housed a few instruments and a few forlorn patients. But even the most prestigious homes of medical learning had credibility problems. As late as 1870, the dean of the Harvard Medical School explained the absence of written examinations on the grounds that too few of the candidates for graduation could write well enough to make such a test fair.[5] This was hardly the kind of comment that would lead people to place confidence in the medical profession.

The prognosis for American medicine began to change slowly in the late nineteenth century. A number of circumstances converged to greatly increase physicians' credibility. The most important was the decision by leaders of the American Medical Association, state medical societies, major medical schools, and major hospitals to hitch their profession's star to the rising success of science. Discoveries in bacteriology were picked up by physicians who applied them to public health concerns, most prominently the control of water-borne and food-borne diseases. Bacteriological research also led to cleaner hospitals as well as to antiseptic surgical techniques. The resulting sharp reduction in hospital deaths (carried out to a large extent by a professionalized nursing staff) was accompanied by two other dramatic developments in bacteriology: the creation of a diphtheria antitoxin in the mid-1890s and, in 1910, the concoction of "the magic bullet," the first major therapy against syphilis.

Physicians also used, and encouraged, development of a range of new technologies during the nineteenth and early twentieth centuries that allowed them to explore the body with more certainty. The stethoscope, ophthalmoscope, laryngoscope, microscope, x-ray, spirometer, and electrocardiograph reduced the physician's dependence on the patient's ability to describe symptoms and diagnose problems. Just as significant, they encouraged the patients to feel that the physician had access to bodily changes that patients themselves could not detect. With their new instruments, doctors could set standards of human physiology, evaluate deviations, and classify individuals. For example, the spirometer, which measures lung capacity, could be used by physicians to judge physical fitness for military service.

Such capabilities did wonders to increase the legitimacy of "regular medicine" in the eyes of the rest of society as well as to encourage people's dependence upon physicians. That was true even though doctors still had little to offer in terms of specific cures for particular illnesses. And medicine's potential for long-term cultural authority was boosted even further from another direction—by an increased ability to wield political power through the American Medical Association.

The AMA had actually been around since 1847. It was not until about fifty years later, though, that it became a powerful representative of medical interests. A number of brilliant moves led it to that position. The organization was restructured to encourage more grass-roots support by physicans, thereby increasing its economic base. It invited medicine's traditional antagonists—the eclectics, the homeopaths, and others—to join the AMA's fold, thus eliminating the main sources of professional rivalry. It encouraged the closing of most of the for-profit medical schools through its support of a Carnegie Foundation study (the so-called Flexner Report) that recommended drastic reforms in medical education. And it played an important role in making the public aware of the dangers of patent medicines, an awareness that stimulated the first Federal Pure Food and Drug Act of 1906.

From the standpoint of the AMA's public image, the campaign against those over-the-counter nostrums marked a turning point in medicine's ability to garner public support. It is not as if the medical association was the loudest voice in condemning the public sale of dangerous drugs; magazines such as the *Ladies Home Journal* with millions in circulation took the lead. But what was remarkable was that the medical profession benefited from all the barbs that were hurled. A central theme in the articles about patent medicines was that the reader should go to a doctor to get help. For example, *Collier's* magazine stated the following "moral" about patent medicine use: "Don't Dose Yourself with secret Patent Medicines, Almost all of which are Frauds and Humbugs. When sick Consult a Doctor and take his Prescription: it is the only Sensible Way and you'll find it Cheaper in the end."[6]

The years that followed saw the American Medical Association and its affiliated state medical associations extend and consolidate physicians' emerging social power. Having triumphed over their nineteenth-century professional adversaries, they proceeded to put their own professional house in the kind of order that would allow them to speak with a consistent voice to society at large. Along with pruning the medical schools, the AMA and state medical associations pushed through tough state licensing laws around the country that limited medical practice to doctors graduating from those schools. Within the profession, the medical leadership negotiated the ways that the increasing number of specialists should practice and the ways that they should relate to general practitioners. The specialists, in turn, organized into groups that would protect their power within the profession and the society.

Collegiality rather than competition was encouraged, with the AMA taking the role as the major resolver of disputes and the major presenter of medicine's face to society at large. Referrals from doctors were to be the major route that patients would take to specialists, and "commercialization"—advertising to the public or the blatant public marketing of services—was outlawed. In the drug market, over-the-counter drugs, available directly to the consumer, were separated legally from the more potent ethical drugs, available only by prescription from a physician. At the same time, the increasingly powerful medical associations and medical specialty groups (by now, deserving the collective title "organized medicine") guided the relationship between hospitals and doctors into an era that made physicians the captains of inpatient care and allowed them to use hospital equipment at no cost. (Patient hospital fees and the communities that built the hospitals carried the burden.)

So the profession that emerged through these and other developments cultivated a self-limiting number of elite practitioners, many of them specialists, who were committed to the private practice of medical care. It did not all come smoothly, or without anger in and out of the profession. Medicine's drastic house-cleaning and reorganization left in its wake the demise of most schools that taught minority physicians (they had closed as a result of the Flexner Report) and, eventually, the downfall of large-scale commitments to general public health programs as opposed to the individual patient's health. Both developments left a considerable hole in the nation's health care net, especially during the Great Depression of the 1930s, when large numbers of Americans could not afford private medical care.

The AMA moderated its political stance slightly during the Depression. Physicians going hungry for lack of patients, along with leverage on the part of the Roosevelt Administration, encouraged medical leaders to support government payment of indigent health care costs as a temporary measure. But organized medicine made clear its insistence that, in the long term, the dominant model of medical care in the United States should be the private, fee-for-service relationship between an individual and a doctor. Given the structure of medical education, that doctor was very likely to be male, white, and Anglo-Saxon. Increasingly, too, he was a specialist who used the hospital and its expensive technology as his workplace.[7]

It was a medical structure that was open to devastating criticism. And, in fact, more than a few writers of the late nineteenth and early twentieth century had cast a cold eye on the emerging health care system.[8] In the 1930s, though, medical leaders worried most about depictions in the nation's most graphic medium, Hollywood movies. They acknowledged that a number of important films—for example, *The Story of Louis Pasteur* (1936), *Men in White* (1934), *Private Worlds* (1935), and *A Man to Remember* (1938)—had shown a lot of respect toward physicians and the advances of medical science.[9] But too many others posed major image problems for the profession, according to the AMA and affiliated societies.

By the late 1930s, organized medicine began to close ranks around movie depictions which its leaders felt harmed the profession. The physician-critics hurled two kinds of objections in their public statements. One was the concern that many motion pictures indulged in too great a departure from reality. For example, a 1939 editorial in an AMA magazine aimed at the general public agreed that "no doubt, for purposes of drama, the writer and producer are warranted to take some license with pure fact." Yet the editorial insisted that some of the greatest medical feats could be filmed effectively without exaggeration. And it worried about the consequences of films such as *Dark Victory* (1939), "the story of a doctor's unsuccessful battle against death for the woman he loves":

> In *Dark Victory* . . . the girl suffers with some sort of brain tumor, not to be found in any of the records of . . . medical science. The public is given the impression that after an operation for tumor of the brain the patient may then be given a definite time in which to live and that the recurrence will take place without any symptom except sudden loss of sight; after that, death is supposed to follow in twenty four hours. This was perhaps necessary for timing and emphasis in the drama but may give many a patient with a brain tumor and the families of many such patients hours of unnecessary anguish.[10]

Still, the AMA admitted that despite these possible ill effects, the popular *Dark Victory* was useful to medicine since it gave wide publicity to "the fine procedures which are the outgrowth of recent advances in medical science."[11] As a result, medical leaders muted their criticism and reserved their pointiest barbs for movies they considered destructive to physicians' social status or to the fee-for-service system they were working so hard to maintain. The AMA editorial reviewed these grievances and was scathing in its denunciation of such films. It concluded, in fact, that Hollywood had targeted the medical profession for criticism. "The medical field," it said, "has of late been more subject to propaganda than any other type of motion picture dramatization."[12]

The editorial singled out as examples two recent movies that had particularly drawn fire from physicians around the country. In *The Citadel* (1938), it said, the producers let themselves be used in the campaign for socialized medicine. However, the editorial admitted, "this aspect of the picture was so completely confused . . . that few observers even remembered it." In the second film, *Doctor's Diary*, movie creators indulged more effectively in what one medical society's leaders called "a malicious attack on the medical profession." The critics insisted that the film's conception of the physicians' code of ethics was absurd. They said that the picture attempted to portray the staff of a private city hospital as "an avaricious crew of vultures who are defied by a temperamental nurse and a heroic intern who is shot by the aggrieved mother of a child prodigy during a suit for malpractice."[13]

In the end, the editorial did hold out an olive branch to Hollywood and implied that as a result of organized pressure more consistently beneficial portrayals might be at hand. Many of the motion picture studios, it noted, had begun to use "competent consultants to assist them in portraying medicine properly to the public." So it hoped that motion picture producers might yet channel the public's interest in medicine into an opportunity for "dramatic education" about disease and health as well as for "the campaign for good medical service."[14] In fact, even before the editorial reached the public, that hope was to be realized in the creation of the doctor-hero Kildare.

Faust, Medicine, and the Kildare Image

It was almost as if Frederick Schiller Faust had volunteered for the job of crystallizing the formula along lines favorable to medicine. If organized medicine had been looking for a paid motion picture propagandist at this delicate point in its history, it couldn't have found a better person. For one thing, Faust as a writer had an almost unbelievable ability to attract millions of people to his material rapidly and repeatedly. With the possible exception of dime novelist Gilbert Patten, he was the most prolific writer that the United States has ever produced.[15] He wrote under at least eighteen pen names, partly because he often placed more than one story in the same issues of a number of magazines at the same time. He is perhaps best known as Max Brand, the name attached to the Dr. Kildare titles as well as the westerns that include such classics as *The Untamed* (1919) and *Destry Rides Again* (1939). He is estimated to have published more than thirty million words during his lifetime, the equivalent of at least 400 full-length books. And it is said that he sold 99 percent of everything he wrote.[16]

Yet Faust was not valuable to physicians simply because he wrote about doctors with rapid-fire virtuosity. Philosophically, he was at one with the science-driven, progress-oriented message that lay at the core of twentieth-century medicine. Just as important, he was an idealist who believed in looking for the best possibilities in American institutions and individuals rather than attacking them. Robert Easton, his son-in-law and biographer, recalled that when Faust finished reading *Main Street*, Sinclair Lewis's hard-edged look at an American small town, he slammed it shut and hurled it angrily to the floor. This was not the world view that he thought writers should go to print with. Faust's work, Easton knew, stood for just the opposite.

Faust himself was a restless man with a zest for living well and a great ability to turn out formula-driven fiction. In creating stories around a doctor, he was not veering very far from those staple popular culture formulas of the day, the western and the hard-boiled detective tale. Obviously, the setting of the doctor tale was quite different from locales that the cowboy and the private eye inhabited. Obviously, the patterns of action that drove the western and the detective story could not be the same as the doctor's. The characters, too, were very different—the former blue-collar types, the latter solidly white-collar.

At heart, though, Faust's approach to the medical arena had important connections with the older formulas. In his scheme of things, the physician was as much a heroic individualist as were cowboys and detectives. The patterns of action, revolving around threats to life and escape from jeopardy, had strong borrowings from the cowboy's West and the detective's gritty urban streets. And the hospital as Faust saw it was as much a frontier setting, with its overtones of civilization and progress hanging in the balance, as were the endangered towns in western stories and the gritty urban streets of detective fiction.

The way Faust came to know physicians and their work helps explain why he thought their profession was a good site for the celebration of untarnished, heroic ideals. He first got a look inside the medical system as a stretcher carrier when he and his boyhood friend Dixie Fish joined the Canadian Army during World War I. It didn't lead to combat (Faust actually left the military because he got bored), but the job gave him a bird's-eye view of basic hospital procedures.[17]

After the war, Faust and Fish ended up in New York. Faust got married and began to sell the poetry and stories that he had been turning out at a rapid pace. His friend decided to go to medical school in the city. When Fish interned at Roosevelt Hospital in the early 1920s, he often invited Faust there to watch operations. Faust also joined Dixie when he visited charity cases and spoke with patients who were in trouble with the police and the courts. The writer found it fascinating, and he was eager to tag along.

A very different development started Faust on a chain of personal encounters with medical professionals that lasted the rest of his life. He had contracted the flu after his army experience, and its effects lingered in the form of a weak heart. The problem climaxed with a painful and frightening "heart attack" in November 1921. Doctors diagnosed the problem as fluttering of the heart, and their advice was that Faust adopt a slower lifestyle.

Knowing that it was impossible for him to rest, yet haunted by the fear of collapsing at his typewriter or in a taxi, Faust sought the advice of two well-known specialists, Evan Evans and Robert Halsey. They, too, urged him to take it easy, to stop smoking cigarettes and drinking alcohol. When he insisted that these were impractical restrictions, they accepted his decision but decided to monitor his progress. Surprised that he could indeed continue his hard living and hard writing, Evans and Halsey wrote journal articles about his case.

Faust was seeing medicine at the top, and he was impressed. Lucky enough to have a buddy who was becoming a distinguished urologist, wealthy enough to afford the advice of renowned specialists even after the Depression set in, Faust had no reason to question the direction in which organized medicine saw itself moving. He felt thanks and he felt awe.

From the standpoint of the doctor formula, it all came together in 1936, in the apartment of Faust's agent, Carl Brandt. Faust mentioned that the idea for a story about a young doctor had been percolating in his mind for some time. He began recalling some of Dixie Fish's experiences as an intern at Roosevelt Hospital. Some of them dealt with the underworld. When Faust mentioned that "interns can't take money" from patients whom they help, no matter who the patients are, Brandt jumped to his feet and exclaimed, "There's your title and there's your story."[18]

"Internes Can't Take Money" is about a poor, country-bred young doctor named Jimmie Kildare. As the story opens, Kildare is having a beer at McGuire's saloon. Two daily beers at the bar are Kildare's only real respite from the hospital. The intern—who is described as not good looking, stylish, or very exciting—is thinking about his financial difficulties. He marvels at beneficence of "the famous Doctor Henry Fearson," whose loans to Kildare have helped him survive. Suddenly, a young man with a badly gashed arm enters and faints from shock and loss of blood. Acting quickly, Kildare stops the bleeding, runs to the hospital for necessary instruments and materials, sews up the wound, and saves the man's life. Soon he learns that the person he has saved is a mobster. Offered a large sum of underworld money in payment, Kildare replies that interns can't take money. By the end, though, Kildare's selfless actions do yield a reward. It turns out that Dr. Fearson owes a lot of money to the mob. He cannot pay, and his life is in danger. But the mob leader, knowing that Fearson is Kildare's mentor, rewards the intern by canceling Fearson's debt.

Faust's agent sold "Internes Can't Take Money" to *Cosmopolitan* magazine for $800.[19] Paramount bought the motion picture rights for $5,000, a high sum for the day. Faust wasn't involved with the screen play; the credits note the film as being "from a story by Max Brand." The main change was the addition of a romantic subplot. Kildare (played by Joel McCrea) befriends hospital worker Janet Haley (Barbara Stanwyck), a young widow who is searching for her abducted baby.

Still, the thrust of the story was Faust's: altruistic young doctor succeeds in hard-boiled mob environment. Even more important, the story's name remained the one Faust had given it. The author had cannily placed the poverty of his intern at the center of his title and tale, perhaps in an attempt to win audience sympathies for a medical professional at the height of the Depression. Paramount's publicity department seems to have recognized this master stroke, for the movie's press kit emphasized the same thing.

The film and its publicists also picked up Faust's subtle theme that Kildare's poverty had a purpose: the development of a noblesse oblige approach to life. Here, the publicists declared, is "a story about an interne—a student physician who, the law says, must toil ceaselessly in a hospital for training at an average salary of $10 a month." They implied, as Faust had, that this real-life poverty was part of a test on the road to success. A student physician's suffering was the grindstone on which doctors honed their sympathy with human problems and crystallized their obligation, even after attaining wealth, to help people in need: "Thus it was that this tale of an interne, some day to win his spurs as a great surgeon, refused to put money ahead of his duty—ahead of his pledge to aid mankind and alleviate its suffering."[20]

It was an idea that was to have lasting impact on the plots and characters of the formula that developed through Kildare. The physician was not to be seen simply as an educated individual who had learned a valuable trade. Instead, he was to be seen as a member of a modern elect: a contemporary knight whose painful movement through the lists of training had shown that he had the heroic stature necessary to link a compassionate nature to the wonders of healing technology.

The approach to setting that Faust and Paramount took would endure, too. The studio committed itself to placing this theme of noblesse oblige idealism against what the publicists called "true backgrounds." To simulate medical realism, technicians constructed a hospital set that filled an entire sound stage. Kildare and company worked in a completely equipped ward room, outer room, waiting room, and operating room. The director used real interns as extras "to give the production proper background as far as personnel was concerned." In addition, "so that technical details in connection with the production would be perfect," Paramount secured the services of Dr. John J. Toma, the chief resident at Hollywood Hospital. Toma read the script before the filming began and made sure that all speeches "were absolutely accurate." He supposedly ordered several changes made. He also studied miniatures of all hospital sets and passed on them. Later he supervised their construction on a large scale. "Every article seen in any part of the picture pertaining to the medical profession was there by his advice and with his approval."[21]

The studio went even further in its claim of realism by associating its hero with the profession.

> Under Dr. Toma, McCrea, who has appeared in several other pictures in the role of a physician, made a tour of Hollywood Hospital and watched several operations performed. Dr. Toma was also on hand whenever any scenes were taken which required technical understanding and dexterity. These included two operations which McCrea performs for the camera.[22]

But Paramount executives did not want to push their pride in the film's medical realism too far for fear of alienating potential moviegoers not interested in such details. Ultimately, they emphasized, the hospital and its surroundings ought to be seen as merely colorful trappings for a story that was compelling by itself. The publicists cautioned exhibitors and reviewers that *Internes Can't Take Money* "is, under no circumstances, to be classed as a hospital picture, although the title may imply it. It is, rather, the story of an interne, the story of a mother seeking her child."[23]

The combination of medical idealism, mob melodrama, and romantic tear-jerker did seem to work for a lot of people when the film was released in 1937. The receipts were quite good, [24] and reviewers' comments were not bad, either. *Cue,* for example, saw in the film "a fast-moving, tense melodrama." [25]

What Faust himself thought of the film, if he ever saw it (he was in Europe when it was released), is not known. What we do know is that the young intern stayed on his mind. He wrote a similarly flavored short story about Kildare titled "Whiskey Sour" for *Cosmopolitan.* And, in early 1938, he generated the idea for a Dr. Kildare film series that catapulted his character to the front ranks of popular culture.

Lassie, Andy Hardy, and Jimmy Kildare

The idea for a film series sprang out of Faust in the midst of personal and professional turmoil. His marriage was reeling from his wife's discovery of his mistress. His income was dipping substantially from its hundred-thousand-dollar mark in the late '20s. He decided to travel to Hollywood to seek both personal peace and more money. Touted by his agent and publisher as a writer of prodigious rapidity as well as the best-selling author in the U.S. and most of Europe, Faust signed an immediate contract with Metro Goldwyn Mayer for $52,000 a year. The studio intended to use his mass-production abilities to produce the so-called "B" or inexpensive pictures that were the company's major money-makers.

At MGM, Faust flabbergasted and frustrated executives by his ability to spin out plot ideas virtually non-stop. They considered most of his ideas vapid, but saw that every now and then he could come up with a gusher. The Kildare idea came at the end of a dry spell. Faust was under pressure to develop a series concept for "B" picture producers Joe ("J.J.") Cohn and Carey Wilson.

The main considerations were these: MGM wanted a series that could be as popular, upbeat, and family-oriented as the studio's Lassie and Andy Hardy films. The setting, characters, and subject matter had to be robust enough to ignite a number of movies. And Cohn and Wilson were also interested in stories that could be developed around actor Lionel Barrymore. Barrymore was severely arthritic with chronic hip problems and hadn't worked in over a year. But he was still under contract to the studio and, not incidentally, he was Louis B. Mayer's favorite actor. [26]

As Faust saw it, MGM's first concern "was to get a gripping new character in the hero, surrounded by intriguing and novel circumstances." [27] J. J. Cohn remembered that the writer pitched a number of series ideas that did not appeal to him or Wilson. Then they hit paydirt:

One day Carey Wilson came into my office and he said, "Max Brand has an idea for a doctor who has cancer. And he's a great doctor and he wants to impart as much information as he can to his young assistant before his time runs out." And I said, "Well, you don't have to go any further." And that's when we did the first Kildare.

Faust wrote a more flamboyant remembrance of the producers' enthusiasm in a letter to his agent:

Finally, this morning, I gave Cohn and Wilson just what they wanted, and they literally pranced around the room, Cohn clasping his hands over his head and exclaiming, "We've got it! We've got it." And Wilson was inspired to say, "Shut up, Joe. Wait till you realize just what it means."[28]

What it really meant was the beginning of a cycle of films that helped keep MGM king of both the "A" and "B" pictures through the 1940s, made Dr. Kildare a household name, and, in the process, reinforced and extended an image of the ideal role medicine should play in society. At the time, though, the chores of assigning a director, choosing a cast and fleshing out a script were uppermost in the producers' minds. For director, they chose Howard Bucquet, who had a reputation for getting the most out of low-budget pictures. The older doctor's role was clearly Lionel Barrymore's. He wanted badly to resume acting and was ecstatic when Cohn and Wilson told him that he could do the role in a wheelchair.

Lew Ayres, a sensitive twenty-nine-year-old contract actor, was tagged for the Kildare role. Ayres had been making a tenacious comeback after years of not being able to live up to the promise he had shown in the 1930 classic *All Quiet on the Western Front*. He took the role with little enthusiasm, though. His ambition was to become a respected character actor. Now he was in danger of becoming a continuing fixture in what he feared would become a "C"-picture series if it succeeded at the box office. Still, it was clear to all on hand that Ayres and Barrymore were clicking as a pair in their new roles. So the studio shot an unusual closing scene for the movie. In what amounted to an epilogue, Ayres and Barrymore appeared on a stage and announced that they would be returning together in a series of Kildare films.[29]

Based on a plot by Faust, MGM writers Willis Goldbeck and Harry Ruskin wrote the screenplay for that first movie, *Young Dr. Kildare*. The story starts with Dr. Kildare returning to his small hometown. He has his medical degree, and his parents expect that he will join his country-doctor father in practice. Instead, Kildare politely tells them that he feels he must continue his medical training to find his own place in the scheme of things. He joins Blair General Hospital as a $20-per-month intern. Dr. Leonard Gillespie, a brilliant diagnostician who is looking to impart his knowledge to the next generation, sees a great future for the young physician. But because of the continual caustic remarks that the older man makes, Kildare believes that Gillespie dislikes him.

Kildare shows his intelligence and tenacity in the case of Barbara Chanler, the daughter of wealthy parents. An expert physician had declared the girl unbalanced. After speaking with her, though, Kildare is convinced that she has a legitimate basis for her mental problems. He investigates the problems in her past, discusses them with the young woman, and in this way brings her back to a normal emotional state. Nevertheless, the hospital's administrator, Dr. Walter Carew, is prepared to dismiss Kildare on grounds of insubordination. The intern prepares to return home, but Gillespie, who appreciates Kildare's talents, chooses him as his new assistant.

At the start of production, someone at MGM became nervous that the name Kildare sounded too much like "dare to kill." They contemplated changing the name, and Faust agreed, but then decided against it because of the recognition that the character already had.[30] In the end, though, the studio showed a lot of faith in the film by arranging its New York debut in the prestigious Radio City Music Hall.

Like their Paramount counterparts on the first Kildare film, MGM's publicists took care to advise the audience that *Young Dr. Kildare* was not overly concerned with the specifics of hospital work. Posters and print announcements stressed that the plot had the elements that lured millions to movies—romance tangled with the struggle of life over death. The publicists spared few of the standard adjectives to herald the adventure and mystery that surrounded the film's men of American medicine. "While sirens scream [the ads said] . . . and adventure lies ahead . . . ride with the ambulance interns of a great hospital! Learn the secrets of Men in White and the Women they love . . . in the split-second drama of "Young Dr. Kildare" . . . and the mystery of the girl in Sables!"[31]

The public responded enthusiastically at the box office. Newspaper and magazine critics also tended to like the film. Much mention was made about the entertaining relationship between the earnest Ayres and the curmudgeonly Barrymore. It is interesting that Metro released its critical look at the medical profession, *The Citadel*, just a few months after it distributed *Kildare*. From the studio's perspective, the two were very different. *Kildare*, the offspring of pulp fiction, had the clear earmarks of bread-and-butter series output. *The Citadel*, by contrast, was a prestige flick. Filmed in England and based on a best-selling novel, it was touted as "MGM's greatest production."[32] The handling of *The Citadel* by the studio and the press was much more sober than that of *Young Dr. Kildare*.

But a *Time* magazine review treated the two as a package and argued that Jimmie Kildare was in some respects a U.S. counterpart to *The Citadel*'s hero. Like the latter film, the review said, *Young Doctor Kildare* champions the ideals of medicine by centering on a physician who wades through medical iniquities. "Scrambling about a Manhattan hospital to see where he can do the most good, Dr. Kildare encounters his full quota of mercenary internes and self-important specialists, but he is also privileged to deal with Dr. Leonard Gillespie (Lionel Barrymore) who, old, morose, and dying of cancer, is still all that a great diagnostician should be."[33]

Film historian Lewis Jacobs, writing in 1939, went even further. He saw *The Citadel* and *Young Dr. Kildare* as part of a cycle of films that were reflecting heightened public and government criticism of the "social irresponsibility" in parts of the medical fraternity. Hollywood, he said, had been stimulated by growing national agitation for "various socialized institutions" and by "the federal government's attack on the American Medical Association as a trust." To support the point, he latched onto elements in several pictures that illustrated what he saw as progressive pattern of negative depictions of the physician in society.

> From *Arrowsmith* (1931), the story of a small-town physician and of the medical scientist's dilemma of a choice between the immediate relief of sufferers and the eventual immunity from disease for all mankind, movies have advanced to *Bedside* (1934), which exposed the seamy side of medical science and the racketeering prevalent in some medical quarters.
>
> *A Man to Remember* (1938) recounted the life of a small-town doctor who is confronted with bigotry and lack of understanding support: despite his practical human experience, because of his lack of degree he cannot continue his investigation. *Men in White, The Young Doctor Kildare, Yellow Jack, Dr. Monica, Main Street*, and *Of Human Bondage* revealed other professional, economic, and ethical problems faced by the doctor. *The Life [sic] of Louis Pasteur* re-evaluated the great scientist's work in the light of social and political pressure that was exerted to frustrate him. The culmination of the exposures of the medical profession came with *The Citadel* (1938), in which not only a protest against injustice but a demand for a new order of things was clearly voiced.[34]

Organized medicine, though, read the whole thing rather differently. As we have noted, medical leaders ripped angrily into what they saw as *The Citadel*'s militantly socialistic intentions for medicine. On the other hand, they were much more sanguine about *Arrowsmith* and *A Man to Remember*. Their attitude toward the goings-on in Blair General Hospital fell into the latter category. *Young Dr. Kildare* ignited no printed comments in medical trade journals. But *Calling Dr. Kildare,* the second in the series, was lauded by the AMA for scenes realistically depicting the joys as well as the travails of internship.[35] The association did take that film to task for getting Kildare involved in murder-related detective work. Yet this was a cavil like the kind directed at *Dark Victory*. The AMA seemed to be saying that dramatic license at the expense of medical realism was a problem, but not nearly as great a problem as negative depictions of the insitution's structure.

As for the people at MGM's Kildare unit, they saw themselves producing a film series that was respectful to medicine at its core. Producer Joe Cohn recalled that one of MGM's mandates regarding *Kildare* was "to be fair to the medical profession." To him and other studio executives, fairness did not mean that every doctor had to be the model of skills and honesty. Rather, it meant that the central characters had to contradict medical evils by portraying the possibilities, the ideals, of American medical practice.

It is unlikely that organized medicine was ever directly involved in guiding this approach. Neither Joe Cohn nor Lew Ayres could remember the AMA or any similar group getting in touch with anyone on the series. Organized medicine really didn't have to do that. In Louis B. Mayer's studio during this period, it was a dictum that "B" pictures were to be idealistic, uncontroversial, conservative. If Andy Hardy's father was the incarnation of the honest American lawyer, if Lassie was the incarnation of the loyal American dog, then Jimmie Kildare had to be the embodiment of the greatness in American medicine.

Cohn pointed out that not only did his writers have to be generally respectful toward the medical profession, he and Wilson had to ensure the technical accuracy of the procedures that were shown. That did not rule out dramatic license in depicting diseases and their cures. An assumption of the storytellers was that as long as something was possible—even if it wasn't probable—it could be used. But to make sure that the plot was indeed possible and to warrant that procedures were authentic, Cohn and Wilson did hire a physician as a continuing advisor and brought in specialists every now and then.

The importance of this technical realism was never questioned. Cohn equated it with cinematic honesty: "First, you have to imbue these things with a degree of integrity. And somehow or other if you don't practice integrity, there seems to be a false premise and the first thing you know is you fall on your ass. The audience can feel it, the doctors will jump on it."

Still, Cohn and Wilson insisted on the same principle that had guided the producers of *Internes Can't Take Money:* despite the emphasis on accuracy, a Kildare film had to go beyond the drama of medical technology. The producers' belief from the start was that Blair General Hospital should serve as a broad stage for examining human relations. And, in fact, they considered a hospital a terrific locale for a human relations approach. As Cohn put it, "When you're dealing with life and death, when a mother comes in and says, 'My child is dying,' where can you find a better situation?" Note the gender here. The central figures in distress did tend to be women.

Most of the elements that were to comprise the Kildare movies could be seen in *Young Dr. Kildare* and its immediate successor, *Calling Dr. Kildare*. Blair General Hospital stood squarely at the center of things. Moving through Blair were several regulars aside from Kildare and Gillespie: Jimmie's dad, Dr. Stephen Kildare; Jimmie's mother, Martha Kildare; Blair administrator Dr. Walter Carew; Gillespie's gruff but lovable nurse, Molly Byrd; Kildare's sweetheart, nurse Mary Lamont; and, for comic effect, ambulance driver Joe Wyman and his gossipy girlfriend, Sally the switchboard operator.

Several plot patterns that became conventional were there at the start as well: Kildare's insistence on sticking his neck out to help a physician or patient (or both) in the face of a difficult medical and/or personal problem; bureaucrat Carew's (futile) threats of disciplinary action against the talented but unorthodox intern; Gillespie's obstreperousness toward Kildare but his eventual display of affection and pride in Kildare's ability and humaneness.

The doctor's impoverished status as an intern was also a recurring theme, most prominent in his inability to marry Mary for lack of funds to support both of them. Kildare displayed a highminded reluctance to ask any woman to play second fiddle to his career, and so he kept his pursuit of Mary low-key. Over and over it was emphasized that Kildare's noble dedication to healing transcends personal love. In *Dr. Kildare's Strange Case* (1939), for example, Kildare risks losing Mary to a wealthy surgeon and forgoes a five-hundred-dollar-a-month research position at the prestigious Messinger Institute to stay at Blair (for $20 a month) and hone his skills as a "diagnostician" with Gillespie, whom he hopes some day to succeed.

The doctors' concentration on medical diagnosis allowed the writers to incorporate detective work and psychological drama into their plots. Hard-boiled detectives were a Depression film favorite, and, Faust noted slyly, "there are as many Kildare stories as there are detective stories that can be given a medical twist."[36] Kildare's occasional performance of skillful surgery in Blair's impressive operating theater added an aura of high technology to the proceedings. Peppering every film were comments—often by the hortatory Gillespie—about the nature and role of the physician in American society.

Dr. Kildare's Strange Case is as good a film as any to highlight these comments. Basic to Gillespie—and to the series—is the idea that a physician is born, then shaped. ("You are a born doctor," he scolds Kildare. "Use your eye, heart, brain, instincts.") Ever mindful of eternal verities, Gillespie knows that, ultimately, whether a person lives or dies "is up to heaven." Still, he and Blair's other doctors believe that as physicians' knowledge progresses, they must work constantly, even dictatorially, to keep patients alive. When a desperately ill patient refuses an operation, Kildare forces it on him and is vindicated by Gillespie even though the patient dies on the operating table. "That patient had one chance in a hundred of getting through the operation," blusters Gillespie, "and one chance in a thousand of living without it! We'd be pretty poor doctors if we didn't do anything humanly possible."

Doing anything humanly possible even extends to dictating the personal morality and life-styles of patients. For instance, Gillespie, concerned about the blood pressure of a fiftyish man, berates his patient for "living too young." He urges the man to leave his mistress and return to the quiet of his family.

Reviews of the Kildare films in both the general and the trade press recognized the predictable patterns that acted out these ideas about the doctor's wide-ranging potential and jurisdiction. They reported the patterns matter-of-factly and implied that the audience picked them up too. *Time* magazine said admiringly that the "professionally precise" series had a "tried and true" formula that was "furnishing satisfactory entertainment to U.S. cinemillions."[37] And the politically liberal *Commonweal* encouraged readers to see *Dr. Kildare Goes Home* (1940). Its reviewer avoided Lewis Jacobs's procrustean tendency to label doctor films of the 1930s as fitting into a cycle of anger about the medical profession. The review said that the movie entertained by predictably invoking comfortable verities and progressive dreams to an audience whose world had turned inside out:

> . . . *Dr. Kildare Goes Home* is so full of the milk of human kindness and worthy ideas on socialized medicine that it deserves your attention. Furthermore, we see so little of Lionel Barrymore these days that his return to the screen . . . is most welcome. Stressing again that the doctor's business is alleviation of pain and postponement of death, this continuation of the Kildare series takes Dr. Ayres to his home town where he starts a clinic with three unemployed young doctors and makes some intelligent statements on preventative medicine. Dr. Barrymore also growls a few sane remarks on marriage and its purpose that come as a surprise considering the flashy kind of escapist entertainment that Hollywood is dishing out in these hectic postwar, prewar, war days.[38]

It was clear to culture-watchers that the young physician had struck a sympathetic chord among the American public. In Los Angeles, the movie's technical advisor found his medical practice swelling so much after word of his film involvement got out that he could no longer consult for the studio. People wanted to call on Dr. Kildare's doctor.[39] In fact, "Calling Dr. Kildare," the title of the third film (1939), became a popular cliché. Even radio performers such as Jack Benny used it to get an easy laugh.

So Metro's Kildare factory was run in high gear. As was the fashion with hit series, the studio required on-screen and behind-the-screen personnel who had started with the show to stay with it. The same cast, the same director (Bucquet), and the same screenwriters (Ruskin and Goldbeck) worked on the first nine movies in the bunch. Faust himself plotted six of those films, paying his personal physician for advice on the medical portions. In addition, he created short stories and novels about Jimmie Kildare that never made it to the screen but helped fan the public's interest in the young physician. In one optimistic letter to his agent he wrote, "I have the feeling the Kildare stories can be made to last indefinitely."[40]

Two Crises

In 1941, though, the well-oiled Kildare engine began to falter under two crises. The first started when Larraine Day, who played Kildare's Mary, told the front office that she wanted to go on to bigger things. Day felt stifled on the Kildare treadmill. She wanted meatier roles and she wanted them in "A" pictures. Louis Mayer kept putting off her requests, but she was so dogged that Carey Wilson finally agreed to arrange her departure. For Day, it would ultimately mean leaving MGM in search of better parts.

But what to do with Mary? After careful consideration—and perhaps reflecting their anger at the actress—Metro's top brass decided to have her killed. More than that, they agree to the most melodramatic time possible, her wedding day. The title of the ninth film, *Dr. Kildare's Wedding Day* (1941) encouraged the sunny thought that Kildare, who had graduated from the poverty of internship to become Gillespie's assistant, would finally marry Mary. Fans were sorely disappointed. Instead of seeing the couple off on a honeymoon, they saw Mary get run over by a truck a few hours before the nuptials. And, they watched her die after telling her bereaved fiancé, "This is going to be much easier for me than it is for you. Poor sweet Jimmie."

Predictably, Kildare's creators found a way to tie the melodramatic death to a medical theme. Kildare's loss turned into a powerful message about the physician's obligation to subordinate his personal problems to the needs of his patients. *Variety* phrased it well:

> The shock, the bereavement, threaten to halt the career of the brilliant young medico. The old doc [Gillespie], with much guile as well as finally with honest appeal and recital of a parallel tragedy in his own life, brings his protege back to hospital labors. Sad, the story, but uplifting and inspiring in its devotionals and the subordination of personal affairs to a creed.[41]

Ironically, it was an actor's subordination to a very different creed that sparked the second crisis, with an altogether less satisfactory ending for those involved. In 1942 Lew Ayres informed his draft board that he was a conscientious objector to armed combat in World War II. The actor who had gained initial fame for his anti-war portrayal in *All Quiet on the Western Front* said that from childhood he had espoused a "Christian doctrine of non-resistance to evil." He believed firmly, he said, in the doctrine's "world healing possibilities." He offered instead to do non-combatant service in the Medical Corps; he had experience working with the Red Cross in Los Angeles. That was refused initially. Ayres was sent to an Oregon labor camp for conscientious objectors.[42]

A *New York Times* editorial of the day observed that it took a lot of courage for someone as famous as Ayres to hold that position in the midst of the nation's most patriotic war.[43] But the film industry wasn't as understanding. Executives at Metro feared that Ayres's pacifistic stance would affect business. There were some early signs in different parts of the country that this was so. For example, in Hackensack, New Jersey, the Fox Theater manager said he withdrew the newest Kildare film, *Dr. Kildare's Victory*, after receiving more than a hundred telephone calls threatening a theater boycott if it were not removed from the double bill.[44] Believing that a trend was developing, MGM president Nicholas Schenck huffed, "Lew Ayres is washed up with us since he's washed himself up with the public."[45] *Variety*, fueling the fire in a front-page editorial, labeled the actor "a disgrace to the industry."[46] Some exhibition chains began to cancel film bookings of all existing Lew Ayres films.[47]

But it soon became evident to MGM executives that they had overreacted. For one thing, the company had more than one million dollars invested in films starring Lew Ayres, and it made little economic sense to dismiss them so abruptly. So, it did not take long for Metro executives to announce that they had conducted an "impartial" and "comprehensive" survey of public opinion in theaters around the country and found little resistance to Ayres films. A studio official even suggested that the public had shown more tolerance in the matter than had theater executives.[48] Accordingly, the three Kildare flicks that were making the theater rounds at the time continued to be shown.[49]

Yet MGM was firm that no other movies with the actor be made. Substituting someone else as Kildare was out of the question; studio executives felt that Ayres was irrevocably identified with the doctor in the mind of the audience. So the next installment in the medical series, which had already begun shooting, was reshaped at a cost of $100,000. The screenplay was rewritten; Kildare references were removed; and the central character was transformed into a Dutch physician.[50]

Frederick Faust, whose unfilmed Kildare scenarios would have to submit to the same fate or go unused, was initially furious that the actor who played his heroic medico should refuse to bear arms. His resentment cooled as he learned that Ayres did eventually join the Army Medical Corps, serving courageously as a non-combatant under fire during a number of Pacific beachhead invasions. Ironically, it was as a non-combatant in the Second World War that Faust met his own end. He got involved as a correspondent for *Harper's* magazine. Unarmed except for a club cut from an olive tree, the fifty-two-year-old writer was shot in the chest while advancing with troops during the 1944 invasion of Italy.

Two years before that, MGM executives had decided how to salvage their lucrative medical series. The idea was to let it go on by keeping the same cast (sans Ayres) and using Dr. Gillespie (Lionel Barrymore) as the central character. With direct creative control remaining with Cohn, Williams, Ruskin, and Goldbeck, the five Gillespie films that emerged from 1942 through 1947 were similar in approach to the Kildare installments. Each movie's three subplots allowed the interweaving of medical mystery (amnesia, mental illness) with melodrama. These were punctuated liberally with scenes in which Barrymore growled comically at the hospital staff, interns (especially Van Johnson in four pictures and the Chinese actor Keye Luke in five), and a succession of patients (most often women or children). The proceedings also gave Gillespie several opportunities to perorate along established lines about the role of the physician in society. In *Dark Delusion* (1947), for example, the old man reminds a young physician falsely accused of malpractice that the public has the right to demand a lot of the medical profession:

> Who's ever fair to a doctor? Does your Hippocratic Oath guarantee that your patients are going to be fair to you? Or does it just obligate you to be fair to them? And remember: A doctor must sink or swim; he must quit or carry on. And a good doctor should always have the courage to make that decision!

Dark Delusion marked the last film in the Gillespie series. Two years later, though, MGM mined its Kildare lode in yet another way. With Ayres back from the war and looking for work, the studio teamed him and Barrymore in a syndicated half-hour radio series, *The Story of Doctor Kildare*. It retreaded the Blair General Hospital routines yet again. This time, though, the cast was new aside from Ayres and Barrymore. The production staff was also new, and writing was done on a freelance basis.

The introduction opened with the announcer shouting, "The Story of Doctor Kildare," then shifted to Ayres reading the Hippocratic oath. "Whatsoever house I enter, there will I go for the benefit of the sick, and whatsoever things I see or hear concerning the life of men, I will keep silence thereon, counting such things to be held as sacred trusts." The announcer, reclaiming the mike, called the program "an exciting, heartwarming series." He then described the setting: "Blair General Hospital, one of the great citadels of American medicine. A clump of gray-white buildings planted deep in the heart of New York, the nerve center of medical progress, where great minds and skilled hands wage man's everlasting battle against death and disease. Blair General Hospital: where life begins, where life ends, where life goes on."

The stories that followed were not nearly as exciting or literate as the introduction implied. The writers typically set a melodramatic situation with a medical pretext—an asthmatic orphan, a fainting truck driver, Kildare needing to perform emergency surgery on himself—against attempts at comedy that took Barrymore's blusterings to even greater lengths than the Gillespie films did. Ayres, who believed that the Kildare films were "soapy," thought the radio show was even more so, even though he wrote a few of the episodes.

The series held on until 1952, but it never ignited anything like the public enthusiasm that the films had sparked. Still, a generation had come to know the pathways and ideals of modern medicine through the eyes of Jimmie Kildare. Moreover, a formula of popular culture had crystallized. The setting was the large metropolitan hospital, a place where a Grand Hotel of interesting patients could reasonably show up. The main characters were two physicians, a neophyte and an older sage, with nurses, orderlies, and the hospital administrator revolving around them.

The patterned plots acted out themes that both glorified establishment medicine and placed heavy responsibilities on it. Doctors were society's champions in the modern struggle against death from disease. The public had the explicit right to demand a lot from their scientific warriors. Physicians had to do all that was possible, even in the face of personal sacrifice, to help patients. And they had to know the importance of getting professionally immersed in patients' problems, of showing that they care even while using increasingly impersonal technologies.

These depictions fit the perspective that the American Medical Association wanted to convey about the health care system. As the organization most involved in reshaping the structure and image of American medicine in the early twentieth century, the AMA was clearly interested in media visions that would help its cause. Yet, as we have seen, the creation of Jimmie Kildare was not a direct result of promotional efforts by any part of the medical establishment. It was, in its most basic sense, the formularized response to a storytelling need by a prolific American writer whose path happened to cross medicine's.

At the same time, the impetus for the Kildare formula cannot be laid fully at the feet of an independent creator. Frederick Schiller Faust was clearly influenced by his era's public messages about medical science, perceptions that the AMA and its affiliates were working to mold. Just as clearly, producers at Paramount and MGM were quite concerned with staying in tune with the medical establishment when it came to depicting health care heroes.

This concern reflected the studios' general policy toward institutions in their pictures, a decision to swim with the mainstream when it came to matters of professional portrayal. In Metro Goldwyn Mayer's case, it seems that caution about offending organized medicine was also a specific response to the AMA's public anger about previous films. AMA film critiques seem to have reinforced the producers' decisions to stay in the medical establishment's good graces when it came to a bread-and-butter film series.

A convergence of a number of mainstream interests at a particular point in time, then, served to cultivate Kildare and catapult him onto the nation's screens. A decade later the Kildare name would attract even larger numbers to a television version of Blair General Hospital. In the meantime, though, as the movies and radio gave way to television as the nation's most shared storyteller, a creator with some similar interests to Faust would try to place his own stamp on the form. The upshot, the most popular doctor show of the 1950s, would try to push medical storytelling in what its creator felt was a very different direction from the course Faust had set.

2

"No Compromise with Truth"

When James Moser, the creator of *Medic*, finally got the show on the air in 1954, it was clear to all who cared that the future of the medical drama on television was at a crossroads. *Medic* wasn't TV's first doctor show, but it was the first hit prime-time program about a physician. More important, the program was pivotal in the development of the form, as much for what it failed to change in the formula as for the precedents it set.

"Realism" was what Moser wanted the show to be remembered for. He saw realism as so important that he actually insisted on living many of his scripts. He wore a hearing aid when writing about deafness, he lay in an iron lung before turning out a script on polio, and he haunted the corridors of Los Angeles County Hospital in search of the kind of realism for which the show had become famous.[1]

The realism theme made a good publicity hook. The Dow Chemical Company, the half-hour show's initial sponsor, recognized this from the start. A full-page ad that Dow placed in magazines and newspapers during *Medic*'s premiere week carried a drawing of a masked surgeon staring at the reader from a television set. The ad's headline shouted that *"Medic* starts September 13! 'No compromise with truth' makes *Medic* top television drama" The copy below the banner supported the claim by pointing to the program's lineage:

> . . . Remember the name. *Medic*. With unparalleled realism and honesty it portrays case histories and carries the official endorsement of the Los Angeles Medical Association. It is produced under their technical supervision by Worthington Miner, originator of Studio One; created and written by *Dragnet* writer, James Moser. The Dow Chemical Company is proud to present a program of such exceptional merit.[2]

An enthusiastic press spread the claim of high-quality realism quickly. Here was a show "whose camera crews had access to nearly every hospital in the [Los Angeles] area," and whose stories dealt unflinchingly with subjects such as unwed mothers, toxemia and pregnancy, manic depression, and corneal transplants.[3] *Newsweek* called the series "impressive."[4] *Look* wrote of Moser's "well-documented scripts," and emphasized that "details are checked, then double-checked."[5] *TV Guide* called the program "a new kind of TV shocker" and said that viewers were calling the series unusual, controversial, startling. The popular magazine said that the series "is telling the story of the medical profession without pulling any punches" and emphasized Moser's deep commitment to his subject.[6]

For his part, Moser reveled in the praise and promised to maintain the program's tone. "So far NBC has been pretty broadminded about it," he told *TV Guide* a month after *Medic*'s premiere. "They're up against something brand new and seem willing to go along, at least until the roof caves in. I don't think it will."[7]

But a year and a half later it did. To understand why, and to follow its implications for the prime-time doctor shows that followed, we have to back up and find out how James Moser fit into the television and medical systems of his day. As with the Kildare film series, several organizational influences that surrounded Moser helped to shape the program. Where Faust had the magazines and movie studios, Moser had the network; where Kildare's fate rested partly with nervous theater owners, Moser had to be wary of jittery local broadcast affiliates. Advertisers, absent in the film industry, played a new and critical part in *Medic*'s rise and fall. So did the Los Angeles County Medical Association, which previously had not been involved as a major player in theatrical or TV storytelling.

It was, in fact, the County Medical Association's entry into the TV arena that was *Medic*'s most important legacy. *Medic*'s advertisers and network pushed Moser into a predicament that virtually invited the use of a powerful medical organization to help produce a "realistic" show. The result was the beginning of a symbiotic relationship between doctor-show producers and powerful medical organizations that was to shape the boundaries of medical portrayals on prime time for decades.

As in Faust's case, however, none of these organizational influences adequately explains the creative spark that ignited the idea or the perspective on medicine that infused the show with an awe toward physicians even before the medical association came on the scene. Bringing the personal, environmental, and organizational influences together means getting a handle on three aspects of the world that fed into Moser's insistent tinkering with the formula: the position of medicine in post-World War II America, the way that Moser related to the medical system and to popular culture's images of it, and the strategies of television's advertisers and networks in the mid-1950s.

American Medicine at Mid-Century

During the 1950s, American medicine was powerful, and its leaders had every reason to be sure that their profession would grow even more powerful. All the signs were there. The United States was on its way to building a medical research and clinical establishment that dwarfed anything that had come before it. The nation was enlarging and equipping the most scientifically advanced hospitals in the world. Its medical work force, 1.2 million people in 1950, was climbing rapidly.[8] So were the nation's health care expenditures, which would soar from $12.7 billion in 1950 to $71.6 billion in two decades (up from 4.5 to 7.3 percent of the gross national product).[9]

It was in the 1950s that medicine began to take center stage in the nation's budget priorities. Organized medicine showed tremendous political clout on that stage. The American Medical Association and its coalition of medical interest groups guided federal and state legislators toward laws and policies designed to shape medicine's growth in ways that medical leaders wanted it shaped. Funding issues caused the greatest controversies. Although organized medicine accepted government support of hospitals and medical schools in the booming postwar economy, medical organizations united in opposing attempts to shape hospitals or health programs along lines that weakened the professional sovereignty of the private physician.[10] In particular, government attempts to intrude into the fee-for-service doctor-patient relationship through publicly sponsored programs raised red flags.

By far the most dramatic example of organized medicine's power in American society at mid-century was the way it went about burying national health insurance. The idea of national health insurance had been around for decades, and it had built up a lot of political support during the Depression of the 1930s. After World War II, President Truman and other government leaders declared that the time had come to institute such a program. The AMA immediately dubbed the idea rampant socialism and added that it would be an unwanted government intrusion into the cherished physician-patient relationship. As an alternative, organized medicine supported private insurance plans that would help defray medical costs but would not disturb the entrepreneurial nature of medical practice.[11]

The ins and outs of the battle are too complex for brief summary here. The relevant point is that one cannot simply attribute the medical establishment's victory to physicians' wealth or the nation's fear of socialism. Rather, it was most of all the result of medicine's ability to garner support throughout America's power structure. The general corporate sector, convinced that national health insurance would increase its costs, fell in with the medical establishment. And media and government representatives fell prey both to formal lobbying by medical interests as well as to informal arm twisting by their own doctors.[12]

At base, though, medical leaders were able to exert their collective will because of their institution's wide social legitimacy: most people felt that the medical system was delivering the goods. Tying medicine to the fruits of science had yielded great benefits during the first fifty years of the twentieth century. By the end of the Second World War, penicillin and the sulfonamides, better vaccines, and improved hygiene had all but conquered yellow fever, dysentery, typhus, tetanus, pneumonia, and meningitis. Malaria could be controlled. Disability from venereal disease had been radically reduced. The hazards of surgery had also been reduced through the increased availability of blood and plasma for transfusions. To many people, this progress was brought home dramatically through the following postwar announcement: compared with World War I, the Army death rate from disease in World War II had fallen from 14.1 to 0.6 per 1,000 soldiers.[13]

Many other medical achievements made the news as well. The term "wonder drug" was in vogue, and periodicals wrote often about the latest ones. Also in vogue was discussion about the limitless possibilities of medical science. Beginning 1937, the American Foundation for Infantile Paralysis started a mass fund-raising effort aimed at eliminating polio. Not only was this March of Dimes hugely successful from a monetary standpoint, it had the good fortune to end eighteen years later in a medical victory. In 1954, the year *Medic* premiered on NBC, millions of Americans participated voluntarily—at risks to themselves and their loved ones—in trials of the vaccine. Then, on April 12, 1955, epidemiologists at the University of Michigan announced that the vaccine had worked. In describing the ecstatic national reaction, one observer wrote that "more than a scientific achievement, the vaccine was a folk victory."[14]

Although political and technological battles were being won handily by organized medicine, some deep problems were emerging. Of greatest importance to doctors of the day was the perception that the traditional physician-patient relationship that they were presumably fighting so hard to preserve seemed to be slipping away. Over and over during the 1950s, articles in medical journals voiced a feeling of declining professional prestige, what one doctor called the public's anger "against the doctor as man and citizen."[15]

Medical leaders were sure that this antagonism was new for their generation and that it was on the increase. A number of physician organizations hired the famous motivation researcher, Ernst Dichter, Ph.D., to diagnose the problem and recommend solutions. In his report to his sponsors, Dichter didn't link that tension to high doctor bills or organized medicine's agressive stance against national health insurance. Instead, he tied it to the general "desire for emotional security" in "modern culture." He argued that the human aspect in the doctor-patient relationship had fallen far behind technological advances. Confronting the modern doctor, the modern patient was often made to feel like an ignoramus confronting a clique. People want just the opposite, the psychologist said. They want to come back to "the kind of relationship on an emotional level that they used to have with their doctor, but in a more developed and scientifically more dependable form."[16]

Dichter pointed out that companies such as General Mills had developed "a personality like Betty Crocker" in order to establish an emotional connection with members of the public. His solution for medicine was similarly image-related, but less media-oriented. It urged a crusade by organized medicine to make physicians at the grass-roots level concerned about providing emotional security for their patients.[17] Still, Dichter's allusion to Betty Crocker was both apt and instructive. Medical leaders were increasingly seeing their profession's image problems through the lenses of contemporary public relations, and that meant active interest in image making at the media level as well as the grass-roots level.

The writers of articles in medical journals seemed optimistic that the image problems could be overcome. Of course, this would not mean that the U.S. health care system would be free of difficulties. The poor still had inadequate care, they admitted. The increasing tendency of physicians to choose specialties was playing down the long-term importance of primary care to the society. The emphasis on research and high technology was introducing a spiral of public investments that would threaten years later to get out of hand. And the ability of medicine to keep people alive without really returning them to society was beginning to raise painful moral dilemmas about the physician's role in life and death.

Yet these issues got drowned in a flood of social optimism. Even the liberals who favored national health insurance marveled at the accomplishments of medical science and looked forward to seeing its future accomplishments. Medical science, they felt, could help bring humane answers to such intractable problems as the social management of delinquency, alcoholism, mental illness, and sexual deviation. The poor may have felt neglected in their everyday health problems. But the broad middle and upper- middle classes had no reason to doubt the existence and value of medical progress.

Moser, Medicine, and Popular Culture

It was in this middle- and upper-middle-class world that James Moser found himself at the start of the 1950s. Solidly in his thirties, married with two young children, with a top scripting job on one of radio's most popular shows; he had come far since his $1.46-an-hour newswriting slot in ABC Radio's San Francisco bureau. Now wasn't the first time that occupational restlessness had bitten him, and it wouldn't be the last. A pre-law major at a college near San Francisco, he had decided to switch to journalism upon graduation. That had led to a stint as a copy boy at the *San Francisco Examiner;* then to a hitch on a steamer to Sydney, Australia; some journalism work in Australia; and back to the States and the ABC job.

It was at ABC that he met Jack Webb, a young actor and producer who needed some radio writing help. Webb was a workaholic. He often expected people who worked with him to be workaholics, too, and by many accounts he was a difficult person to like. But Moser inhaled Webb's fascination with the everyday heroics of the police detective. Working with Webb on *Dragnet* from its beginning in 1949, Moser found a terrific entry into a new career. For his part, Webb seemed to find in Moser's journalistic flair the kind of writing he needed for his new police detective show.

After two and a half years, though, Moser concluded that Webb's spartan work demands got to be a bit much. By then, too, Moser had become excited about developing a series of his own. He wanted it to be for television. *Dragnet* had made the move to TV and was doing very well. Moser was certain that a *Dragnet*-like show about another institutional hero, the doctor, would catch on too.

Writing about doctors was not totally new for Moser. In 1949, Metro Goldwyn Mayer had hired him freelance to write a couple of scripts for MGM's syndicated *Dr. Kildare* radio drama. Moser was sure that he wasn't asked back because the show's producers judged his scripts not melodramatic enough.

In 1951, he had tried his hand at medical drama again. He and Jack Webb had written and produced a half-hour radio pilot called "The Doctor" for NBC. Both had felt that since that network was flying high with *Dragnet*, its executives would welcome a similarly styled show about medicine. They were wrong. NBC ran the program, which starred Richard Boone, as a one-shot in the summer but declined to let it go to series. Thirty-five years later, Moser remembered little about the show, which was described by *Look* magazine as a "radio medical documentary." He did remember thinking that it was a little too "clinical" for network executives.

That might have been Moser's last foray into medical drama had it not been for William House, an intern at L.A. County Hospital. Moser's wife had been close with House's wife when they were growing up in San Francisco. When Bill's residency took the Houses to Los Angeles, the two women re-established their relationship, and the two husbands became friends as well. Bill House became for Moser what Dixie Fish was for Frederick Faust. One day, House suggested that his writer friend visit County to see what hospital medicine was like. Moser did:

And boy, it was really fascinating [he recalled]. Seeing all these young kids—the interns and the residents—at work, really covering the territory. The realism—wow, this was it. And, you know, it was positive, it was really great. Instead of killing somebody, they were saving somebody. And the drama was there.

Moser hadn't quit *Dragnet* yet, but he told his agent, "Listen, the first chance I get I'm gonna take off and do some research at County." A short while afterward, he used a falling out with Webb as the pretext he needed to leave and gather materials for the medical series of his dreams.

While he wasn't quite sure what he would come up with, he knew what he didn't want. He had "checked out everything that had been done" on TV and radio during the past several years. That confirmed his expectation that "it was all soapy." Moser used the term "soapy" to mean overly romantic and unrealistic programming that focused on relationships between people and not on medicine. NBC had run *The Doctor* on TV in 1952 and CBS had *City Hospital* as a drama in 1954, and Moser knew that they fit his description. But he singled out in particular the two most popular doctor images of the time, Dr. Jimmie Kildare and Dr. Paul Christian.

They were a tough pair to move against. If there were any fictional images of doctors that were ingrained in the collective national psyche of the early 1950s, they were Christian and Kildare. Though no longer in first-run theaters or on the radio, Kildare was still a symbol of the young American medical hero. Christian, on the other hand, was America's friendly uncle of medicine, the epitome of the family doctor. He was played by Jean Hersholt, a Danish immigrant who came to America in the 'teens to work in silent films.

Hersholt's involvement with doctors started with a role in *A Man to Remember,* the popular 1936 film about a general practitioner. Soon after, Twentieth Century-Fox signed him for a movie about the physician who delivered the Dione quintuplets, *The Country Doctor.* The fifty-year-old Hersholt became infatuated with the character to the point of wanting to bring it to radio. When he couldn't get the air rights, he decided to press ahead with a doctor series anyway. He mulled over names, and settled on his favorite author, Hans Christian Andersen. He felt that the name "Christian" was strong, and he particularly liked the religious connotation, which he reinforced with the first name of his physician.[18]

The idea clicked. *Dr. Christian* became a staple of CBS Radio's prime-time lineup from 1937 through 1953. It became so popular that RKO decided to do a number of Dr. Christian films beginning in 1939; a novel about the physician appeared in 1944. A large part of his lure seems to be that the actor's persona in the popular press was virtually indistinguishable from the personality of the radio physician. Hersholt's name was linked to many charities (the Motion Picture Academy still gives an award in his memory), and his personal philosophy was tied to a "help others" theme.[19] In fiction, it was expressed through Dr. Christian's involvement with his patients. The good doctor was always leaving his office to deal with the psychological or monetary problems of his friends in the small Minnesota community of River's End. In the film *We'll Meet Again*, for example, Christian is so concerned about the ill effects that a father's arrest is having on the man's daughter that he coordinates a private investigation that proves him innocent and finds the real criminal.

That was typical, and it was encouraged by a script-writing contest that the radio show began in 1941. Instead of turning to professional writers for plots, the producers invited the audience to write the show. The prizes ranged from $150 to $500 a script, with a grand prize of $2,000 for the year's best.[20]

Apparently, the contributing public saw no limits to the general practitioner's jurisdiction, for the new policy had the physician acting as an all-purpose humanitarian. He moved from town philosopher to town cupid to town detective and more. In 1947, the winning script had Christian convincing an about-to-be-born child that the earth wasn't as bad as the child feared. The approach brought the show hordes of loyal fans, but it also drew humor-tinged criticism. *Newsweek*, for example, noted that Dr. Christian led "one of the most active lives in radio." The magazine suggested that the good doctor was actually far too busy at non-medical things to do anything more clinical than dispense a few pills.[21]

A Plot with Zoom!

Moser scorned this approach to medical drama, but he wasn't quite sure what an alternative formula could be. To find out, he decided to crash L.A. County Hospital. To support his family, he took a job writing potboiler Westerns during the day. At night he followed Bill House and the other residents through County. He poked around the various departments and took notes on what people were doing.

It was critical to get a feel for "the whole scene," he said, "because I knew that if you were going to do it right, . . . to present a fairly accurate picture, you simply had to immerse yourself in it. . . . You put on greens and looked like you knew where you were going, and no one bothered you. I got a meal ticket from Bill's brother [also a physician there], and so that was my home for a long time."

"A long time" turned out to be two and a half years. Much to the chagrin of his wife and young daughters, Moser stalked L.A. County's night corridors on the schedule of an overworked intern. Finally, after getting what he felt was a good grounding in every area of the hospital, he forced himself to confront the notion of a TV pilot. His first idea was to script a story about a general practitioner in his mid- to late thirties. He refrained from pitching the idea to a network before writing because he valued the autonomy that went with the risk. He was adamant about not being "beholden" to television executives. Being "beholden," Moser said, inevitably meant that "right away they'd start tinkering."

Writing the pilot became an obsession. When he wasn't at the studio churning out Westerns, he was at the hospital typing the doctor script and sharing it with the people there. His intention was to depict a day in the life of a G.P., the succession of cases that a typical family physician might see. He wanted to show how human relations in medicine worked hand-in-hand with science. The trick, he felt, was to merge the art of Dr. Christian with the wonders of medical technology.

But it soon became clear to Moser that the G.P. script would not get him a TV doctor series. The writing was accurate, but it didn't have the dramatic tension necessary to place a program on the network schedule. Showing it to a number of writer friends, Moser heard comments like, "Gee, it's sure nice, but don't you think it needs a little zoom?" Moser agreed, but following the writers' old dictum not to throw anything away, he did eventually use it as a segment of *Medic*. Still, it seemed clear that the episode could not be the first one.

By now, though, Moser was revved up about the possibility of finding a plot with "zoom" that would make the airwaves. Things began to fall into place. He told his agent that he definitely wanted to do a realistic medical drama. The agent started to get the word out to TV executives. Then came a new idea for the the *Medic* pilot. Moser's summary was concise and stark: "Pregnant woman comes up with leukemia. Acute. Dies right before the child is born."

Moser himself had witnessed it. Visiting the obstetrics section one day, he was hailed by a senior resident.

[The resident] said, "Come on, let's go get a beer." So we went across the street. And he said, "This gal is really something. She's gonna die; she knows she's gonna die. And all she wants to do is stay alive long enough to have a baby."

I said, "That's it. That's it!" And that's the plot I used for the *Medic* pilot. It ended with the baby being born. They finally get the baby to breathe. And the mother's dead, of course. And the nurse says, "Doctor, should we tell the husband that his wife has died?" and . . . Dr. Styner says, "No, no. Tell him that the baby lived." And that was it.

Styner's last line may sound like dramatic license, but it wasn't. It was exactly the line Moser had heard the physician use, and its dramatic appropriateness bolstered his insistence that medical reality lent far more punch to storytelling than medical soapiness. Moser liked what he had. The trick now was to get the show on the air. It turned out to be quite difficult, despite his track record with *Dragnet*.

In 1954, bringing a series to TV meant clearing two major obstacles, the sponsor and the network. The sponsor hurdle was a holdover from network radio. When radio networks developed in the 1920s and 1930s, their executives saw their business as selling time to advertisers that wanted to reach the public, much as magazine and newspaper executives were in the business of marketing space commercially. A network would sell a company a block of minutes (in radio it was typically fifteen minutes, a half hour, or an hour), and the company and its ad agency would be responsible for filling them with attractive material. Companies were identified with their entertainment. Everyone knew that Chase and Sanborn supported Edgar Bergen, that Hertz was Abbott and Costello's sponsor, that Lux mounted quality dramas, that the weepy afternoon melodramas sold various kinds of soap.

For radio networks intent on making the expensive leap to television in the late 1940s, this "full sponsorship" system was a lucrative engine that could be transferred easily to the new medium. But the high-stakes competition over ratings between NBC, CBS, and ABC heated up as TV fever swept the nation. Network executives began to get increasingly concerned about the kind of programs that some sponsors were bringing to the air. They were worried that the size of the audience for any particular program would be influenced by its placement next to other shows. Since the price a network could charge an advertiser for time during a period of the day (morning, afternoon, prime time) was directly related to the past size of its audience during that period, network executives had a strong interest in guiding sponsors toward programs that they felt were appropriately competitive.

The message that Moser kept getting from network executives was that his show did not promise to be appropriately competitive. He pitched *Medic* as a series that would cover the exciting waterfront of medicine. It would be introduced by the actor who played Dr. Styner, the G.P., but the series would be an anthology. Its stories would zero in on a different aspect of the profession each week.

Moser insisted that the approach would allow him flexibility to target the most riveting aspects of medicine. At the networks, though, executives worried. The first decade of television is often remembered nostalgically as a "golden age" precisely for anthology series that were aired live, often from cramped New York studios. Moser, however, found that, as early as 1954, network executives began to discourage sponsors from supporting serious anthology dramas, particularly properties as potentially upsetting as *Medic*. Anthologies were not drawing large audiences as predictably as were variety series, detective series, and situation comedies. *I Love Lucy*, a hilarious sitcom filmed in Hollywood, was the top show of the day, and that signaled the main road TV was to travel in prime time.

It took an unrelated development at NBC to open doors for Moser. The network had been urging Worthington ("Tony") Miner to create programs for the network. Miner had made his reputation as the dynamic producer of *Studio One* on CBS. His name signaled popularity as well as prestige, and NBC executives wanted both in the same package. To lure him from the other network, NBC offered Miner the freedom to make three pilots a year without getting approval from anyone in the corporation. If the pilots attracted a sponsor, they would make the airwaves.

Miner's agent knew Moser's agent, so the *Medic* script came up as one of the possible pilots. Miner saw in *Medic* potential for suspenseful live drama. But Moser's mind reeled at the logistical complexities of creating a realistic medical drama live each week, and he used all his persuasive powers to do the show on film. Miner finally agreed, and the network allocated $25,000 to the project.

Since Miner had other program coals in the fire, he took the title of executive producer. Moser, the writer, needed someone to do the day-to-day production chores for the potential series, but he was afraid to look for a producer along the traditional Hollywood route. He sensed that a person with TV or movie experience would bring to the show the very clichés that he was working to expunge from the doctor drama. To Moser, the logical solution was to hire a journalist for the producer's slot. He contacted Frank LaTourette, the news executive who had given him his first job in radio. LaTourette was now heading ABC's news bureau in Los Angeles, and Moser coaxed him into coming on board the new venture.

The venture was not bursting with cash. Twenty-five thousand dollars was not much for a half-hour show even in the early 1950s. Moser, Miner, and LaTourette realized quickly that building realistic hospital sets was out of the question. They determined that the county hospital would have to be their principal stage. So, with the help of hospital administration and the Los Angeles County Medical Association (LACMA), they got the actors into a real operating room and filmed an actual childbirth for the climactic scene. Moser had chosen Richard Boone to play Styner because he had developed respect for the actor's ability to play a doctor on radio. Beverly Garland played the dying mother, and Lee Marvin her husband. Bill House served as technical advisor and as a key intermediary between the medical powers and the TV company.

When network executives saw the result, they realized that they had a strange property on their hands. NBC programmers intended to use the program in a kind of suicide time slot—9 to 9:30 on Monday evening. That period was dominated by CBS's *I Love Lucy*. The show seemed impervious to anything NBC or ABC could throw against it, and a cynic might say that in slotting *Medic* as *Lucy*'s competition NBC relegated the curious program to a lost time period, where even if it faded quickly it would not do any real harm. A more charitable view was to look at *Medic's* scheduling as a classic counterprogramming ploy. In this interpretation, NBC's hope was to lure enough people from *Lucy* to *Medic* to cause the comedy to give up its number-one position in the overall Nielsens. Taking over that rank would be the current second-place series, NBC's own *Dragnet*. By either version, though, *Medic* was a kind of sacrificial lamb for its network.

NBC shopped the result around Madison Avenue and received a cool reception. In the end, it was the quick thinking of Michael Dann, the network's Vice President of Program Sales, that landed Dow. Dann was traveling the country trying to convince major advertisers to support the new programs that his network was scheduling on Monday evening. Monday night had been NBC's stronghold, but the huge success of *I Love Lucy* had encouraged a large part of the national audience to switch network loyalties for the evening.

Dann flew into Dow's home base, Midland, Michigan, at the invitation of McManus, John and Adams, the firm's ad agency. Dow would soon be introducing a major new product oriented toward women, Saran Wrap. Dow and McManus executives were looking for appropriate TV sponsorships to tell Saran Wrap's story. Dann was hoping to convince them that he had just the vehicle: a one-third sponsorship of the *New Sid Caesar Show,* which was to air between 8 and 9 Monday evenings.

Dann launched eagerly into his prepared sales pitch to Dow's top marketing executives, but he was interrupted in midstream by an urgent call from New York. The caller said that NBC had just sold the last third of *Sid Caesar*. "Don't sell them on that," the caller admonished. Dann asked what he *was* supposed to sell. "You can sell them *Medic,*" the caller responded, knowing that it came after *Caesar* and was still untouched. "Well," Dann asked, "For what price?" "Whatever you can get it for," was the answer.

Dann returned to the executive conference room and again faced his audience. He had the *Medic* pilot with him because he had intended to show it to other prospects. The trick to selling, he knew, was to hit the right buttons. With Dow executives, the biggest button was pride.

The Dow people were very serious people. They were very proud of their community. Midland, Michigan had these marvelous modern houses built by Alden Dow who was the son of the founder and an architect. And all the people owned part of the company. It was a company town, but a very fancy one. Looked like Rochester and Eastman Kodak.

So I said, "But what we're really most proud of"—and at that point everybody straightened up a little—"is a new show called *The Medic*." And there were only men in the room, and I showed it to them. They thought it was marvelous. But it showed the birth of the baby. Umbilical cord and all. Not the baby actually coming out of the womb. Still, enough of a suggestion that it was difficult for us to clear it with our program practices department. And these men were uncomfortable with it.

So what I said to them is "What I'd like most of all, because women buy Saran Wrap, is for the women to see this, whom you respect." And the women of Midland, Michigan who were involved with Dow Chemical were smarter than the men, all university trained and sophisticated. . . . And that night there was a screening [for them]. Which I wasn't at.

Dann was told later, though, that the women of Dow considered *Medic* the most important TV show ever done. He sold the series to the company for the maximum price. "And even though it went against *Lucy,* they didn't care. And I remember how proud I was of that sale," he recalled.

In negotiating the sponsorship contract, Moser insisted on the highly unusual stipulation that there was to be no middle commercial in *Medic.* The doctor drama was to run straight through without interruption. To Moser, that meant that Madison Avenue messages would not be able to interfere with the realistic atmosphere that he hoped to generate in every episode.

But *Medic's* creators understood from the start that their positions were far from autonomous. For one thing, Moser, Miner, and La-Tourette knew well that Dow was looking for prestige and quality, but definitely not controversy. They also knew that NBC, which insisted on owning half of the show (the other half went to Miner and Moser), expected that each episode would be produced for the same amount that the network had used to finance the pilot.

The show's modest budget combined with its creators' hard-headed awareness of Dow's needs had a critical consequence. It led Moser, Miner, and LaTourette into the tight embrace of LACMA. The budgetary considerations meant that the show couldn't afford episodes that took place outside a doctor's office or hospital. But the producers determined that even these locales would cost too much money if sets had to be built. The bottom line was that *Medic* continued to need real hospitals for low-cost filming, and LACMA held the key to medical access throughout the area. In addition, Moser and Miner saw the organization's imprimatur as an important signal to Dow that the series had credibility with the establishment.

They had a non-cash price to pay, though. LACMA executives were nervous about starting a long-term relationship with a TV drama series. It hadn't been done before, and the organization's leaders worried that mistakes and controversies in the show would be blamed on them. So, in return for their seal of approval and a commitment to help open doors for the producers, the physicians required that Moser and Miner sign a contract that gave the Association control over the medical accuracy of every *Medic* script. That supposedly meant control over only mistakes of fact. In practice, though, it meant that LACMA had leverage over the entire range of *Medic's* portrayal of medicine.

Moser recalled that tensions ran high on both sides. "Apparently it got out in the medical journals that L.A. County Medical was going to put their seal on this show," he said. "And some of the Eastern journals said a 'lunatic fringe on the West coast is at it again!' And so boy were they careful!"

He remembered that at the start a twenty-one-person committee had to pass on every script. "Oh, Jesus! That was the first six to eight months. And then we said, 'Look, we can't operate like this,' so we got it down to five."

Even the smaller group looked over every script for the most minute problem. Accuracy was only the first step. The reviewers pursued their concern about the doctor's image even to the level of sentence construction. The sentences that caused the problems were those with contractions and slang. Moser found himself in a running battle over the use of phrases such as "why'd you" and "how'd you" in his scripts. The reviewers were concerned about the public seeing TV doctors talking improperly. He tried to explain that the merging of words would not be noticeable on the tube, that he wrote that way merely so the actors would not camp on their lines. The explanation hardly helped. It was an issue that the Association's reviewers kept bringing up.

An even more common concern was the show's portrayal of relationships among medical professionals, and between medical professionals and patients. The Medical Association would not let Moser get away with showing anything but the most proper of interactions. Bill House recalled a scene where a patient had been taken to intensive care after an accident and the script called for two doctors to talk about the victim while drinking coffee (to give them something visual to do). It turned out that one of the physicians on the review team objected that showing doctors drinking coffee in that circumstance would give viewers the impression that they did not have grave concern for the patient. As a result, the coffee was dropped from the scene.

Although Moser and LaTourette capitulated to many tinkerings of this sort, they did manage to hold firm on some. One was a change that House himself tried to instigate. He had taken three months' leave from his residency to serve as an on-site advisor to the program. An ear specialist, House had counseled Moser on the particulars of a plot dealing with a rather new surgical correction of a certain kind of deafness. Moser's dramatization depicted the person with the hearing problem as poor. That annoyed House, who argued that both the drama and the physician-patient relationship would be better served if the patient were a famous musician or scientist—"someone worthwhile," as Moser wryly remembered it. Moser objected strenuously in front of House and to the review committee, and in the end the character retained his poverty.

But victories such as this had their down side: they took time and energy, and they ultimately encouraged a self-censorship that conformed to the physicians' views of the world so that the show could continue on an efficient track. In fact, Moser was quite aware of the important limitations that both the network and LACMA were placing on his scripts. For one thing, the need to pack realistic medical dialogue and action into twenty-two and a half minutes (the half-hour minus commercials) meant that character development suffered. Week after week, the protagonists were cardboard figures. Much to Richard Boone's dismay, even Dr. Styner turned out to be simply "a good doctor" with no memorable idiosyncrasies.

Another limitation Moser noted was his inability to deal in any detail with medical personnel other than physicians. The reason related partly to the show's length and partly to the program's focus on the physician's central role in the technology of healing. Even nurses got short shrift as a result of that focus. In addition, conflicts between health professionals were nonexistent on *Medic* as a result of nervousness by leaders of the Medical Association. And because Moser associated hospital administrators with conflict, they didn't appear either. *Medic*'s patients, on the other hand, benefited greatly from the pressures that the show's creators felt. A cure was almost always in the cards. "I don't think we lost many patients," Moser recalled. "That would not have sat too well downtown at the Medical Association."

There was, as well, turf-protectiveness on the part of some of the physician-reviewers. Moser came to realize that all the specialists on the review team expected him to write about their various bailiwicks. So, he learned to rotate medical areas in order not to anger anyone.

It was because he did not have any philosophical quarrel with medicine's supremacy that Moser found he could write all twenty-three of the first year's episodes rather comfortably according to the Medical Association's requirements. There were many possibilities within those boundaries. A few of the *Medic* episodes even reached to the past to illustrate advances of medical science. For example, one focused on the doctor who treated Abraham Lincoln after he was shot. Another centered on a turn-of-the-century physician who pioneered investigations into the pain-numbing qualities of cocaine and similar substances. A third told of a World War II Army Air Force officer who determined the factors that caused pilots to suffer pain and blackout upon parachuting from planes at high altitudes.

Most of the time, though, *Medic* presented cases that could unfold in a contemporary doctor's office and hospital. Moser, Miner, and La-Tourette intended each episode to be part human drama, part medical documentary. For instance, one story depicted the devastating impact of hearing loss on a musician, and the help that medical specialists could offer. Another centered on the weakening effect of undiagnosed diabetes on a professional boxer. It stressed how doctors, after properly diagnosing the disease, could teach the boxer to treat himself.

The creators were particularly attracted to medical problems that linked up with obstetrics or gynecology, for they believed that plots relating to childbirth would draw the largest audiences in that baby-boom era.

Certainly the premiere show—the pilot about the leukemic mother—fit the bill. Another that did was about a nineteen-year-old who found out from Dr. Styner that she was pregnant, too late to give her baby proper prenatal care. A third episode illustrated the emotional trauma that infertility could cause and identified recent medical advances in that area.

The latter story, titled "Candle of Hope," typifies *Medic*'s general approach. According to Dr. Styner's stylized introduction, the "object in point" here is "the eye of the microscrope." The "case in point" is Nick, a Greek immigrant who wants a son. The story begins at his wedding, where, somewhat older in marriage than most, he is already praying for an heir. In documentary style, the narrator (George Fenneman) tells us that months go by. Nick lights a candle of hope in church during Easter, and still his wife is not with child. He blames her, and their relationship suffers severe strains. Nick begins to entertain thoughts of adoption, but he has severe qualms. He is in anguish. He gets violent with friends who talk about children.

The breakthrough comes when the head of an orphanage advises that he and his wife should see their physician, who turns out to be Styner. The doctor conducts a number of tests and concludes with the help of a microscope that the fertility problem lies with the husband, not the wife. The husband's sperm count is low, Styner explains. Using charts and semi-scientific jargon he describes the nature of that kind of infertility and its implications ("It can't be overemphasized that infertility in the male has little to do with virility"). He suggests a new technique called testosterone rebound therapy to increase the sperm count, but cautions that it may not work.

In Nick's case it does, and he gets his heir. But in a concise lecture about sterility at the end of the show, Styner emphasizes that "testosterone rebound therapy is highly experimental. At best, it works in 18 percent of the patients." Styner adds, though, that medical science is continuing research in this area. The *Medic* theme signals the episode's end, and the credits roll.

What the Doctor Ordered

Medic's premiere was a hit with the press. The *New York Times* reviewer was especially enthusiastic. About the scene depicting the cutting of the umbilical cord and the doctor's efforts to start the baby breathing, he wrote:

> Undoubtedly some viewers oppose such stark reality on television, but the manner of presentation had no more hint of sensationalism than the ringing of a church bell on Sunday morning. The scene reflected the seriousness and high mindedness with which *Medic* craftsmen go about their job.[22]

Equally excited, other writers gave much notice to the precarious time slot in which NBC had placed the show. The typical assumption was that the network had decided "to fight farce with often tragic drama."[23]

It seemed to work. *Medic* didn't knock the sitcom out of the number-one slot, but it did manage to rack up a higher rating score than any other Monday *Lucy* foe. A strong blizzard of initial publicity undoubtedly helped. The tack, reminiscent of Paramount's approach to *Internes Can't Take Money* in 1936, was to frame the program as so authentic that all involved became engrossed in the drama of real-life medicine.

Moser was depicted as a layman who had sacrificed years of his life to learn the intricacies of medicine. Boone, on the other hand, admitted that he had not learned much more than medical terminology from playing Dr. Styner.[24] He did say, though, that the power of medicine had impressed him. And he added that working on *Medic* had gotten him to truly appreciate physicians. "I suppose that we actors seemed just as strange to the doctors associated with *Medic* as they seemed to us. I think they all wear a protective veneer, a sort of professional aura. But when you finally break through to them, they're pretty real people. And you have to respect them, because where everybody else is dealing with money, they're dealing with human lives."[25]

Reinforcing the theme of respect and credibility, the press touted the involvement of the Los Angeles County Medical Association as a major plus for the show. *TV Guide*'s piece on the Association's connection with *Medic,* for example, emphasized LACMA's careful review of symptoms, diagnoses, and treatments in the show. At the same time, it and all other articles avoided any larger discussion of issues relating to the management of doctors' images. The potential problem of using a TV drama as a direct vehicle for the expression of organized medicine's power never came up. *Medic, TV Guide* said flatteringly, was "just what the doctor ordered."[26]

Reviews of the show were not totally flattering, though. Several critics opined that while *Medic*'s approach to medicine was authentic, its stories and dialog often verged on insufferable melodrama.[27] That was ironic in view of Moser's avowed determination to get away from the alleged soapy tradition of doctor shows. On the other hand, a number of writers suggested that the program sometimes went too far in its use of medical jargon. A lukewarm review in *TV Guide* at the start of the program's second year concluded that "with the occasional injection of some leavening humor (as opposed to comedy) and a realization that medicine is not all scalpels, test tubes and grim foreboding, it can become one of television's outstanding shows."[28]

But progress in this direction was not swift enough for executives at Dow's advertising agency, McManus, John and Adams. In spite of the program's decent ratings and its ability to generate publicity, they were convinced that Dow had made the wrong move in sponsoring *Medic*. The key problem kept coming up in a word that the executives repeated over and over: starkness. The *New York Times* reviewer had enthused about the *Medic*'s boldness in depicting medicine's "stark reality" on television. To the ad executives, though, *Medic*'s vivid approach to problems was a psychological downer that could only have negative effects both on viewers' decisions to keep viewing and on their perceptions of the sponsor. Agency representatives kept imploring Moser, Miner, and LaTourette to loosen their reign on "reality," to soften their approach to illness.

But *Medic*'s creators would not allow any interference from the sponsor. They saw their stand as a matter of principle related to the integrity of the series. (At the same time, they saw the Medical Association's tight rein on the program as enhancing its integrity.) There were lots of arguments. "We were pretty independent in those days. We told those sons-of-bitches off so many times. . . . [We said,] 'Here's the show. Now, you like it or you don't like it.' "

Perhaps it is not surprising that Dow did not renew its sponsorship of *Medic* for the 1955–56 season. But Procter & Gamble and General Electric picked it up jointly, and the year looked as if it would sail along uneventfully as a top-rated program. Moser had cut his scripting to about half the episodes. Sharing the role of producer with La-Tourette, he encouraged freelance material for the other installments, and spent a good deal of time editing what he got from outside. As it turned out, though, two scripts that he oversaw caused *Medic*'s cancellation.

The public problem—the episode that officially got the series yanked off the air—was another OB/GYN theme. Titled "The Glorious Red Gallagher," it included film of an actual caesarian birth, incision and all. The thought of that airing on national prime-time television angered the Reverend Timothy J. Flynn, Director of Radio and Television of the Roman Catholic Archdiocese of New York. Flynn somehow found out about the graphic depiction a few days before it was due to air in March 1956. He wrote a letter to NBC arguing that childbirth information was part of sex education, which was the responsibility of the church and the family and not a proper subject for an entertainment medium.

NBC's program censorship department agreed that the scene ought to be removed. A repeat episode was substituted for the offending installment, and the network made plans to get rid of the childbirth scene. A network spokesperson claimed to reporters that NBC censors were acting independently of Father Flynn's letter. The letter just happened to be received at the same time the decision was made, he insisted. From the network's point of view the portrayal of the actual incision in a Caesarean section was "too stark" and "too realistic" for a family audience. The fact that a childbirth was involved had no effect on the decision, he said.[29]

Over in Hollywood, the *Medic* crew was furious. Moser, a Catholic himself, was sure that the Archdiocese had learned of the childbirth scene through Cardinal Spellman's friendship with NBC Chairman David Sarnoff. The Church and the network were colluding to get an important episode off the air, he insisted. He and LaTourette balked at NBC's decision to delete about 90 seconds of film and replace it with stock surgical operation footage or have Richard Boone cover the deletion with talk. They insisted publicly that "it goes as is or not at all."[30] Part of a news release that LaTourette issued in the midst of the controversy attempted to justify their all-or-nothing approach to the episode:

> People fainted at the preview [of the first *Medic* birth-of-a-baby program]. I never thought we'd get an actual birth on the air. We wanted to show actual operations, but the network and even doctors were against it. Finally we tried one operation. Viewers loved it. The reactions convinced doctors and the network that people want to see operations. So we have a rule now— our camera doesn't go into surgery without filming the entire operation. People feel cheated if you just show the nurses' faces. . . . People lose faith in our program if we don't show more.[31]

But LaTourette's comments fueled further controversy. Some critics began to claim that *Medic* was using the operation as a vehicle for "sensationalism."[32] The Catholic magazine *America* editorialized that LaTourette in his memo "sounded more like a producer of a Roman gladiatorial show than of a serious 'educational' program."[33]

Ultimately, neither NBC nor the sponsors were swayed by the producers' tough talk.[34] The scene was deleted from the episode when it aired in mid-April. But LACMA, angered that changes in medical aspects of the show had been made without its permission, withdrew its seal of approval from the episode. LACMA's action was picked up by newspapers around the country, adding further fuel to the controversy.

Frank LaTourette tried to calm things down, but it didn't help.[35] A large part of the difficulty was that another problem came up right on the heels of "The Glorious Red Gallagher." The episode that caused new trouble starred James Edwards, a black actor who had won acclaim for his role in the pathbreaking Hollywood film about bigotry, *Home of the Brave*. In the story, Edwards, having just finished his residency at a medical center, has to choose between two paths: to follow big money possibilities in the big city, or to return to practice in the small Southern town where he had grown up. His mother, who has scrimped all her life for his success, urges him to stay in the metropolis. In the end, though, he decides that what he really wants is to go home.

It was a classic plot used numerous times, most notably with a Jewish doctor in the 1936 film *Symphony for the Millions*. But in an era still steaming with anti-black prejudice and crackling with tension over a recent Supreme Court decision that mandated integration in schools and other public places, the *Medic* episode was a firebrand. Moser recalled that the show was already in the can, ready for showing, when executives at four or five NBC affiliate stations in the South heard about it. They insisted that the network not schedule the episode and emphasized that if NBC did decide to send it down the line, they would not air it. NBC programmers gave in. *Medic*'s producers argued with them vigorously, but it was futile.

Moser claimed years later that he, Miner, and LaTourette decided not to push that argument into the public arena because "the black doctor plot followed on the heels of our big beef with Spellman and we figured that 'if we raise a stink now, we're really dead.' " It turned out that they were dead anyway, or at least the show was. Moser figured that together the two arguments turned out to be all the network and sponsors wanted to handle.[36]

It was an ironic end for a series that was billed by the sponsors and the network as making no compromise with truth. Moser's preoccupation with realism had been made *Medic*'s defining characteristic, its justification for crossing the boundaries of typical prime-time standards of taste, its claim to fame among the increasingly escapist programs of the late 1950s. The emphasis on authenticity also had proven to be a terrific hook for getting publicity for the program. Magazine and newspaper writers seemed to revel in a show that took great pains to be genuine in portraying medicine. To the press, even the unfavorable reviews, the controversies, and the final decision to yank it off the air showed that *Medic* meant realism at its utmost.

Actually, of course, a particular meaning of realism was being touted. The meaning got created through a variety of very different influences. It had been impelled by Jim Moser's fascination with the advances of medical technology and his disdain for the melodramatic leanings that the doctor-show formula had taken to that point. It had been channeled through Moser's experience with the tight, matter-of-fact style of *Dragnet*'s detectives. And it had been crystallized through the time constraints of the network, the interests of the advertiser and ad agency, and the relationship that *Medic*'s creators had established with the Los Angeles County Medical Association.

The result was a portrayal of medicine that was different in style from the portrayals offered by the creators of doctors Kildare and Christian, yet quite similar in its notions of cultural authority. In all three versions of the medical formula, highly solicitous white male physicians stood at the center. Apart from nurses, hardly any other health-care workers existed. The hospital was the doctor's workshop for the most important problems. Those problems could typically be handled by means of the newest technology, with which the physician was immediately familiar. Long-term, intractable diseases rarely complicated the plot. Patients sometimes died, but it was clear that medicine was marching forward in its curative abilities. It was also clear that the duty of the physicians was to spare no resource to try to help everyone—poor and rich alike—live the best life possible.

This was an attractive vision, squarely in line with the image that mainstream medicine had of itself and that seemed to be circulating through the gamut of public media. Keeping guard over it on the *Medic* set were the LACMA advisors. They didn't need to contradict any of Moser's major beliefs about medicine; these were about as mainstream as one could get. Yet their presence did serve to deepen and sharpen the ideology that the program presented about the medical institution week after week. And it set a precedent for the control of TV doctor shows by the medical establishment in the years to come.

Jim Moser realized that it was certainly not the ideology that led to *Medic*'s downfall. Still interested in working with medical drama, he concluded that next time he would have to go back to the older, standard elements of the formula, to drop the documentary style, to reach for less clinical plots. By early 1958, the time seemed right to try again. This time, he would come up with *Ben Casey*, a series that would not be just a doctor show; it would be a national phenomenon.

3

The Gentleman and the Bull

"What the hell are you using for brains?"

These unfriendly words were among the first spoken on TV by Ben Casey, a nasty neurosurgeon who is Topic A in show business these days. The character has become such an entity in its own right that many viewers forget that Casey is a piece of fiction played by a relatively unknown actor named Vincent Edwards. On the weekly show (Monday on ABC), Casey is an irate surgeon who has no qualms about tangling with the hospital board, patients' relatives, other doctors, and most of the human race. As played by Edwards, he runs the gamut all the way from snapping to snarling. . . . And yet Dr. Casey is making feminine hearts go pit-a-pat as they haven't in a long time.[1]

Nobody quite like Richard Chamberlain has come along in many a video moon. . . . He had only a few bit roles to his credit when the studio cast him as young Dr. Kildare in the NBC-TV series built around the role created for the movies by Lew Ayres. The show went on the air in September, 1961, clicked almost immediately, and has been in the top 10 for nearly a year. In this short time, Dick Chamberlain has become one of the biggest stars in Hollywood, drawing more fan mail than anybody in the history of MGM. . . .

And the nicest part of all is that Chamberlain wears the success like the gentleman he is. . . . He is hard-working, has the great potential of a lasting star, and everybody likes him. Even the hard-bitten studio hands, who can spot a phony clear across the lot, treat him with the fond affection reserved for favorite sons.[2]

Ben Casey and *Dr. Kildare* were the hottest television topics of the early 1960s. For their creators, being hot was a heady and lucrative experience. But it wasn't easy. Young actors with aims that went beyond their medical parts were startled to find themselves central to a huge fad that often did not separate their medical images from their private personalities. And producers, writers, network officials, and medical leaders often found themselves struggling over medical depictions in an unusually public way.

[46]

No one working on the programs had predicted the extent of their popularity, or the extent of public discussions about them. The people who had created the show, however, had purposefully chosen track-record elements of the doctor show. For them, the doctor formula was clear.

The mold had begun to be set during the 1930s and 1940s with Dr. Kildare and Dr. Christian. On television, *Medic* had pumped new excitement into the form while also indicating what shouldn't be done. Now the trick was to mix what producers and network executives saw as the combination of setting, characters, and plots that would draw the largest audiences. For the programs' creators, it meant placing storytelling routines in motion that could navigate the complex, and sometimes contradictory, concerns of networks, advertisers, medical organizations, and medical advisors. What the creators did, and the impact it had on discussions of medicine in public and in the TV industry, is the subject of this chapter and the one that follows.

"This Guy Had Balls!"

Ben Casey's beginning is really a continuation of James Moser's story after *Medic*. By late 1958, Moser was getting tired of the hack writing he was doing. He was well regarded and he was making a lot of money, but he was unhappy. He recalled:

> All the other writers I knew, they were at Universal or Warner's and I looked at the shit they were doing and I said, "I don't want to do that." In that interim period I went over to Warner's and they wanted me to do *Colt 45* [a TV western series]. Nice solid little deal. Turn out 26 of them. And I said, "Boy, this is gonna take a year and a half—wow. Who needs it!"

Moser's agent, sensing his client's frustration, reminded him that he had a lot of unused material left over from *Medic* and suggested that he find a way to use it. For his part, Moser had by then gotten past his anger over what he saw as NBC's refusal to let him deal honestly with medical reality. He also began to see new possibilities for medicine in American television. Increasingly, series episodes were an hour long. He and Worthington Miner had initially pushed for *Medic* to be an hour, but that had not been the fashion and NBC executives had turned them down. Moser reasoned that a new medical show with an hour format might give him the room to explore medicine more deeply and dramatically than he had been able to do before. He was sure that he had just the subject: neurosurgery. Neurosurgery pulsated with the human drama that Moser knew TV required. He himself had become intrigued with the precarious specialty during his first sojourn at Los Angeles County Hospital.

His adrenaline pumping again, Moser's next move was, knowing him, rather predictable. He returned to L.A. County Hospital in 1958 for ten months in the neurosurgery ward. Certainly, American medicine had changed quite a bit since he had begun his research on *Medic* at County in the early 1950s. Technology that was nonexistent during his first tour was now routine, and new drugs and surgical techniques were coming on-line every week.

All was not rosy. Professional articles and speeches especially emphasized three interrelated concerns. The first was what doctors saw as a continued decrease in the trust that Americans placed in medicine. As in the early 1950s, some physicians warned that the decrease augured terrible times ahead for the profession and urged organized medicine to take additional steps to protect and improve its image. Others, though, noticed another, equally important trend. Surveys consistently showed that middle-class wage earners had high regard for and confidence in their own family physicians, even if their verdict on the rest of the medical profession (especially specialists) was less endearing. As a widely quoted poll conducted by *Good Housekeeping* of 1,744 of its readers concluded, "[M]ost readers view their own family physicians with warmth and affection."[3]

Many physicians who were sanguine about their relationships with patients were alarmed by a second development that they felt grew out of the public's declining respect for their profession—Medicare. It was first introduced by a Rhode Island congressman in 1958 to cover only hospital costs for the aged on social security. The proposal was modest compared with earlier attempts to secure national health insurance; coalitions led by the American Medical Association had always managed to defeat those. Yet organized medicine saw even this small step as a dangerous infringement on physicians' autonomy. The AMA again tried to frame this government interference in the medical marketplace as a threat to the doctor-patient relationship. Medical leaders picked up the AMA's verbal banner and even colored it with the popular anti-Communist rhetoric of the day. The president of the American College of Surgeons insisted, for example, that "the great conflict in which we are currently involved both in politics and in medicine is the totalitarian ideology versus that of the democracy."[4]

The third development also centered on physician autonomy but in a different way. At issue was the physician's changing role in the hospital. As the hospital became more complicated from an organizational standpoint, a professional administration emerged to challenge the virtually absolute authority that physicians formerly enjoyed in that domain. Harvard Medical School sociologist Robert N. Wilson wrote that the high tide of the doctor-dominated hospital had lasted from 1900 to around 1950. That period, he said, recalled "Dr. Kildare bracing his men (and women) in white." While a fictional stereotype, it did encapsule the truth that "the doctor was not only the central figure in the hospital but a towering one."[5]

Times were changing drastically, Wilson said. He and other commentators pointed out that the physician was becoming increasingly bound by the dicta of the hospital as an organization. No longer did "nurses open doors for him" or "administrators always bemoan his uncontrollability" or trustees "confine themselves to financial surveillance." Nor did sophisticated patients "grant [doctors] quite the omniscience that they [once] did." While the core of the physician's interaction was still the two-person system of doctor and patient, effective treatment of the patient could less and less often be restricted to this framework. Rather, "the physician must be prepared to engage in several types of concerted effort with non-physicians (nurse, social worker, medical librarian, administrator) as well as with those specialists whose medical competencies adjoin his own."[6]

Increasingly, then, many physicians in the late 1950s were being forced to confront the possibility of becoming "team players" on teams with rules that might not be totally of their choosing. The single doctor treating the hospitalized patient with all but total independence was gradually becoming an anachronism in the face of hospital bureaucratization, medical specialization, increased patient distrust of specialists, and impending government involvement. Certainly, these developments were not evenly distributed. Nor did they mean that physicians had lost their ultimate power to define and treat disease. In most situations, that remained intact. What it did mean, though, is that some enduring challenges to this power were emerging.

But these challenges were frankly not foremost in Jim Moser's mind as he patrolled Neurology Ward 57 W. New developments in medical technology did interest him because they could make his program both more accurate and more exciting. On the other hand, building the series around developments that questioned the direction of U.S. medicine or challenged the power of physicians could weaken the dramatic interest of his doctor-hero. Besides, Moser believed in the ever-advancing movement of American medical science. To him the best kind of image to portray was of the doctor as the all-powerful captain of that most progressive of medical ships, the hospital.

Because he had decided to write what he thought TV executives wanted, Moser ended up relying much more on the doctor formula of the 1930s this time than he had done with *Medic*. Concerned with getting a show on the air, he had come to terms with the idea that selling a series to a network meant giving network executives "something they want and something that will sell; otherwise you're never going to be looked at." That meant combining clearly popular elements and updating them.

He decided that what would grab network TV executives was emergency ("You know, right away. Red blankets"). Another selling point, he decided, was a central character with the gruff style of a number of the surgical interns. The idea gelled at the sight of the chief neurosurgical resident, Dr. Allan ("Max") Warner, snapping into a telephone: "Damn it. Stop having hysterics!" Here, Moser thought, was the perfect medical counterpart to the popular anti-hero of the late 1950s. Here was James Dean—the "Rebel Without a Cause"—in surgical gown. "It struck me," Moser recalled, "that that was a pretty good hook. It was believable, argumentative—you know, challenges his superiors—the whole bit!"

Working on the script, Moser pragmatically decided to place less emphasis on realistic hospital structure than on the tried and true conventions that he had worked so hard to avoid in *Medic*. He knew all the tricks of the popular culture trade and had become an avid reader of successful medical novels. For example, after first resisting the idea, he decided to insert a younger doctor/older doctor relationship that could add to the dramatic tension. "I figured, if it was good enough for A. J. Cronin [the physician who wrote *The Citadel*] and a few other guys, you'd better do it this way."

Similarly, he gave Ben Casey a sidekick, Dr. Ted Hoffman, because "the convention for an hour show [was that] you've got to have a sidekick." He also put in a love interest, Dr. Maggie Graham. He knew that in most doctor novels the love interest was usually a nurse or another kind of physician's helpmate. Still, he made Maggie an anesthesiologist, in the hope of sparking more compelling interactions between her and Casey. "You had to have an equal," he contended. "I hoped that [Ben Casey] would be so strong that you needed someone strong to work against."

As it turned out, Moser did not have to write the script on speculation. His agent had convinced Basil Grillo, head of Bing Crosby Productions, to become interested enough in the subject to fund a script and buy the rights. Moser loaded the pilot with tension and conflict. The "A" plot had Casey trying to save the life of a nine-year-old boy through a series of intricate brain operations. During the same hour, his hero also found it necessary to face off against an archaic hospital administration and to worry that he might have accidentally contracted meningitis from a needle scratch during a spinal tap. There was, in addition, the requisite introduction of characters that one expected from a pilot. Especially important were his frictional but caring relationships with the old and wise head of surgery and the attractive anesthesiologist.

Grillo gave the go-ahead to film the story. Moser's agent suggested another client, Howard Koch, as line producer, and the two plunged into a frantic search for an actor who could play Casey. The problem was not finding someone with talent; it was finding someone who would cut against what Moser saw as the rather effeminate grain of most "nice" TV heroes. They searched for months, first in Los Angeles, then in New York. Back in L.A., a well-known agent named Abby Greshler suggested Vincent Edwards, an actor who was not then his client and who had been bouncing around Hollywood playing small hoodlum parts. Greshler, finding Edwards at a racetrack, had to convince the skeptical actor to audition for the doctor role. Moser recalled the climactic casting moment:

> . . . Someone [in Los Angeles] said, "Vince Edwards." I didn't know Vince Edwards. The guy said, "He played in the show *Mr. America*; he wore a blond wig." I said, "You've got to be kidding! Save my time." He said, "Look, see him." I said, "OK, fine. Christ. I've looked at everybody else."
>
> And he walks in the room with a lousy dirty t-shirt and a couple of days growth. And he says, "What's all this shit about a doctor?" That was the opening line. Now, this guy had balls. He was a real bull. And I said, "Son-of-a-bitch, now if he can just act, I've got him!'

Fortunately, Moser determined that Edwards's acting was adequate, so he and Koch turned to choosing the supporting cast. The key foil to Casey, everyone agreed, would be the older physician. In an implicit bow to his agent, Moser had called the doctor David Rosenberg. The Jewish handle then led him to provide lines that reflected a Yiddish intonation and cadence. Sam Jaffe's name came up as perfect for the role. The dedicated sixty-five-year-old actor was doing plays in New York and didn't want to commit himself to the series. But he was won over by the charmingly dogged determination of Howard Koch. Jaffe's much younger wife, Bettye Ackerman, accompanied him to Los Angeles and was persuaded by the pilot's director to take the role of Maggie.

Although executives at Bing Crosby Productions were enthusiastic about the *Casey* pilot, they had a hard time getting it on the air. As it turned out, NBC had already committed itself to a previously tested medical name, *Dr. Kildare*. CBS was simply not interested. Neither was ABC, but Bing Crosby held leverage over that network. BCP owned the rights to the Pebble Beach Golf Tournament and a few other items that were garnering good ratings for the perennially number three network. When Basil Grillo threatened to move his hits elsewhere, ABC executives realized that they had to give in.

Having given in, they moved to deal with two major concerns. One was to tinker with Moser's designation of Sam Jaffe's character as Jewish. Programming executives felt that a Jewish doctor would not sit well with Middle America's viewers, and they insisted that his name be changed. At a give-and-take session with ABC executives, Moser felt he had to capitulate on the name to keep clout in other areas. His solution was to keep the name ethnic but to make it Greek. So David Rosenberg became David Zorba (as in "Zorba the Greek"). Still, the script's Yiddish cadences remained, leaving Jaffe to sound like a Greek American with a Yiddish accent.

A second concern of the network executives revolved around the show's central character and its medical environment. Moser had written Casey—and Edwards had played him—as glum and sometimes even nasty. The medical terminology was realistic, and the pilot was actually shot in L.A. County's neurosurgery ward. In black and white—in 1961 ABC had not yet gone to color—the series would accentuate what many executives saw as a depressing atmosphere. Even the show's opening trademark had stark foreboding. Recalling Moser's style on *Dragnet* and *Medic*, it had the camera focus on a chalkboard drawing of the life cycle while Sam Jaffe's voice intoned "Man, woman, birth, death . . . infinity."

ABC's programmers were afraid that *Ben Casey*'s tone would scare advertisers away from the show. But this tone lay at the heart of the program and Moser was firmly against changing it substantially. So network advertising executive Bert Briller was charged with finding ad support for what was there. His job was made a bit easier by the general shift from full sponsorship to participating sponsorship that was occurring in the TV industry. That meant that he did not have to find one advertiser willing to devote its resources to *Ben Casey* week after week. Rather, he could locate a number of advertisers interested in purchasing a minute or two of time during one or more episodes of the show. The approach required less commitment, and it was possible that more advertisers might be willing to take a chance.

Briller found it easy to get ad people to see the pilot. Having seen it, though, they were hesitant to lay out cash because they thought it would turn audiences off. To make his selling job easier, Briller hired the well-known marketing psychologist Dr. Ernst Dichter to view the *Ben Casey* pilot and suggest what kinds of sponsors might be most appropriate. Dichter offered the opinion that since a medical show such as this would get viewers concerned about their own mortality, products that would soothe their troubled minds—for example, wine and beer—would be most appropriate. Briller dutifully looked in that direction.

In the meantime, ABC's audience testing department had found that *Casey* was disliked by preview audiences because the Edwards character was too gruff. It all made ABC's programming and marketing executives very nervous, until the start of the season. Then it quickly became clear that ABC had a solid hit. Finding advertisers was no longer a problem.

"The Arrow Went Way Up!"

Around the same time, across town at MGM's Culver City studio, NBC's *Dr. Kildare* series was getting off the ground. Actually, an earlier version of the show had been tried and abandoned the year before. That idea had been to continue the chronological life of the hero that Frederick Faust had originated back in the mid-1930s. By 1960 Kildare would have replaced Doctor Gillespie at Blair General Hospital and would have his own young intern to deal with. MGM even got Lew Ayres, who had played the young intern in MGM's original movie series, to continue the Kildare role. A young Metro acting hopeful (no one seems to remember his name) was chosen to play the medical neophyte.

Unfortunately for the studio, the pilot was by several accounts a scripting and acting disaster. Worse, it was part of a string of failures that Metro was experiencing in getting its new TV production division off the ground. As a result, the head of the division was fired and CBS Television's West Coast Director of Programming, Norman Felton, was brought on board to start anew.

Soon after arriving, though, Felton astonished the studio's top brass by announcing that he would like to take another stab at Kildare. He argued that the first effort had suffered from an overly melodramatic script compounded by Ayres's unconvincing attempt to be as boisterous in his role as Lionel Barrymore had been as Gillespie. He insisted that a different cast and a better approach to storytelling would revitalize the concept.

In truth, Felton had never really had much respect for the Kildare series. His excitement about the intern's TV potential actually related to his longtime fascination with things medical. The fascination started during his childhood in England, when sickness forced him in and out of hospitals. It continued after he moved to the States and began to work for the NBC Radio network in Chicago during the early 1940s. There he came into contact with officials of the Chicago-based American Medical Association who were making a deal with the network to support a Sunday afternoon "public service" program that dramatized the achievements of American medicine.

Under the auspices of the AMA, Felton wrote, produced, and directed the weekly sixty-minute series first called *Doctors at War*, then *Doctors Today*, then *Doctors Then and Now*. He also developed and directed NBC Radio documentaries for the AMA on medical subjects. Felton knew that the Medical Association's aim for both formats was to "show medical advancements and the things that made doctors look good." The AMA had two physicians constantly feeding him subjects that reflected that aim. Felton went along with that, but the dramatist in him was more interested in exploring people's relationships with physicians in times of trouble. He also found that the episodes that seemed to be most popular were in fact the ones that focused on the people.

AMA leaders were generally pleased with the way Felton integrated personal matters into stories about the technology of healing. They did get irked now and then, though, when his concept of relevant medical stories seemed to go farther afield than the Association's self-interest mandated. For example, for a Fourth of July weekend broadcast he dramatized the importance of careful driving during that busy period. His AMA advisors were disappointed, saying, "[W]e're getting far from medicine now." An exasperated Felton found himself retorting that it was a medical story because, after all, the accident victims in the show ended up in the hospital.

In the late 1940s, Felton left the AMA programs and Chicago radio for the hotbed of live television drama that was then percolating in New York. He earned a good reputation working on such highly regarded drama anthologies as *Robert Montgomery Presents* and *Studio One*. He started out as a director but ended up producing several segments of the programs; three related to medicine. He moved with *Studio One* to Los Angeles in the mid-1950s and then got involved producing *Playhouse 90*, another critically acclaimed anthology series. It was from there, in 1958, that he moved out of active producing to become the West Coast Director of Programming for CBS.

By that time, James Moser's *Medic* had come and gone on NBC. Felton admired the show greatly. He tried to convince the executives above him at CBS to allow him to develop a realistic medical series. But his bosses insisted that such a show would drive viewers away, for, they asked, "who wants to go to a hospital and see sick people?" They contended that *Medic* was a bad example to bring up because although it was well received critically, it was not really a strong commercial success.

That argument stymied Felton since he found it difficult to cite other radio, TV, or film fare that had done with medicine what he wanted to do. The Kildare film series was certainly not a good model. He found Barrymore's Gillespie totally unbelievable, and he saw the plots as mostly irrelevant to medicine. He felt that they were merely "melodrama without strength of character and with an emphasis on adventure in which there was suspense and a happy ending. The medical side of it was purely in the background."

When he left CBS for MGM, though, Felton saw Kildare as his chance to get into real medical drama. He had come to Metro with an agreement that his own company, Arena Productions, could produce a pilot of his choosing. Felton was developing several scripts to that end, but he was most interested in working on a medical show. He grabbed the Kildare name for pragmatic reasons. The bottom line, he kept telling himself and his MGM colleagues, was that "it was foolish not to use such a terrific title."

Felton took his pitch to programming executives at NBC. He wanted to keep both Gillespie and Kildare in the new version, but he made it clear that he would not duplicate the film and radio characters. Rather, he would do " a slice of life in a hospital." He added that it would be interesting for the audience to follow the progress of an attractive young doctor.

The network gave the go-ahead for a half-hour pilot, and Felton went looking for a script. He turned to E. Jack Neuman, a TV writer with a fine reputation for earthy realism who had been doing some work at the studio. Felton was a bit chagrined when, during their first conversation about possible Kildare stories, Neuman began to spin out an "Internes Can't Take Money" type of tale, about two gangsters who are patients at Blair General Hospital. Clearly, he thought that that was what Felton was looking for. But the producer explained that he wanted *Dr. Kildare* to resonate much more realistically with the actual goings-on among residents, patients, and staff. And he stressed that he wanted a story built around people, not medical machines. He said that he had learned from his Chicago experience that viewers are less interested in technological gizmos than they are in families and individuals who come together with doctors over sickness.

Felton's desire to reshape the Kildare approach was fine with Neuman, for he had come to despise the Kildare movie and radio series. During World War II he had contracted a near-deadly case of tuberculosis. The illness had given him extended experience with hospitals and their routines to the point that he had even considered enrolling in medical school. Thus he scorned what he considered the flagrant inaccuracies of the Kildare/Gillespie material, from the way doctors interacted to the kinds of clothes nurses and physicians wore in operating rooms. He found Gillespie's professional designation as "a diagnostician" especially preposterous, since, he said, there was no such specialty. Moreover, he pointed out, the premise that Gillespie had decided to take Jimmie Kildare on as "his intern" also had no basis in the way teaching hospitals actually functioned.

Neuman and Felton agreed that the best way for the writer to infuse realism into his script for the new *Dr. Kildare* was to investigate what life was like in a hospital. So, with Metro arranging the contacts and picking up his expenses, Neuman embarked on a tour of Los Angeles area hospitals. In the beginning, he was sorely disappointed. He wanted to know how doctors acted, what they felt. But his guides were giving him public relations trips through fancy equipment and exotic diseases.

Fortunately, the approach changed when he got to L.A. County Hospital. There an intern named George Andros had been assigned to show him the works. Andros, exhausted and pained from working the previous night on a patient who finally expired, determined to give Neuman a gritty view of the facility. It started with forty-five minutes in the morgue—"the ass end of the place," he called it—and worked up from there over the next three and a half hours. Neuman saw the gamut—from babies being born to old people dying. He was tired and startled but fascinated. He felt that Andros was testing his willpower and that he had passed. In the end, he was pleased that Andros said he could tag along with him on other days to learn what living as an intern was like.

Neuman spent three months at L.A. County at the same time that

James Moser was working there on his doctor pilot. They saw different things. While Moser's central concern was with neurological realism, Neuman's focus was on the lives of the interns. It struck him that they were bottled up in a little world. They were so busy that they hardly had time to go outside the hospital. The unmarried interns' sex lives revolved around the nurses and secretaries in the building. The interns who were married hardly had time for their wives and children. George Andros became his model of the intern obsessed with being an expert at his profession.

Neuman became convinced that the intern's struggle to be a great doctor should be the dominant theme of the *Dr. Kildare* series. Kildare was not to be a perfect intern but an intern who was constantly trying for perfection. The pilot script, "Twenty Four Hours," contained elements that Neuman hoped would set the pattern for the ensuing episodes. In one subplot, a weary Doctor James Kildare works through a difficult day of his rotating internship. His main goal is to please the stern Doctor Gillespie under whom he hopes to be accepted for a general medicine internship. He bungles these attempts comically. A related subplot has Kildare trying to help an alcoholic patient who is depressed about a court's removal of her legal rights to visit her young daughter. Over the course of the episode, we see that Gillespie is increasingly impressed with Kildare's compassion for the woman and his desire to do the right thing. In the end, we are sure that Kildare will get his hospital appointment.

It ought to be noted that despite Jack Neuman's avowed desire to stay away from the original Kildare pattern, he did bring to the script significant connections with Frederick Faust's vision of the medical world. The hospital was still the center of the medical universe. The doctor was its ruler. Professional administrators were absent and unimportant. (In later episodes they would typically take on their "bad guy" role as futile contenders against what was medically right.)

A specific link to the earlier Kildare was the intern's trip to the familiar bar near the hospital when off duty. More subtle connections came through several references to the poverty of interns and the ideals that their superiors expected them to hold. Reflecting his hospital experience, Neuman added grueling twenty-four-hour shifts to the poverty theme. When it came to ideals, he gave Gillespie a speech about a physician's obligation that echoed many of the sentiments in Barrymore's cinematic perorations:

> You know, there's nothing special about a doctor. But the attitude towards him is always special. You've got M.D. after your name, and no matter how a patient may say "doctor," or snarl it or scream it, he's asking for help. And by your oath that's just what you've got to give him, whether he's worthy or not. . . . A doctor doesn't escape from his professional obligations. He escapes *into* them!

To Neuman, this was what Kildare's struggle was about: understanding professional obligations fully and acquiring the knowledge to carry them out. It was a challenge similar to the development of a noblesse oblige approach to life that Faust had discerned in the interns of his day. Creature discomforts came with the territory. They were part of the gauntlet that interns had to run to prove themselves worthy. As Neuman's Kildare says to a fellow neophyte, "We're not paid . . . we're not anything . . . unless we train under the best in our specialty."

But Neuman's approach to physicians did diverge from Faust's in a significant way. To Faust, as well as to the people who worked on the movie and radio series, all physicians who made it through the training gauntlet were members of a modern elect. To them there was indeed something typically special about both the physician and the calling; Doctor Kildare was a symbol of this. Neuman, on the other hand, explicitly brought the physician down from such heights to the more common realm of the modern professional. Doctors were not special, he had Gillespie say. It was the medical calling that was special. Good physicians had an obligation to try to attain the unique combination of humaneness and knowledgeability that their chosen profession required of them.

Yet Neuman also believed that there were some individuals who did, in fact, comprise a medical elect. Unlike the rank and file professionals, these people were born physicians. Even untutored they could intuit problems and the way to deal with them. For such potentially great doctors, internship and residency was a way of harnessing this intuition to modern science and letting their talents glow. James Kildare, as Neuman wanted to depict him in the series, was such an extraordinary talent. Not a symbol for the typical physician, he stood beyond the medical crowd.

Norman Felton was impressed with Neuman's script. Reserving the title of executive producer, he brought Herbert Hirschman on board as day-to-day ("line") producer. He also hired a director, Boris Sagal, and the three proceeded to assemble a cast. Felton hoped from the start that he could get Raymond Massey to play the new Gillespie. The two had been friends since Felton had directed him in live TV during his New York days. In fact, one of the shows they did together had Massey in a tour de force as an aging surgeon. The sixty-six-year-old actor said he would take the part, but only if he approved the actor selected as Kildare.

"Dr. Kildare is the story of two men and their effect on each other," he later explained to a reporter. "It is important that the two be compatible because acting is teamwork. I'd had my belly full of these pipsqueak method actors. They are moody, selfish, and a pain in the rear."[7]

Felton interviewed several actors for the role of Dr. Kildare, but found that he was not excited about any of them. Nor were good young actors terribly excited about working on the show. Part of the reason was that they were afraid of getting mired in a mere reprise of Lew Ayres's insignia. Part of the reason, too, was MGM's poor track record in television. The studio's shows seemed to have the kiss of death.

Richard Chamberlain was a kind of afterthought. A Beverly Hills native, he had attended Pomona College and become interested in acting. MGM had taken in the former sprinter as a contract player during the last days of the studio's star system. As a cowboy, a federal trooper, an adventurer, and a skin diver—minor roles he played in TV and in feature pictures—Chamberlain was far less than a smash. Nor did he excite MGM executives in 1960 as the lead in a pilot film for a proposed television series called "Paradise Kid," which landed on the scrap heap.[8]

To Felton, though, Chamberlain had the handsome, slightly vulnerable look that he wanted for James Kildare. It was only a few days before shooting was scheduled to start, and Felton was willing to gamble. Sagal and Jack Neuman, though, were very uneasy.

In the meantime, another serious glitch popped up. Felton got a call from NBC saying that the network programmers had changed their minds. They did not want the *Dr. Kildare* pilot because they were not confident enough in it, and, besides, they really did not want another half-hour program.

Felton and the head of MGM rushed over to network headquarters. They convinced the programmers that *Kildare* could easily be converted into an hour show without jeopardizing the shooting schedule—and that, in fact, both the pilot and the series would be better because of it. What that meant was that Jack Neuman had to rewrite the entire half-hour script into an hour over the weekend.

He did it, and NBC approved it. Next came the trial by fire of Chamberlain working opposite Massey. Massey had tentatively approved of the choice. But Chamberlain was terribly lackluster in readings with actors who were to play other interns on the show. Massey had not been at the reading to see the fiasco, but Felton and Sagal were very distressed. The next day actual filming began. The first scene to be shot had Gillespie chewing Kildare out for allowing the alcoholic patient to leave the hospital. Felton braced himself for a disaster, but it didn't come. Instead, he recalled, the two worked against each other very well. "It was truly marvelous. It was as though they had been working together for years."

Excited, Felton had the scene edited in time to screen it for NBC's programming chief before he returned to New York. Also impressed, the network executive committed himself to putting the show on the fall schedule without seeing any more of the pilot. The word began to spread that something unusual was happening on the *Dr. Kildare* set. Felton remembered his experience showing the pilot at a test theater. As the episode unspooled, audiences were asked to turn dials to indicate interest or boredom. In the control room, a rising arrow meant that the audience liked that part of the picture; a falling arrow meant that they disliked it.

> Well, the film opened, it's outside, it's dark, it's a night scene. You see three or four interns in their white uniforms coming out of the place they live and they came across what looked like a little park and they leaped over the fences and the camera took them to the door of the hospital. They went in, and then three of them went down the hall and the other one went to the elevator. The camera stayed with him as he went into the elevator. And he turned to face the camera and for the first time you see it's Dick Chamberlain.
>
> Well, believe it or not when he turned to the camera, and *no* word had ever been spoken, the arrow went straight up. It really was—It was unbelievable! As long as he was on, it stayed up, and they loved him. It was incredible!

Dramatic License

Getting the pilot accepted was only the beginning. The next stage involved turning out from twenty-six to thirty-three episodes for the September to May television season. For the creators of both series, that meant continually trying to recreate the energy and attitude that they had brought to the premiere. And it meant bearing the additional tension of continually having to do it on time and on budget.

That meant making sure that the freelance writers employed by the show understood well the rules of storytelling that the various parties to the show had negotiated. To keep *Ben Casey* on track, James Moser drew up a short manual about the show and its characters that would be a bible for potential script writers. It sketched the general premise of the series and the ground rules for characterization. He wanted to bathe the program in an aura of tension and suspense. The hospital, he wrote, should not be given a name or a place. Nor should the main characters' background be discussed. Ben Casey, especially, should remain a mystery, with a raw masculinity that was puzzling and intriguing in a physician.

But at the same time Moser stressed that the series was to be a "dramatic documentary." Accurate medical situations in the hospital were to drive the program. Characterization was critical, but it was to be intimately entwined with highly charged situations that touched on neurosurgery.

To carry out this goal, Moser hired Max Warner, his model for Casey, to help writers develop the medical aspects of the plots. Warner's routine typically worked this way: Moser would go through medical journals or talk to physicians (including Warner) about diseases or issues that seemed dramatizable. Then he would call a member of a small group of writers whom he trusted and who knew the show's ground rules. He would present the writer with a list of possible story ideas, and after discussion they would choose one. Then he would refer the person to Max Warner, who would help with the technical aspects or provide the name of a specialist who would give more information. That done, the writer would return to Moser or story editor Jack Laird with a specific human situation to place within that medical context. They would talk it over and a *Ben Casey* script would emerge.

Norman Felton's approach to *Dr. Kildare* was subtly but significantly different. It started from his belief that, while medical accuracy was important, human relationships were the key to a successful show. He was interested in using a hospital "as a place where patients come under great tension and meet with healers," healers who were often not perfect. That meant that he and story editor David Victor had to get freelance writers to understand that for *Kildare* the human situation came before the medical situation. He recalled, "I'd say something like, 'Everyone has a pet interest in life. Whatever yours is, start from that. Start from whatever passion you have to write about.' "

Many writers appreciated the unusual amount of scripting freedom Felton and Victor seemed to encourage. E. Jack Neuman saw the matter a lot differently, though. He agreed that the drama should center on the human condition. But in his mind *Dr. Kildare* was primarily about the progress of an intern moving through the lists of training. And he felt that the joys and agonies of the internship experience that he had seen in L.A. County Hospital—and that he had underscored in the pilot—should be a central aspect of the series.

Neuman tried to carry this theme into the several scripts he wrote for *Kildare*. Yet the producers would not accept his version of the formula. He was chagrined by what he saw as Felton, Hirschman, and Victor's lack of interest in authentic hospital experience. It was clear that they would keep the pilot's stress on Kildare's hard work and on his aura as an especially intuitive intern. But they would play down the actual experience of being an intern in favor of having Kildare learn more universal lessons about life from his patients and Gillespie. The plain fact was that hospital activities didn't interest them, Neuman complained. In fact, he said, Hirschman and Victor were squeamish at the sight of blood and medical procedures. Victor, who replaced Hirschman as line producer toward the end of the first year, firmly rejected Neuman's suggestion that he get first-hand experience about the way interns train.

"You're too picky," Neuman recalled Victor saying. "Fifty million people watch us and like us. Besides, we don't have the time to go through the kind of work that you're talking about to find out how interns live."

Accuracy about diseases and medical procedures was another matter, though. Here Felton, Hirschman, and Victor were fastidious. Neither they nor the network wanted to mislead the public or incur the anger (or laughter) of America's doctors. As their first line of defense, they decided to hire a technical advisor. The first one was George Andros, the intern who had been Jack Neuman's major model for James Kildare. His job was to review the script and filming for medical accuracy.

But Andros had become too loyal to Jack Neuman's conception of the series to limit his role to simple fact-finding. He saw himself as "Jack's defender of the product" to Felton, Hirschman, and Victor. He would constantly insist that the producers emphasize more of an intern's gritty view of Blair General Hospital than they wanted. His fights with them ranged from a desire to have interns comment in frustration about the horrors of their training (Victor wouldn't allow it) to an insistence that the choice of a thirty-eight-year-old actor to play a patient with a ruptured abdominal aneurism was unrealistic (Victor eventually agreed to make the actor look older).

The second technical advisor, hospital pediatrician Phyllis Wright, did not hold allegiance to Jack Neuman's approach; that made life a bit easier for Felton and Victor. She did, however, agitate the producers and writers by insisting, like Andros, that the age of patients match the typical age at which the chosen disease took hold. And, more committed to the medical establishment than was Andros, she chose to champion another topic: the proper public image of the physician.

A good example was the consumption of alcoholic beverages by the Blair doctors. When Wright joined the series toward the beginning of the second season, she was chagrined that Faust's legacy of the interns' visit to the bar between patients was alive and well. She also was horrified that the writers were not above suggesting that Dr. Gillespie reach for the bottle during moments of excruciating medical decisions. Taking a strong stand, she got David Victor to agree that the TV physicians would drink only coffee while on duty.[9]

Technical advisors were not the only medical forces with which Victor had to contend. Agents of the American Medical Association were heavily involved in supervising the depiction of medicine in both *Dr. Kildare* and *Ben Casey*. James Moser had set the precedent when he called on LACMA for help with *Medic*. After that, Hollywood producers needing accurate medical information joined network executives concerned about the credibility of their medical programs in besieging LACMA with questions. By 1956, the requests were streaming into the Association at such a rapid rate that its leadership called on their national organization, the AMA, for aid.

Jerry Pettis, the AMA's public relations counsel in Los Angeles, suggested that the national organization set up an Advisory Committee for Television and Motion Pictures. The resulting committee positioned volunteer physician-reviewers in New York and Los Angeles. Five years after they started, Pettis and his assistant were fielding an average of two hundred phone questions a week from Hollywood writers and producers. And they were referring physicians to shows as varied as *The U.S. Steel Hour, the Loretta Young Show, Armstrong Circle Theater, Have Gun Will Travel, Hennesey,* and *The Donna Reed Show.*[10]

Ben Casey and *Dr. Kildare* were special cases for the Advisory Committee. The shows with which the AMA had dealt previously had not involved medical stories on an ongoing basis. By contrast, such stories promised to be at the core of *Casey* and *Kildare.*

Remembering the public relations mileage *Medic* got out of its formal association with organized medicine, the *Casey* and *Kildare* production companies wanted a permanent seal of AMA approval. After some negotiation, the Association allowed both shows to post a written statement noting its cooperation at the end of each episode. In return, the Committee had the right to review each script for medical authenticity. The physicians also saw it as their duty to consider each script's possible effect on the public and the image of medicine. The producers were not obligated to respond to every demand. But they knew they had to cooperate if they wanted to keep the AMA imprimatur.

The committee members took their work quite seriously. They talked publicly about how they encouraged a *Kildare* episode that saw an unwed girl die in childbirth. The lesson, they stressed, was that she hadn't sought medical care during pregnancy. The physicians also pointed to their role in an episode where a patient had acute leukemia. They insisted that the actors emphasized the word "acute" throughout the show so as not to mislead people with chronic leukemia into thinking that the symptoms and prognosis applied to them.

Yet another proud moment related to a script in which an apparent malingerer was diagnosed as having a tumor. Committee reviewers worried that it might incite a cancer panic among people with shiftless friends and relatives. So they insisted that the disease be changed from a tumor to an involvement of the optic nerve. Presumably, that was more esoteric and less panic-inducing.[11]

Studio personnel preferred to remember different sorts of AMA demands. They said that the Advisory Committee was concerned much more with doctors' images than with factual accuracy. One producer recalled that a Committee member was aghast that a *Kildare* script called for a physician to sit on the edge of the patient's bed. It was too informal, he said, and he insisted that the physician stand. Similarly, *Ben Casey* reviewers constantly tried to tone down the hero's gruff speech. They particularly cringed when Vince Edwards ad-libbed slang into his dialog.

A more general prohibition related to cigarette smoking by doctors. The Advisory Committee didn't allow it in front of patients. But the physicians did occasionally allow their TV counterparts to take a drag in the doctors' lounge.

To the producers of *Kildare* and *Casey* this kind of tinkering could be a real bother. They realized that their aims and the aims of the AMA were often in unavoidable collision. The physicians wanted to "assure an authentic portrayal of medicine and the profession" from the AMA's viewpoint. The creators, on the other hand, placed dramatic and audience-drawing considerations ahead of what they considered the often-parochial concerns of the AMA.[12]

The studios would yield to unambiguous mistakes of medical terminology or action. But when the Committee moved against dramatic license that would spice up a plot—grayer areas of medical possibilities or doctors' personalities—the producers' tempers would boil. One ploy that sometimes helped them have their way in factual disputes played one medical side against another. The idea was to maneuver the non-AMA technical advisor (say, Max Warner or George Andros) into supporting a more dramatically interesting but admittedly less probable medical path than the AMA people wanted. Since the technical advisors were bona fide physicians, the Advisory Committee had little recourse but to agree.

Even touchier was the image of medicine. James Moser recalled that the studios and networks had to be pragmatic about their dealings with the medical establishment if they wanted its support. Moser admitted that there were stories—about doctors shielding one another from legitimate complaints and about turf fights between medical specialties— that he and others on *Ben Casey* felt were too sensitive for TV.

Still, he said, the creators of *Ben Casey* and *Dr. Kildare* had a lot more freedom to deal with medical images than he had while working on *Medic*. Producers from both shows did agree that their continuing doctor roles had to match a medical ideal. Viewers wanted to be uplifted by their medical heroes, they contended. At the same time, the storytellers insisted they knew that not all doctors were terrific. And they insisted they knew that the audience knew it. So, for audience credibility reasons as well as for dramatic conflict, they wanted to air some episodes about doctors (guest stars) who were unsavory or incompetent.

As it turned out, the AMA's Jerry Pettis was a pragmatist about the extent of control that his organization could exercise over the doctor shows. Seeing *Kildare* and *Casey* as excellent public relations opportunities for organized medicine, he urged his Advisory Committee to take a "you scratch my back, I'll scratch yours" attitude. One result was that early in the relationship the physicians moderated their accuracy fetish to allow for the dramatic telescoping of time and the use of inappropriately large syringes that would look good on camera. Pettis and Advisory Committee Chair Eugene Hoffman, M.D., even convinced the physicians to approve scripts in which physicians lied and made mistakes.[13]

In fact, as Norman Felton and David Victor told it, *Kildare's* first malpractice episode arose during one of their early meetings with the Advisory Committee. Committee members said that the one topic that they didn't want the producers to touch was malpractice. Partly to show their independence, partly because they thought it was a good idea, Victor and Felton decided to commission a script on just that subject.

The idea struck fear into AMA leaders. But they were relieved when that episode, and the handful that followed it on *Kildare* and *Casey* over the years, took the medical establishment's side on a number of issues relating to the suing of physicians. Yet the Advisory Committee could be hard-nosed when it perceived a direct attack on organized medicine's accreditation process. At least one "bad doctor" plot, a *Ben Casey* script about a quack, was forced out of production by the AMA. The physician-reviewers insisted that the bad guy's lack of knowledge was so outlandish that he could never have become a physician in the first place. Therefore, they concluded, the script was unrealistic and inappropriate.

As if the AMA were not placing enough sentries around the model of medicine, advertisers and the networks got into the act as well. Sponsorship considerations affected *Kildare,* and they were to the point. *Kildare* writers couldn't mention the word "cancer" in their dialog because of a cigarette sponsor. And, because Bayer was a weekly benefactor, they couldn't say that a patient died of an aspirin overdose.[14]

As for NBC and ABC, they assigned the requisite "Program Practices" person to keep their shows within TV's boundaries of propriety. These censors provided a flow of medically related objections in addition to their standard arsenal of prohibitions against sex, violence, and blasphemy. For example, they nixed words such as "urine" and "pregnant." They disallowed the exposure of sensitive body parts and the showing of blood or the body cavity during operations. And they refused to let them deal with venereal disease. The limitations they set were often strangely selective and sometimes paradoxical. David Victor once found himself coordinating an episode about a woman going through a mastectomy without being allowed to let his actors use the word "breast."

Collectively, Program Practices, the AMA, and the technical consultants could have made life intolerable for the creators of *Ben Casey* and *Dr. Kildare.* They didn't. Even before the end of the first year, the producers had accepted those forces as part of the process. The producers clearly had their own storytelling priorities. But they accepted the idea that each of the parties involved also had a vested interest in particular approaches, in certain types of dramatic license. And they learned how to live with those approaches, fight against them, or compromise with them, depending on the situation.

The same was true for the medical and network personnel. Living together in the hothouse of series production day after day often led to a more sympathetic consideration of the producers' needs. Technical advisor Phyllis Wright said as much in an unusually revealing article for *Redbook* magazine:

. . . I am gradually developing a keen appreciation for the difficulties encountered in the production of a dramatic medical television series (another way of saying it might be that I've been brainwashed). I now know that the most difficult chore for my TV employers is to get good scripts. All too often, what is to me a medically honest script is a washout dramatically, and vice versa.

There still are times when I complain that a particular script is just too far out medically, only to be gently reminded by the producers that we are "not making a documentary film." It took me quite a while to find the appropriate comeback to that one; but recently I discovered that I can usually get the desired results by saying, "No, you're going to make a medical *Western!*" We then end up with a compromise script—satisfactorily full of 'conflict' (big word in TV), yet more acceptable medically.[15]

Cultivating this attitude helped the producers turn out their episodes efficiently. So did hiring reliable writers who knew the way the shows worked. There was a definite pattern to follow. James Moser described *Ben Casey*'s this way:

It was doctor/patient/hospital. . . . The patient comes in with a physical problem, and [we see] the relationship between the doctor and the patient [or] the patient's relatives. Or doctor-doctor relationships. One's Casey, and he has a difference of opinion with the other. Or it's a patient, Casey, the staff, the front office.

Ideas to fit this form could come from all sorts of places. Moser found that he could adapt material from *Medic* very easily to fit *Casey*. He even found it useful to dredge up old *Dragnet* scenes and transform them for hospital use.

Knowing how to put an episode together also meant knowing that there had to be guest stars. Guest stars were indispensible to both shows as patients and doctors. That was because the primary focus of the episode was rarely Kildare and Casey or Gillespie or Zorba or Maggie. The viewer really learned little new about them. Instead, they were catalysts. They sparked an exploration of the visitors and the visitors' concerns.

The exploration often targeted a personal psychological trauma or tied into a contemporary social issue that the visitor represented. In that sense, creators from both series agreed, *Dr. Kildare* and *Ben Casey* were very much like anthologies. With their continuing characters, they were more salable versions of the critically acclaimed but commercially unsuccessful TV anthology format of the 1950s.

Of course, one part of the guest character's concern almost always had to be medical. So, to find medical ideas for plots, producers and writers poured over newspaper articles and medical journals. They talked to the technical consultants, to the AMA advisors, to physician friends. Fortunately, from a dramatic standpoint, the legitimate playing field was broad; the illnesses that drove the episodes of both shows could be quite varied. Since James Kildare was an intern in general medicine, the entire range of diseases—and the entire range of medical specialities—could come into play. Ben Casey's neurosurgical residency status constrained that show's medical geography somewhat. But Moser was quick to remind writers that as long as a patient started or ended in neurosurgery, a broad swath of problems was available.

Yet there was pattern amid variety here, too. Since a hospital stay was needed, the medical problems tended to be rather complex. Because each episode was generally expected to tell a story that stood alone, the patients' difficulties were typically acute or in their acute stages. That allowed the patients to slide towards a cure or death that, while realistic and dramatic, also gave the situation closure.

To accommodate a neurosurgeon or other expert, the maladies tended to be specialist-oriented. And, as befitted a major teaching hospital (and the producers' need for high melodrama), the illnesses tended to be pretty unusual. George Andros quipped that each show became a kind of medical zoo. It gathered a collection of "the lions, the tigers, and bears of human problems, not the little puppies and kittens."

But while the shows had certain broad elements in common, their creators preferred to dwell on the differences. They pointed out that *Kildare* made more of the nonmedical aspects of stories than did *Casey*. And they emphasized that James Kildare matured and progressed through time while Ben Casey did not. They also pointed to the fact that different people scripted each series. In fact, the producers entered into an informal agreement not to raid each other's stable of writers so that the two series could continue to draw on distinct talents.

Overall, though, *Dr. Kildare* and *Ben Casey* cast up approaches to the TV doctor that were similar enough to one another to constitute a clear program type. Whether or not the TV audience saw similarities and differences in the shows' approaches to physicians is difficult to say. But articles in popular periodicals from the early 1960s suggested that an excitement about the shows was sweeping the nation. The fad would lead network executives and producers to see the *Casey/Kildare* elements as classic patterns from which subsequent TV efforts about medicine ought to flow. At the same time, the fad would force leaders of powerful television and medical publicity machines to decide how much to talk publicly about the considerations that were knitting fictional images of medicine together for vast audiences.

4

"Oh . . . Doctor!"

Press coverage of *Dr. Kildare* and *Ben Casey* reached avalanche proportions. Magazines and newspapers claimed to reflect the excitement that millions of Americans seemed to be feeling as both shows rocketed toward the top of the rating charts. But the press clearly did more than act as a mirror. It explained and channeled the excitement and played certain ideas down while it boosted others.

Encouraged by networks interested in promoting the programs and an AMA interested in promoting physician cultural authority, the press recited similar themes about the series across a variety of media. Many of the articles reinforced an illusion that the actors and the roles were in many ways interchangeable. This slant was not new. Claiming that the realism of doctor shows extended to the behavior and personalities of their stars was a publicity approach that harked back at least to *Internes Can't Take Money* in 1936.

But now magazines and newspapers carried the activity to new heights. They sustained their attention to the programs until the ratings for *Kildare* and *Casey* started to drop. When the fervor died, a variety of chefs scrambled to reshape the series. That they were unsuccessful ultimately didn't matter. The excitement the shows ignited, the image of medicine they presented, and the way the press talked about it had created a solid frame of reference by which creators, production firms, networks, and organized medicine would judge other programs for years to come.

"He's a Doctor"

Magazines and newspapers confided that Richard Chamberlain *was* James Kildare. Likewise, Vince Edwards *was* Ben Casey. True, neither of them knew that much about medicine, nor cared to. But when it came to their bedside manners, the articles said, each actor was a spitting image of his TV counterpart.

Chamberlain's mother was quoted in *TV Guide* as saying, "I do sometimes get the feeling that Dick is a doctor. I think it's because this part suits him more than anything else he has ever played. . . . A casual friend of mine . . . turned to her husband right after watching the show last week and said flatly, 'He's not an actor, he's a doctor.' "[1]

His press coverage said that he was "a real doll," and "squeaky clean." As soft-spoken as the Blair intern, he could also be as quietly stubborn and intent about his career. He was callow but eager to learn, and he looked up to Raymond Massey much as Kildare looked up to Gillespie. He was described by the same adjectives that Chamberlain used to describe his TV alter-ego: "good, high-minded, trustworthy, loyal, warmhearted, friendly, sincere, and chaste."[2]

Vince Edwards's press image was almost the opposite, and very close to Ben Casey's. Writers trying to capture him used words such as surly, snarling, and growling. They found him blunt and self-assured. They said he was an inveterate horse gambler who made life difficult on the set by holding up the shooting schedule. He was said to be a good actor only when it came to emoting anger—and then only because he basically played himself.

Nevertheless, the public gossip said, he was dedicated to his TV character. He told reporters that he was committed to perpetuating the "Godlike kind of man" he felt Ben Casey represented. They obligingly cemented that commitment by blurring the lines between Casey and Edwards. The following headline was typical: "Vince Edwards, the scowling star of the *Ben Casey* series, electrifies women . . . with his cantankerous bedside manner."[3]

According to the press, both Chamberlain and Edwards appealed to women, but definitely different kinds of women. The accepted wisdom was that Kildare ignited the fifteen- to thirty-five-year-old population. Casey, it was felt, was especially attractive to females aged thirty and up. One writer compared their effects to a two-pronged epidemic which reached its weekly peak when the shows aired. Common symptoms of the supposed epidemic were raised blood pressure, faster pulse rate, occasional hypochondria and, "as the psychiatrists might put it, transference of affection."[4]

This kind of hyperbole was not rare, and it was not always tongue-in-cheek. Magazine and newspaper stories alleged that the two medics had kindled an awesome fever. Speculation on why it was happening yielded two curiously traditional reasons: sex and violence. Richard Chamberlain expressed the consensus opinion about his character's (and his own) appeal when he ventured that his medical posture had a sort of soft-sell sexuality: "With a doctor, a women envisions security, both emotionally and materially. [In addition,] Kildare looks pure. He is waiting to be taught sin. To women, this is encouraging."[5]

The attraction that hordes of women were said to have for Ben Casey (and Vince Edwards) seemed to require a more complex diagnosis. Most observers were sure that the magnetism was a subtle combination of sex and violence. They noted that Edwards's rugged handsomeness (often compared to Burt Lancaster's) exuded sexuality and that the anger he projected added sexually violent overtones to even the most pristine scenes of healing. One writer suggested that, to many women, "Casey is sexy because he is violent."[6]

Another commentator suggested that Casey's personal aura of physical tension emphasized the violence inherent in his weekly battle against disease. Network programmers were well aware that violence ran to the core of such programs, he contended. Under siege from Congress and the Federal Communications Commission for such gangster shows as *The Untouchables*, the executives found *Ben Casey* a perfect substitute because of the implicit ferocity that shot right threw it. In other words, argued the writer, what the networks had in doctor shows was "high minded violence." And, he said, the muscular surgeon with the permanent scowl was the perfect embodiment of this approach.[7]

The *Casey/Kildare* mania fueled a battalion of products that played on the shows' aura of medical realism. Among the items marching to market were Ben Casey surgical blouses, sweaters, watches, and jewelry (with dangling miniature scalpels). Stores stocked Blair General Hospital miniature ambulances, Doctor Kildare Nurse's and Doctor's Kits, a Doctor Kildare surgical smock and mask, and a Doctor Kildare Board Game with "diseases, symptoms, and hospital administration." Paperback books and comic books based on the TV series showed up nationwide. In New York, the *Journal American* began running a daily *Dr. Kildare* comic strip. *The New York World Telegram & Sun* carried a daily *Ben Casey* strip. The title characters looked just like Richard Chamberlain and Vince Edwards.[8]

It all plugged into an army of anecdotes with a loud message: television's handsomest doctors had developed a powerful real-life following.

—Both Vince Edwards and Richard Chamberlain found themselves besieged with letters and people asking for advice. According to *McCall's*, in the 3500 letters a week that Chamberlain received, women opened their hearts to him, some discussing gynecological problems. Edwards likewise found that people identified him with his doctor role. "Ministers, little old ladies—everybody is asking me for advice," he told *Look*. "Even real doctors discuss cases with me."[9]

—In a number of hospitals, the gruff surgeon's name became part of hospital lingo. When a doctor exhibited his temper or extraordinary diligence or notable exasperation, underlings would say that the physician was "pulling a Ben Casey."[10]

—*Ben Casey* changed at least one hospital's time schedule. The curfew for student nurses at St. Vincent's Hospital in New York was 10:30 p.m., except on nights when *Ben Casey* was on duty. Then they were allowed to turn in when the show ended at 11.[11]

—The two actors found that everywhere they went they were subjected to mobs of screaming fans. When Vince Edwards agreed to participate in the opening of a new housing development in Phoenix, Arizona (for $10,000), he found himself surrounded by an estimated 75,000 fans. Many wanted to touch him, call him "doctor," and ask his advice about everything from high blood pressure to liver problems. According to one report, a fortyish housewife joyously informed Edwards that she had been trying to get pregnant without success for fifteen years, but that she had conceived after watching *Ben Casey* for three weeks. "That's nice," mumbled Edwards, "but I can assure you, madam, I had nothing to do with it."[12]

—Richard Chamberlain found that he could not even walk through Central Park without being surrounded by admirers. *McCall's* noted that he was recognized by a teenage girl, who promptly screamed. "Soon she was joined by a small squealing mob. One girl slipped her class ring on his finger. Others threw scarves at him. Another . . . rested her head on his back and moaned rapturously, 'Oh, Doctor.' "[13]

Magazines and newspapers reported stories like these with a chuckle. There was a split among physicians, however, on whether or not to be as good-humored about it. The ones who went public with their opinions made it clear that their judgments were based on the value the shows brought to the profession. Typical of the positive reactions was that of one physician who wrote to *Ben Casey*'s producers, "You're performing a service to medicine by making people aware of the importance of such preventive measures as smallpox vaccinations and antitetanus shots." But doctors who opposed the programs argued that physicians around the country would suffer from what they felt were the negative images that the series were selling.

"The way Casey treats sick people on the air, you're setting doctor-patient relationships back a hundred years," one physician exploded at *Casey*'s producers. Another sent a letter to the *Kildare* show complaining that the "insipid, forceless, and sometimes thoughtless character" of the young intern would wreak havoc on doctors' image. And a hospital chief of staff objected that the producers of both shows were teaching "bad habits and ridiculous concepts of medicine."[14]

The American Medical Association found itself in the middle of this crossfire. The organization seems to have been caught between an awareness of the medical failings of the programs and a feeling that *Kildare* and *Casey* were on the whole good for the profession's image. Besides, the Association had made a strong commitment to the series. Its approval paraded across the end of every episode. It had become part of the promotional process, and its power and reputation were on the line. Medical leaders did not seem to know how straightforward to be about their arguments with producers, or how much of their compromising over dramatic license to wash in public.

Perhaps as a result, the widely distributed public comments by AMA leaders about *Ben Casey* and *Dr. Kildare* often were chock-full of inconsistencies. For example, Eugene Hoffman told *Today's Health* that the two series "have given the public an accurate picture of the long, tough struggle to become a practicing physician." Similarly, Richard Reinauer, a physician who took Eugene Hoffman's place as the Advisory Committee's head, was quoted in the *Wall Street Journal* as saying that *Ben Casey* and *Dr. Kildare* "are the best public relations the AMA ever had." [15] Yet just a few months earlier, Reinauer had complained to the *New York Times Magazine* that his Committee was appalled by *Ben Casey*'s scripts as well as by Casey's "excessive bad manners." He had said that the AMA had considered pulling out entirely from its advisory capacity but felt it best to have some influence over the show rather than none at all. [16]

The behind-the-scenes problem was that in spite of the AMA's highly publicized imprimatur, the Advisory Committee's influence had to be renegotiated every working day. The AMA's power varied constantly depending on immediate clout of the technical advisor, the sponsors, the network censors, the writers, and the producers. Fewer than a handful of articles mentioned this point, though. With many opportunities to get quoted on it and encourage public discussion, AMA leaders never brought it up. Clearly, they had no interest in exposing the extent, and the limits, of their power. Instead, they floated a blurry, shifting notion of their power to bring medical realism to TV dramas, a notion that seemed to change with the speeches of AMA leaders. Sometimes they implied that they oversaw only inaccuracies of medical fact, but other times they suggested that AMA advisors had the power to guide depictions of larger aspects of the medical world.

Skirting Issues

The American Medical Association's failure to publicly confront the more sensitive implications of its involvement in TV's medical reality did spark a short controversy. By the end of *Kildare* and *Casey*'s first season, a few newspaper columnists argued that this involvement was more politically motivated than anyone in Hollywood was willing to admit. The central concern was the Kennedy Administration's Medicare program, which was then winding its long way through Congress.

The *Wall Street Journal* noted that AMA involvement in the series via the Advisory Committee may well have deterred their producers from depicting any forms of socialized medicine. Jack Gould of the *New York*

Times suggested that doctor-show writers were using a crafty device to avoid mentioning the bank-busting cost of health care. He observed that the shows concentrated on acute cases, the ones that required immediate attention. That gave doctors a realistic reason to rush the patient into the hospital. Under such circumstances, Gould said, medical expenses rarely came up.[17]

Lawrence Laurent, the *Washington Post*'s television columnist, told of congressional complaints that *Ben Casey* was lobbying subtly against Medicare. The lawmakers insisted that the series placed "too much emphasis on [Ben Casey's] poverty and too much emphais on bureaucratic red tape." As a result, they argued, the unspoken message to viewers was that Medicare's cost controls would cripple already poor physicians and tie the already bureaucratized hospital into knots that even the muscular neurosurgeon couldn't undo.[18]

Columnists were given more fuel for their fire when in June 1964 the Association presented an award to Raymond Massey, Richard Chamberlain, and David Victor "for furthering public understanding of the medical profession and the practice of medicine." *New York Daily News* scribe Kay Gardella opined that she didn't know why the AMA had decided to bestow that honor, "unless a public association with the popular TV series helps the AMA in its fight against Medicare."[19]

Comments such as these yielded no replies from physician-leaders, who were otherwise quite voluble about the shows. With no argument to report, the press dropped the issue quickly and stayed with its more typical coverage. It's not clear whether this silence was a strategy on the part of the AMA. Nevertheless, it had the effect of limiting a potentially far-reaching debate about medicine's power over America's media agenda.

It paid for AMA's representatives to tolerate quietly a few disparaging pieces about their organization's manipulation of TV's medical reality as long as they were sure that those pieces didn't end up turning the creators of the shows against them. That assurance was often part of the negotiation that producers used with the Advisory Committee over plots that made the members nervous. For example, part of the way in which Norman Felton and David Victor soothed Advisory Committee concerns about shows with bad doctors or controversial medical themes was to point out that Raymond Massey would vigorously state the case for high-quality mainstream medicine. That virtually made Committee members stand up and cheer. Raymond Massey was widely considered to project a terrific image for America's physicians.

One oration that Massey as Gillespie presented in an episode about medical risks and malpractice thrilled physicians so much that many asked for copies. It took place in a climactic courtroom scene. The defendant, a Blair Hospital specialist (a guest star), had risked the use of a potent medicine on his patient but she had quickly and unexpectedly died as a result.

"Those risks must be taken," Gillespie insisted. "If every time I pre-
scribe a drug, every time I administer an antibiotic, I have to stop and
say, 'No, you can't do it because you may be held legally responsible
for that unforeseeable accident, because you may be taken into a courtroom like this and punished for trying to save a human life,' then medicine is not worth practicing."

Clearly, Gillespie was expressing beliefs about doctors' autonomy and
scientific progress that many physicians hoped the American public
would cherish during that time of regulatory uncertainty. *Dr. Kildare*
was at root, a booster of American medicine. Issues such as malpractice
and incompetent physicians did take center stage now and then, but
those episodes clearly and intentionally defended the overall goals and
idealism of doctors and their hospitals.

Understandably, then, the three *Kildare* stories that sparked the greatest
public controversy didn't blame medicine for anything. Instead, they
dealt with areas of life that doctors would find convenient to flail against:
malpractice lawyers, greedy funeral directors, and society's refusal to
deal frankly with sexually transmitted diseases.[20]

Generally, though, the easiest path for writers and producers wanting to avoid problems was simply to sidestep any subject that might
conceivably lead to trouble. But that raised an opposite danger. Following standard, uncontroversial plot lines could lead to unmitigated
blandness in the medical dramas and a different kind of audience alienation, boredom. Not only that, the producers and writers of TV's "serious" dramas liked to believe that they could deal with significant social issues.

So they learned a trick to navigate between this dramatic rock and a
hard place: pick up on a cutting-edge societal tension—drug abuse,
malpractice, divorce, mental retardation among adults, the right to die.
Package it with titillating devices that imply controversy and so help
network promotional spots entice curious viewers. But take care not to
jab medicine too hard. And, in any case, write a "balanced" script that
will offend as few viewers as possible and give all major disputants on
the issue reasons to be happy.

It was ultimately a cop-out, as Richard Chamberlain came to understand: "[I]n *Kildare* they'd often write around problems. TV never gets
to the heart of a problem. Producers have a tendency to skirt issues or
merely suggest them."[21]

Running Out of Arguments

By the middle of the decade, it seemed that the press was losing interest in the problems that the shows did touch on. Whereas episodes
during the first three years of *Casey* and *Kildare* saw "closeup" articles
in *TV Guide* on a routine basis, after that the nation's most popular

weekly magazine rarely highlighted the shows' stories. Some observers contended that there was definitely a drop in the quality of the writing. Richard Chamberlain said simply that the writers "ran out of arguments to use for plots."[22]

Judging from declining ratings, audience interest appeared to be declining as well. There ensued a low-level battle between network programmers and the series producers to define what was going on and what to do about it. For network programmers, the easiest tactic was to point to the audience. Viewers, they said, get tired of even the best shows after a while. The producers, for their part, insisted that the declining ratings of *Kildare* and *Casey* had less to do with that than with scheduling and strategic errors by network programmers. A number of creative personnel blamed the rating dives on an almost pathological need by top studio and network executives to shift time slots and meddle with plots.

But some of the ability of network personnel to do that to a greater extent than before related to weaknesses in the production companies themselves. During the last years of their runs, the people whose zeal began the programs had little to do with them. The restless Jim Moser left *Ben Casey* after two years to start *Slattery's People* and film it in Sacramento. Matt Rapf vacated the producer's chair of the show after the third year. Norman Felton got increasingly removed from daily affairs of *Dr. Kildare* as his Arena Productions became involved in other programs. And even David Victor, who took immense joy in shaping the medical stories, dropped out of daily work on the program to work for Felton as producer of the espionage/adventure series *The Man From U.N.C.L.E.* Richard Chamberlain saw the problem this way:

> [O]nce a show has made it, they cut the budget every year. The top producers move on to other projects and turn it over to their assistants. And later their assistants turn it over to *their* assistants.[23]

The producers who took over—Wilton Schiller, Irving Ellman, and Fred Freiberger for *Casey*, Douglas Benton for *Kildare*—were by no means inexperienced TV storytellers. Benton, in fact, had been associate producer of his show before being lifted to the key spot. But, looking back, Felton, Moser, and Victor agreed that the new people simply didn't have the clout or credibility to battle network programmers over changes they didn't like.

The storytelling changes that the network people imposed at the beginning of the 1964–65 season were rather drastic. They reflected the influence of what many in Hollywood were sure marked a new trend in prime-time dramas, *Peyton Place*. A twice-a-week evening serial based loosely on the popular novel by Grace Metalious, the program seethed with extramarital affairs, dark secrets, startling coincidences, and only rare nods to contemporary social issues. It was a runaway hit for ABC, creating the kind of huge public stir that *Ben Casey* did when it emerged.

After *Ben Casey*'s ratings began to dip in the third season (when it was pited against CBS's comedy smash, *The Beverly Hillbillies*), ABC programmers were sure that they had just the solution. The order went out to include serialized elements into the plot à la *Peyton Place*. In addition, and also à la *Peyton Place*, more emphasis was to be put on the personal lives of Casey and Dr. Maggie Graham.

Dutifully, the producers set up a new creative approach for the show. Each hourly episode would have what they called a running plot and an anthology plot. The running plot had romantic elements designed to continue for several weeks. It was written in-house. The anthology plot was the more traditional self-contained story. It was written by one of the show's trusted freelance writers. But now, to make room for the running plot, the stand-alone story could only run a total of about a half-hour.

Weaving the two plots together week after week for the next two seasons became a hassle. The writers and on-line producers found themselves breaking many of Jim Moser's original rules about keeping the central characters' pasts a mystery and dealing foremost with a realistic medical story so as not to make it "soapy." For example, one plot line brought Maggie's mother into hospital and explored their relationship. Another pulled out the operatic stops for a stormy romance between a new doctor on the series and a disturbed patient.

Undoubtedly the highlight of the new approach was Casey's strangest love affair. Beautiful twenty-six-year-old Jane Hancock has just awakened from a thirteen-year coma. Jane (played by Stella Stevens) falls in love with Ben, and he is attracted to her. The situation is further complicated by the emergence of a short-lived love triangle between Casey, Hancock, and a young intern. Still, it becomes clear to Casey that, while Jane is now physically a woman, she still has the emotional makeup of a girl. After five angst-filled episodes, Jane realizes it too, and they part.

This sort of story made *Ben Casey* old-timers shudder. It gave them little solace to learn that it was happening at their chief rival as well. After *Kildare*'s ratings dipped somewhat during the 1964–65 season, NBC's bigwigs decided that the series needed a new time slot and an overhaul along the lines of *Peyton Place*. So, during its next (and final) year, *Dr. Kildare* became an evening serial, with continuing stories across two separate half-hours a week (Monday and Tuesday, from 8:30 to 9). In addition, Kildare took a steady girlfriend, head nurse Zoe Lawton. Presumably, the relationship was to grow, and attract viewer interest, as the serial progressed.

The complete stories varied in length. Some of them took up only two episodes, others filled as many as six. The aim was to give Jim Kildare more zip, to get him out of the hospital more, to put more physical action into the show. The storytellers tried to put the most positive public face on the changes. Norman Felton emphasized that the serial form would allow time for medical case histories in which the patient didn't have to die or recover within an hour. He also pointed out that the new format would allow writers to tackle subjects "such as young medical students, loneliness, and medical procedures" that wouldn't fit the hour limit.[24]

Richard Chamberlain echoed Felton's contentions and added that his continuing on-screen romance would be a refreshing change. He recalled that in past years his several brushes with romance had ended with tragedy for the women that conveniently kept Kildare an eligible bachelor. "I'm the kiss of death," he had once joked. "Every time a girl gets involved with me, she ends up being run over by a truck or something." This time, he said, things would be different.[25]

Only Raymond Massey, the elder statesman of an actor who had the least to lose professionally, admitted concern about the format that had been forced upon the producers. "I think an hour is a more integral dramatic unit than a half-hour," he suggested. He didn't feel that stories would be able to keep a sense of cohesion with parts strewn across two days or a number of weeks.

Many of the show's creative personnel agreed with him privately. "Cry in the Streets," one of the stories of the final year, illustrates the difficulties. Kildare goes to the slums to help a former colleague, a black private practitioner, find the source of an epidemic among some of his poorest patients. He intrudes upon a conflict between the poor-but-proud doctor (played by James Earl Jones) and his materialistic sister (Ruby Dee). She financed his medical training and is constantly pushing for him to choose wealthier practice options so that they can escape their depressing environment. In the end, the sister is unmasked as having caused the "epidemic" by selling impure whiskey (unknowingly, she contends). In a triumphant declaration of his free will, the brother makes it clear that now he must stay with his people, that he will stay no matter where his sister goes.

"Cry in the Streets" followed the new Kildare mandate of getting out of the hospital and stressing action in a multi-part approach. It also continued the program's tradition of rubbing against contemporary social tensions with the help of strong guest stars. Though melodramatic and clichéd, the story had its powerful moments. The tale was reminiscent of the *Medic* script about a black doctor that NBC had turned down in the mid-1950s. But this was the mid-1960s, the height of civil rights turmoil, and "Cry in the Streets" was now acceptable as a TV version of the contemporary black predicament.

Still, the program had to be chopped into four half-hour parts instead of two hourly episodes, or even one tightly constructed sixty-minute drama. That slowed the story's momentum severely. It clouded the drama's themes. And it made the whole thing pretty long-winded and boring. Creative personnel considered this problem typical and blamed it on the new format.

The Legacy

In the end, everyone had to agree that it was low ratings that finally killed off *Ben Casey* and *Dr. Kildare*. The Nielsen numbers at the start of the 1965–66 season had *Ben Casey* in 85th place among 102 evening shows. *Dr. Kildare, Part I* fell into 72nd place, and *Dr. Kildare, Part II* ended up in 58th place. Neither ABC nor NBC had announced a cancellation so early, but TV sources were telling reporters that the series would not return for 1966-67.

They hobbled along for the duration, lame ducks in an industry that had not yet gotten into the habit of yanking turkeys early in the year. ABC did pull *Ben Casey* in March. NBC allowed *Kildare* to expire after normal reruns in August 1966. In reruns and in memory, though, their heroes long remained Americans' favorite young doctors. And to Eugene Hoffman and others connected with the AMA Advisory Committee, the characters were continuing to counter what organized medicine saw as a general perception in society that doctors were much too interested in money, too reluctant to make house calls, and often involved in charging excessive fees.

In other words, AMA leaders contended that *Casey* and *Kildare* were doing precisely what they hoped they would do to boost their profession's image. They were making physicians seem devoted, idealistic, and dedicated—but still human. They were educating viewers about the "financial plight" and "tough struggle" of interns and residents to become practicing physicians. They were attracting the best young people to the professional study of medicine, nursing, and allied health careers. And they were encouraging viewers to be conscious of their health and to consult their family physician "at the first signs of illness."

Ben Casey and James Kildare seem, indeed, to have become widespread norms for the most modern of physicians. As cultural anthropologists Barbara Meyerhoff and William Larson pointed out in 1965, what separated TV's Kildare and Casey from Dr. Christian and the Kildare of yesteryear was the emphasis on scientific training.[26] Casey and the new Kildare did retain the inborn, "charismatic" traits of their predecessors. Jack Neuman purposely drew Kildare to be a "born" doctor, and James Moser claimed that the character of Ben Casey was "based almost directly on the Hippocratic oath and what it stands for, allowing for some personal idiosyncrasies which make Casey interesting."[27]

But they also made their characters the most contemporary of doctors. Training in scientific medicine was an area that was getting the most play throughout society, whether in raves about the March of Dimes anti-polio success or hype about new medical machines and procedures. The doctor shows, following *Medic*'s lead, plugged right into this new world. "Operations, drugs, and machines are currently given so much time and attention on television programs," wrote

Myerhoff and Larson, "that *they* emerge as the virtual heroes of modern medicine."[28]

A general air of contemporary authenticity rubbed off on press portraits of Kildare, Gillespie, Zorba, and Casey. Writers depicted them—and, by implication, the best of the era's doctors—as state-of-the art scientist/humanists who would fight to ensure their patients' optimal comfort while curing them with the best technology available. Anything less (on TV or in real life) might be grounds for scorn, or malpractice suits.

Magazines and newspapers spread the word that *Ben Casey* and *Dr. Kildare* were also highly authentic in their portrayal of the hospital. What stood for "hospital" in those series was the high-technology, specialist orientation of the modern teaching institution. Their hospitals pulsated with an awareness of, and a pride in, the inexorableness of medical progress. Acute life-and-death problems pumped dramatic adrenaline into a "damn the costs," immediate-response atmosphere where physicians were kings. Sick people rarely lingered with chronic problems. Patients were saved or, rarely, they died. And everyone learned something useful in the process.

It was a cultural model that TV storytellers had built from blocks as diverse as Faust's *Kildare, The Citadel, Arrowsmith, Dr. Christian, Dragnet,* and *Medic.* It was a medical world that was created quite self-consciously for dramatic effect, to convince the public about its "realism" and to cultivate the credibility and support of organized medicine. In the end, it was a picture of American medicine that a self-interested American Medical Association could both encourage and point to with some pride as reflecting its own values.

Yet—and perhaps because of all of that—it all had a terrible flaw. The world that James Kildare and Ben Casey navigated may have been realistic enough to reinforce certain public beliefs about their doctors and the medical system. It might even have been realistic enough to encourage people to make some insistent demands of their doctors and that system. But it was not real enough to point out that many of these demands might well be impossible to satisfy. The day-to-day political and economic concerns that shaped and limited health care were absent both from the shows themselves and from public discussions of them. The driving assumption behind TV's premier doctor series was that the physician was the unquestioned king of health care in a society where medicine was an infinitely expandable commodity.

It was an assumption that reflected both the wishful thinking of organized medicine and the optimistic medical environment of the early 1960s. Medical progress was on its broadest march in history. Conservatives and liberals both had reasons to crow. The conservative medical system was being pushed by liberal reformers determined to bring the benefits of medical progress to all the people. The passage of the Medicare bill in 1964 was only one of a clutch of Great Society programs designed to distribute the health care wealth more broadly. To keep the medical establishment satisfied, though, lawmakers agreed to shape the programs so that the basic structure of medicine—its private, fee-for-service nature, above all—did not fundamentally change. Government intrusion and hospital bureaucracy were seen by medical leaders as a small price to pay for increased income, subsidized training, and continued power to define and treat illness. And it did indeed appear to many people that society could have as many medical services as it wanted without changing anything, including doctors' power.[29]

For producers wanting to move forward with the doctor show in the late 1960s, the most pressing concerns were also unrelated to the politics and contradictions of Great Society medicine that lay beneath their model of the medical institution. Their immediate need was to find ways to adapt the successful *Kildare/Casey* framework for the next cycle of medical dramas, which they were sure would come soon. Already, beginning in the early '60s, a number of series had capitalized on the doctor craze. The producers intended to be innovative with the form. However, their fate at the hands of the networks signaled that the options for expanding the formula were really quite limited.

5

Witchcraft

In the late 1950s, when producer Norman Felton told the higher-ups at Metro Goldwyn Mayer that he wanted to do a television series on psychiatry, he got nowhere. They knew that the psychiatric profession had been depicted in theatrical films from *Spellbound* to *Lolita*. But they were convinced that a weekly series on the subject would drive away a high percentage of the audience. In the mid-1950s, Warner Brothers had tried to make a series out of *Kings Row*, a romantic drama about a turn-of-the-century psychiatrist based on the Henry Bellman novel and the 1941 movie classic. The program, on ABC, had lasted only a few months. "Psychiatry is like witchcraft to the general public," Metro executives told Felton. "Viewers would simply find it too scary."

But after Felton hit paydirt with *Dr. Kildare*, the idea took on a different value. Now some Metro executives were actually elated that Felton's company, Arena Productions, would be working in association with MGM on that kind of show.

Felton's interest in the subject was re-ignited by a *Kildare* episode that Herbert Hirschman had guided to completion during the 1961–62 season. Based on a script by Harry Julian Fink, it depicts Anna Costigan (guest star Vera Miles), who is charged with pushing her husband to his death. The district attorney thinks that she also killed her husband's first wife. Denying the wife's murder but admitting her husband's, Costigan pleads innocent by reason of insanity. She is ordered to undergo psychiatric examination and is brought to Blair General Hospital. There Kildare and Gillespie have opportunities to push the story along. The court appoints Dr. Theodore Bassett, a noted forensic psychiatrist, to determine Costigan's mental condition. Insanity is indicated, but Bassett is still hounded by an element of doubt, even after questioning her under sodium amatal, a truth serum.

In a climactic scene demonstrating the use of post-hypnotic suggestion, Bassett hypnotizes the woman and then orders her to her room. She is to pick up scissors on her dresser and, if she did, in fact, willfully push her husband off a cliff, to cut her long hair short. When she returns to Dr. Bassett's office, Costigan first breaks a mirror, then severs her hair. Bassett is now sure that the report he has already completed is correct: Anna Costigan is a cruel psychopath, but she is legally sane.

Felton was excited. He was sure that here lay the basis for a new series built around the psychiatrist, who was played by Wendell Corey. An versatile actor with formidable film and stage credits, Corey had shown that he was capable of carrying a TV series. He had been featured in a number of key dramas on prestigious anthology series of the 1950s, and he had been a star of two situation comedy series in the late 1950s and early 1960s, *Peck's Bad Boy* and *The Nanette Fabray Show*. Felton decided that since Kildare and Gillespie had minor roles in the episode anyway, they should be edited out. Scenes were reshot and the drama was reshaped as a pilot for the 1962–63 season.

It was the birth of *The Eleventh Hour*, the direct programming descendent from the *Casey/Kildare* craze of that year. Two others followed. *The Nurses* made its debut on CBS the same season, and *The Breaking Point*, a psychiatric series from the *Ben Casey* stable, followed a year later. Undoubtedly, network executives expected to add more doctor shows. After all, the Western craze of the late 1950s had saturated the medium to the point that twenty Westerns graced prime time during the height of their popularity. Moreover, a clutch of medical ideas and been pitched to them that were copies of *Kildare* and *Casey* with but anemic variations.[1]

Now, however, the networks seemed willing to be experimental with producers (as long as they had track records). Programmers accepted ideas that clearly aimed to point the doctor formula toward roads they hadn't traveled before—toward issues of the mind and toward other health professions. Essentially, they were testing the limits of the formula.

The test didn't last long, as this chapter and the next one indicate. *The Eleventh Hour, The Breaking Point,* and *The Nurses* made producers and network programmers wary. The shows instigated tensions between physicians and two other constituencies of the medical institution, psychologists and nurses. Network programmers' concerns about getting embroiled in jurisdictional battles between health care professionals stayed their attempts to experiment with the central heroes of the formula. Their wariness regarding innovation ended up reinforcing the cultural authority that acute-care physicians long held over the medical system in popular culture.

Paladin and Freud

Network experimentation with medicine after the success of *Kildare* and *Casey* certainly didn't represent a radical shift in attitude. Network programmers still approached new ideas with strong doses of caution and conventional logic. When Norman Felton brought his pilot to NBC, executives spent time worrying about the title. Felton had originally chosen "The Psychiatrist," but network programmers felt that "The Eleventh Hour" would give the show a sense of urgency, as in people coming to the psychiatrist in their "eleventh hour" of need.

Felton agreed, and NBC picked up Felton's pilot rather quickly. After all, his company had already struck gold twice for the network, with *Kildare* and with *Hazel*, a situation comedy about a maid. In addition, Felton had greased the series' path to NBC acceptance by hiring writer Sam Rolfe as its producer. Sam Rolfe was a hot property. His star started climbing when he won an Academy Award nomination in the early 1950s for the screenplay of a Western, *Naked Spur*. A tough little film about a bounty hunter, it quickly was tagged one of the best Western movies ever made.

The film earned Rolfe a reputation for being a Western writer of great ability. Westerns on TV and in the movies were very popular during the 1950s, and opportunities to concoct new scripts kept coming his way. One TV series that he created about a dapper bounty hunter named Paladin turned out to be an overnight sensation after its premiere in September 1957. Called *Have Gun, Will Travel*, it starred Richard Boone in his first continuing TV role since *Medic*. From 1958 through 1961, the series was consistently among the top five shows on the air.

Felton's psychiatry pilot was certainly no Western, but that was precisely why Rolfe was drawn to the assignment. A self-described "kid from Coney Island" who had never experienced the Wild West, he hated being typed as a Western writer. In fact, he hated being typed as a writer of any specific genre. Yet he knew that it was an occupational hazard of the entertainment business. He wanted to avoid being pigeon-holed, and he saw working on a psychiatry series as one way to do it.

The ironic thing is that NBC executives *were* typing him. Having seen the pilot, and aware of the new producer's track record, they assumed that they would be getting a weekly crime-based mystery that would be resolved by the daring psychiatrist—sort of Paladin playing Sigmund Freud. Rolfe didn't know that, though, and he proceeded to rework the show from a totally different angle. He recalled:

> I looked at [the pilot] and I said to myself: "What kind of series is this going to be? Is everyone going to want to say they are legally insane? I can't deal with this; it's kind of silly. But what's never been done is a series with a psychiatrist."
>
> Now, the storyteller in me—not the doctor or anything like that—says

that there are a lot of stories that can be spun out of people. What's more natural than people with their problems coming to see a doctor and saying, "Here is my problem: My husband hates me, my kids are walking out on me, I think I'm going crazy, I'm being fired from my job"? I said, "With all of these wonderful stories of people, let's do that."

Rolfe shared his ideas with Felton. Felton agreed with him and urged him to continue. But Felton did caution Rolfe against letting NBC programming executives in on the direction he was going with *The Eleventh Hour*. The shrewd executive producer seems to have understood that NBC's programmers thought they were buying a crime-based program. Even the press release that the network put out after they sealed the deal with Felton hinted that crime would be a continuing element. The circular pointed out that in addition to his private and hospital practices on the show, Dr. Bassett served as an advisor to the state's correction department, juvenile authority, and police department. It added that "in these latter capacities, he has earned a growing reputation as a court alienist," that is, an expert witness. Felton knew that these aspects of the show were important to network programmers. So, while he agreed with Rolfe's intended path, he anticipated arguments about it from the top NBC brass, and he wanted time to prepare his response.

In the meantime, Rolfe began to learn about psychiatry. He got in touch with the head physician at a local psychiatric institute and in long conversations began to soak up a feeling for what psychiatrists do, how, when, and why. It didn't bother Rolfe that he knew little about the subject, or about medicine in general. He saw himself as a storyteller, and he felt that "psychiatry is just the arena, just the theater" through which he was going to tell a good story. Yet the physician did make him more sensitive to the possibility that his series could cause great harm to some people if he didn't hold to a measure of accuracy and responsibility.

One problem of accuracy that concerned him right away was that, from any reasonable standpoint, a psychiatrist was not a desirable TV hero. "[I] had discovered that a psychiatrist is a very placid protagonist," Rolfe recalled. In television, your protagonist is usually a man who forces action. But a psychiatrist just says, 'And then what happened?' "

Rolfe concluded that to allow the potential for more youthful action he would add a continuing character. Doctor Paul Graham, in his thirties, would go up against the fiftyish Dr. Bassett in ways that fit the well-tested *Casey/Kildare* formula. His first thought was to to make Graham a psychiatrist as well; the two would share an office. But with the discovery that "psychiatrists do not share offices," Rolfe decided he had to change Graham's vocation. Still, he wanted to keep what he felt was the key attraction of the older man/younger man relationship: its father/son, tutorial nature. "I wanted someone in a more dominant position and someone working for him, and learning and growing," he remembered.

From talking to psychiatrists about clinical psychology, it struck him that here was a field that could be well represented in his show. He decided that Graham ought to be a clinical psychologist who would do the legwork for Bassett and help him with the testing of patients. Sometimes they would argue about appropriate methods. Their relationship would lend interesting conflicts to the program.

Jack Ging, the actor who read for Dr. Graham's part and got it, thought so too. The thirty-one-year-old Ging had a reputation of being brash; *TV Guide* called him "a fighting bantam-cock of a man."[2] He had recently left a co-star slot on the popular *Tales of Wells Fargo* Western series after announcing publicly that the shallowness of his role made him sick to his stomach. Now he was looking for one that would give him meaty, challenging things to do. He thought he found it in Dr. Graham. Ging was enthusiastic that Sam Rolfe saw his character's relationship with the psychiatrist as carrying a basic tension that could cause great dramatic sparks to fly. He might even get the kind of public notice that Chamberlain or Edwards were pulling.

What neither Ging nor Rolfe knew, though, was that they were conceiving of the clinical psychologist's role mostly from the standpoint of the psychiatrists Rolfe had consulted. They also didn't know that there was a fierce conflict taking place within and between the worlds of psychiatry and psychology as to what role the clinical psychologist really ought to play in relation to the psychiatrist. Both disconcerting realizations emerged slowly as Rolfe relied on the head of the institute to help him assemble an advisory panel for the show.

The panel consisted of nine psychiatrists and one psychologist. Their task was to scrutinize scripts for problems as well as consult with writers on plots-in-progress. Serving as head of the panel was Dr. Harold Arlen, a psychiatrist who was appointed by the American Medical Association to be the on-site technical advisor for the show in return for the use of the organization's seal on the credits. Rolfe had not intended to seek the AMA's imprimatur. Network programmers, demanding a voice of the medical establishment backing the show, would have been happy with the American Psychiatric Association's blessing. But contacts in the Psychiatric Association told Rolfe the AMA insisted on representing medicine in TV advising.

In the beginning, the advisory panel served as a fountain of information for the freelance writers who wrote the show. Rolfe demanded only that the writers know how to tell a good story, not that they know the art and science of the mind. If the seed of a tale was a good one, Rolfe would turn the freelancer over to a member of the panel, and they would meld scientific issues about the mind into the story.

But Rolfe and his writers soon found that they had to constantly push the advisory panelists hard for ideas that were action-oriented.

As they turned to magazines and books for additional ideas, it chagrined them to learn that what they considered the most telegenic of mind-exploring subjects—group therapy, hallucinogenics, psychodramas—were coming not from the physicians (i.e., the psychiatrists) but from various corners of psychology. Psychologists, Rolfe concluded, "were always more daring, thrusting, looking around, trying to bring things out. From our point of view they were more daring than the psychiatrist."

One couldn't have picked up that conclusion watching *The Eleventh Hour*, though. Like other doctor shows of the day, large sections of the plots tended to revolve, anthology-like, around the guest stars who often played patients. But when one of the two leading characters did participate, it was much more likely to be the M.D. rather than the Ph.D. One reason was that Wendell Corey, who played the M.D., was a major talent who had been hired as the "big star" of the show. His part could not be pushed aside for lack of something to do. Another reason was that psychiatrists on the panel were absolutely insistent that the psychiatrist on the show be shown as dominant over the psychologist. As Sam Rolfe put it, "There was a tendency on the part of the psychiatric group to keep the psychologists in the trained nurse business."

The physicians were particularly sensitive to situations where Bassett and Graham would argue about the proper course of clinical action. The medical doctors didn't want it to appear that a clinical psychologist could have a legitimate beef with the actions of a physician. The image of the physician was particularly important to Dr. Arlen, the AMA representative. Sam Rolfe recalled that Arlen was less interested in the program's approach to the mind than he was in what the psychiatrist and psychologist wore and how they spoke. He coached the stars on proper behavior: never touch the patient other than shaking hands, learn areas of restraint—when to be gentle or harsh, when to lead in questioning and when to follow; and learn how to look objective and compassionate at the same time. He was even concerned about the car the psychiatrist would drive. It had to be expensive enough so that the established physician would not look poor and modest enough so as not to make viewers jealous.

Rolfe and Felton accepted Arlen's dicta, partly because they wanted the AMA's imprimatur and partly because they felt the image of the physician the AMA wanted to project was suited dramatically. "[The AMA] wanted the image of a country doctor," said Rolfe. "And the reason we never had a conflict, really, is that that's the image we were looking for. We wanted someone friendly; you know, somebody you'd like. So there was no problem between us and the AMA."

Rolfe also found that there was enough divergence of opinion among the psychiatrists of the panel that, even if one physician did not think a medical approach in the script was acceptable, it was likely that Rolfe could find another one who did. He began to conclude that "psychiatry was a very inexact science, or at least one in which several schools were at war with one another." He knew that the psychiatrists would never stand for revealing their internecine wars and ambiguities on the home tube, so his plots had to choose between treatment possibilities.

But this raised a terrible responsibility for him as a storyteller: "I'm trying to tell a good story and I'm trying not to hurt anybody. I'm actually trying to help somebody if we can. And yet you can't find exact answers [to psychiatric problems]." In the end, he learned to trust his instinct about the best combination of story and medical advice. He noted that making that decision gave him "a sense of responsibility—[but] not enough to get in the way of a good story."

Rolfe found that one area where the psychiatrists did unite was their attitude toward psychologists. As a result, following the advisory committee's suggestions meant giving up a large portion of Jack Ging's role. Jack Ging remembered that beefy arguments between him and Corey were yanked out of scripts and whole plots turned around due to the psychiatrists' insistence. Rolfe remembered that to keep Corey's character in the center stage, the producers often gave him activities that psychologists (i.e., Ging's character) would typically do. "We pushed the psychiatrists further than they really went," he admitted.

One place the scripts didn't go was into the courtroom. Even after filming ten episodes, Rolfe and Felton were still nervous that network higher-ups would pull the show's plug because the scripts that they were developing didn't revolve around violent criminal action that ended in some sort of trial. In those days, the large number of episodes per season often required a production company to complete several well in advance of airing. Moreover, the network decreed that only an episode's story outline had to be approved by the programming department; if approved, the script could be contracted and the episode filmed. So it was perfectly possible, though risky for a show's future, to have a number of episodes in the can before network decision makers took a look at the script of even one of them.

Felton and Rolfe had taken the risk. Rolfe managed to get several story outlines without crimes approved by the network without comment. For example, the episode after the "Ann Costigan" premiere dealt with the problem of caring for a mentally retarded youngster. The one after that explored the agonizing difficulty faced by a teenage girl and her parents when the girl becomes pregnant. Rolfe sent the NBC programming department copies of the scripts while he was filming them. He had ten episodes in the can and still heard no comments. He was pleasantly surprised. Perhaps network programmers weren't going to object after all, he thought.

To be on the safe side, though, Norman Felton and MGM had arranged for a private testing organization to have studio audiences evaluate five completed *Eleventh Hour* entries before their fall premiere. Just around that time they received a call from NBC. A number of West Coast programming executives wanted to meet with Felton, Rolfe, and Robert Whiteman, who was head of MGM's TV division at the time. They had viewed episodes that Rolfe had sent to them right after they were finished. Led by Grant Tinker, NBC's West Coast programming head, the men were friendly but their questions were ominous. "Are you people satisfied with what you're doing?" Tinker asked mildly. Rolfe was sure that this approach was merely a workup to the angry exclamation, "We bought murder mysteries and we're getting psychological dramas!"

But Bob Whiteman was ready. Keeping the friendly tone that the NBC executives had helped set, he said, "Yes, we're very satisfied. But we weren't sure that's what the public wanted, so we started running some tests on it."

"Oh, we'd be interested in the results of the tests," was the equally measured response. But Sam Rolfe could see that the NBC executives were leaning anxiously in their seats. He assumed that they knew Whiteman wouldn't have brought up the subject unless he had a bombshell. Whiteman opened the drawer and pulled out the findings. He said that he intended to send them over the following week, but that he would summarize it for them. He started modestly and built to a strong finish: "None of the shows we tested got the highest rating ever. But, the report will tell you that they have never had a group where every one of them has rated as highly as this series has run in the test. The audience reponse was high and stayed high on every one of the shows. What we learned from the test is that if people tuned into *The Eleventh Hour* they would stay with it and like it."

Felton and Whiteman had played their game well. Tinker and his colleagues seemed buoyed up by the research findings. The meeting became a collective pat on the back and a bidding of good luck on the upcoming season. Curiously, though, network publicity continued to use many of the phrases about "police department," "correction," and "courtroom" that had marked earlier publicity. That may have added fuel to the angry attacks on *The Eleventh Hour* that broke out soon after "Ann Costigan" aired on October 3, 1962.

Curtain of Doubt

The first highly visible salvo came from *New York Times* television critic Jack Gould. Reviewing the initial episode, Gould was convinced that the new series would make the criminal insanity plea a weekly affair. Gould's aversion to "Ann Costigan," and to the idea of a series about psychiatry, ran deep. He resented that Dr. Bassett deceived Costigan in order to get her to confirm that she was only faking madness. To associate psychiatrists with such tactics is most questionable, he argued. More generally, he resented TV's "trafficking in illnesses of the mind for no other discernible reason than to provide a weekly show."[3]

Gould suggested that the airing of dramas about insanity was an inevitable result of the popularity of *Ben Casey* and *Dr. Kildare*. For a new program to try to enter the charmed circle of successful series, he said, it is usually under pressure to exceed its predecessors in vividness of content. With its ability to focus on the intense morbidities of life, psychiatry was almost an automatic choice, argued Gould. But, he suggested, TV's programmers' difficulties in developing series did not excuse the use of insanity as a regular staple of coast-to-coast video. He concluded:

> Problems of the mind do not lend themselves to the degree of license often necessary for the achievement of dramatic effect. Moreover, for reasons of pictorial emphasis, TV tends to accent the physical behavior of a patient, not what underlies its cause. To trifle with the details of mental illness, to adopt elastic diagnostic procedures to suit script requirements, is not a sensible pastime for TV.
>
> No one can foretell the possible influence on viewers who may be under some form of psychiatric care, and frequent recourse to the subject of insanity only invites distortion of the many forms of mental health that lie far short of that extreme. What . . . problems may arise with respect to the [insanity] rules are better left to bar and medical associations, not the broadcasters' association.[4]

Gould was not alone in these concerns. The *Saturday Review*'s Robert Lewis Shayon was put off by what he considered the unrealistic portrayal of the psychiatrist as an action-oriented sleuth whose beat extends as far as the homes and businesses of his patients. He also disliked the emphasis on the hour of ultimate crisis (the eleventh hour) to the neglect of what he felt was the essence of psychiatry: finding the roots of maladjusted behavior in "the first hour," the critical moments of a patient's past.[5] Echoes of these complaints appeared in letters to The *New York Times*'s "TV Mailbag" section a few weeks after the premiere.[6]

The complaints also emerged in a more academic setting at a conference on broadcasting and mental health that took place later that year in West Point, New York. *The Eleventh Hour* became a kind of lighting rod at which many bolts against television were hurled. Participants from the mental health field suggested that the networks had been making some progress toward meliorating unfeeling jokes and stereotyped illusions involving the mentally ill. *The Eleventh Hour*, they said, raised concerns that even this small progress was about to be undone. According to one participant, many present feared that "the stigma of the mental patient as a violent person berserk in hospital corridors would recapture public consciousness and the psychiatrist would be falsely presented as a charismatic wonder worker."[7]

This last point was important. Psychiatrists wanted to be portrayed well, but not too well. They didn't want to promise miracle cures and not be able to deliver. A good image would be to portray them as scientifically guided humans, not gods.

Norman Felton and Sam Rolfe tried to dampen the chorus of complaints by depicting *The Eleventh Hour* in magazine and newspaper interviews as taking an upbeat and progressive approach to mental illness. Specifically replying to Gould, Felton suggested that the writer's concerns would be allayed after seeing more than the first episode. The series, he said, was going to cover "many forms of mental health that lie far short of [the insanity] extreme." Answering other criticisms of the program's authenticity, he emphasized that *The Eleventh Hour*'s policy was to avoid showing psychiatry as a quick fix. From the start, he had agreed with his advisory panel that scripts would not wrap up a patient's problem neatly in sixty minutes. Instead, he said, "we will show where and how they can get help." He also spoke vaguely at the West Point conference about adjustments in scripting policies that his staff had made as a result of other criticisms.[8]

Above all, Felton and Rolfe tried to frame the show publicly as educational. Here they fed right into the psychiatrists' professional self-interest. The goal, the two agreed, was certainly not to portray psychiatry as magic or its practitioners as wizards. It was, rather, to reinforce the acceptance which that branch of medicine was beginning to find among mainstream Americans. Rolfe recalled speaking to a group of critical UCLA faculty and students and telling them, "We are careful. We are responsible. And, we make this point over and over again, we're not treating people on television. We're saying, 'If you have a problem this is the person you go to with this problem.' That's the point we keep trying to make over and over. There is a thing called a psychiatrist. And you really can't imagine how many people there were throughout middle America who don't know what a psychiatrist does."[9]

"Actually," Sam Rolfe told *TV Guide* a few months after the series premiere, "we really are trying to help the cause of psychiatry. We want to let people know that when a man is boxed in, when it's a case of 'I lost my job and my world is tumbling down'—there are doctors for that, too. In *The Eleventh Hour* we have just such a doctor."[10]

Rolfe also remarked that "happy endings" were not at odds with the need to portray problems of the mind authentically. " 'The Eleventh Hour,' the title, implies a sense of time running out, but all our stories are resolved affirmatively. A happy ending could be that the patient has taken a first step toward a more purposeful life. We are stressing mental health, not mental illness."[11]

"Millions of viewers could profit from the show," Norman Felton told a reporter. "Psychiatry is opening up now and people are beginning to accept it as a normal means of healing people. Perhaps our show can help move the curtain of doubt a little further aside."[12] But that was where compromise between television and the psychiatric community had to come in. Giving psychiatry widespread legitimacy required combining a sense of medical responsibility with a sense of dramatic license, Felton argued. "[W]e want to entertain and hold an audience so that our program doesn't end up on the Sunday morning schedule."[13] This approach pacified many who agreed that the dilution of realism was mandatory for gaining widespread publicity for the profession. The American Medical Association thought well of the series. Its public relations counselor Jerry Pettis, by now a veteran at TV's dramatics, observed that his organization had learned to accept a lot of latitude in the portrayal of medicine. AMA leaders "realize[d] the show must be interesting and entertaining."[14]

But the American Psychological Association would not play that game. APA leaders were riled by organized medicine's ability to take control of the program and define the psychologist's position as subservient to the psychiatrist. In a public relations blitz two months after the program's debut, the Association charged that "the actions of the psychotherapists in this series too often have little resemblance to the realities of today's methods for care and treatment of the emotionally disturbed." It also contended that the one psychologist on the advisory panel had not been able to place his imprint on the program.[15]

The public should know, the APA said, that "there has not been any professional preview by psychologists of the episodes in this series." This point would not disturb psychologists so much if the series were not accompanied by publicity that implied some measure of authenticity, the Association stated. "It seems to us this is too large and too grim a problem to present in a misleading or morbid entertainment, for the ultimate purpose of selling mouth wash and other commercial products."[16]

NBC tried to dispose of the APA's complaint quickly with a statement clearly designed to be reported with the APA's criticism (it was) and to make the Association seem petty and entirely self-concerned. The network mentioned the turf war between psychiatrists and psychologists and charged that the APA was preoccupied "primarily with advancing the status of psychology." NBC declared itself more interested in authentic portrayals than in status, and it stressed that "the producers at Metro-Goldwyn-Mayer, where the program was produced, had the advice of the Physicians Advisory Council of the American Medical Association." The panel included a clinical psychologist, the network press release said, and it added that "existing arrangements should satisfy any legitimate requirements that the APA professes a wish to satisfy."[17]

The network's sharp rejoinder seems to have had its desired impact. The psychologists' complaints were not brought into the other debates surrounding *The Eleventh Hour*. Maybe physicians and others who publicly discussed the drawbacks and benefits of the show agreed that the issue was too parochial. Maybe the network's curt response telegraphed to interested parties that while NBC was willing to talk about the depiction of mental illness on TV, it considered the psychology/psychiatry debate off-limits for useful discussion. Members of the show never raised it. Even when Jack Ging exploded in public anger about his diminished part in the show, no one, not even Ging himself, mentioned that it related to the reduced role for psychology in the series. "Jack chafes," Norman Felton explained Ging's attitude cryptically to *TV Guide*. "He's like to play the king each week, but he often finds himself portraying the prince."[18]

From the standpoint of its bottom line, the network had no reason to complain. Perhaps partly because of the controversies that kept bringing its title to the fore in magazines and newspapers, *The Eleventh Hour* was taking off like gangbusters in its time slot. It was quickly edging out its competitors, CBS's *U.S. Steel Hour* anthology and ABC's long-popular police drama *Naked City*. One TV reporter wrote at the end of the first season that *The Eleventh Hour* had inspired writers throughout television. "[P]robably one of the few TV shows now on the air which hasn't made use of mental illness of one sort or another is *Lassie*. Derangement has been the theme of episodes on *Ben Casey* and *Dr. Kildare*, both of whom are having trouble finding new diseases. Even the lawyers on TV, like *The Defenders*, have taken a crack or two at showing and prescribing for crackpots who have become entangled with the law."[19]

There was some evidence that *The Eleventh Hour* was performing the kind of educational function about psychiatry that Normal Felton and Sam Rolfe hoped it would. The head of the psychiatric institute found that he could use his connection with *The Eleventh Hour* as an audience draw. Before the show's debut, he would regularly send members of his staff around the country to lecture about mental illness and the psychiatric profession. In many places, turnout was small. Then, when *The Eleventh Hour* began to air, he began advertising his organization's connection with the TV show. Audiences quickly got larger. In addition, the people coming seemed to be less fearful of psychiatry and more eager to learn about it.

Over the course of the season, the series settled down to quite respectable, if not spectacular, ratings. Fast to capitalize on what looked like a successful wrinkle in the doctor-show form, Bing Crosby Productions and ABC announced *The Breaking Point* as a new psychiatry series for the next fall season. Starring Paul Richards as the older physician and Edward Franz as the younger one, the program would revolve around the psychiatric clinic of a fictitious Los Angeles hospital.

In announcing the show, the program's producers showed that they had done their homework about the points that raised psychiatrists' ire. They were careful to state that their show would not be interested in quick solutions. "It is very difficult to stage a believable cure in the space of a one hour drama," ABC's press release intoned.[20] Good intentions aside, however, the ratings were weak. The show lasted only one year.

The Eleventh Hour was pulled after its second season. During its first year, 1962–63, ratings were fine. Sam Rolfe happily recalled that he presided over a program that was essentially a weekly anthology drama draped in the psychiatrist's coat. "[W]e were getting very good stories," he said proudly. "Everyone was letting me do the show that I wanted to do. All of us connected with it were very pleased with it. I would take any of those [episodes] that I did that first season and show them off because they were all exceptional. Some of those were so [good] that actors and actresses were fighting to get on the show."

The one dark spot of that time was the discovery of Wendell Corey's alcoholism. The wardrobe man who was supplying Corey with liquor was fired, but the problem did not go away. Aware that the star was increasingly difficult to handle, and afraid that it would become public gossip that *The Eleventh Hour*'s psychiatrist was a drunk, Felton and Rolfe decided to look for another lead. They cast around and found Ralph Bellamy. Corey himself left with a ray of hope. He had sought out the head of the psychiatric institute and had begun to see him regularly about his problem

With Corey's departure after the first season came a downturn in the show's Nielsen fortunes. It limped through the second year and wasn't renewed for a third go-around. As usual, network programmers, producers, and cast offered various, often contradictory, explanations for the demise. Looking back, however, it seems clear that NBC's controversy-filled experience with *The Eleventh Hour*, the care with which ABC treaded when presenting *The Breaking Point*, and the eventual mediocre ratings of both, crystallized for network programmers notions of which health care professions might be worth working with on TV.

Doctors came out on top; psychologists faded away. Eventually, psychiatrists took a far back seat to other types of physicians, since it became clear to executives that matters of the mind weren't amenable to the acute-care, hospital-based excitement on which *Casey* and *Kildare* had thrived for so long. Ironically, the same sort of thinking and narrowing was going on at the third network, CBS. There a different medical profession was being tested for a starring role in the formula: nursing.

6

Narrowed Options

Wanting to build an entire series around nursing was considered a brash idea in the early 1960s. Previously, the only series to center on nurses had been *Janet Dean, R.N.*, in 1954. Starring Ella Raines as a private-duty nurse in her thirties, the program had not been carried by a network. Rather, it had been syndicated to stations around the country.

Aside from that one, not terribly successful show, the opportunities for nurses to involve themselves deeply in medical issues in continuing TV dramas were slim. One exhaustive study of nursing images on television concluded that when nurses were depicted in the 1950s they revealed few professional skills. Often, the study found, physicians were shown to solve complex problems that nurses would typically handle in real life.[1]

To the producers of *Medic*, *Ben Casey*, *Dr. Kildare*, and *The Eleventh Hour*, the failure to give continuing attention to nursing was a dramatic necessity. While invariably pointing out individual episodes that highlighted nurses, they admitted that the series revolved around docotrs, not nurses. Packing all the elements necessary for a good doctor show into an hour while worrying about the nurse's role would have been impossible, they contended. So, said David Victor, the nurse on *Dr. Kildare* was typically a "functionary." Similarly, James Moser said of Nurse Wills, a regular on *Ben Casey*, "She was a standby. We got into nurse stuff, but it was always peripheral."

Now, in 1961, Herbert Brodkin proposed to redirect the formula by moving the nursing profession to center stage. Brodkin had not worked on a medical series before, but he had the kind of track record that would lead network executives to take the idea seriously. Yet as in the case of *The Eleventh Hour* and *The Breaking Point*, an attempt to move away from standard approaches ironically helped narrow the options for characterizations and plots that producers and programmers came to see as useful for medical drama. When it came to portrayals of medicine's cultural authority, direct intervention by physicians to protect their cultural authority was only one avenue that helped to keep their traditional role in the formula intact.

Schizoid Values

Despite the bias in Hollywood against centering shows on nurses instead of doctors, Brodkin considered the project a more opportunistic and commercial venture than some of his other TV work. He knew that, after NBC and ABC struck gold with *Kildare* and *Casey*, CBS would reach for some of it with a medical show of its own. Trying to take advantage of the need, Brodkin remembered "Diary of a Nurse," a 1959 episode from his *Playhouse 90* anthology series.

Written by Arthur Hailey, it was the story of the conflict that a young nurse felt between modern scientific nursing practices and her patients' needs for human and emotional involvement. Inger Stevens was the inexperienced woman in white and Mildred Dunnock her older and wiser boss. The play earned good reviews and appreciation from the nursing profession.

Shrewdly, the producer recognized that "Diary of a Nurse" had several of the elements that network programmers had come to associate with successful doctor shows: the tension between neophyte and experienced supervisor; the interplay between scientific progress and human emotion in a modern hospital; and the ultimate tension of life versus death. The pilot script for the series, written by John Vlahos, pulled out all the stops on these elements as it dealt with student nurse Gail Lucas's turmoil in a maternity ward where a Greek woman dying of rheumatic heart disease was about to give birth.

Ted Ashley, Brodkin's powerful Hollywood agent, pitched the show to CBS. During the early and mid-1960s, when he turned to drama series after the downfall of the anthology programs, all of Brodkin's work was for CBS. CBS was a network with a schizoid sense of programming values—torn between the high-minded image that William Paley, its founder and chairman, liked to project and the coarsely pragmatic view that the network president, James Aubrey, took.

Producers such as Brodkin appealed to Paley's image of TV as a creative force. Brodkin's name had been established in TV's creative pantheon during the 1950s, when he had become a major figure in the development of live television dramas. He had also developed a reputation for creative independence. People knew that he continued to work out of New York when most prime-time TV activity was shifting to Hollywood. He paid writers more than the going rate (and actors less) on the conviction that the script was still the essence of the program. He encouraged his writers to deal with volatile social themes on the belief that TV drama should goad viewers toward thought as well as entertain them. And he demanded near-total freedom from network interference.

For Aubrey, on the other hand, Brodkin was the kind of producer who could be a major liability. Aubrey knew that his job was to make CBS television into a money machine. To him programming had to be least-common-denominator entertainment for the masses. Social issues brought needless controversy. They belonged on news programming, a money-loser at the time, which Aubrey considered an unfortunate drain on company resources. He spread that philosophy through the company. "Your job is to create shit," an Aubrey lieutenant once told a Hollywood producer.[2]

Nevertheless, James Aubrey understood ratings success. So when Brodkin's social issues series revolving around a father-and-son law team, *The Defenders*, did extremely well in its Saturday evening time slot, the producer had an "in" with the network. Aubrey had initially hated *The Defenders*. Michael Dann, CBS's vice president of East Coast programming, had commissioned the pilot with an eye on the 1961–62 season. Dann was a self-styled programming expert who had learned the craft in program sales at NBC (he was the one who sold *Medic* to Dow). He saw Brodkin as one of the best sources of product on the East Coast. Nevertheless, Aubrey ordered the pilot shelved. He disliked the idea of a law series tackling timely social issues. His notion of a good lawyer show, he said, was another *Perry Mason* murder-mystery.

A few months later, though, *The Defenders* pilot made a comeback. It happened that Dann and Aubrey were talking with William Paley about a program to replace the ailing *Checkmate* in the Saturday 8:30–9:30 slot. Dann casually mentioned *The Defenders*. Paley, who was often involved in programming decisions, remembered seeing the unaired pilot and liking it. He ordered Aubrey to give it a try. *The Defenders'* subsequent success with controversial stories gave CBS prestige as well as good ratings. And it gave Brodkin the credibility to do more for the network.

Mike Dann felt that Vlahos's script for *The Nurses* combined the literate style of *The Defenders* and the pathos of *Medic's* premiere installment, the one that had so captivated the women of Dow. He was impressed and ordered a pilot. Lewis and Brodkin turned to choosing the two leads. Both knew Shirl Conway, a fortyish, good-looking actress whose show business experience spanned variety, comedy, and drama. Brodkin remembered her for a recent guest star appearance in *The Defenders* and was sure that her versatility would be perfect for the puritanical, severe, yet humane and dedicated older nurse. He chose a seventeen-year-old ballet dancer, Zina Bethune, for the younger nurse. Bethune had little acting experience. Presumably, Brodkin's idea was that the youthful enthusiasm and real naïveté that Bethune would bring to her new role would lend an air of authenticity to her role as an inexperienced student nurse.

The pilot turned out well, though in the process Dann and Brodkin had the expected (and successful) struggle with the network censors over showing the baby's birth. *The Nurses* was given a slot on CBS's 1962–63 schedule. The position, 9 to 10 o'clock on Thursday night, was a disappointing one. *The Nurses* did get *Perry Mason* as a strong lead-in. But its competition would be intimidating. On NBC, *Dr. Kildare* would continue to make its rounds between 8:30 and 9:30. That show would be followed by the hit half-hour sitcom, *Hazel*. ABC would start its popular half-hour situation comedy *My Three Sons* directly against *The Nurses* and follow it with a new entry, *McHale's Navy*.

The severity of the opposition was indicated by the realization that, the year before, *Hazel* had been the number 4 Nielsen show, *Kildare*, number 9, and *My Three Sons*, number 11. CBS was clearly attempting to counterprogram with drama against the comedy shows. But with a proven drama leading into NBC's hit comedy, it seemed doubtful that the 30 percent of the viewing audience that was typically needed to keep a show alive would make it to *The Nurses*.

Nevertheless, work on the series continued. As it did, Brodkin's sense of creative autonomy began to poke through even in this admittedly opportunistic venture. Breaking with the pattern of the past decade, he refused to invite the American Medical Association, the American Nurses Association, or any other branch of the health care system onto the set. Instead, he hired his neighbor, Florence McManus, a head nurse at New York's Roosevelt Hospital, to be the show's chief technical advisor.

Arthur Lewis remembered that Brodkin was wary of the power structure and "extremely sensitive about the influence and pressures put upon the rank and file by the establishment." Publicly, Brodkin told a reporter that his refusal to get an AMA imprimatur related to independence. He believed that "an organization's objectives would necessarily be different from his own."[3]

And, in fact, Brodkin and Lewis felt that they had to be free to raise issues central, and possibly sensitive, to medicine. Still, they insisted that their primary aim in the series was not to explore or critique the health care establishment.[4] Like their counterparts on *Dr. Kildare, Ben Casey, The Eleventh Hour,* and *The Breaking Point,* Brodkin and Lewis saw their running characters and setting as a frame that would allow them to dramatize in an anthological manner a range of subjects from different points of view. But the emphasis was more on moral and ethical choices (à la *The Defenders*) than on urgent, life-saving interventions (à la *Casey/Kildare*).

The range of plots was wide:

—"Frieda" depicted a sympathetic, dedicated nurse who is a former Nazi involved in horrid medical experiments. She is exposed by an unsympathetic refugee who insists that she be fired. Although it is clear that justice has been served by the dismissal, it is also clear that the writer wants the viewer also to have unresolved positive feelings for the former Nazi in a new life.

—"The Prisoner" centered around a black prisoner (Lou Gossett) who is recovering in a guarded hospital bed from wounds that he received after killing two policemen during a bank robbery. Gail Lukas (Zina Bethune), who expresses sympathy for the man while working in the guarded room, has to deal with the inescapable moral ambiguity of the situation: a team of doctors and nurses are saving his life so that he can stand trial and be put to death for first-degree murder.

—"A Kind of Loving" dealt with a Puerto Rican father who is upset over his wife's delivery of a son into his already large family. A religious Catholic who will not use contraceptive devices, he prays that the baby will die. He deserts his wailing wife and runs from the hospital. Shocked, Liz Thorpe (Shirl Conway) follows him and tries to get him to cheer up his wife. In the end, though, the viewer follows the father and another son to their one-room hovel. Ending with the father asking "Where is he going to sleep?," the episode implies that perhaps the father's prayer hadn't been cruel, after all.

—"For Mice and Rabbits" concerned a veteran nurse (Geraldine Fitzgerald), who decides not to administer a prescribed experimental drug to a young patient. After reading the literature, she is convinced that the risks outweigh the possible benefits. As it turns out, the nurses's fears prove correct, for dozens of patients who have taken the drug are soon reported to show serious side-effects of the drug. Despite the physician's relief that the patient didn't receive the drug, he and the nursing administration fire the nurse for not following the doctor's orders.

Episodes such as these were bound to shock or offend some groups of viewers. At a time when NBC wouldn't allow *Dr. Kildare*'s characters to use the word "pregnant" or deal with venereal disease, at a time when the American Medical Association successfully prevented *Ben Casey*'s producers from using a script about a quack physician, *The Nurses* was marching consistently through a range of controversial subjects. Brodkin and Lewis saw drug addiction, abortion, euthanasia, and venereal disease as issues that could be treated well within a hospital setting, and they didn't flinch at trying.

They even aired one story about a middle-aged nurse who is harassed by physicians and threatened with the loss of a desperately needed job transfer if she discusses her support of Medicare (then still a congressional bill) with the press. The episode ends tensely, with the eager reporter knocking at her door and the frightened nurse sitting in her chair, afraid to answer and exercise her right to free speech.

It's not totally clear how Brodkin and Lewis managed to get away with such plots while others couldn't even try. Their refusal to establish ties to the AMA when they aimed their volleys at physicians might have made it easier. More important was Herb Brodkin's bull-headed stubbornness when it came to the right of his programs to handle social issues. Because of the success of *The Defenders*, CBS allowed him to be stubborn. Mike Dann noted that Brodkin knew how to handle volatile issues in a manner that would not turn the network censors too red. Brodkin was also seen as a rare kind of series producer, someone who brought the high ratings that executives like Aubrey needed and the prestige for which patriarchs like Paley hoped.

Press reaction to the initial installments of the series was decidedly mixed, however. In an industry-savvy critique that mirrored other reviews, *Variety* expressed exasperation with what it called TV's "overexpanding 60-minute anthology series" in the *Kildare/Casey/Defenders* mold.[5] Of course, *Variety* realized that melodramatics need not be a negative factor in audience pulling. More ominous for prime-time success, it said, was the gender of its lead characters. Reflecting a growing interest in programming principles, the review noted that the major departure from the *Kildare/Casey* format in the area of sex might well spell doom for the show:

> [Even] if the [format of *The Nurses*] particularly fits the *Kildare* or *Casey* show, there is, however, this inevitable difference (as basic to Madison Avenue as the slide rule): the predominantly femme audience attracted to such anthologies would rather dig a Dick Chamberlain and a Vince Edwards than a nurse. Plus the inescapable fact, that since it's competing with *Kildare* Thursday nights, *Nurses* is bound to get the worst of it on the Nielsen fever charts.[6]

The show's emphasis on female leads was to haunt the series as it hung around for the next three years. During the first few months of the program's existence, the ratings for *The Nurses* were so dismal that rumors circulated early that it had little chance of being renewed.[7] In an effort to save the series, Ted Ashley persuaded Jim Aubrey and Mike Dann to move it from its deadly time slot. The idea was to place it an hour later, where it would be opposite less lethal competition, ABC's ailing *Alcoa Premiere* (an anthology series) and *The Andy Williams Show* (a variety program). In the early 1960s, changing the time of a show in mid-season was highly irregular, but Ashley had the clout to force the unusual. The strategy worked. In its first outing at 10 o'clock, *The Nurses* won its time period with a 44 share. It was quickly renewed for the 1963–64 season.

Sensationalized Images

One audience that wasn't sure it was happy about *The Nurses*'s newfound popularity was America's real-life nurses. Letters and articles in nursing journals indicate that many nurses were sensitive to the influence of the rash of medical shows in the early 1960s on the public's image of their profession. They were most vocal about *The Nurses.* Thelma Shorr, senior editor of *The American Journal of Nursing*, wrote in October 1963 that nurses had been besieging the network, the sponsors, the producers, and the American Nurses Association with opinions about the series.[8]

By far, the consensus was negative, Shorr wrote. A chief concern was the image of nursing student Gail Lukas. Many of her real-life counterparts felt that she was embarrassingly and unrealistically inept. Another source of irritation was with the "soap opera situations" in which they said the nurses were depicted. The generally melodramatic plots gave uninitiated viewers strange ideas about what goes on in a true hospital, they felt. The general lack of humor around the nursing station would turn off prospective applicants to the profession. Even more dismaying to nurses were the sensationalized images of the women in white who were often the center of attention in guest roles.[9]

Said Shorr of her constituency: "Why, they ask, are nurses portrayed as alcoholic, luetic, unmarried and pregnant, Nazi, or neurotic? Many agree vehemently with the critic who wrote off an early show with the comment, 'These nurses should never have been registered.' "[10]

Brodkin's insistence on independence from outside forces meant that he didn't have the imprimatur of the American Nurses Association to help buffer the show from such complaints. He and his chief technical advisor, Florence McManus, did, however, try their best to ingratiate themselves with the profession they were depicting. Publicity stressed that McManus was a nurse of broad experience. To work on *The Nurses* she had taken leave from her position at Roosevelt Hospital. Concern with technical accuracy was so great on the show that when McManus found she could not both check scripts and set props for authenticity, she hired Sandra Pascual, also a Roosevelt Hospital nurse, to do the latter.[11]

At the same time, Brodkin and McManus added a plea for understanding the constraints of dramatic television. McManus noted what other consultants had learned—that on television the medically possible often takes precedence over the medically probable. And she repeated what by then had become a medical show consultant's familiar refrain: "I have learned to recognize the director's problems and sometimes I have to adjust to them. For example, even when the patient should be flat in bed, the head of the bed will have to be raised a little for a good camera angle. I realize now that many of the things I criticized when I watched the show myself, before I came to work here, involve dramatic or camera requirements."[12]

Some of these requirements were frustrating her attempts to deal with legitimate criticisms, McManus allowed. For example, she agreed with many who wrote letters noting that in a real nursing school clinical instructors separate from the hospital-based Liz Thorpes would guide novices such as Gail Lukas. McManus revealed that she had argued vociferously for adding such a character to the cast, but she had been turned down.[13]

As for humor among nurses, McManus said she had tried to inject some into the script. However, time requirements often forced the creators to drop that on the cutting room floor. "Besides," noted the show's story editor, Earl Booth, "in the treatment of a serious subject, attempts at humor are too apt to be offensive."[14]

It was Brodkin who tried to defuse the most sensitive issue, the allegedly repugnant depictions of nurses in guest star roles. Brodkin told Thelma Shorr that using the series to raise powerful social issues such as drug addiction, abortion, and euthanasia often meant using guest nurses as embodiments or vehicles of those controversial subjects. "I want this show to say something, to be truthful," he said. "I try to portray reality so I must show nurses as human beings."[15]

Brodkin emphasized his firm belief that his program was good for the image of nursing. Yet this, he stressed, could not be his primary goal: "Our purpose is to entertain. We respect nurses here, and our intention is honest. We mean to give a good picture [of nursing] but our first loyalty is to the public. Our job is to entertain."[16]

Ironically, it was the imperative to entertain that ended up lowering the status of nurses on the show. Two forces were at work here. The first was what people on the set regarded as Zina Bethune's low acting ability. Arthur Lewis recalled that while Brodkin hoped that the chemistry between Conway and Bethune would be right for the show, it didn't work out that way. Being a novice actress did not make her good at playing a novice nurse.

The program's producers and directors agreed that her acting range was narrow. At one point the producers even considered replacing Bethune with a young singer who was making a name for herself in a Broadway musical comedy called "I Can Get It for You Wholesale." But they ended up deciding that Barbra Streisand's face "could stop a truck" and wouldn't work well on TV. They'd stick it out with Bethune.

The consequences were severe for the image of the student nurse. Important scenes had to be rewritten so that Conway or someone else could say lines originally intended for Bethune. That affected the range of experiences that viewers could have with the characters. For example, vignettes illuminating Liz Thorpe's background were dropped into episodes fairly frequently. Program loyalists could get to know her. She was shown in her apartment, talking about her past (she was a widow), socializing with friends, and engaged in a long-term (but never deeply examined) romance with Anson Kiley, a hospital physician.

Gail Lucas, on the other hand, was not depicted in nearly as much detail. True, she did graduate to become a staff nurse in the third season. And plots did hint of romantic interest she had in an intern. But, at least in part because of a concern about the actress's range, plots tended not to give her meaty bits to work through. Little wonder that many nursing groups thought that the student had "a unidimensional quality" and "less depth and believability" than did her mentor.[17]

The second force that lowered the status of nursing on the show was an entertainment programming principle that network officials seemed to be relying on more and more. James Aubrey and Mike Dann had come to see in *The Nurses* a disastrous flaw: the show revolved around women. It was the point that *Variety* had mentioned in its 1962 critique. Unlike *Variety*'s reviewer, though, Dann and Aubrey were bothered not only by the possibility that women viewers were leaving the program for handsome male leads elsewhere on the dial. Their additional, more serious concern was that *The Nurses* drove male viewers away because it had no male leads.

By 1964, Dann had moved up from being CBS's Vice President of East Coast Programming to being vice president of all programming activities. Given a modest degree of autonomy by Aubrey (who was soon to be fired for unrelated reasons), Dann was developing a hard-headed programming style designed to maximize his network's competitiveness. Perry Lafferty, who joined CBS in 1964 as the West Coast programming chief, recalled that Dann built his prime-time drama strategy around a straightforward principle: the series that get the best ratings are "franchise" shows based on men who are involved in struggles of life against death.

Life-and-death was important, Dann felt, because the subject riveted viewers. A franchise was key because it gave the continuing characters an excuse to involve themselves in life-and-death adventures. And men were necessary as central characters since (1) a prime-time show had to attract both sexes, and (2) men would not be lured to a series revolving around women.

It was a simple brew, and Dann insisted on it. Lawyer shows, cop shows, detective shows all had to use formats that fit the recipe. Clearly, *The Defenders* didn't because it dealt more with social issues in a naturalistic way than with murder and action-filled jeopardy. *The Nurses* had the same problem, but it was compounded because women were central to the cast.

Actually, executives at Plautus Productions were also regretting the choice of central characters, but for somewhat different reasons. Not long into the first season, Arthur Lewis and his writers found that writing powerful stories around hospital nurses presented major difficulties. Buzz Berger, an executive at Plautus, recalled that "*The Nurses* proved harder to do meaningful scripts than . . . *The Defenders*. We went through a series of producers and story editors in the first year or so of *The Nurses* because of the inability of some writers to come to grips with the nurses."

The problem, Berger and others at the company decided, was basic to the series: "It's hard because nurses are not usually involved in the kind of life and death situations that either doctors or lawyers are involved in, where somebody's life or liberty may be dependent on how well he works at his job. Nurses—while they're desperately important, . . . like teachers—don't really do the kind of things that make great drama."

Joel Katz, one of those who produced the show after Arthur Lewis left after the first year, said that a basic difficulty was a perception by writers, producers, and network officials that nurses realistically did not have enough power in the hospital to believably command life-and-death situations. The storytellers tried to face the problems head-on, he said. "We tried to give Liz strong stature running the joint. But it was a problem, and it was one that we could never really deal successfully with." The writers included physicians when they needed them, he noted. But that didn't solve the larger problem. "We sold a concept, and once you sell that concept, you're stuck."

At CBS, people seemed to feel that the problems of profession and gender in *The Nurses* were linked. Certainly, their proposed solution combined both issues, as Mike Dann remembered: "There was a great feeling about how do you get more masculine appeal into *The Nurses*. There were arguments going on with Brodkin constantly about how you get masculine appeal. They did try. There were always men involved. But Herbert used to say, 'The name of the show is *The Nurses*.' And later we said . . . 'Why can't we make it *The Doctors and the Nurses?*' "

Finally, the solution was forced on Katz and Brodkin as condition for the show's renewal for a third season. Two doctors who had appeared in earlier episodes, a supervisor of residents (played by Joseph Campanella) and a resident (Michael Tolan) were added to the continuing cast. Speaking to the press about the changes, Mike Dann conceded that he hadn't felt "altogether secure" about the show from its start because "it was a completely female-oriented show." Brodkin himself admitted the difficulty of finding good stories for a pair of nurses.[18]

CBS's press release about the "new male stars" accentuated the positive. It made the new slant sound like a Brodkinized *Ben Casey* with nurses thrown in. "Tolan plays a young resident, Alex Tazinski, who frequently finds himself at odds with American medicine," it quoted Herb Brodkin as saying a month before the new season."He is a hot-head, a fighter, always bright but sometimes wrong. Campanella is Ted Steffen, an attending physician on the neurological staff of the hospital, who is beset by moral doubts. Tazinski and Steffens are often in conflict with one another and with the characters played by Shirl

Conway and Zina Bethune. This widens the range of subjects we can dramatize."[19]

Shirl Conway was gracious in public about the addition of two co-stars. Nevertheless, she did go out of her way to knock the new title. "Out of sheer diplomacy, I think it should be called *The Nurses and the Doctors*," she told *TV Guide*. "The producers have made a lot of money out of the nursing profession, and it would have been more politic to give the nurses top billing."[20]

It soon emerged that the name and the men were not the only changes in the show. In line with Dann's desire to tilt toward the macho, physical violence was added. Nursing researchers Philip Kalisch, Beatrice Kalisch, and Margaret Scobey found that of the seventy-two episodes that made up the first two seasons of *The Nurses*, only four (5%) depicted scenes of murder, suicide, crime, or the "malignant occult." By contrast, eight (28%) of the third year's twenty-eight installments of the series saw that kind of brutality.[21]

Yet the new approach did not bring higher ratings. Opposite ABC's *The Fugitive*, an adventure drama, and NBC's *The Bell Telephone Hour*, a variety show, *The Doctors and the Nurses* failed to attract an audience larger than *The Nurses* had lured the year before. By contrast, *The Fugitive* turned into the number 5 Nielsen show of the season. It had just the premise Dann hungered for: a physician found guilty of murdering his wife escapes from the police and travels the country incognito trying to find the real killer. Every week gave the fugitive a new setting, a new reason for both male and female viewers to get involved with people's lives, and a new kind of jeopardy.

The Fugitive was judged a hit, and *The Doctors and the Nurses* was not renewed. Years later, Buzz Berger admitted that the series deserved to go off. He recalled that "it was tired and it wasn't doing so well in [the ratings]." At the time, though, the cancellation infuriated Herbert Brodkin. Part of the problem was that it came with two other bits of bad news. CBS announced that in addition to terminating *The Doctors and the Nurses*, the network intended to yank from prime time Brodkin's other two series—*The Defenders* and his wobbly new law show, *For the People*.

In spite of the brouhaha that Brodkin raised about the cancellation,[22] *The Doctors and the Nurses* was absent from the CBS prime-time lineup during premiere week of September 1965. Yet it was far from absent from TV altogether. Taking comments about the "female oriented," "soap opera" nature of the program to their logical conclusion, CBS programmers scheduled repeats of the show on weekday afternoons in search of a distaff audience. ABC executives went one step better. They transformed the program, re-dubbed *The Nurses*, into a daytime serial tilted toward women. With a different cast and a totally different thematic slant, the program sold soap on weekday afternoons for two and a half more years.

Dramatic License

The Nurses lasted a year longer than The Eleventh Hour, which endured for two seasons. The Breaking Point survived only one season. After that, only Ben Casey and Dr. Kildare remained. When they were pulled from prime time in 1966, the first doctor show cycle on American TV came to an end. By then, network programming executives had begun to feel that the potential of prime-time medicos was gone for a while.

Part of the reason seems to be what was hot in the mid-1960s. Situation comedies and variety hours were the staple of Nielsen's Top 20, with Westerns taking up most of the remaining slots. Kildare and Casey had dropped off the hits list and were weighing in with mediocre numbers. The time didn't seem right for running with medicine.

Then, too, the programming principles that increasingly began to guide schedules advised against a general influx of doctor shows. Consensus in the industry was that while hourly dramas tended generally to attract women, the doctor shows had especially strong female appeal. At a time when raw audience size was the name of the prime-time game, it seemed like a bad idea to mount more than a couple of series that might turn off the men of U.S. households. The most successful drama programs of the 1965–66 through 1967–68 seasons were The Fugitive, Bonanza, Daktari, The Man from U.N.C.L.E., and The Wild Wild West. These shows mixed high macho with high melodrama in an effort to appeal to both sexes.

The Man from U.N.C.L.E. and The Wild Wild West, two mindlessly rollicking spy adventures, point to another consideration that seems to have made TV people insecure about doctor shows. The medical series had gotten a reputation of being too cerebral. With their emphasis on dilemmas of the human mind, the creators of The Eleventh Hour, The Breaking Point, and The Nurses had tried to continue what they considered the literate tradition of TV's anthology shows from the 1950s.

But that was a tradition that network officials wanted to put behind them. They felt that poetic stories about immigrants and minorities in ethical or emotional quandaries were simply not the kinds of tales that held huge audiences over the long haul. Even Norman Felton came to admit ruefully that sometimes the writing in such programs was "above the heads of the masses." Network programmers also know that advertisers weren't enthusiastic about these shows, since their sometimes downbeat scenes didn't contribute the kind of upbeat excitement that they wanted around their commercials.[23]

These reservations, however, did not mean that network programmers were ready to write doctor shows off as not viable. There had been too many hugely popular precedents for them to do that. It did mean, though, that the doctor cycle of the early 1960s had taught them to worry about how far afield to let the form go in the future. Mike Dann at CBS was an opinion leader for the industry. To him being

Frederick Faust (left) with George W. Fish, Venice 1930. Under the pen name of Max Brand, Faust created the character of Dr. Kildare, which was influenced by his friendship with Fish. *(Courtesy of Robert Easton)*

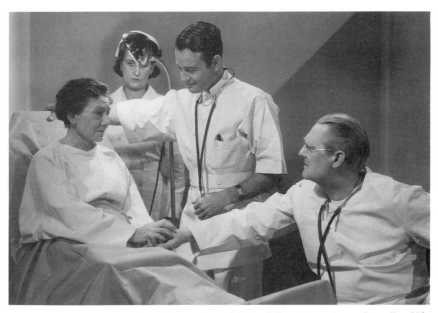

Lew Ayres (standing with stethoscope) and Lionel Barrymore (seated) as Dr. Kildare and Dr. Gillespie. The two were the mainstay of Metro-Goldwyn-Mayer's popular Kildare film series. *(Courtesy of Turner Entertainment Company)*

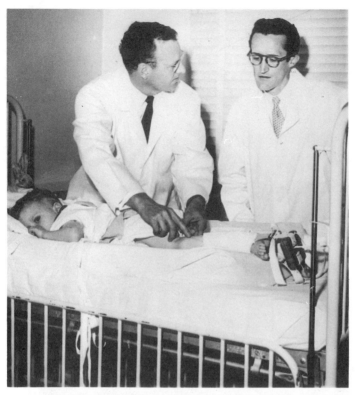

James Moser (right) conducting research for his NBC-TV series *Medic*. It was network television's first hit doctor show. *(Courtesy of TV Guide)*

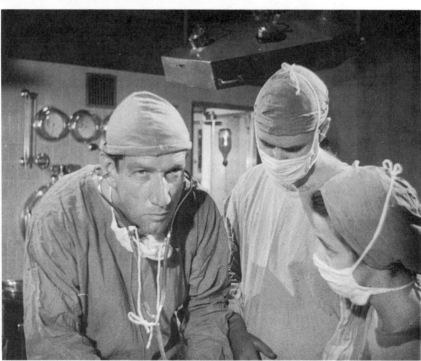

Richard Boone as Dr. Konrad Styner in *Medic*. He was host of the anthology series as well as an occasional participant in the cases. *(Courtesy of TV Guide)*

The casts from Arena Productions' two contributions to the TV doctor-show cycle of the early 1960s. *Dr. Kildare* starred Richard Chamberlain (center) as the young intern and Raymond Massey (left) as Dr. Gillespie, his mentor. *The Eleventh Hour* starred Jack Ging (standing at right) as a young psychologist and Ralph Bellamy as a psychiatrist who was his partner and mentor. *(Courtesy of Norman Felton)*

Richard Chamberlain and Yvette Mimieux in "Tyger, Tyger," a 1961 episode of *Dr. Kildare*. The romance between the doctor and the epileptic water skier received much press attention, as did Mimieux's scanty bikini. *(Courtesy of Norman Felton)*

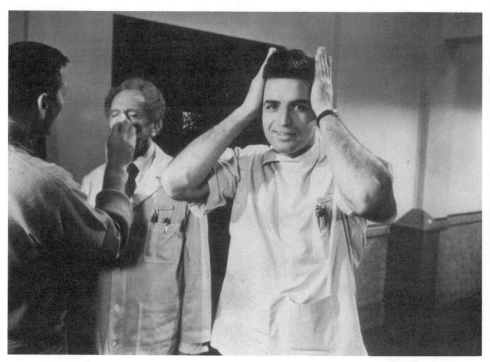

Sam Jaffe (left) and Vince Edwards (right) on the set of their enormously popular series, *Ben Casey. (Courtesy of TV Guide)*

The stars of *The Nurses* in 1964. A year later the program was retitled *The Doctors and the Nurses. (Courtesy of TV Guide)*

James Brolin as Dr. Kiley and Robert Young as Dr. Welby in *Marcus Welby, M.D.* To the producers Kiley's motorcycle was a sign of youthful rebellion. *(Courtesy of TV Guide)*

The cast and crew of *Emergency!* on Engine 51. *(Courtesy of Hannah Shearer)*

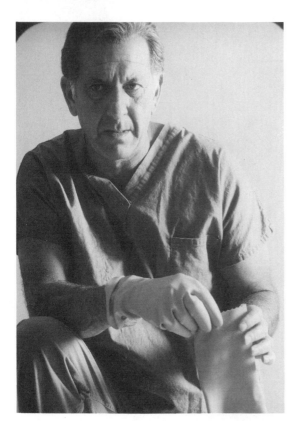

Jack Klugman as the crusading pathologist Quincy. *(Courtesy of TV Guide)*

A scene from "Antagonists," the first presentation in the *Medical Story* anthology series. Beau Bridges starred as a young intern who opposes a noted gynecologist (played by Jose Ferrer) when the latter orders a hysterectomy for a young patient. *(Courtesy of Columbia Pictures Television)*

Roscoe Karns, Abby Dalton, and Jackie Cooper in *Hennesey*, one of the first situation comedies with a medical theme. Kent cigarettes was a sponsor, and the producers often looked for ways to include the product in the action. *(Courtesy of TV Guide)*

"Mentor and Tormentor" is what Screen Gems, the production company, titled this publicity still for *Temperatures Rising*. In the first version of the situation comedy (there were three) intern Cleavon Little (left) sparred with chief of staff James Whitmore. *(Courtesy of Columbia Pictures Television)*

Patricia Kalember as Kay O'Brien in the show of that name. Like most other women physicians in TV history, "KO" was great at medicine but terrible at romantic relationships. *(Courtesy of TV Guide)*

Members of the large cast of *St. Elsewhere. (Courtesy of MTM Enterprises)*

cautious meant following three broad principles in dealing with the formula. First, doctor series had to be placed in the late evening, preferably at 10, because (he said) that was when female-oriented dramas traditionally scored best. Second, the shows had to revolve around male physicians, not nurses or women. And third, the dramas had to enact clear, high-emotion issues of life and death, not the politics of the hospital or the medical system.

It was perspective that pointed the doctor show back toward its core approach: human emotions entangled in a male physician's technological struggle with death. By this view, the best recipe was to have the aura of scientific exactness confront the anguish of mental and physical turmoil. James Moser had taken that approach when he had decided to build *Ben Casey* around neurosurgery. Here, he knew, was a frontier science where clear-cut decisions often had to made in seconds. Here was a field of prestigious battle, where the knife could meet the mind in legitimate and tension-filled climaxes.

To a network programmer, the trick was to come up with something that embodied the basics of this *Kildare/Casey* form but appeared different. In the mid-1960s, *The Eleventh Hour*, *The Breaking Point*, and *The Nurses* underscored for programmers and producers the dramatic difficulties of getting even a little far from the mold. Producers on *The Nurses* said they were hard-pressed to make their heroines the center of life-and-death engagements. The producer of *The Eleventh Hour* found that building a doctor show around psychiatrists was unwieldy for the very reason that they tended not to see themselves in short-term technological struggles with disease. He also complained that, unlike other areas of medicine, psychiatry was hard to portray as an exact science. Medical struggles, he felt, were more effective when the medical answers were clear, even if they were not always attainable.

In addition to highlighting dramatic difficulties, the creation of *The Eleventh Hour* and *The Nurses* also pointed to the political headaches that could come from straying too far from the traditional core of the formula. Sam Rolfe found that using psychologists with psychiatrists invited a tumultuous rivalry between the two professions to play itself out behind the show's scenes. Similarly, Herbert Brodkin and his associates learned that centering a medical show around nurses rather than doctors raised thorny questions about the depiction of sexual and professional power. When it came to portraying physicians, Hollywood had already answered those questions. To would-be medical show creators wanting to avoid trouble, the message was that doctoring (rather than nursing or psychology) was the craft to use.

Despite the portrayal of doctors as health care kings, some physician leaders were unhappy with television's image of physicians during the 1960s. According to Eugene Hoffman, a longtime member of the AMA'a Advisory Committee, two especially conservative members of the Association's board of trustees argued that the Committee was allowing unfavorable images of doctors to hide behind the AMA seal of approval. Especially worrisome to them was the AMA's impotence over what they considered the unacceptably sexy image Ben Casey projected as a physician.

Yielding to these concerns, the Board decided that the Association's seal of approval should not go to shows that didn't allow complete AMA supervision. So, the trustees made it clear to public relations counselor Jerry Pettis that his office would lose a good deal of funding if he didn't withdraw the seal from *Dr. Kildare, Ben Casey,* and *The Eleventh Hour.* Pettis complied, but he tried to keep the spirit of cooperation alive. He reminded producers that the advisory committee remained. He also told them that they could still say their show had been produced with the help of the AMA, even if they couldn't display the seal.

Hoffman felt that Jerry Pettis and the advisory physicians understood what the AMA's trustees did not: television's producers had no intention of creating programs that attacked the legitimacy of the nation's health care professions. Doctors, especially, were the central heroes of TV medicine's struggle against death, and it would be dramatically self-defeating to make them fundamentally unsympathetic.

Direct attempts by the AMA's Physicians Advisory Committee to monitor scripts was only one of several forces leading producers to continue emphasizing the centrality of physician-heroes in prime-time medical dramas. Herbert Brodkin's refusal to deal with the AMA may have allowed him unusual freedom in a few plots, but it didn't affect the network thinking that led to restructuring the series with doctors in command. Even *The Doctors and the Nurses* never ended up making the consistently weighty arguments against organized medicine that Brodkin suggested it would.

At the same time, Pettis knew that the producers of all doctor shows felt a need to build their own credibility with the public by showing their awareness of issues that sometimes strained public sympathy for the medical system. They typically did it through guest stars who, as bad examples, often got caught by the good examples, the continuing medical heroes. Still, some criticisms against medicine needed to be toned down, Pettis and the members agreed. It was here, they felt, they could be of special help to organized medicine. The members of the Committee operated under the belief that cooperation with TV even under conditions of incomplete power would still yield image benefits in times of need. At least organized medicine would be calling some of the shots.

In the end, a melting pot of considerations surrounded the creation of programming. Public and professional controversies, programming principles, and dramatistic concerns served as guideposts for producers trying to come up with the next hit medical series. Despite a few failures, there were many people working at it. Michael Dann recalled that he and his counterparts at NBC and ABC were flooded with proposals for doctor dramas in the mid-1960s.

At it happened, the race was won by a producer who was already familiar to doctor-show players and who understood the narrowed options. His series, *Marcus Welby, M.D.*, was to become the biggest hit in the history of ABC to that time. It was to enshrine the image of the TV doctor and lead to a new generation of medical shows. Yet, reflecting the continuing tensions inherent in the relationship between physician leaders and the television industry, it was to raise new concerns about the doctor show on the part of organized medicine. For the first time, the medical establishment would consider that the big issue might not, after all, be that doctor shows were doing a bad job with their image. "Instead," medical leaders wondered, "might it be that the job they are doing is too good?"

7

Doctor Knows Best

Sid Sheinberg was gambling the whole wad, David Victor knew. It had come down to a little projection room at Universal Studios. The group was small but powerful: Sheinberg was head of Universal's TV operation; Grant Tinker, previously with NBC, was a prominent Universal executive; Marty Starger was programming chief at ABC, and he had brought one of his assistants. And David Victor was executive producer of the proposed Universal series, *Marcus Welby, M.D.*

The tension was not about whether ABC should finance the two-hour pilot movie for its 1967–68 season. Network programmers had already agreed to that after they had read the script. What the men sitting in the projection room had congregated to decide was whether the actor they had just viewed on the screen, Robert Young, should play Doctor Welby. Young wanted the role. David Victor insisted that he would be perfect for the part. But the ABC people demurred.

They knew that the issue was not Robert Young's acting ability. The sixty-one-year-old Young had been a genuine movie star longer than some of those in the room had been alive. In addition, he had helped create, and had starred in, the classic family television situation comedy, *Father Knows Best*, first on radio and then on television. That had made him a household name and a TV rerun king.

The issue, everyone understood, was Young's alcohol problem. Though it was not a public matter, people in the industry knew that Bob Young had longstanding difficulties with the bottle. It had caused troubles on the *Father Knows Best* set; it had caused unpleasantries elsewhere. ABC executives didn't want to risk having it crop up in the new series. They wanted Ralph Bellamy for the role. Apart from the alcohol issue, they felt that Bellamy fit their curmudgeonly image of the older physician better than Young did.

David Victor again repeated his case for Young. First, Young had vowed that he had been on the wagon for nearly three years, and Victor trusted the man. Second, Young had worked for him in 1965 on a *Dr. Kildare* episode and had been thoroughly professional. Third, Young had recently done a guest star stint on Universal's *The Name of the Game,* a series that Victor had produced, and had won rave reviews. He had the public image and the talents for the role of a general practitioner. Bellamy, while a fine actor, was already tagged as a psychiatrist by many viewers because of his role in *The Eleventh Hour.* In addition, he was now doing medicine commercials on TV. Victor contended that this would further confuse viewers as to what Marcus Welby really was.

Starger and his assistant were still not visibly won over, so Sheinberg decided to force the issue. He asked Victor to say again with finality whom he wanted to play Marcus Welby. Victor repeated Robert Young. Sheinberg then turned to the ABC programmers and said, "Gentlemen, you heard him. Either we go with Robert Young, or we'll take the project somewhere else."

Victor was astonished at what he heard because it was a bluff. The Welby script had already passed through CBS and NBC but no deal had been made. CBS ended up going with *Medical Center,* and NBC had chosen *The Bold Ones* as its new doctor series. ABC was the end of the line. Starger didn't know that, though, and Sheinberg's pressure worked. A deal was struck. Victor and his producer David O'Connell had their series. And Robert Young had a new character.

The character was to have a major impact on the public discussion of physicians in the United States. More than even during the *Kildare/Casey* fad of eight years before, an actor became associated almost inextricably with both a role and a profession. Over the show's seven-year life, Robert Young as Marcus Welby became the embodiment of norms for the American family physician.

It was not the series alone that held that image up to such adulation. What makes the enshrinement of Welby/Young as a quintessential people's doctor particularly interesting is the role that media in general—especially newspapers and magazines—played in the process. As in earlier years, the media hype was fueled from a number of sources—studio and network publicity, publicity from organized medicine, desire on the press's part to capitalize on interest in a highly rated show. But the publicity for *Welby* was raised to more fascinating levels by the determination of its star to live his role outside the sound stage.

The combination of influences led to so many good words about TV's good doctor that a backlash of sorts began to develop in some quarters. Some medical leaders even began to ask whether physicians were being portrayed too well on the home tube. In the future, that would raise important issues of credibility for producers tinkering with the formula. But to Welby creators the best response to the criticism was simply to restate that Welby was a good model. Ironically, physicians found that television was dictating their behavior, rather than the other way around.

Kildare Leaves the Nest

For David Victor, the Welby character was in many ways not a new model at all. He was James Kildare grown older. Producing *Dr. Kildare* for Norman Felton at MGM, Victor had seized on the idea that the central character should develop. He had moved Richard Chamberlain from intern to resident to chief resident. As ratings dipped and NBC strategists prescribed the serial format for the show in the manner of *Peyton Place*, Victor had tried to convince them to drop the twice-a-week plan and go with the logical next step: having Kildare leave his student days at Blair Hospital and open up a practice on his own.

The change, he felt, would allow new dramatic possibilities. He admitted that he had never been stuck for stories on the program. A hospital, he knew, is "a Grand Hotel, and you can have a zillion stories." Nevertheless, "in a hospital you're constrained because you only see people when they come in and you lose contact with them when they go out." Taking Kildare from the box and giving him legitimate reason to roam through the world would freshen up the series, he was sure. He added that it was the realistic thing to do. "You don't remain a yeshiva bokker [boy] all your life," he chastised NBC programmers. "Let him legitimately go now!"

They didn't listen, and Victor turned his energies to producing two adventure series at Metro that had nothing to do with medicine, *The Man From U.N.C.L.E.* and *Jericho*. He left MGM for a short stint at Filmways and moved again around 1966 for a lucrative Universal producing contract. He started at Universal by helping to develop Robert Stack's segments for the glitzy three-in-one NBC series, *The Name of the Game*. But the idea of doing another doctor show stuck with him.

"That thought never left my mind," he said years later. "So after I was at Universal for six months or so, making *The Name of the Game*, I never stopped thinking that what really should have happened is that the man should have gone out. Except that I didn't want to encroach on *Dr. Kildare*. I couldn't use the name; Metro owned it. And I didn't want to have a young man going out because that was too close to Doctor Kildare. And because I'm a creative man, and there's more than one way. And because I thought, 'Why not have a middle-aged or elderly man who's been in practice a long time, and make him a family practitioner. What gives you a better arena for drama?' "

A couple of years before, David O'Connell had pitched a show at the studio about a general practitioner, but it had been rejected. O'Connell, a jack of all film trades who had recently moved from editing into production, had received a letter from the doctor he used when he had lived on Long Island suggesting a series about a family doctor. He liked the notion and brought the idea to Jennings Lang, Sid Sheinberg's predecessor as the head of Universal's TV division. Lang had turned him down with the statement that as good as the notion might be, the time was wrong. "Nobody at the networks wants a doctor show now," he said. "Kildare has been cancelled and the Vince Edward thing is being cancelled. You just can't sell doctor shows. I wouldn't even attempt it."

O'Connell was working on another set of segments for *The Name of the Game* two years later when David Victor began to try out his doctor show idea on people at the studio. Sheinberg was now the TV chief, prejudices at the networks had changed, and Universal's top brass seemed receptive. O'Connell was enthusiastic about the possibilities, and the two put their heads together on some of the specifics. For example, they decided to place the show outside of a big city because they felt that most viewers associated family doctors with more easy-going locales.

"People don't believe that compassionate family doctors who make house calls operate in the city of New York," explained O'Connell. "You see, when you have a family doctor you can either put them in a rural area or small town, but then you don't have many stories. Or you can put them in a medium-sized city, like Santa Monica or Spokane, Washington."

For logistical reasons, the choice was more likely between Pasadena and Santa Monica. They chose Santa Monica, partly because the executives at St. John's Hospital there were willing to cooperate with the shooting schedule. St. John's even allowed them to use the actual hospital sign for the show. This was important to Victor since he believed that rooting a program in a concrete locale lent it a realistic air.

Then there was the matter of the character's name and the program's title. Victor wanted to call it something like "Family Doctor." But O'Connell persuaded him that the audience would remember the title better if it were the physician's name. O'Connell liked Victor's choice for a last name but the first name caused both of them trouble. After working on Mark for a while, they settled on Marcus because they thought it just sounded better. Years later, both Victor and O'Connell insisted that the sound of the word "well" in their healer's surname was purely accidental and didn't occur to them at all at the time.

At any rate, the two got along and agreed to work on the pilot together. Victor would be the executive producer and O'Connell would carry out the on-site production chores. Victor also took responsibility for sketching the characters and writing the initial plot which would set up the proposed series.

Made into a script by veteran writer Don Mankiewicz, the plot used all the storytelling approaches that Victor had gleaned over the years, For example, he was aware that the show would be a switch from *Casey* and *Kildare* in that it focused on a middle-aged rather than young physician. Yet for interpersonal conflict and youth-oriented sex appeal he decided to retain the young man/old man relationship of the traditional formula by giving Welby a "coltish" young colleague, Steven

Kiley (played by James Brolin, a Universal contract player). In the pilot film, Welby is slowed by a heart attack and must hire a partner. Kiley, who not-so-secretly disdains family practice, bitterly forgoes a neurology residency to work with him because he needs money to help his kid brother get through college.

Victor's choice of Lew Ayres for a small but important role of hospital administrator in the film underscores that he was knowingly working in the doctor-show tradition. In some of the ground-level premises that Victor and Mankiewicz set up in the series pilot can be seen variations of the noblesse oblige assumptions that lay at the core of doctor shows going back to the Kildare short stories of the 1930s.

There are obvious differences. Marcus Welby drives a Chrysler; he is not an ostentatious physician but he is well off. Similarly, Steve Kiley is not crying poverty in an era when even interns earn a living wage. Yet both must make basic sacrifices to their profession and the audience is meant to sympathize with that. Welby's illness is clearly caused by overwork and overconcern for his patients. His sacrifice is compounded by a further development that echoes in an ironic way the selfless waiting of nurse Mary Lamont, Kildare's girlfriend in the Lew Ayres movies. In the pilot we see that Welby, a widower, loves a woman (actress Ann Baxter) who refuses to marry him unless he gives up his time-robbing and heart-breaking practice.

These establishing themes weave through a self-contained story that would become a model Welby plot. It concerns the treatment of long-time patient Lew Sawyer who has lost his power of speech and is reduced to the helpless status of a child. Sawyer's wife wants him committed to a hospital that specializes in aphasia. Welby refuses to sign the commitment papers until he has exhausted every resource. Finally, he is forced to do it.

Sawyer escapes from the hospital and takes refuge in Welby's office. There he becomes infuriated when he finds that his doctor has agreed to commit him. Burning the commitment papers, he sets the premises afire. He reaches for the phone and calls for help in one word. The fire department responds and he is rescued. Dr. Welby now knows there is hope. Lew Sawyer will regain his speech.

"Once he hangs up the shingle," said Victor of Welby, "he leaves himself open to get himself involved legitimately in any phase of a man's life." The key word was "legitimately," and he repeated it again for emphasis. He wanted to show the audience a character "you can go up to . . . with any problem. He's the father confessor, the family friend."

To authenticate this premise and build credibility for the entire show, Victor decided to follow the lead of James Moser and Norman Felton by getting the imprimatur of an established physicans' organization. Victor knew that the American Medical Association had stopped giving out its seal. But he learned that the American Academy of Family Physicians (AAFP) might be useful. It was based in Kansas City and its leaders were more than willing to help. They volunteered to let Victor post their formal blessing at the end of the show.

Victor's contact came at a critical point in the history of the AAFP. The organization was the spearhead of a newly recognized branch of American medicine, and it needed all the good publicity it could get. The basic idea behind family physicians, under the label general practitioners (GPs), was actually quite old. But as American medicine had become increasingly specialized after World War II, the status of GPs declined markedly. Internists and pediatricians and even gynecologists had become primary care physicians for many people. Yet the general practitioners insisted that there was a national need for well-trained generalists who could coordinate patient care of an entire family (especially in places where physicians were scarce) and decide which specialists to use, if they were needed.

In the late 1960s, an important AMA-sponsored commission on the future of graduate medical education agreed with them. One of the major conclusions of the commission, however, was that hospital residencies after medical school should guide medical school graduates toward specialization. Rotating internships, where the new M.D. got a taste of everything in the hospital, were to be phased out. To remain viable, family practice had to be considered a specialty. That was exactly how the politic committee saw it—as specialized training in broad-based medical care. As a result, it suggested that an American Board of Family Practice be formed as the official certifying unit of the specialty. Receiving organized medicine's approval, the Board started operation in 1969.

So just as the *Marcus Welby* pilot was getting off the ground, the family practice association was trying to familiarize the public and medical students with its presence and purpose. As a result, AAFP officials were eager to help Victor. What he needed really didn't take much work. Victor had already found a physician as his L.A.-based technical consultant. He had also hired a nurse to help with in-studio details. The AAFP's role would be to provide long-distance advice when necessary about the authenticity of Welby's activities and character. To do that, the organization got its six-member Public Relations Committee to read the scripts that Victor sent through the mail. The reviewers could call Victor or O'Connell if they had complaints or suggestions. In return, Victor could place a statement at the end of the pilot movie stating that the Academy had granted the program its approval.

Hanging Up the Shingle

ABC had already scheduled *Marcus Welby, M.D.*, as a series for a fall 1969 start when it aired the pilot film as an ABC Movie of the Week on

March 27, 1969. It got good ratings but only fair reviews. Bob Williams of the *New York Post* shuddered over "the cluttered story of what was presented as a movie."[1] Ben Gross of the *New York Daily News*, on the other hand, liked the story and complimented the scripting, producing, and directing. But Gross snickered that Welby was too good to be true, more dedicated that any doctor you could ever meet.[2]

Daily Variety's critic sided with Gross about the technical credits. Rather than dwell on Welby's astonishing bedside manner, though, the review zeroed in on the "formula approach to the subject" and its bottom-line implications for the network: "[The movie] demonstrated conclusively that there is the makings here of a popular series. The same set-siders who religiously turned on *Dr. Kildare* and *Ben Casey* . . . and followed Young and his family in *Father [Knows Best]*, are natural audiences."[3]

This was obviously the kind of prognostication that ABC and Universal executives liked to hear. The show was certainly going to have a good chance at making it. It was scheduled to air Tuesday at ten, opposite *CBS Reports* (a traditionally weak performer) and the last hour of NBC's Tuesday Night Movie. In addition, word in the trade was that the late-evening slot was best for doctor shows.

In the meantime, Victor and O'Connell got busy putting the hour-long series episodes together. A string of early decisions related to the regulars on the show. It soon became apparent that there would be little time for Welby's daughter and girlfriend in the weekly episodes. As in the doctor shows that preceded them, Welby and Kiley's past would have to take a far back seat to the problems of the guest stars they would deal with week after week. Ignoring the histories of running characters was a TV tradition, O'Connell noted. "I learned that from Jack Webb, because I had worked with Jack Webb on the original *Dragnet*s. You never knew if Sergeant Friday had a mother, a father, if he was married, or single or anything."

Some of Welby's personal attachments couldn't be merely ignored. A daughter, girlfriend, and housekeeper had shown up in the pilot. To clear the deck for Welby's patients, the daughter was married and sent to South America, and the girlfriend appeared very infrequently. Victor and O'Connell also decided to dispense with the housekeeper and instead get a nurse who would help the doctors in their office. Out of concern for portraying minorities (a growing public issue), they wanted to find someone with a Mexican background. But they saw their choice, Elena Verdugo, as someone who could bring to the part of Consuelo Lopez more than just a legitimate Hispanic background. An experienced actress with a joyously expressive face, Verdugo could lend lighthearted relief to an episode that might otherwise be grim. In fact, the producers made it a rule that writers had to include two scenes— one in the middle of the show and one at the end—where Verdugo would banter with Welby and Kiley. "She is one of the main reasons the show lasted so long," O'Connell maintained.

Other approaches began to fall into place as the series took shape. The creative impulses of the producers and writers came together with the standard demands of TV storytelling in such a way as to generate a flow of routines that became rather predicatable after a while. David Victor had it down pat. "The ideal show," he said, "would have to do with a good strong human theme. And you get involved with somebody in the opening minutes of the show . . . so that there's an emotional tie to somebody—the patient—in the early moments. So then you care what happens to them through this travail."

That meant the introduction, before the title. In those days, such prologues always included the main character. But Victor and O'Connell argued that sometimes it was less important to see Marcus Welby or Steven Kiley in the prologue than it was to get audience sympathy with the person who, anthology-like, would be the focus of the episode. ABC programming executives allowed them to do it.

Then came the body of the program. "First of all," Victor explained, "you're burdened with the fact that you have three acts with commercial breaks. Certainly, anybody who can write weekly series can write anything. We give them impossible demands. Here you go to a good writer. First of all, he's got to research the medical part of it. Then he's got to tell a dramatic story and arbitrarily break it just when it's getting good. Three times we legitimately have to have climaxes that will carry you over past the commercial. You have to have high points at which you drop off the story and then be able to pick it up again without losing momentum.

"Act One is the longest. You're allowed the longest period of time to develop your character and hook the story. To draw audiences in. It's like a good lay; it gets shorter and shorter until you have the orgasm at the end."

Medical incidents had their proper place in this scheme. "If an operation takes place, it will take place at the end of the second act. Carrying it into the third act. Usually it's a cutting edge of a medical problem, whatever it is. And there are not always operations. There are relapses and emotional adjustments. . . . But you do carry some crisis over that you can build on and bring to a resolution in Act Three."

Victor saw the "coda" at the end which brought Verdugo, Young, and Brolin together as a useful fillip. "It's an afterthought. There's no resolution, no additional material. We don't cheat in that we explain [the medical problem] away at this point. It's essentially a reaction to it, or a moment of lightness. To keep a continuing interest in our particular characters who may have been slighted a little bit in the episode. Since sometimes we would give the thrust of the story to Kiley and sometimes to Marcus Welby."

With the exception of the coda, the structure he described had applied to his work on *Dr. Kildare* as well as to *Marcus Welby*. Searching for plot ideas to feed writers during the first year, Victor also reached back to *Kildare* for tried and true inspiration. The first Welby episode, for example, redid "A Shining Image," the classic story from *Kildare's* inaugural season. The plot explored Kildare's first emotional relationship with a dying patient. Now, Victor figured, it was young Kiley's turn. The Welby script, "Hello Goodbye Hello," updated "Image" to resonate with and gently startle audiences in the late '60s. For example, the beautiful yet quickly dying young schoolteacher (played by Susan Clark) admits ruefully to Kiley that her one true love turned out to be gay. Yet the basic theme—the dying process as a self-exploration for doctor and patient—is the same.

The ending is upbeat in spite of the woman's death. After she dies, Kiley receives a note she had written thanking him for his help in her time of greatest loneliness. It is a heartwarming moment that ends the third act. The coda lifts the spirit even higher. Welby mentions that he is on his way to teach a boy how to use insulin. The youth will learn quickly, says Welby, and live until he's eighty. So much of what he and Kiley do does have hope, he stresses. The message is to the viewer as well as to Kiley.

The uplifting ending of "Hello Goodbye Hello" set a pattern for the several Welby episodes where the patient wasn't cured. True, *Welby* followed other doctor shows in that a cure was usually in the cards. But *Marcus Welby* did have one slant that made it different from *Kildare,* or the more contemporary *Medical Center* and *The Bold Ones*. The other shows stressed short-term illnesses that paralleled or ignited certain unrelated personal problems. *Welby*, on the other hand, dealt consistently with long-term medical problems that were tied directly to the patient's psyche and interpersonal behavior. Acute episodes of the difficulty often sparked movement toward a cure, but only after Welby or Kiley uncovered the root causes of the behavioral problems. For example:

—Dr. Welby and Dr. Kiley become concerned about Enid Cooper, a counselor in an orphanage, when they learn she's addicted to pills. The doctors are unable to persuade the young woman to give them up. Then, under the influence of pills, Enid is responsible for a car accident in which one of her charges is hurt.

—At a rehabilitation center, Dr. Welby and Nurse Consuelo help a young woman who has become a paraplegic because of meningitis. Their goal: to help her realize that despite her lifetime confinement to a wheelchair, she can still fulfill her ambition to become a writer.

—A young girl who goes from an orphanage to live with a couple who lost their own daughter has recurring attacks that require medical attention. Whether the illness is physical or psychosomatic (related to parental fears communicated to the child) is a diagnostic problem for Dr. Welby.

—Over the course of a summer, Dr. Welby helps an overweight teenage girl lose a lot of weight. Now she is an attractive person. That, however, causes new problems. Her mother, who has always wanted her child to be popular, begins to push her into promiscuity. When Welby sees her again in the fall, she is pregnant. Helping her become slim has opened a Pandora's Box. What can he do now?

These problems were precisely the stomping ground for the family physician as Victor, O'Connell, and their technical advisors saw the profession. David O'Connell recalled that both he and Victor would scour medical journals, magazines, and newspapers for diseases that fit their program's approach. They learned that by varying the patient and the family problem, they could reuse diseases like epilepsy many times through the show's life.

O'Connell sent the AMA's Advisory Panel on Television, Radio, and Motion Pictures scripts as a courtesy. The panel was asked for help infrequently. Thomas Stern, the family doctor on call for the show during most of its run, was the primary resource. He saw his job as lending an authentic air to the proceedings by checking the script, and, before that, by consulting with writers on medical facts once they had discussed their basic plot with Victor, O'Connell, or the story editor.

With respect to broader aspects of the show, Stern did come to accept the producers' insistence that dramatic license often had to be introduced. He knew that no physicians could devote the time to a single patient that Welby and Kiley did every week. Victor and O'Connell had the writers stress that in most cases the physicians had known the patients long before the episode's start. Even so, Stern knew, it was unrealistic.

There were other compromises with authenticity. To be as dramatic as possible, *Welby* writers sometimes portrayed certain medical tests or other events out of sequence. Sometimes, too, the symptoms or social consequences of a disease were pushed to their realistic limits in order to hype the story. Stern learned to accept it, and Victor made no apologies. "If it were incorrect," he said, "we'd never use it. But with a matter of dramatic license, [we'd ask] 'Is it possible?' It's as simple as that. The dimensions are, either you play that game and stay on the air for seven years and teach a lot . . . or you don't stay on the air. And then you are more sociologically correct, but nobody watches."

According to the deal Victor had made with the American Academy of Family Physicians, the physicians on its public relations committee would get a script about a month before it went in front of the camera. The doctors were invited to write or call David O'Connell if they had complaints or suggestions. Dr. Robert Young, a family physician who would often be ribbed about his name, served on the committee throughout the seven years *Welby* was on the air.

He recalled that he and his colleagues realized the unmatchable attention Welby and Kiley gave their patients was necessary dramatic license, out of their control. Beyond that, neither he nor any of the other five members had many suggestions. "The interesting thing to me was how well the writers did," he recalled. "Here I was, a man who'd been a family physician for many years in a small town and taught medicine in the university, and I was impressed with how close the writers got to the spirit of what it meant to do what I do."

When the AAFP physicians did have a complaint, it tended to be about aspects of the family physician's image that Tom Stern had missed. Dr. Young remembered getting a script toward the end of the show's run in which Dr. Welby treats a Native American medical student who is expected to return to his tribe as a family physician. But the student starts getting violent headaches and Welby is concerned at first that he has a tumor. Ruling that out, he comes to believe that the headaches stem from psychological tension. In the script, Welby refers the young man to a psychiatrist.

That upset Dr. Young. He phoned David O'Connell. "I called and said, 'By God, don't have the show with him getting psychiatric counsel. Welby should be his counselor. All the family doctors in America will be mad if you refer him to a psychiatrist for a headache when a headache is our forte. . . . And all the psychiatrists in the country will be mad, because they're so doggone busy doing other things that may be more sophisticated.' "

O'Connell changed the ending. It made Dr. Young feel proud. The AAFP public relations committee didn't do it often, he noted, but it could shape Marcus Welby's image if it saw a problem.

The Honest Burgher

Many people had a lot riding on the Welby image, but none so much as Robert Young, the actor. The concern surely wasn't money. Young was wealthy, and he'd continue to be wealthy as long as *Father Knows Best* reruns kept showing up on local stations around the country. Rather, the need was for personality and self-esteem. Young needed Welby's personality and self-esteem as a psychological anchor, a substitute for the character he felt he didn't have. It was a pressing issue for the aging actor. He had made extraordinary efforts to secure the role.

This view emerges from discussions with colleagues and from a series of interviews that Young gave to journalists after *Marcus Welby, M.D.,* was a solid success. Only in these after-the-fact revelations does the tortured, struggling psyche which reached out to play Welby make itself visible. Before that, until around 1971, the press pictured Young's private self in the most benign, easygoing fashion. Just before the *Welby* premiere, for example, Jack Robbins of the *New York Post* called him the incarnation of "comfortable rectitude, the honest burgher." He also noted, though, that the experienced actor "deftly and quickly sketches out his biography, pausing now and again for an anecdote, avoiding telling more about himself than he would care anyone to know."[4]

What Young didn't want the public to know at the time was that the past thirty years had been a continual battle with severe depression. The condition was so serious that he often resorted to alcohol to simply get through the day. At times he was so despairing that he seriously considered suicide. "As I look back now," Young told a reporter in 1985, "I realize that I was full of fright most of the time. Actually a more accurate word for it was terror.

"A few drinks were just enough to modify the terror sufficiently that it wasn't predominant," he recalled. Ironically, he managed to make it through his one-hundred-plus films and his TV family situation comedy often playing the soul of congeniality. Backstage, it was a different story, and many of his coworkers knew it. Young himself saw himself as a man totally adrift, without any clear identity: "The last person I talked to—that was my opinion," he remembered. "You can't get along too well like that."[5]

Young asked Betty, his wife since 1933 and mother of his four daughters, what made her stick around. She said, "I knew all the time that the guy you kept talking about wasn't you at all." He asked her, only half-facetiously, if she knew it by his behavior after two martinis. "No," she answered. "There were moments that I saw flashes of the real you. I saw it when you didn't."[6]

But Young wasn't at all sure what the real him was about. Painfully insecure, he knew that he was like many actors who use the mask of drama to fill a character void.[7] "When I acted, when I was playing a role, I wasn't Robert Young," he admitted in 1985. "That was my escape. That enabled me to be what I wanted to be, which was anything but myself."[8]

Doctors told Young that his depression seemed to stem from a chemical deficiency. But they didn't know what to do about it, and he continued his bouts with booze. It began to affect his work substantially. In 1966, when he was starring in the road company of the show *A Generation*, in which he played an alcoholic, he drank himself into a severe emotional breakdown and had to be replaced.[9]

That marked his lowest point. With the encouragement of Betty, Young pushed slowly yet consistently toward a new life. He checked into a hospital in Detroit for three weeks, where a friend, a psychiatrist, helped him to begin the rebuilding process. He joined Alcoholics

Anonymous. And, most important from Young's standpoint, he began to take seriously the philosophy of life that Betty had been sharing with him in an effort to carve out a path toward recovery.[10]

Called "the science of mind," it was a cosmology that combined Christian ideals with psychological insights to develop a theory of health and disease. The basic premise was that "there should be order within us." Young called it "sort of the power of positive thinking." For him, it worked. "Betty tried to implant in my mind that I was worth something. I became more sure of myself. Nothing in the outward world changed, but something happened within."[11]

Young was feeling quite a bit stronger when the script for the Marcus Welby pilot movie arrived a couple of years later. It was Betty who persuaded him to go for it. She thought it would be good for him to get back to work.[12] Undoubtedly, too, both of them realized that here was an acting "mask" which would reinforce the kind of personality that she and Young had been trying to create for him. Here was a character that wore the qualities of "love, compassion, and trust" as his major attributes.[13] Moreover, said Young, "I've always had a great affinity for the healing profession. I spent most of my life feeling that kind of exasperation of needing help."[14]

He indicated to David Victor that he wanted the Welby role, but ABC executives balked. Young then made an unusual offer for a major star. He would do a screen test and pay for it himself. Victor felt that this approach would persuade the network programmers, but he had Universal Studios pick up the tab. ABC executives found fault with the scene, though. Young, undaunted, offered to do another. That was the film clip that instigated Sid Sheinberg's bluff and brought the decision, finally, to give Young the Welby role.

It was a role that Young reveled in from the start. Many of the problems that Victor, O'Connell, the story editors, and the writers had the TV doctor tackle were addictions, fixations, or other psychological problems that had reached an acute stage. The difficulties resonated with the challenges that Young himself had overcome, and he enjoyed the idea of showing people around him (and the home audience) ways out of their crises. He even encouraged scripts on that subject.

People working on the show recalled that Young tried to express his "science of mind" philosophy on the *Welby* set and through his TV character. At eight in the morning, when shooting started, Young had the camera man toot the "quiet while filming" horn and everyone on the sound stage was expected to pause for a moment of prayer and meditation. Often in conversation he would say something like "true wisdom is recognition that there is order in the universe." He would invoke God and the Bible to emphasize his message. And he would link the idea to health.

"There should be order within us," he would say. "The body has the most incredible resistance . . . if let alone, if not harassed or harried by the mind. Psychologists tell us some people are accident prone. I contend others are sickness prone. If a person is full of hate, frustrations, anxiety, fear, he lowers his level of resistance."[15] Young believed that people should rely on modern medicine once diseases get the upper hand. But he emphasized that the more important steps related to preventative psychological health.

Elena Verdugo said that Young was so convinced by his role as the paternalistic physician that he often exceeded the typical bounds of acting. One time, when he was supposed to feign the giving of an injection during a scene, he actually punctured the "patient's" arm with the needle. Another time, off-camera, when Verdugo mentioned that she didn't feel well, he took her pulse. She also recalled that he often took a doctor's pose when talking to her husband, a psychiatrist.

Verdugo found Young a curious person. On the one hand, he had a major streak of insecurity that gave him a tentative air. On the other hand, he was a highly competitive actor who insisted on playing a scene the way he understood it and who would not let anyone steal the show from him. Young himself admitted that he could be a bit of a martinet when it came to getting work done. His contract required that filming take place only four days a week and that he have afternoon rest periods to keep his strength. So Young made sure that there was "very little foot-dragging," as he put it. "Once in a while," he continued, "you have to remind people we can laugh our way into seven o'clock. The crew works like a well-oiled machine. I'm reduced to just learning my lines."[16]

Verdugo recalled, too, that when it came to giving advice à la Welby, even off-camera, Young's tentativeness vanished altogether. Get him into a conversation that allowed him to philosophize about science of the mind and the ways of the world, and the talk turned into an extended monologue.

"It was a one-sided conversation," James Brolin agreed. "He's a very funny guy. One of the makeup boys would say, 'Every morning in makeup, all you have to do is ask him a question in the direction you want him to go and he'll just keep talking.' Maybe he'll be different now, but in those days it was like you got the feeling that he knew all the answers to everything, to life.'"

Brolin found this Welby-like mien particularly irksome because while Young identified increasingly with his character, Brolin distanced himself from his. The problem had to do with the on-screen relationship between Welby and Kiley. As Brolin saw the pilot, Kiley came to Welby's practice cock-sure that "the old man really didn't know any of the latest medicine but [did know] a lot about this general practice and holding hands and how to deal with people." Kiley may have been wrong about the extent of Welby's knowledge, noted Brolin, but his approach laid seeds for interesting friction between the two. Here was the impulsive motorcycle-driving young physician disdainful of family practice versus the kindly practitioner dedicated to showing his new colleague what the best kind of medicine was like. It was this conflict that drew Brolin to the part.

After about six episodes, though, O'Connell and Victor told the writers to play down the Welby-Kiley conflict. The producers claimed that the decision was in the interest of realism—that given their personalities Welby and Kiley would become good friends soon into their partnership. From then on, Kiley would learn from Welby as Kildare had learned from Gillespie.

Brolin saw in the move a fear by ABC strategists that viewers would not like his character. To him, though, the decision obviously took the identifying edge off the person he had contracted to play. Kiley became just "kind of a nice guy who was great to the kids." He felt that he was being made into a Milquetoast sidekick, and it made him bitter. He stayed because the money, training, and visibility were good. But, he said, "from then on I lost interest."

The Show and the Self

Brolin may have lost interest in the part, but he remained fascinated by the enormous public response that the series was generating. "On the first show we were a smash hit," he marveled. "And by the sixth show we were bigger than *Lucy [I Love Lucy]* ever was."

Marcus Welby, M.D., became the biggest hit in the history of the struggling ABC television network to that time. It ranked number eight among all network shows during its premiere year. More important, it was the first series on the perennially number-three network to be counted as number one among all TV programs for a full season (its second, 1970–71). Cynics objected that the show was a great example of a "placement" hit. They pointed out that for its first two years *Welby* ran against a CBS news documentary hour and frequently against documentaries on NBC as well *(First Tuesday)*. The limited appeal of these shows practically forfeited the audience to ABC, they contended.

But once viewers got used to *Welby*, they stayed even when the competition was much stronger. The series averaged a number-three slot on the Nielsen chart during the 1971–72 TV year and a number-thirteen berth during the year following. It slipped out of the top twenty-five during its last two seasons. But it retained a large, loyal following, and its stars continued to maintain high national visibility.

The highest visibility was given to Dr. Welby himself. Magazine articles celebrated Robert Young as "television's newest phenomenon," in many ways the embodiment of the character he played.[17] *McCall's* magazine, for example, wrote that his personality was often "indistinguishable" from Welby's.[18] A number of the pieces did go into detail about Young's years of alcoholism and inner anguish. But far from separating the actor from his role, Young's private triumph came through as a kind of trial by fire that helped him really feel the sympathy for patients that Welby felt.

Young encouraged that thought. "I have always been sensitive to other people's problems," he told *Good Housekeeping*, "perhaps as an escape from my own."[19] "I really *am* Marcus Welby," he declared in a *Saturday Evening Post* feature.[20]

What did that mean to him? "A doctor is looked upon by the whole family as a person on whom they can rely for sound advice on almost anything," Young told a reporter.[21] And, in fact, Young often peppered his interviews with advice based on his philosophy of life and its relevance to contemporary issues. During the early years of the show the country was racked by civil strife over the military action in Vietnam as well as concerns about youth's alleged aimlessness and the so-called "generation gap." Young stayed away from an explicit stance on Vietnam. But he was eager to share his views on how to keep the country and the home intact. Often he came out sounding like the nation's family physician, a sort of conservative Doctor Spock.

"When I see a youngster in a hurry," he told the *Saturday Evening Post*, "I feel like saying, 'Don't be in such a rush to get the job done. The world is going to fall apart anyway.' Of course, I really don't believe the world is actually going to fall apart. Sometimes distressing things give us the impression that we are headed for doomsday, but mankind has been saying that for the last thousand years."[22]

And: "We say that as a nation we are having a difficult time because of corruption and pollution, and the difficulty of making the machinery of government work. We blame it on the president, we blame it on the Vietnam War, we blame it on anything and anybody. . . . The easiest way out is to think all of those things are forces beyond our control. So long as we believe that, we are off the hook. The truth is that the only place where those problems can be corrected is within ourselves. . . . When enough individuals change, everything else will change."[23]

It got around that Young's seriousness about his new position extended to the way he handled fan mail. Much of the mail contained appeals for free medical advice. "I know you're not a real doctor, but—" they would typically begin. According to *Good Housekeeping*, Young would answer "a select number of letters" he considered significant from the five thousand or more addressed to him each month.[24]

The ones that the magazine highlighted related to the kind of psychological complexities both Young and Welby considered up their alley: ideas on sex education (it must be "an ongoing thing," he wrote back); fear of marital commitment ("sexual promiscuity is not freedom," he answered), attacks of inexplicable fear ("recovery from fear is a do-it-yourself proposition," he wrote); and a pregnant teen deserted by her boyfriend and wondering whether she should get an abortion (having the baby may "jolt your boyfriend out of his adolescent attitude," Young suggested).[25]

Clearly, what was emerging through the program, the mail, and the articles was a mutually reinforcing identification of Robert Young with Marcus Welby. "James Brolin . . . and I build trust and confidence in what we do," he told an interviewer. "It works. We identify with our roles to such a degree that recently, when I was having my annual physical checkup, and a young doctor was making routine tests, without realizing it I was watching him intently. He eyed me quizzically, then asked, 'How'm I doing, Doctor?' "[26]

Jim Brolin did not feel comfortable being associated closely with his role. While he wasn't getting nearly as much attention as Robert Young, his bitterness about the direction of the Welby-Kiley relationship led him to look down on any attempt to peg him to the program. He had little patience with people on the street who joked with him or confused him with one of the show's characters.

"It would happen pretty much everywhere," he recalled disconsolately. "I mean, the common thing was, 'Hey, Doc, my arm's hurt.' And they'd laugh like I'd never heard it before. You can't believe how many times down the block I've heard 'Marcus!' where they got the name mixed up. Or, 'Aren't you Steve Brolin?' "

Publicly, Brolin's refusal to be Steve Kiley off the set became evident soon after *Welby* took to the air, in Brolin's first interview with *TV Guide.* He didn't mention the issue that irked him, but he came out sounding sour and angry. "This series will be a great school for me, a stepping stone," he predicted. "I will use the show to the utmost; it will not use me. The series will be my last TV series. If it is a success, I want to go on to something with more quality. If it dies, I will have built my reputation."[27]

Elena Verdugo had very different feelings about her relationship to the show. At the start, she was chagrined when the publicity departments at both ABC and Universal decided to work on hyping only Young and Brolin. Not wanting to be ignored, and knowing that a strong impression in the media would get her larger parts in the show as well as a salary raise, she hired her own publicity agent. After a while, she persuaded Universal's public relations people to get her a *TV Guide* interview.

The media attention helped Verdugo a lot with the producers. She was successful in instigating a number of plots that centered around her. One, inspired by her real-life hysterectomy, dealt with Consuelo's pain on realizing that because of a required hysterectomy she could never bear a child. That story and others like it—for example, one where Consuelo's mother is dying—had the downside of making her melancholy. In fact, she remembered, the realistic personal problems with which *Welby* often dealt lent a generally low-keyed atmosphere to the set. Made more intense by the no-nonsense pace that Young enforced, some of the plot lines drove her and others in the crew to wash their somber mood away with two-martini lunches.

There was another negative side to her bigger role. Engineering a public identification of her with her character also brought some difficulties that Verdugo hadn't anticipated. She had starred in other TV programs, but this was the height of her visibility. Many people told her that they wished when they were sick that they had had a nurse like Consuelo. Worse, everyone she met expected her to act as genial and helpful as "good old Consuelo."

She felt compelled to oblige. "It was a tiger by the tail," she recalled. "It changed my life. It created different concepts of myself and forced me to change my approach to people. I felt that I couldn't let the world down." It was a painful experience for a while, but she managed eventually to accept her new self. A more immediately happy consequence of merging with Consuelo was that she met and married a physician as a result of publicity associated with the show.

Kudos and Controversies

After just a short time, most of the publicity for *Marcus Welby, M.D.*, did not have to be engineered by Universal or ABC. With the comet-like ascent of the program in the ratings, droves of feature writers from the print and broadcast media began their hot pursuit of material about the show and about Young, Brolin, and Elena Verdugo as she gained popularity. In addition, true to the tradition of organized medicine's wooing of successful TV doctors, physician organizations gave Young and Brolin awards for representing doctors well. In addition, they were contacted often to represent one or another health benefit, or to give speeches at medical conventions or graduations.

Young immersed himself in publicity about health care (especially Easter Seals) as well as in a celebration of his Welby character. Jim Brolin, more hesitant, went along with him to a few conventions and medical award ceremonies. Brolin spoke to medical groups a couple of times after receiving awards, when the organizers beseeched him to tell anecdotes about the show for a few minutes. He involved himself in a number of telethons. Young encouraged him. "All you have to do is get up there and say a few things and smile a lot," the older man would say.

But Brolin began to see disturbing aspects in the charity appearances, the awards, and the speeches. Sometimes he felt exploited. Most often he felt that receiving an award from a medical organization had a kind of humiliation connected with it. Getting decorated for playing a TV doctor at the same time that real physicians were getting kudos for saving lives made him wince. It happened, for example, "when Bob and I went back to Chicago in 1974 for the AMA convention and got one of those Life Achievement Awards. We got one for being Kiley and Welby and the other guy got one for fifty years of cancer research—which made me feel like shit!"

Whatever effect the public adulation had on the show's stars, it allowed the producers to breathe easy about potentially provocative plot lines. The belief around Universal Studios and ABC Standards and Practices was that with the wise and fatherly Marcus Welby at the helm, the producers could navigate virtually any topic. That didn't mean the network had a hands-off policy. Even in the program's seventh year, David O'Connell had to get approval of story lines from network executives before filming. But generally, David Victor recalled, the thrust of network involvement was to make sure the plot was powerful enough and that the climaxes before commercial breaks stayed tantalizing enough to keep viewers around.

It was, Victor conceded, a much more liberal era for topics than it was during his *Kildare* days. In fact, one of the first stories he commissioned for *Welby* was a variation on a *Kildare* venereal disease tale that had been vetoed by NBC in the early 1960s. The Welby image wasn't the only reason for the widened window of acceptability. Tom Kurzy, an ABC Standards and Practices executive at the time, recalled that people in his department, as well as officials in prime-time entertainment, were trying to get a handle on how the tumultuous currents running through the country should affect their programming philosophy.

"The sixties brought about many changes," Kurzy said, reflecting on their thinking. "They brought about an openness, a frankness in public attitudes. They brought forth the strength of the word called 'truth' in professions, in advertising, in everything. And, because of that, as well as a general awareness and a general enlightenment in the viewership, we were able to do things that were not done previously."

Kurzy said that this perception of changes in the American psyche fit into a key evaluation that a team of top network executives conducted about ABC's programming image. Their aim was to spark more viewing of the network's fare by Americans in the eighteen- to thirty-five-year-old group and to generate more interest from advertisers who wanted to reach the youthful, big-spending audiences. The executives decided that ABC should develop a youth-oriented image, not only through the ages of its stars (Welby certainly wouldn't fit there) but by showing people it wanted to "broadcast to the edge of things, not play it safe."

But if the network censors were given more liberal cues from their bosses, they knew they had to remain cautious. "Everything is gradual in this business," Kurzy reminded. "In Standards and Practices, we don't take large steps in anything."

As a result, even in *Marcus Welby* there were occasional tiffs between the censors and the producers over scripts. David Victor described himself as "a diplomatic sort of fellow" who understood the network's public relations predicaments and knew "how to give an inch." Yet he wouldn't budge when it came to the basics of story selection. He knew that ratings and attention would continue to follow his show if he dealt with problems that TV was afraid to cover. So, invoking the purview and legitimacy of medicine, he insisted to Standards and Practices that his show gave him the right to deal with virtually any topic.

"I'd always tell them, 'I'm too mature to write dirty words on the toilet. I'm not doing it for exploitation. If we're going to do a story on venereal disease or homosexual rape, my only requirement is, is it true and does it really come under the purview of a family physician. . . . A doctor, especially a man like Robert Young—[when] a patient comes into his office; he closes the door. Anything he can tell the doctor in the privacy of that room, as long as [the doctor] can handle it, is grist for our mill.' "

The upshot was that except for minor bows to the network censors, Victor and O'Connell invariably did what they wanted. And, in fact, few of the show's 175 episodes that aired over its seven years caused even a ripple of controversy. The one that created the greatest stirs was a 1974 episode called "The Outrage." The central incident of the episode is the rape of a teenage boy by a male teacher. Most of the plot deals with the doctor's concern for the physical and psychological well-being of the youth. David O'Connell told a reporter that the story had its genesis in several actual child abuse cases brought to the program's attention by its medical advisors.[28]

But to gay activists, the central issue was the episode's stock implication that homosexuals molest children, an implication that the episode would pictorialize in millions of American homes. They angrily told ABC executives that there could be nothing redeeming about the program and it should be halted. As word about the impending episode spread through the gay and mainstream press, the American Psychiatric Association, which had only a year earlier voted to remove homosexuality from the list of mental illnesses, issued a public statement condemning the portrayal. The National Education Association put out a press release protesting the airing of the show for its negative portrayal of the teaching profession as well as the "misconceived, stereotypical portrayal of a homosexual." Sensing the storm brewing, several sponsors withdrew their ads, leaving only one minute of time sold on the program.[29]

Then a number of local network affiliates announced that they would not broadcast the episode. People picketed ABC buildings. It began to look as if network programmers might withdraw the show. But ten days before air date, members of the Gay Activist Alliance announced that they had negotiated with the network and had produced some substantive changes. The episode was now acceptable to them. One notable addition was the use of the term "pedophile" as the label for the sex offender. Network officials said that they had insisted throughout the protest that the program was not about homosexuality but about child molestation and the extreme emotional problems such physical assault can cause its victim. A *Los Angeles Times* writer actually lauded the episode just prior to its airing.[30] But many in the gay community were still very angry.

The "Outrage" controversy took a while to blow over. Gay activists sought to make sure that it did not get into ABC's summer rerun schedule (it didn't) or in the package of *Welby* episodes that Universal was beginning to syndicate to local stations (they stopped it). In addition, the episode led activists in the rising women's rights movement to look closely at the series and decide that it had a strong anti-feminist bias, too. One trenchant observer wrote in an article titled "Is Dr. Welby a Menace to Women?" that Welby's many female patients have no understanding of themselves or control over their lives. "What's worse," she added, "is they don't need either of these qualities [since] Dr. Welby is on the scene (whether anyone wants him there or not) and all the plots revolve around the daddy-will-kiss-and-make-it-well syndrome, a.k.a. the white-knight-to-the-rescue syndrome."[31]

These were scathing criticisms. Yet they made up a rather small portion of the public discussion of the series over its seven-year primetime life. One issue did, however, lace through the program's entire existence and come to be discussed virtually in the same breath as the series itself. That was the controversy about *Welby's* ultimate impact on physicians' images. Was it true, as one writer-physician contended, that the series couldn't help "but make things better for American doctors and their patients"? Or, was it the case, as others claimed, that *Welby* was among the factors contributing to the rise of malpractice actions against physicians?[32]

It marked the first time that the physicians establishment got involved in a large-scale argument over whether fictional images that were *positive* actually had negative effects on their status. Previously the concern was with cultivating as favorable an image as possible. Part of the new wariness undoubtedly came from the cultural environment in which organized medicine found itself. The cynicism that many people were feeling in the late 1960s and early 1970s applied to medicine, too. The general public's increased mistrust of the "establishment" led many traditional physicians to see even highly positive images of traditional medicine as depictions that could be and were being turned against them.

Each side of the argument about *Welby* had its vociferous defenders. Physician Michael Halberstam, writing in the *New York Times Magazine*, lauded the show for its presentation of a humane and heroic approach to family medicine. He and others pointed to young adults whose choice of a physician's career had been clinched while watching the program.

Halberstam suggested that in an era when medicine and other professions were being denigrated, it was important to have a widely popular program that romanticized doctors.[33]

"The need for scientific knowledge, for compassion, and for relentless dedication is not a trick bag decked out by the AMA, but the deepest want of any human in trouble," he contended. *Welby*, he said, continually reminded the public that the best of America's physicians abided by that credo.[34]

"That's just the problem," responded physicians who disliked the show. They argued that the credo that the show enacted was totally unrealistic for the modern physician. Focusing on one patient and his (or her) family per episode, Welby and Kiley seemed to be running a two-person intensive care service. Their attendance to medical problems included spending much time counseling them and their family, driving them to the hospital, adjusting their oxygen, sitting with them through the night, and standing by in the operating room while the surgeon did his thing. Beyond these duties, the doctors found time to take patients to ball games, serve them elaborate dinners, stop by their workplaces, and attend their weddings.

Beyond that, ran more complaints, diagnosis of major problems on the *Welby* series was typically quick even in the case of chronic problems. This gave viewers the impression that good physicians can disentangle serious illnesses rather fast. Another unrealistic element was that illnesses began to clear up during the course of the episode, giving the impression of quick turnarounds for difficulties that were typically long-term. To top it off, the anti-Welby faction railed, money was never an issue, either between Welby and patients or Welby and Kiley.

No doctor could possibly run his or her practice that way and survive, many physicians pointed out. Yet, these critics argued, the air of clinical realism which permeated the show's episodes made viewers feel that Welby's norms for patient care were as authentic as his medical advice, which the press touted as impeccable. The upshot, they complained, was that millions of Americans were becoming resentful of their physicians for not living up to the image of the wise and caring physician.

Anecdotes galore were recited at many professional conferences to validate the presence of this Marcus Welby Syndrome. While a few might be energized toward medicine because of the show, the contention went, on balance it did more harm than good for the profession. "People see *Marcus Welby* and other [doctor] shows and then expect miracles from us," ran the typical complaint. The view by some was that the increased readiness to sue physicians came at least partly from a feeling of betrayal that physicians were not acting the way viewers had been told they ought to act.

Victor and O'Connell heard the complaints at every professional gathering they attended. They developed a defensive arsenal that included the claim that if plaintiffs viewed more episodes, they would see that *Welby* was more realistic than they thought, especially in the area of medical costs. The producers admitted dramatic license on several issues. But they didn't retreat on the subject of Welby's approach to his patients. David Victor recalled:

> People would say, "Doctors don't work that way." I said, "Fine. He is an example for doctors to follow. I know that there are doctors who every Wednesday play only golf, and [who care only for] their conversations about tax shelters and all that. Do you want me to give that kind of an image? I mean, we can."
>
> My choice is that I'd rather give the image of an idealized doctor. Because I think that people need reassurance in this world. I think that they take their particular intimation of immortality much too hard. And I think that when it comes to the end of a day, right before the news at eleven o'clock—which is full of weltschmerz—this is a comfortable, reassuring spot.
>
> If I am going to err on the side—I don't want to do *Hospital*, the [1970] movie with George C. Scott, which shows it as a charnel house. On a long-running series, I'd rather explore the likes of a good man, of an idealized doctor. Let the others, the bad doctors, look up to him.

Following this reasoning, Robert Young went even so far as to chide physicians publicly for not living up to his Welby image. At one convention of family physicians, for example, a doctor said to Young, "You're getting us all into hot water. Our patients keep telling us we're not as nice to them as Doctor Welby is to his patients." Young didn't mince words. "Maybe you're not," he said.[35]

It was evidently taken in good humor. But neither it nor Young's other reported pronouncements on the responsibilities of the American physician did much to answer those who felt that the Welby ideal was so unreachable, it was a burr in the side of every contemporary physician.

Back to the Hospital

Burr or not, *Marcus Welby, M.D.*, Tuesday evenings at 10, was a staple on ABC's schedule. Then, before the 1974–75 season, there were changes in both ABC's programming department and in Universal Television's management. They decided that *Marcus Welby* was becoming stale, that the show ought to try format changes that would appeal to younger audiences and get it more in line with the demographic profile that the network was pushing to Madison Avenue.

Specifically, they suggested that the producers shift Welby and Kiley to a hospital setting where they would teach young family practice students. That could introduce new problems, more stories with dramatic surgery, new guest doctors, and a new flair. Victor and O'Connell resisted the move. Their perspective was that if the ratings were good, and they were, people should leave the format alone.

"The network executives, who were kind of bored with it, wanted to tinker with it," he recalled. He kept trying to tell them that by making Welby a teacher of doctors, they would be removing Welby's direct relationship with the patients and their families. That, he and Victor concluded, was the central point that had made the series a success.

"Well, I didn't win," he said simply. Trying to conform to the new concept yet keep as much of the old as they could, O'Connell and Victor solicited Dr. Tom Stern's help in shaping a realistic family medicine preceptorship. St. John's in Santa Monica was not a teaching hospital, so they had to invent a new place, Lang Memorial (named after O'Connell's mentor at Universal). They created a Family Practice Center at Lang, and Welby and Kiley, as supervisors of the Center, were involved with teaching interns as well as seeing more acute-care cases. A good-looking young hospital nurse, Kathleen Faverty (played by Sharon Gless) was added to the cast to supplement Consuelo.

But ratings began to drop; the concept didn't take hold. "It lasted about a year," O'Connell remembered a decade later. "Because before the season was over I had started changing it back. We got rid of the interns because it didn't really work. All in all, it was quite a season. And then the network people changed again, and even though the show was getting a higher rating than most of the top shows are getting now, they cancelled it [after another year] because they wanted to do something else. They were tired of medical shows again."

To network strategists, though, the problem with the series was straightforward. In the mid-1970s prime-time television series were expected to garner about 33 percent of the audience in addition to favorable demographics in order to stay alive. *Marcus Welby*'s pulse began to flutter during its sixth year, and people at ABC began to wonder whether it could be steadied. Was this the handwriting on the wall? Was it time to put the kindly old physician to rest?

James Brolin, still angry after all those years, felt that the show had indeed become near-moribund. He said: "I remember being told by David O'Connell, who worked under David Victor, that when you have a successful thing, you don't touch it. Which I totally disagreed with. . . . We started to lose our audience like crazy all of a sudden because the show was becoming redundant. It was becoming disease of the week. They were afraid to do something fresh. They wanted to stay by the old formula that worked."

"As a matter of fact," he continued, "they were hiring the same faces back too, altogether too often. A lot of actors said, 'I *did* this. I'm not going to take the show unless you come up with an original script.' So they'd hire guys back in six months who would just come back. [Those actors] didn't care. They'd just say their lines, pick up their check on Friday, right?"

David Victor remained insistent that *Welby* was on-track. Nevertheless, he became increasingly nervous about the cavils on ratings, demographics, and sameness that he was hearing from the network brass.
"You know," he said, "it's a big pressure on the producer. When they
come to you and say, 'Come on, it's getting a little too similar,' you
begin to doubt yourself, to say, 'Am I falling into a rut?' And that's not
fair, because the audience likes what you're doing. . . . But you're at
a disadvantage. Because I'm a creative man. If you come to me with
some kind of feeling [of] 'How about something new?' I begin to justify it in my own mind, begin to worry, and come up with something
new."

The major "something new" that Victor reached for to inject some
youth, excitement, and sexiness into the series was actually a variation
on things old. "There are tried and true ways to handle the problem,"
he admitted drily. The decision was to point Steve Kiley toward romance and marriage at the beginning of the next season. Victor knew
that steady romance toward marriage had been used to hype both the
Kildare film and TV series as well as numerous other shows with declining audiences.

The strategy was as follows: the debut episode of fall 1975 would
introduce the prospective bride, Janet Blair, as a public relations expert
at the hospital who would suffer paralysis when thrown from a horse
during a picnic with Kiley. The key medical question would be whether
delicate neurosurgical work to avert permanent loss of limb power would
succeed. That drama would be paralleled by Kiley's growing attach-
ment to the woman and by competition from her present boyfriend.
Both surgical science and Kiley would triumph, and the next four episodes would cover their courtship and the climactic wedding.

"Building toward a wedding is always good viewer bait," *Variety*
agreed. The trade journal predicted that *"Welby* should have strong
first five weeks, which conceivably is long enough to reestablish a viewer
pattern for the skein [i.e., network]." Word also got around the trade
and popular press that in an additional effort to hype the ratings, the
producers were having Welby's (now divorced) daughter moving back
to live with him along with her six-year-old son. As a result, for the
first time, both Welby and Kiley would have problems in their personal
lives moving parallel to the main medical episode. This was counter to
the original philosophy of the show, the producers knew, but maybe
it would save the show. It didn't. True to industry predictions, the
number of Nielsen homes turned to *Welby* soared to the top of the
chart the week of the wedding. A week later, however, the show was
down to number 64. The hype had helped with only short-term resus-
citation. *Marcus Welby, M.D.*, limped through the 1975–76 season and
was then pulled from the evening lineup.

Even before its prime-time demise, though, the series moved into
syndication on local stations around the country. Full-page advertise-

ments in *TV Guide* heralded the daily afternoon visits of "Robert Young, Family Doctor."[36] Rarely in the history of U.S. television had an actor become so associated with both a role and a profession. In his seven years on prime time, Robert Young as Marcus Welby became the quintessential family doctor. *Good Housekeeping* noted that "through his glorification of the family doctor, he has become TV's most revered actor, and the nation's father confessor."[37]

Like Dr. Christian, his closest soulmate in popular culture, Marcus Welby had the time to help people with the deepest of problems. True to his late-twentieth-century status, however, Welby combined his profound solicitude with a scientific acumen that understood the value of sophisticated medical specialties. This family doctor rushed people into the hospital and referred people to specialists quite often. He may not have made miracle cures, but he made sure that his patients received cutting-edge care in the shortest possible time.

Precisely what effects this image had on a generation of viewers is impossible to say. Medical journals and the popular press of the time certainly suggested a number of possibilities to viewers. One, by then a standard response to doctor shows, was that it was creating a nation of hypochondriacs. Another, more friendly, was that the kindly Welby was helping to "peel off some of the fears we all have when confronted by the mysteries of illness and death."[38]

But by far the most enduring discussion of the program's impact centered on its depiction of physician. As we have seen, the public was told again and again by the show's star and producers, by press writers, by some in the medical community, and perhaps even by the AAFP through its imprimatur that Welby was an ideal for doctors to live up to. Certainly, some young viewers were energized toward becoming physicians because of that; David Victor's own grandson became a family physician, the producer noted proudly. Still, it seemed that in the context of the troubled late 1960s and early 1970s, the most consistent response to the kindly practitioner was to blame other physicians for not being like him.

Many in the medical community were becoming anxious because of it, and over the next few years doctor-show producers would feel forced to find a way to deal with that. In the meantime, though, a number of other programs were entertaining millions with images of the medical system that picked up at the hospital where Welby left off. Mapped against the public suspicion of the medical establishment, they would parade possibilities of medicine that might, image-wise, put organized medicine into an even more uncomfortable position.

8

Long Hair, High Tech, and Mod

What surely must be the strangest press release created about a doctor-show episode was distributed by CBS Television during May 1971. Titled "Medicine and Long Hair," it began:

> If you find yourself in a hospital being cared for by someone with long hair, you may have to look twice—it could be a doctor rather than a nurse.
>
> That's on the authority of Frank Glicksman, who, as executive producer of *Medical Center* on the CBS Television Network, keeps a sharp eye on modern medicine.[1]

Glicksman's eye was not peering at the increasing number of woman physicians who were beginning to swing through medical school doors. Instead, his interest was in the way that anti-establishment styles of the younger generation were making their way into the hospital scene. "One reason we did [an episode] with this theme," Glicksman said, "was the shocked reaction of a friend of mine when he visited a hospital and saw that interns and residents alike had joined the trend to long hair."

The story concerned what the press release called "a hippie style doctor," played by Gary Lockwood. In the drama, said the release, "Lockwood's unconventional appearance and his partiality for motorcycles put him in sharp conflict with an establishment surgeon," played by Andrew Duggan. The two disagree on the treatment of a girl (Stefanie Powers, Lockwood's real-life wife) who is facing a leg amputation. In the end the younger surgeon proves correct in his medical approach. He even wins the girl.

"Our idea was to show that a man, whether he's a doctor or not, shouldn't be judged by the length of his hair or the cut of his clothes," Glicksman explained in the press release. "Those external factors have nothing to do with a man's medical skills." The circular added that Gary Lockwood was enthusiastic about his role because, he said, "[i]t makes a statement we need today."

Lockwood's statement could itself be taken as a banner phrase for the period. In the late 1960s, "now" and "relevance" were words that Hollywood television producers and network executives tossed around furiously. Young adults in conflict with establishment figures seemed like good plot directions. Doctor shows were part of this trend, as CBS, NBC, and ABC executives increasingly gave the nod to medical series.

The new medical-program cycle had started in earnest during September 1969, when each network ushered in a prime-time doctor series. ABC introduced *Marcus Welby* on Tuesdays at 10. CBS gave *Medical Center* a 9 p.m. Wednesday berth. And NBC mounted *The Bold Ones* on Sunday at 10.

The first two shows climbed quickly toward the top of the hits chart, with *Medical Center* just a few notches below the heralded *Welby*. In fact, it ultimately would beat *Marcus Welby* by a few months as television's longest-running doctor show to that point (seven years). *The Bold Ones* didn't do nearly as well with the numbers, but NBC executives were nevertheless satisfied with the show's performance. It would stay on the air four years.

Seeing the beginning of a good thing, executives scheduled two more doctor series for the 1970–71 season, *The Interns* (CBS) and *Matt Lincoln* (ABC). All the programs, including *Welby*, carried the burden of a television industry nervously trying to keep up with its society. The trick was to parlay strong ratings out of a multitude of contradictions: be challenging but harmless, relevant but escapist, immersed in social change but comfortably familiar.

The creators of *Medical Center* and *The Bold Ones*, especially, showed that it was easier to do than it might seem. They found ways to adapt the traditional doctor-show formula that fit comfortably with contemporary marketing, dramatic, and censorship considerations in such a way as to actually evade painful realities of social change while pretending to face up to them.

As we will see, this evasiveness applied to the doctor shows' depiction of the medical system at least as much as to their portrayal of any other part of society. However, with the failure of *The Interns* and *Matt Lincoln* to gain high Nielsen ratings, the issue for producers and programmers became one of tactics. Their mission was to determine what new elements could be merged with the traditional formula so as to create certifiably huge audience grabbers that could, in turn, be copied.

Such were the needs of the commercial storytellers. But in view of the many new issues facing the medical institution that were starting to boil in the early 1970s, it is ironic that producers' dominant concerns spoke only to the surface of change. At a time when relevance was a TV industry buzzword, the home tube's portrayal of American medicine was increasingly out of touch with the fundamental perspectives that government agencies, insurance companies, hospitals, and other health care policymaking bodies were adopting to shape the health care system that viewers were using.

The Winds of Change

The considerations that encouraged the new medical cycle and the networks' preoccupation with relevance fed into one another. Some of the influences were more subtle than others. In the case of doctor shows, it was clear to many of those involved that the decision by network executives to take another try at medicos (as *Variety* called them) was not simply due to an upsurge in their awareness of the profession's dramatic value.

Marcus Welby's creator, David Victor, said that "the most important, immediate catalyst" was the general public's outrage over TV violence.[2] Frank Glicksman agreed with him. "The trend is away from violence," he told a reporter in 1970. "So what better way to do dramatic life and death than a medical show."[3]

The situation was even more complicated than Glicksman or Victor let on. Violence was at the root of the new doctor-show cycle, but it was the intertwining of real social violence with TV violence with which all three networks were trying furiously to cope. This was an era of extreme social unrest. Civil rights riots, mob rampages through slums during hot summers, the assassinations of black leader Martin Luther King and U.S. Senator Robert Kennedy, violent protests against the escalating war in Vietnam, youth alienation from the establishment, the police riot against angry young protestors at the 1968 Democratic National Convention in Chicago—these threatening events cascaded into people's living rooms through the television evening news.

Many social critics linked the violence in society to the high level of violence on TV. They claimed that the shootings and illegal activities on the home tube were encouraging the TV generation to use illegal aggression to solve social problems. The Federal Communications Commission, which had the power to renew the licenses of network-owned stations, voiced its concern over TV violence. Two federal task forces were set up to study the matter.[4] Network executives were on the hot seat.

Lowering the temperature meant cutting down on the aggression. But the network officials were convinced that it was physical jeopardy that hooked people to the tube. As Glicksman's comment suggests, one way around the problem was to make that jeopardy more acceptable by tying it to a medical situation. CBS's programming chief, Michael Dann, was so convinced that a successful doctor show could benefit his network that he commissioned half a dozen pilots on medical themes with the idea that at least one would be good enough for a prime-time slot. Dann was sure that with *Ben Casey* and *Dr. Kildare* gone for a few years, a new cycle of doctor shows could be successfully encouraged. He felt that CBS had gotten in on the earlier doctor-show cycle too late and that CBS's entry, *The Nurses*, had not been on target. He didn't want to lose out again. Glicksman and his partner Al Ward, veteran TV writers who had worked on *Ben Casey*, were among those invited to submit a script.

Yet a series' acceptance by political groups against TV violence was clearly not a sufficient criterion for network acceptance. Perry Lafferty, CBS's West Coast programming head during the late 1960s and early 1970s, recalled that in addition to a low-violence profile, network personnel were insistent on series that projected youthfulness and a contemporary feel. That, in fact, was an industry-wide preoccupation.

A young, contemporary aura had always been part of the medium. During the late '60s, though, Madison Avenue executives began to develop a preoccupation with relatively young adults in the TV audience. The baby boom, coming of age, was the hot market. Americans 18 to 49 years of age—or, even better, 18 to 35—were more desirable than older ones. City dwellers were more desirable than country folk, since they tended to be richer. And urban women 18 to 35 or 49 years old were a particularly prized catch, since they controlled most of the typical household's income.[5]

The black audience was also of growing interest to advertisers. The civil rights concerns of the 1960s had made marketing executives more aware of the need to portray an integrated society in their ads. But the move toward targeting more blacks for commercials was really more mercenary than that. An economically powerful black middle class was emerging. Major marketers were recognizing its strength and wanting its business. And they also recognized that a lot of blacks watched network television.[6]

All three networks felt these new pressures, especially the youth-oriented ones. Programs that had strong overall popularity but catered to undesirable demographics—for example, *The Lucy Show, Andy Griffith, Lawrence Welk*—were yanked off the networks. And new shows were sculpted to appeal to the young urban market that advertisers wanted.

One of the ironies was that corporate and political leaders perceived a good part of that desirable market to be untrusting of the very establishment that network TV had come to represent. Certainly they didn't consider their targets to be as rabid in their beliefs as the hippies and yippies on the network news seemed to be. But the feeling was that most younger Americans had picked up some of the same restlessness and desire for change. To reach them, CBS President Robert Wood announced, TV drama had to begin facing up to "the gut issues of our day."[7]

The trick for industry storytellers, then, was to lure an unpredictable youth market while keeping the other TV age groups loyal. Storytellers had to come up with shows that announced to young and old, black and white, that TV was on their side. The message to the young and black had to be that TV was changing with the times, was willing to explore new ways of doing things, new social norms. The message for older and more conservative viewers had to be that, despite the changes, the American verities would be upheld.

This was the mandate that the creators of *Marcus Welby, Medical Center*, and *The Bold Ones* had to face. It was a difficult line to walk, and the different production companies chose different ways to do it. *Marcus Welby* took the most traditional path, using the familiar older man/younger man relationship to evoke some of the generational tensions of the day. Creator David Victor's most explicit bow to the rebellious generation in the show's continuing elements was Dr. Kiley's motorcycle. That aside, the "now" issues of the society that intruded on the upper-middle-class comfort of the continuing characters came in the form of weekly plot lines.

Frank Glicksman and Al Ward put *Medical Center* together using many of the same traditional notions of character and plot that Victor relied on in *Welby*. Most prominent was their anchoring the show with a relationship between a younger doctor, surgeon Joe Gannon (played by Chad Everett), and his older chief of staff, Dr. Paul Lochner (played by James Daley). Yet Glicksman took great pains to point out that the relationship was more youth-oriented than the well-known previous cases. Lochner was not nearly as old as Doctors Gillespie or Zorba (or Welby, for that matter). In addition, the goings-on between the younger and older doctor were not based on a father-son disciplinary model but on a model of mutual respect and friendship. As he put it, "[W]e don't have an old guy like Raymond Massey lecturing a young upstart like Dick Chamberlain."[8]

Even more important to a show "designed to appeal to the young as well as to women," said Glicksman, was a setting tailor-made for plots that would attract the target audience.[9] "From the beginning," he noted in 1970, "we thought a university would be a perfect setting because it would give us a chance to deal with the young and with a good many contemporary social and medical problems at the same time."[10] To Glicksman, getting away from the hospital walls was a key to being contemporary. "A university medical center works closely with a wide variety of people in life science, athletics, free clinics, and similarly provocative areas. It gives us a chance to get outside, to be youth oriented, and still to set our story and our people, in the thinking of viewers, in the medical center."[11]

The Bold Ones also had the idea of relevance built directly into its format. But for Cy Chermak, developer of the show for Universal Television, the key twist was to excite viewers with the potential of technological change rather than to have them identify with the problems created by youth-oriented social change. The series glorified state-of-the-art medicine. It showcased a team of brilliant surgeons at the fictional Craig Institute, a combination hospital and research center, which had the prestige and funding to pursue breakthroughs. Dr. David Craig (actor E. G. Marshall), an aging but masterly physician, ran the elite operation. His chief of surgery was a brilliant young heart transplant specialist, Dr. Ted Stuart (John Saxon), while chief of medicine Dr. Paul Hunter (David Hartman), worked on nonsurgical techniques for treating disease.

Strictly speaking, the title of Chermak's program was *The New Doctors*. *The Bold Ones* was actually an umbrella name for three series, one of which was *The New Doctors*, that rotated through the 10 p.m. Sunday slot during the 1969–70 season. The other shows were *The Protectors* and *The Lawyers*. The collective idea was to highlight brave modern men of America's key institutions. But the other shows didn't catch on as well as the *Doctors* segment. The fourth year saw only the physicians returning, and *The Bold Ones* became a description of the medicine men alone.

CBS and NBC tried hard to position their respective doctor shows in ways that reflected their individual thrusts toward relevance. NBC press releases exulted that *The Bold Ones* concerned "men in the forefront of medicine, developers of new techniques who are dedicated to breaking down the barriers of disease and ignorance."[12] CBS press releases, for their part, stressed that *Medical Center* was filled with "provocative themes involving people and medicine."[13]

But how did the producers and writers of each series draw human dramas from their characters, settings, and broad descriptions of intent? What did they end up saying about social change, about medicine, and about the relationship between the two—and why? How did their approaches to the formula set precedents for *The Interns* and *Matt Lincoln*, and the blizzard of doctor shows that followed them? To answer, we have to explore the creation of *Medical Center* and *The Bold Ones* in more detail.

Astronauts and Embryos

The aim of *The Bold Ones* medical series was to stress the technologically bold. The program's creators went out of their way to find plots that used machines or techniques that were at the vanguard of medical abilities. "Our stuff was so sophisticated that it was sometimes hard to find an expert in town to consult with," Joel Rogosin, a producer with the show during its first two years, said with some pride.

The show's look was subsidized by medical technology companies. They bombarded the producers with offers to lend them their newest equipment, even suggesting plots that might showcase the machines' capabilities on national TV. Byron Bloch, a writer and "human factors engineer" who helped design the famed Cardiovascular Research Center in Houston, was the show's on-site consultant regarding the gadgetry.[14]

"We had medical equipment on the show that some hospitals didn't," Rogosin remembered. "We had a heart pump machine on the show operated by a heart pump specialist from UCLA. And our heart lung machine was more advanced than the one at UCLA. I found it disturbing that we had better equipment than a top-notch hospital."

To feel secure about the accuracy of the state-of-the-art plots, Chermak and Rogosin asked the American Medical Association's Physicians' Advisory Committee on TV, Radio, and Motion Pictures for help. An Advisory Committee representative was consulted throughout the script creation process. He read every script and suggested specialists who could give definitive answers to questions. He also helped the producers with suggestions of possible topics.[15]

Of the three late-'60s medical series, *The Bold Ones* placed the most reliance on the AMA's Advisory Committee. *Marcus Welby* and *Medical Center* were helmed by people who had a lot of previous experience with TV medicine. While they sent scripts to the Committee for technical review, the AMA was not their main arbiter of medical dramatics. To them, the best way to achieve plot-making autonomy along with medical realism was to hire physicians and nurses as full-time technical advisors and use representatives from disease associations (such as the American Heart Association) for extra plot advice.

By contrast, *Bold Ones* Executive Producer Cy Chermak and his producers (Universal assigned a number of them in rotation) hadn't worked on a medical series before. While they began to search early in the series for specialists in university hospitals around Los Angeles, they nevertheless appreciated a central agency that could supply them with advice and references, including contacts in disease associations. Exotic issues piled up. The show's scripters and producers asked the AMA panel questions about when death really occurs, about developing human life outside the womb, about the steps of changing a man into a woman. They inquired into a new technique for heating blood in the treatment of cancer, into the work by a Russian doctor on the use of low-voltage current to cure peptic ulcers and asthma, into the current state of knowledge and progress on the use of artificial hearts for transplants.

Several of these issues were a source of frustration for the Advisory Committee's chair, surgeon William Quinn. The artificial heart especially raised hackles. The physicians tried to convince the storytellers that an artificial heart was so futuristic as to be unacceptable as a theme for a TV drama. The producers responded testily that they had no intention of excluding a good story just because professional caution suggested the time was not right. The Advisory Committee backed off, retreating to its chairman's posture that "mostly . . . we read these scripts for medical accuracy and that's all."[16]

While the AMA Committee had no power to censor the treatment of certain medical problems in *The Bold Ones*, NBC's Standards and Practices Department did. According to producer Rogosin, the issue came up infrequently, but when it did it tended to revolve around "something that was in the realm of possibility but had not really happened." Liver transplantation was an example. With kidney transplants rather common at the time, it was clear to the producers that liver transplants were around the corner. If they wanted to explore that procedure dramatically, though, they had to be very careful.

"If you projected a story a little bit into the future, the network was very keen on making sure that everything was thoroughly authenticated. We were conditioned to avoid the temptation, unless we could justify that it could happen in a certain way."

One *Bold Ones* presentation was actually kept off the air for a few weeks by the network because it was too true to life. Called "A Small Step for Man," the episode concerned an astronaut who lapsed into a coma while orbiting the moon. Dr. Ted Stuart of the Craig Institute, who is monitoring health aspects of the flight for NASA, risks his life to find a cure by introducing the astronaut's symptoms into his body. As Rogosin told it, around the time the episode was to air, an astronaut actually orbiting the moon became seriously ill. NASA's furious attempts to determine the cause of the problem and find a cure had eerie similarities to depictions in *The Bold Ones* script. Not wanting to appear to be taking advantage of a potential tragedy, NBC programmers substituted another episode. Only after the astronauts returned safely to earth was "A Small Step for Man" allowed to air.

The creators of *The Bold Ones* prided themselves on the cutting-edge realism of their plots and expected that viewers were excited by it as well. At the same time, they were aware of the importance of balancing the display of awesome technological capabilities with compelling human drama. One way they tried to build that into the show was to create lives away from the hospital for their continuing characters.

This was an approach that hadn't been tried on a doctor show before. They gave E. G. Marshall's character a wife and grown children. They created a love relationship for David Hartman's character. John Saxon was placed in a long-term intimate relationship. (It was not a live-in situation; network censors wouldn't have accepted that out of wedlock.)

Chermak and Rogosin's idea had been to serialize the physicians' personal lives across episodes while depicting self-contained medical stories each week. Sometimes, they had the two areas intersect. For example, Dr. Craig's discussions with his wife about his fear of death were injected into a story on patients with terminal illnesses, and echoes of that conversation came up in other episodes.

But people at the studio and in the network began to feel that concentrating on the medical story as well as the sometimes unrelated personal lives of the physicians was detracting from both approaches. "We didn't find the proper balance," admitted Rogosin. The upshot was that the serialization of the physicians' meanderings outside the hospital didn't have a chance to take hold. When Rogosin handed the program to other producers, they fell back on the tried and true technique of building human drama out of a patient's illness, the doctor's professional dilemma, or the relationship between the two.

Typically, the human dramas grew out of the physical problems. An episode called "Broken Melody," for example, unfolded two separate plots: a popular female rock singer who seems to be going deaf and a small boy who is kept at the Institute because Dr. Hunter fears he was beaten by one of his parents. In the end, the singer helps the boy, who had been repeatedly assaulted by his mother, come out of his shell. In the process, we learn that her problem stems from child abuse, too. As a child, her parents forced her to play music. She now resents her draining singing schedule but is inhibited from stating it because of her childhood memories of coercion. As a result, she has become deaf psychosomatically. She learns of this with the aid of understanding doctors and through her concern for the boy.

"Broken Melody" wasn't filled with the kind of high-powered medical gizmos that were hallmarks of *The Bold Ones*, though John Saxon did give an impressive lecture about new techniques for curing deafness. At the same time, it was typical of most episodes in its celebration of the potential of high-powered doctors to solve medical and emotional problems.

But a number of episodes did go beyond this celebration of technology to explore some of the moral dilemmas associated with cutting-edge medical procedures. One tale investigated the excruciating family tensions involved when a brain-dead man is still breathing with the aid of fancy machines while a patient on the same floor needs a heart. Another episode related the story of a woman who is paralyzed from the neck down and suffering from hopeless kidney damage. She demands that her treatment be halted so that another patient may have a chance to live by means of dialysis. A third was about a futuristic attempt at embryo transplantation from an ailing woman to her sister.

The case of the paralyzed woman on dialysis raised important questions about "The Inalienable Right to Die," as the story was called. Robert Van Scoyk wrote the script with Gustave Field. He recalled that the producers bought the concept because it brought an opportunity for conflict between the patient and the physicians as well as among the physicians themselves. Van Scoyk said that the producers would let him explore issues of medical morality and politics as long as he presented the arguments for all sides of the question and didn't overtly favor one. Thus, he had Dr. Craig vehemently oppose the notion of physicians allowing a patient to die. On the other hand, he made Dr. Hunter not quite as philosophically secure with that position as Craig was.

At the end of the episode, the patient gets a court order telling the physicians to cease dialysis. As she leaves the hospital with her husband, it is clear she will die. Van Scoyk said he wrote an upbeat tone into that scene to suggest that the decision was right for that patient. He also tried to convey an awareness that the issue was really unresolved, that here was an argument that would have to be thrashed out again and again as new technologies kept people in a state between life and death.

The heart and embryo stories have even more ambivalent and/or ambiguous endings. The heart episode concludes with the doctors and families still agonizing over the transplant; the embryo story stops short with a miscarriage. As producer David Levinson admitted about the latter case, "[L]egal entanglements that could ensue if embryo transplants become commonplace stagger the imagination. But we [did] not get into that area since the emotional drama generated by these women is enough."[17]

There were, then, considerations that muted the power even of episodes where creators tried to deal seriously with the relationship between medicine and society. The limitations of time, the need to balance all the arguments, the desire not to get away from the medical arena into the legal sphere, the need for upbeat (if not always happy) endings: these TV realities were often insurmountable. The issues may have been dwarfed further by the show's continuing theme of the Craig Institute's inexorable medical progress. Still, it is noteworthy that the creators of *The Bold Ones* tried now and then to step back and explore ethical and legal dilemmas that were cropping up precisely because of that kind of progress.

Cooperative Bodies

The same could never be said about *Medical Center*, and it is doubtful that the creators cared. The point is important because *Medical Center*'s substantially better ratings and longer life than *The Bold Ones* gave it greater credibility with industry personnel looking for clues about what would work in doctor shows of the '70s. Again and again, Frank Glicksman and *Medical Center* producer Al Ward insisted that doctor dramas were not really about medicine, anyway. Illnesses, they averred, are merely an excuse to get a good tale going. As Ward put it, *Medical Center* was simply "a life-and-death formula with an authority figure to handle it and solve it."[18]

"[W]e're doing sociological stories rather than medical or disease stories per se," Ward continued. "In fact, the medical aspect is usually quite incidental. We don't start with a disease; we begin instead with some sort of social premise which we've read about in newspapers or magazines. Then we'll have a four or five hour session with a writer about the premise, and most of the time we won't even mention the disease. It's only when we have that premise worked out that we ask our medical advisor to come up with an appropriate illness."[19]

"The human body is very cooperative," Frank Glicksman agreed. "It always comes up with *something*."[20] Glicksman admitted, though, that there were certain rules of the formula-driven game that the producers and writers had to follow. One was that every episode required at least one character to be confined to a hospital bed. Subplots were often created with this dictum in mind. So, Glicksman said, one main story line revolved around an ill doctor. "He was walking around apparently cured, and it detracted from the drama. So we had to drag in a young girl—as one of his patients. She had a melanoma, a virulent case, and her breast had to be removed. That worked out fine."[21]

The show's technical advisor, Chris Hutson, added that the most appropriate illnesses tended to be acute problems that were amenable to climactic operations. Hutson, a registered nurse, had experience with doctor shows dating to *Ben Casey*. While the medical consultant helped on scripts mostly from afar, Hutson brought on-set expertise to *Medical Center* during the show's entire run. Her job was to ensure the accuracy of the equipment, the actions of the physician-actors, and all the little things that lent an authentic feel to the show for the non-medical viewers in the audience.

"There are some things that we have used all the time," Hutson said. "Every series that I have ever done, maybe every fifteen [episodes] you've got a ruptured spleen. Because, it just fits. And somebody falls off a motorcycle, or has a car accident, or comes in and we have to take them to surgery. Well, ruptured spleen is perfect, or appendix, broken bones, head injury, closure bypass, heart problems."

Severe problems of the heart were particularly useful in *Medical Center*, since Joe Gannon, the show's hero, was billed as a cardiovascular surgeon. Yet any number of other ills that fit the storytelling needs were acceptable. If the plot required it, Gannon would even get involved in surgery outside his specialty. To justify this bit of dramatic license, the writers would have someone point out in passing that Gannon was assisting an expert in the procedure. Then it was OK.

In fact, the clinical domain of *Medical Center* was purposely immense to accommodate virtually any kind of plot that the writers could dream up and any area of relevance that seemed ripe for plotting. Medical accuracy ruled when it related to the facts of a disease and its clinical treatment. But when it came to the actions of patients and hospital personnel, the mandate to be melodramatic got priority. In fact, the producers and writers used the university setting as a kind of hip Grand Hotel with a surgical theater. And when, in the show's second season, Dr. Gannon became Director of Student Health, that crystallized even more his role as a kind of roving master of ceremonies and *deus ex machina* for contemporary problems.

To the show's producers, contemporary problems often meant human interest topics that had been off-limits for television before the late 1960s. According to Don Brinkley, who was head writer on the show, the CBS network's programming people encouraged their experimentation with such topics in the hope that it would help build the audience. On the other hand, Program Standards and Practices, the censorship division of the TV network, took a much more cautious approach.

One area that was not negotiable—and the producers understood this from the start—involved the images of the continuing doctors. A doctor still had to be treated "like god," to use Brinkley's phrase. As in past series, troubled and potentially dangerous physicians could, and did, show up as guest stars. But their inadequacies had to be exposed and remedied, often with a Joe Gannon exemplifying the correct way to handle the situation.

Other aspects of the plots were open to negotiation with the censors. "So far," said Frank Glicksman in 1971, "[the CBS censor assigned to the show] has let us do stories on abortion, homosexuality, drug addiction, venereal disease, impotence, artificial insemination, and rape. All of these themes were absolutely unthinkable on TV in the *Casey-Kildare* period, and now we can use them."[22]

Glicksman, Ward, and Brinkley had many fights with CBS Standards and Practices—"they questioned everything," said Brinkley—but the *Medical Center* crew often prevailed. Things got better especially after the first year, when it was clear the show was a hit. Another reason for the greater freedom was the changing network censorship philosophy in that time of changing public norms. Now, in line with their counterparts at NBC and ABC, the criterion for building a plot around a topic was rarely the acceptability of the subject itself, but its handling.

There were exceptions; Brinkley noted that menstruation could never be mentioned on *Medical Center*. Generally, though, the network censors wanted to be sure that explorations of social controversies gave due recognition and respect to all the prominent sides. The censors wanted to ensure that no pressure group could claim that an episode was being used as propaganda for a cause or as advertisement for an immoral act. Words such as "legitimate" and "balance" came up in verbal jousts over scripts.

"We did a . . . two-parter about a transsexual," Brinkley recalled. "And we went to great lengths to keep it as legitimate as possible. We did a very detailed outline on the thing, and they said, 'You can't do it.' Robert Reed played the role. I don't remember what his profession was, but he was white collar, a professional, an intellectual. . . . So the network felt it was much too touchy, too squeamish a situation. They were afraid we would exploit it, cheapen it, and so on. . . .

"And we said, 'Trust us.' And we fought like crazy; [we said], 'At least give us a chance to put this in script form.' Because in outline form everything is bold and cold and none of the subtleties are there. And we fought like crazy and they liked the script. They were on our side."

Alienation from the establishment and generational misunderstandings with a contemporary flair (between "straight" adults and their long-haired offspring) often complicated Dr. Gannon's attempts, typically successful, to straighten out his patients' physical and emotional crises. The producers said they wanted to avoid preachiness. "We don't make moral judgments like we had to do by mandatory command of the networks in the old days," Glicksman remarked. "A young girl comes in to see Chad Everett with gonorrhea and he doesn't say, 'You shouldn't have done it,' but 'let's cure it.' The kids dig that—a young hip doctor who relates to them and doesn't moralize."[23]

The creators admitted the bottom-line significance of using previously verboten subjects. These "helped nicely in building our audience," Glicksman said bluntly. *Medical Center*, he continued, was "specifically designed to appeal to the young and to women," and they were attracted to that kind of contemporary plotting.[24]

Using patients with whom the target audience could identify was another ratings-oriented strategy. *Medical Center*'s population tended to be white, middle-class, and young, though a few plots did revolve around blacks and Hispanics. More women than men needed Gannon's bedside manner, and they were more likely than not to be good-lookers in their twenties.[25] In addition, trading on actor Chad Everett's sex appeal, the producers worked up a number of episodes in which Dr. Gannon fell in love. For those who knew the formula, it was needless to say that the women were dying or otherwise unattainable; one, it turned out, was a lesbian. After a while Glicksman and Ward gave Gannon an on-again, off-again romantic interest who was a staff psychiatrist at the center. Perhaps they were drawing from their experience writing for anesthesiologist Maggie Graham, Ben Casey's subtle flame.

In the end, it all had to get distilled into an hour-long story about the patients, the doctors, and the attempt to cure physical and emotional problems. Veteran TV writer Shimon Wincelberg, who created a number of scripts for the series, developed for himself a kind of shorthand guide to what he saw as the most typical *Medical Center* storyline: the patient is his own worst enemy.

And, in fact, many episodes did revolve around the efforts of Dr. Joe Gannon and Dr. James Lochner to get patients (who were sometimes friends or loved ones) to follow medical orders that they didn't want to hear. Although it was rare that their medical bag of tricks let them down, the overall atmosphere was more important than whether the guest star died or not. The producers had strict rules about the kind of medical tension and atmosphere a writer could bring to the show.

"There really isn't a subject which we can't or won't treat," Al Ward told a reporter. "Our only basic rule is that a story can't be downbeat. That so far has ruled out senility, and for a long time we couldn't handle euthanasia—until we came up with a humorous character who made the story work."[26]

Mod Squads and Mind Bombs

Medical Center's strategy of placing watered-down youth-oriented tensions side by side with hyped-up medical problems had strong parallels in the early evening medical series of 1970, *The Interns* (CBS, Fridays at 7:30) and *Matt Lincoln* (ABC, Thursdays at 7:30). But while *Medical Center* was clearly a precedent for the two shows (much more so than *The Bold Ones* or *Marcus Welby*), the most direct impetus for them came from an early evening police drama called *The Mod Squad*.

To understand how a cop show could serve as an impetus for a doctor show, we have to map network executives' turn-of-the-'70s concern about TV violence and relevance onto the special requirements they made of early evening series. It was a holy network principle that youngsters and preteens controlled the set before 9 p.m. In an era where one-set homes were more prevalent than they are now, network programmers' fervent hope was that the youngsters and their parents would agree on those shows and then stay with the flow of that network's programs through the evening. Traditionally, the type of series that played best in the evening lead-in time slots was the situation comedy. Solid sitcoms such as *The Lucy Show, My Three Sons*, and *Bewitched* tended to hold up for years.

But, recalled CBS's Michael Dann, the start of the 1970s was a time when creators of good situation comedies were hard to find. Most masters of the form during the 1950s and 1960s had retired, passed away, or gone on to theatrical films. One second-best programming solution for the early-evening period was to schedule adventure tales that would lure teens and preteens as well as their parents. The key question: how to devise an attractive adventure that would (a) plug into the contemporary rebelliousness that the young audience was seeing in the streets and on the news, while (b) reassuring adults about the solidity of fundamental institutions and values.

ABC came up with a solid-gold answer when it mounted a one-hour show called *The Mod Squad* at 7:30 on Tuesdays during the 1968–69 season. The series unfolded the adventures of three young cops—a white man, a black man, and a young woman. Each had dropped out from "straight" society and had tangled with the law. Led by an older police captain, their purpose was to infiltrate the counter-culture and ferret out the adult criminals who took advantage of the often naïve "now" generation.[27]

The Mod Squad's attempt to work both sides of the establishment fence was painfully obvious. There was hardly an attempt at sophisticated drama here. But it worked in the ratings, and as a result the next two years saw a clutch of programs across the networks that were aimed at applying the same idea to different situations. So, for example, *The New People* (ABC) centered on a diverse group of forty young Americans stranded on an abandoned (but fortunately modern) island who had to create their own society in the absence of adults. *The Young Lawyers* followed a diverse group of law students (a Jewish man, a black woman, and a male Anglo) as they operated a law office for indigents in Boston under the watchful eye of an older male supervisor. And *The Storefront Lawyers* (CBS) followed a diverse group of recent law school graduates (a white man, a white woman, and a Hispanic man) as they operated another law office for indigents, this time in a poor section of Los Angeles.

With *The Interns* and *Matt Lincoln*, the medical establishment got its share of attention in the youthful relevance dramas. *Lincoln*, for example, had action, contemporary issues, and interesting surroundings (the central character lived by the beach, enjoyed sailing, and drove a sports car). The show also had nostalgia built into it. It starred Vince Edwards, whom turn-of-the-'70s parents would remember as Ben Casey in ABC's medical blockbuster of the early 1960s. Then Edwards had been a neurosurgeon; now he played a psychiatrist.

His new series, an association between Edwards's production company and Universal, appeared at a time when it looked as if psychiatry might get another chance on TV despite the lukewarm reception to *The Eleventh Hour* and *The Breaking Point* in the early 1960s. Norman Felton, executive producer of *The Eleventh Hour* and *Dr. Kildare*, was developing a psychiatry show for the 1971–72 season. In addition, Quinn Martin Productions, creators of several high-voltage cop series before the latest violence purge, had already mounted a psychiatry pilot called *Crisis*. It had aired on CBS in 1970 but had not gone to series.

The three attempts reflected the conviction of at least some programmers and producers that psychiatric drama could make it on TV if only it could move away from the inherent slowness of traditional psychiatry. Norman Felton stressed in an early description of his new project that he would have the leads deal with acute problems—"emotional explosions," he called them—in a manner that could be resolved dramatically by the hour's end.[28] *Crisis* followed this line as well, revolving as it did around the blowups that mobilized a hospital-based psychiatric crisis center.

In the *Matt Lincoln* pilot, the emotional explosions started on the telephone. Called "Dial Hot Line," it was a made-for-TV movie that aired at 9 p.m. during the 1969–70 season. The two-hour drama places psychologist/social worker David Leopold (Edwards) in charge of a walk-in and phone-in clinic for people with problems.

Four aides, two black and two white, cover the phones. Their goal: to try to prevent tragedies from happening and, if possible, to bring desperate callers to the clinic for help. They certainly get their chance. The flick jumps back and forth between stories of drug dealing, suicide on the phone, youthful runaway, nymphomania, and lack of parental understanding.

Daily Variety's reviewer was impressed. The film, he said, "has the jolt of a power line, the morbid attraction of a sideshow, and the coiled intensity of Vince Edwards." He added that "following through on each case, 'Dial Hot Line' provides unswerving insight into characters of the clinic crew and its callers [and] doesn't avoid any grim realities it sets out to explore."[29]

On the way to a weekly series, though, the concept lost a good deal of its jolt. The lead character got a more zippy name (Matt Lincoln) and more professional clout (he became a psychiatrist instead of a social worker). But by running the series in the 7:30 to 8:30 slot, ABC placed the show in the same ballpark as *The Young Lawyers* and the other relevance dramas. As such, it put restrictions on the writers regarding the portrayal of themes and the use of language. That gave the show less bite.

The biggest change had to do with Matt Lincoln's personality, a personality that had resonated with the gritty reality of the pilot. Now it had to be more acceptable for family viewing. The "coiled intensity" was toned down drastically. ABC's press relations department tried to make it clear that in the series Lincoln would come off as "a gentle man" who was the best kind of establishment hero. A press release said that "Lincoln will be characterized . . . as an aware contemporary human being, forthright in his beliefs, but also displaying warmth, humor, and compassion. A concerned man, he is committed to using his medical training within and without the hospital walls, endeavoring to reach out into the community."[30]

The Interns was toned down for series television as well. The title originally caught the public's eye as a novel by Richard Frede that became a popular theatrical film from Columbia Pictures. That was in 1962, at the height of the first TV doctor fad. One movie reviewer, reflecting on the fad, called the flick "a glossy renovated *Dr. Kildare* soap opera."[31]

But the movie was actually quite different from either the *Kildare* or *Casey* series. The latter involved a procession of patients' physical and psychological ills and revealed few, if any, deep-seated flaws in their heroes. On the other hand, the movie *The Interns* and its sequel, *The New Interns*, positively wallowed in the personal problems of its central

doctors. Fixating on the image of medical training as a torturous gauntlet that tested would-be physicians to the utmost, the theatrical films
emphasized the "survival of the fittest" aspect of medical training.

"The Interns are on duty thirty-six hours at a stretch and off twelve,"
said the promotional page of the novel's paperback edition. "That's
when they study, sleep, drink, and make love—furiously and ardently,
for they are young, eager, and bursting with life." [32] The key question
in the book and the movies: "Which MDs would follow the medical
track they wanted, which would have to drop out, and why?"

This was not the key question in the television version, which came
from Columbia's Screen Gems TV subsidiary. The basic structure seemed
to be similar to the movie: a chief of staff (Telly Savalas in the film,
Broderick Crawford in the TV series) served as an authority figure to a
diverse group of young interns in New North Hospital. But this was
early '70s television, and the early evening to boot. There was little
chance that network censors would allow *The Interns*'s plots to writhe
soap opera-like with overheated personal lives of the continuing characters.

And, in fact, that wasn't necessarily the idea that Jackie Cooper, head
of Screen Gems, had in mind when he suggested to Robert Claver that
he work up a medical series based on *The Interns*. The notion was just
to exploit Columbia's well-known title for the attraction it would have
to people who were teens when the movie came out and who were
now the networks' prime targets. Claver and his associates, recognizing the title's basic strengths, reshaped the theme to come up with a
tack they knew network executives wanted: youth-oriented "relevance"
that would attract teens and their parents through stories of both the
interns and their patients. The interns they chose reflected the cast of
all relevance dramas. There was one black man, one woman, one young
married man, and two adamantly single males.

The publicity rhetoric was also standard. Claver told the press that
the series would be about young people struggling against authority to
change the establishment from within. It would not be another medical
melodrama, he assured viewers, but a story of five young people who
incidentally are doctors. [33]

It didn't quite work out that way. Over time, the producer and his
head writer, William Blinn, found themselves concluding that the relationship between Dr. Sam Marsh, the married intern, and his wife,
was the only good source for drama among the continuing characters.
As a result, they veered the plots toward the guest star-centered anthological air of other medical series.

The story lines were definitely in tune with *Medical Center*'s. A young
man who fears he is inheriting a brain disease demands that his girlfriend have an abortion. A go-go dancer disrupts hospital routines. A
hospitalized executive becomes suspicious of his pregnant wife and an
intern. Dr. Marsh, traumatized by the death of a teenaged addict, gets

out of the hospital to learn about the drug rehabilitation activities of Synanon.

Bob Claver remembered the Synanon episode as one of the most riveting of the short-lived series. The drug habit of young adults was a common TV theme at the time, on and off doctor shows. Claver said the catalyst for his decision to use *The Interns* to explore the subject was a White House conference President Nixon hosted for Hollywood executives at the turn of the '70s. Nixon said the aim was to enlist storytellers' help in drawing attention to the problem and possible solutions.

At the time, Synanon, a commune with a strong counter-cultural image, was considered to have a model drug rehabilitation program. Veteran TV medical writer Barry Oringer, a Synanon resident, wrote the script. The climax of the episode was the "Synanon Game," a confrontation session where the residents bluntly hurl ego-bursting comments and challenges at one another.

Oringer and Claver would later confess to regrets about glorifying the game and the participants. By the mid-1970s, news reports were characterizing Synanon as fascistic and violent. In fact, Oringer (who later left the place) admitted feeling when he worked on the plot that the organization was beginning to veer toward culthood. But for personal and dramatic reasons, he kept that feeling out of the script. His aim was to portray the Synanon approach as an unblemished solution to the drug habit.

New Vestments, Old Villains

Oringer's portrayal of a counter-cultural community with unorthodox methods but establishment goals (at least when it came to drugs) was precisely the compromise between the old and the new that producers and networks were striving for in their relevance dramas. But *The Interns*'s Nielsen numbers were marginal. So were *Matt Lincoln*'s. *The Interns* lasted through the summer and then was pulled. *Matt Lincoln* didn't even get a chance to go that far. Responding to dismal ratings, ABC yanked it off the air after just three and a half months.

Lincoln was most obviously a victim of its NBC competition, *The Flip Wilson Show*, which was second only to *Marcus Welby* in Nielsen popularity. "*Matt Lincoln* was a good idea but the people didn't want to deal with relevance," Vince Edwards sighed. "They put us on at 7:30 opposite Flip Wilson [comedy] and our first show was [guest star] Patty Duke dealing with the abortion problem. Who the hell would watch it?"

With the exception of *The Mod Squad*, in fact, all the relevance dramas expired rather quickly. *Variety*'s TV editor Les Brown wrote that "relevance may have been the shortest program cycle in the history of the medium."[34] In a 1972 book on "the business behind the box," Brown mentioned that network analysts cited the failure of the early evening relevance series as proof that viewers wanted television for escape and not for confrontation with society's problems. Brown argued quite differently. The public was not shying away from relevance, he contended, but from bogus depictions of it. He wrote scathingly that the rather simplistic writing level of those early evening programs made obvious what may not have been as clear in other prime-time programming: that the industry's bow to contemporary issues was often merely an insipid way to repeat messages about the ultimate right of the establishment.[35]

TV script writers had "merely found new vestments for their old, reliable evildoers," Brown said.[36] He brought up one example from the premier episode of *The Interns* where, he noted, the criminality of one character was "telegraphed in one of the earliest scenes by his preoccupation with smut. Crude speaking, seedy, and having a distracted look suggestive of being stoned, he sells to a terminal patient looking for the means of committing suicide an injection that does the job."

Brown's point was that this criminal was costumed as a philosophical dropout of the system but was really an old-fashioned psychopath. In other shows, he said, militants were not angry revolutionaries but paranoics or agents of hostile countries. Draft evaders were not really opponents of the Vietnam War but "neurotics rejecting their fathers in return for having been rejected by them." Recalling the CBS president's commitment to "the gut issues" of the time, he added: "Instead of shedding light on the ailments of the social system and the divisions within it, the playlets distorted the questions and fudged the answers."[37]

These trenchant comments about the early evening dramas could have been made about most of the programs after 9 p.m. as well. Voiced by a mainstream trade paper journalist not known for radical leanings, the harsh words reflected a crescendo of complaints that were circulating against the television networks' portrayal of reality. Liberals as well as radicals who were to various degrees disaffected with the American power structure saw the media in general, and television in particular, as the voicebox of an unresponsive establishment.

Brown's comments were also typical in another way: liberal press critics of doctor shows might well mention the general depiction of social power in those series. But they didn't discuss the specific depiction of *medical* power in those shows, or its possible impact. Nor did they discuss the extent to which (or the way in which) *Medical Center, Marcus Welby, The Bold Ones, The Interns,* and *Matt Lincoln* were mirroring changing social policies toward the actual medical institution.

The critics' silence on this topic is particularly curious because in other quarters concerns about health care policies were not only deep, they were loud. As social historian Paul Starr noted, "Medicine, like many other American institutions, suffered a stunning loss of confidence in the 1970s."[38] Previously, Starr pointed out, two premises had guided U.S. health policy: first, that the government had an obligation to provide Americans with a continually increasing amount of medical care; and second, that medical professionals and private organizations were best equipped to decide how to organize that care.

At the turn of the 1970s, both these notions hit a logjam. Rapidly escalating costs of the major health entitlement programs of the 1960s, Medicare and Medicaid, led many politicians to fear that the notion of automatically adding to these and other health budgets had pushed things terribly awry. The system of medical financing, experts said, was fattening hospitals and encouraging hospital-based care while neglecting (and discouraging) desperately needed ambulatory and preventive health services. It was encouraging doctors to settle in wealthy suburbs rather than in rural or inner-city areas. It was paying specialists more than primary care physicians, even while generalists were critical to keep track of patients' overall health and guide them efficiently to specialists when needed.[39]

Many reformists pointed to the Kaiser Health Foundation as a model for providing high quality health care at lower costs. Kaiser was a leading early example of what was to become known as the health maintenance organization, or HMO. The idea, encouraged by legislation, was to prepay an organization a flat sum to care medically for a broad population of individuals. Using a "health team" approach of doctors, nurse practitioners, physicians' assistants, and other "physician extenders," the HMO would improve access to health care as well as improve its efficiency. Efficiency was supposed to be stimulated additionally through peer review of surgery and hospitalization which would discourage unnecessary procedures.[40]

The new experiments, laws, and proposals quickly bogged down a mire of bureaucracy that was made even more obscure because of blatant attempts by the medical establishment to derail and overcomplicate them. The government activities were further weakened in the mid-1970s, as inflation made federal funders hesitant to lay out money for new programs. But as the philosophical tilt toward structural change increased, more radical critiques of the medical system began to appear.[41]

Observers from a variety of ideological persuasions began to question some of the basic arrangements of American health care—the emphasis on acute, hospital-based problems instead of preventive health care and chronic problems; the unhealthy paternalistic attitude of the medical profession toward women (a particular concern of recently reborn feminism); and the tendency of the profession to claim domination over broader and broader areas of life, from school discipline to drug addiction to mental health.[42]

Whether or not they agreed with these critiques, the people in government and in private industry who administered the health care bills of a large portion of the population were shocked at the effect their payouts were having on the costs of goods and services. The steadily rising health care premiums insurance companies were demanding for workers were making American products too expensive on the world market, corporate leaders complained. Government leaders, too, worried that the escalating costs of Medicare and other health programs were a noose around the neck of a nation trying desperately to deal with ravaging inflation.

The bottom line, these private and public policymakers said, was that medicine was being stretched to impossible limits. They were sure private and public policy on health care had to change, with the guiding priority being cost containment. Moreover, for the first time in a long time, "the economic leadership of American society seemed ready to bring about changes in the organization of medical care over the opposition of providers."[43]

In the process, they found they had to go beyond costs. To guide their debates in the face of new realities, policymakers had to develop a set of ground-level assumptions about the nature of medicine that was significantly different from the one of just a few years before.

The people who shared these emerging premises did not necessarily agree on how to handle the medical world. But they did agree on the assumptions that made certain issues more important for debate than others. Daniel Callahan, an ethicist involved in the policy debates, characterized the new approach concisely: "Scarcity—restraint—limit: these are rapidly becoming the slogans of the times, and it is difficult to foresee that they will cease to be so very soon."[44]

Callahan predicted that setting constraints on medical care would increasingly be the responsibility of both the government and the individual:

> [Trends] point toward, if not a theory of medical limits, at least the ingredients for one, toward the establishment of . . . more self-discipline and self-restraint (not only in terms of what people do but also in terms of what they desire). . . . The most discussed ethical issues are all likely to reflect the force of [this idea], as some new balance is sought between public needs and private desires.[45]

Shallow One-Sidedness

At the time Callahan gave his prediction, in 1975, most of the philosophical debates about American medicine were limited to a small sector of decisionmakers and intellectuals. It is true that popular magazines, newspapers, and the broadcast media were shouting the message that medicine was in crisis. And, in fact, pollsters were finding that one-third to two-thirds of the population agreed with the general proposition that the health care system was going through a "crisis."[46]

But while this message of the popular media was loud, it was also typically short and discontinuous. That was especially true about the main trumpeters of national events for most Americans—the three network evening newscasts. An analysis of topics on the newscasts from October 1969 through October 1971 found only a handful of pieces that covered debates about medical care in the U.S. Those brief spots centered on the need for more money, the more efficient use of money, and the possible need for national health insurance. The bulk of network coverage of health care had to do with the clinical side of medicine, not its philosophical side. In fact, the newscasts shed light on the same kind of stories that the doctor dramas were covering: the triumphs and frustrations of heart transplants, the dangers of illicit drugs and cigarettes, the mixed blessings and uncertainties of the birth control pill.[47]

Actually, one could argue that *Marcus Welby, The Bold Ones, Medical Center, Matt Lincoln,* and *The Interns* could have a big advantage over the news when it came to letting viewers in on the new emotional and ethical tensions involved in health care's clinical side. Like the doctor shows before them, these prime-time dramas went deeper and more broadly into the tensions, frustrations, dangers, and triumphs of medical knowledge than the journalistic spots ever could. In addition, they were watched by far more people than watched the newscasts.

But the doctor series showed almost no awareness of the sociopolitical changes that were beginning to reshape the medical system. More significant, they showed almost no sensitivity to the new assumptions that corporate executives, labor leaders, congress people, hospital administrators, and physician leaders were bringing to the emerging medical environment. As we have seen, the programs continued to depict medicine as an unlimited resource. They acted out a high-technology, ever-advancing sort of medical science with a damn-the-cost, always-do-everything-possible attitude. Social policy toward the poor and the elderly was not a problem because they hardly existed on TV's doctor shows. In fact, policy didn't come up as a major problem at all. It was shaped not by legislators or insurance company executives (or even hospital administrators), but by physician-heroes.

It isn't as if new premises guiding real-world medicine were unworthy of prime-time scripting. To the contrary, the notions of scarcity and restraint raised a crop of dilemmas that begged for exploration. Here was a wonderful agenda for human drama. "Medicine is in part a moral enterprise," Callahan pointed out, "one that seeks human good. Now we can ask once again about that good which medicine is said to serve, and about what its role in the quest for a larger good might reasonably be. The question has forced itself upon us whether we are ready or not."[48]

It would be too easy to say that the creators didn't have a way to find out what was going on. Producers David Victor and David O'Connell (*Marcus Welby*), Cy Chermak and Joel Rogosin (*The Bold Ones*), and Frank Glicksman and Don Brinkley (*Medical Center*) made a point to review medical periodicals in search of ideas. Many writers did the same thing. In addition, the producers and writers were in continual touch with representatives of the medical system at a number of levels—from permanent technical advisors to one-shot medical school consultants to medical equipment manufacturers to AMA Advisory Panel members to officials of disease foundations.

But some of these information sources were actually part of the reason that doctor shows ignored the new perspectives shaping medical care. Technical advisors really had no clout to encourage new perspectives even if they had wanted to. They realized they were being paid because they knew how to serve the tried and true approach. Their job was to ensure a semblance of medical accuracy without making a fuss about certain kinds of dramatic license.

As for AMA physicians, equipment manufacturers, and disease foundation executives, they had a vested interest in trying to ensure, respectively, that TV doctors came through as the dominant medical force, that the latest technology was showcased, and that the plots encouraged viewers to feel that medicine should continue to receive increasing percentages of society's resources. Clearly their priorities challenged the emerging policy of reduced medical expenditures and reduced physician control over the system. It was therefore in their interest to encourage stories that took their perspective for granted and did not even acknowledge that very different positions were beginning to hold sway.

The traditional influences on the doctor show, then, were arrayed to reinforce rather than subvert the longstanding formula with its traditional perspective on medicine. David Rintels, the outspoken head of the Committee of Censorship of the Writers Guild of America, West, sensed this as he spoke as early as 1972 to the Senate Subcommittee on Constitutional Rights. Ranging across a variety of program types to show the difficulties that television writers have in overcoming the rigidities of their industry, Rintels made a special pause at doctor shows:

> At least two Senators on this Subcommittee—Senator Kennedy and Senator Scott—have strong feelings about the cost and availability of health care in this country; they stand up here, in one of the two most influential forums in the country, and they say so. It's their right, not to say their obligation. Many writers agree with them. Those who do are absolutely prohibited from standing up in the other most influential forum and suggesting that American medicine could be improved, its costs reduced, its scope expanded. . . .
>
> The consequences of this shallow one-sidedness are tragic. No debate ensues, no national awareness of a problem which some of you and some of

us believe may have reached crisis proportions. Pesonally, I don't know whether there is a health care crisis in America; I'd like to know. I do know that it is a gross disservice to the country to refuse to discuss whether such a crisis exists.[49]

Rintels' speech was excerpted in the *New York Times*. His comments did not, however, spark extended discussion in the popular press. Magazine and newspaper writers continued to ignore the relationship of doctor shows to the changing politics of the medical world. Instead, they continued to grab eagerly onto the images that network publicists, who had eyes on their own companies' competitive problems, wanted to convey about the series. The themes were basically updated versions of the ones circulated during the *Kildare/Casey* heyday: doctor shows had life-and-death excitement, were youth-oriented, were in tune with the turbulent times, yet firmly supported the establishment.

The publicity about *Medical Center* bore by far the most fruit, the greatest proportion of it centered on the show's younger star, Chad Everett. Of the new crop of medico heroes, Everett qualified best for the label of sex symbol. His modish long hair, his athletic profile, his Hollywood name (invented by Henry Wilson, the same agent who coined Rock Hudson), his devotion to his medical role, and his female viewers' reactions to him intrigued members of the press.[50]

The fan mail was particularly intriguing. *TV Guide* noted that much of it was sexually blunt. Many of his fan letters, it said, "rhapsodize over Everett's provocative walk," and more.[51] Everett himself admitted to liking the idea of being adored by women throughout the nation. He told *TV Guide:* "I could be a big sex symbol, but with the white coat and stethoscope I can't be as animal as in a pair of tight Levi's with a gun slung low on my hip."[52]

But there was another part of Chad Everett that came through in the press as well. He was, writers confided, a conservative man in many ways. He was wealthy and liked showing it off. He was traditional in his views of woman's place in raising children and serving her husband. He was a staunch Republican who knew by heart the names of the numerous speakers he had to introduce at the GOP Convention.

He was so removed from the intellectual warfare of the late 1960s that he didn't recognize the then-controversial feminist names of Gloria Steinem or Bella Abzug. Still, he was refreshingly honest about his ignorance of some of the upheavals taking place in American society. "I didn't even know about women's lib," he told a reporter, "until some script we were doing kept mentioning a male chauvinist pig."[53]

Chad Everett was, in other words, an embodiment of the very qualities the producers and network programmers were trying to project in that period's prime-time shows. One part of his persona fit perfectly with the network's desire to be perceived as plugging into contemporary looks, youthful honesty, and sexual frankness. The other part fit well with the programmers' desire to curry favor with mainstream

America and older America, to appear to be avant-garde and reaching toward a new consensus, but really, in the end, celebrating traditional values.

And if a show's healthy ratings are a measure of the strategy's success, it can be said that it worked. No matter that both *Marcus Welby* and *Medical Center* were said to be in easy time periods where their chance to build an audience was assured. (*Welby* stood opposite a low-rated news hour on CBS and *Medical Center* competed with the NBC's ailing *Kraft Music Hall*.) What counted was that the ratings were solid and stable, pointing well toward the long haul.

An added value from the networks' standpoint was the favorable reception the programs and their stars often received. *TV Guide* even countered the trend to snicker at the hypochondria doctor shows were said to reinforce. The magazine carried an article that detailed incidents in which viewers learned valuable health care facts from the series. People's lives had been saved and illness-torn families had been brought closer together as a result of the authentic medical details on *Marcus Welby* and *Medical Center*, the author stressed.[54]

Doctor shows also won kudos in public polls and from community groups and other established organizations. *Welby's* Robert Young, of course, typically received a special respect. But *Medical Center* and *The Bold Ones* got their share of high status, too. For example, *Medical Center* was named the "most liked" television program in a 1971 poll of high school students and community influentials conducted by the American Council for Better Broadcasts, a consumer organization devoted to improving TV. And *Bold Ones* star David Hartman, who became involved in various charitable efforts while working on the show, was honored in 1972 by the National Conference of Christians and Jews for his "promotion of human relations in the entertainment industry."[55]

As a result of such all-around good news in a treacherous environment, and despite the failures of *The Interns* and *Matt Lincoln*, doctor dramas seemed versatile and programmable to network executives. They became known as vehicles with which program creators, taking a cue from the networks, could exploit the tremendous changes that were coursing through American society without having to really explore those changes or face up to them.

The five turn-of-the-'70s shows became good and bad examples for producers and network people concocting new series during the next few years. *Welby* and *Medical Center*, the most successful of the bunch, particularly indicated clear-cut directions to others who thought gold could come through tinkering with the formula. So, in a negative way, did *Matt Lincoln* and *The Interns*.

And producers did tinker: by the mid-1970s, the amount of doctor activity on television was dizzying, with thirteen more dramatic series and a clutch of made-for-TV movies on medicine hitting the airwaves.

Gold did not come easily, though. As the next two chapters show, the creation of those shows turned out to be a roller-coaster ride of more failures than successes as producers and programmers worked nervously to find the best ways to make something new out of the same old stuff. That had important implications for the direction of the formula.

9

Sexism, Stiffs, and Speed

It was one of Norman Felton's more painful joustings with network censors. He was working at Universal Studios on the pilot movie for his 1971–72 TV series, *The Psychiatrist*. The film was called "God Bless the Children," and it dealt with widespread teenage drug addiction in a small town. Dr. James Whitman, the title character, tries to fight the problem with the aid of a thirty-two-year-old former addict and current resident of an L.A. halfway house.

At issue was a key scene that made all connected with the program proud. The scene's purpose was to highlight the physical and emotional self-destruction that was part of the drug-abuse problem. In it, Felton recalled, "a fellow is going to shoot up. He has a spoon, he's going to heat it, and he's in the back room of a church.

"It was not frightening—yes, it was, to a certain extent—but I felt it was borderline. The whole idea of it was how degrading it was. We shot it, the film was given to [the network programmers], and they thought it was wonderful. They called; they said it was marvelous.

"But two days later they said, 'We've changed our minds, you've got to take that scene out.' " The word from people in command was that the scene was too stark, too shocking, for the TV audience.

Angry, Felton held firm. But the pressure mounted, especially from the executives in New York. "The network finally sent one of their senior vice presidents out because I made such a big to-do about it. Universal was putting pressure on me."

Sid Sheinberg, head of Universal Television, accompanied the network VP to Felton's cutting room. "I was in the editorial room," Felton remembered, "and I opened the door. I ran the film to this particular point, and I made my point of why the scene should stay in. I knew I couldn't stop it. No way I could stop it. But they heard from me. I don't know—there comes a time. And the editor, a fine editor . . . he cried."

John Furia, an experienced TV writer-producer, found himself facing off against censors twice while working on a 1973 TV movie/pilot called "The Healers." The first incident had to do with a subplot about a dying boy. In the script, Dr. Robert Kier, the hospital's chief physician and the movie's central character, decides that he must be honest with the youngster about his prognosis. Network censors balked at that, fearing that discussion of the boy's death might frighten children and their parents in the audience. But Furia convinced them to leave it in. He argued that the scene was not only dramatically sound, it was the approach that many physicians were recommending.

Furia had to compromise on the second objection, which involved the major network bugaboo, frank allusions to sex. Toward the middle of "The Healers," Kier falls to professional and personal low points, both at the same time. As if to compound the doctor's frustrations, in comes a colleague, a woman physician, who suggests that they become romantically and sexually involved. Having just had a major blowup with his wife, Kier finds the offer tempting. But, though flattered, he rejects it, saying something like "not now." To that, the woman replies angrily, "I don't take rainchecks."

The entire exchange raised the censors' hackles. But it was the woman's aggressive retort that made them especially nervous. Quibbles back and forth finally led to an agreement that the scene would be toned down.

Anybody involved in a network doctor drama during the 1970s is likely to tell at least a couple of stories about interference by network censors on the grounds that a scene was too startling. Anecdotes such as these, however, do not contradict the assertions by virtually everyone who worked on the shows during that time that network airwaves were a lot more open to plot ideas than they had been in the past, even if those ideas were controversial. The late 1960s, with its questioning of traditional standards and its emphasis on youth culture, had encouraged a new permissiveness in prime time.

Yet, as the anecdotes suggest, the extent of that permissiveness can be exaggerated easily. Producers often assumed that they had to concoct plot lines at the boundaries of acceptability if they were to lure audiences during that decade of intense competitive pressures linked to furious social change. It was true that a producer had to stretch hard to think of a social issue that couldn't make it to a dramatic TV script. But it was also true that the network standards and practices divisions placed a barrage of requirements on the handling of those issues that often limited the sharpness and depth with which they could be etched. A middle-of-the-road approach to morality, with balance and caution at the helm, remained the norm.

The result was that when doctor-show producers and writers did deal with issues at the forefront of people's consciousness—and they were likely to deal with the same ones: drugs, abortion, venereal disease, heart transplants, homosexuality, and a few more—they tended to feel limited in terms of the moral and political perspectives that they could bring to them. They knew that the trick to creating an acceptable script didn't lie in the moral or political distinctiveness of the plotting. Rather, it lay in being good at tinkering with the formula's surface: making variations on old themes appear new.

It is significant that, while TV storytellers eagerly recall scuffles with network censors from the 1970s, they tend to have few, if any, tidbits to tell about restrictive pressures by the American Medical Association, which had been such an intensely direct force on programs during the previous decade. At least part of the reason seems to relate to the declining status of the AMA in society at large. Producers and writers, who had never been comfortable with agents of the AMA Advisory Committee looking over their shoulders, began to see in the early 1970s that network executives were no longer worried when creators distanced themselves from the major public arm of organized medicine.

This did not mean that the strong influence of the medical establishment disappeared. The basic framework the AMA had helped to set up during the doctor shows' formative years was very much in place.[1] It was guarded by technical advisors and consultants who, while not AMA agents, were nevertheless deeply committed to its perspective. In addition, as producers and writers looked to dramatize new ailments, or to find new wrinkles on old ones, disease foundations such as the American Cancer Society and the American Lung Association came on board with free advice. In the process, they reinforced the science-driven, ever-progressing, resource-rich, apolitical view of health care that had become standard.

For its part, the American Medical Association began to find that it had to use a softer tone in trying to influence programming. The turn of the '70s had AMA leaders agreeing that the major problem with doctor shows was that their central physicians were often too heroic. In an era when physicians were increasingly under attack for incompetence, inattention, and materialism,[2] some doctors saw their television counterparts as models of perfection who couldn't possibly be imitated. These gods were inciting people to make unrealistic demands of their physicians, the observers claimed.

The charge had become widespread because of the national adoration of Marcus Welby. Now it was directed against other doctor shows as well.[3] The AMA's official response to the issue seems to have been to treat it gingerly, to jawbone for change publicly but not to damn existing programs too much. William Quinn, M.D., the Advisory Committee's head at the time, said that he was trying to convince producers to lay off the grandeur, the life-and-death tensions, and instead focus on the humor and ordinariness of physicians' work in the hospital.[4] Presumably, that dose of "realism" would allow viewers to feel more empathy with their doctors and lead to better feelings about them in the real world.

It is doubtful that Quinn's requests had a direct effect.[5] Yet his pronouncements and those of other medical leaders may have made network programming executives and censors breathe a bit easier when they allowed main characters in their new doctor show cycle to be less than always heroic. There seemed to be general agreement that this was an approach that would make doctor shows of the 1970s different from their predecessors.

Coming up with something different was deemed important. Yet among the thirteen series, thirty TV movies (often series pilots), and two miniseries about doctors that network executives had accepted for airing during the decade, there was much that was tiresomely familiar. For example, TV series *Doctors Hospital, Westside Medical*, and *Julie Farr* and TV movies *The Healers* and *The Critical List* took the traditional *Medical Center/Bold Ones* path in following physicians in state-of-the-art hospitals as they fought administrators and other obstacles to save patients' lives. Similarly, the series *Rafferty* and *Doc Elliot*, the pilot *Dr. Max*, and a TV movie remake of *The Last Angry Man* nodded to the *Marcus Welby/Dr. Christian* strain by focusing on a general practitioner who eschews the hospital setting in favor of working closer to the people.

The copycat approach was obviously aimed at lowering the risk of failure on the assumption that the audience would go for proven scenarios. But the welter of high-powered TV competition demanded more than just imitation. Creators of new shows had to offer something unusual so that network buyers would notice their products above others. The network people, in turn, needed that holy grail of TV: an idea different enough to stand apart from the competition in viewers' minds but similar enough to previous hits to (virtually) ensure success.

Producers and their network counterparts agreed that one way to make doctor shows appear different despite the sameness was to go against the grain with the personalities of lead characters. The belief was that viewers of the cynical 1970s would now accept heroes who were less godlike than before. This meant showing that great doctors sometimes have personal problems—like all of us, but more so.

"It's one of the things that I felt was interesting about doctors and not very different actually from people in my business," said John Furia about creating *The Healers*. "They get so heavily involved in their work that the adrenaline pumps all day long and there's not much left of them outside of their work environment. . . . It's hard to go home and deal with 'take-out-the-garbage.' "

Furia gave his central doctor in *The Healers* a troubled family life and an alcoholic physician on his staff. William Blinn and Jerry Thorpe, who adapted *The Lazarus Syndrome* series from Michael Halberstam's book, emphasized their central character's doomed marriage in the pilot film. Sterling Sillaphant, who wrote *Dr. Max*, gave his hero a variety of personality quirks. Jerry Isenberg and Gerald Abrams injected Julie Farr with a number of insecurities. There was no doubting that these were still good doctors with first-class medical intuitions. The idea was that the audience would find the characters more believable if they were more "real," which to creators meant more torn by inner conflict.

Yet it was understood that touches such as these alone could not, in the end, make these series stand out. Except for the two miniseries, which were drenched with the problems of doctors and nurses, the medical dramas of the 1970s were based overwhelmingly on the notion that the patient had to be the focus. From a dramatic standpoint, the new TV physicians could not be self-indulgent about their own rather minor difficulties if they were to be the dedicated healers the publicity promised they were.

Doctor-show creators were forced in the end to soft-pedal the personal difficulties of their heroes. As a result, they felt obliged to take additional turns with their formats to make their products look different from the previous decade's medicos as well as from contemporary competition. Two twists got special attention. One involved making a main character female—or, more rarely, black or ethnic—with the intention of sparking audience attention and unusual story lines. The other involved linking the doctor show to the action area, getting it out of the hospital and into the streets.

While each path had its successes and failures, industry insiders judged the overall pattern disappointing. Interpreting the meaning of the failures and successes became the way that programmers and producers, incrementally and jerkily, charted directions for the form.

Paramedics and Greek Sailors

As early as the fall 1971 season *Variety* was announcing the action trend. "Time was," noted one of the trade journal's TV reviewers, "when medical dramas could find enough material within the walls of the institution itself to satisfy their theatrical needs. But practical considerations arising from the public's surface familiarity with almost every variety of organic malfunction have forced medics out into the real world. The real world, that is, of violent crime, sadistic parents, perverts, pickpockets, and psychopaths."[6]

The reporter was referring specifically to the season's opening stanza of *Medical Center*. Yet he could have been writing about several shows that were already on the air, or would soon be on. *Matt Lincoln* had its hero out on the streets, or in his boat. *The Psychiatrist* tried hard for outside action, as did *The Interns*. As for *Marcus Welby*, one of the reasons David Victor made him a family practitioner was to get him out of a hospital setting that Victor felt had become too confining.

By and large, though, these shows were still tied to an indoor locale, if only because the diagnosis and treatment process had to take place inside. *Welby's* creators found that to be both realistic and life-and-death dramatic, they often had to send their patients to the hospital. And *Medical Center's* producers, while boasting in publicity releases about shows shot outdoors, nevertheless needed their simulated corridors, operating theater, and nursing station. A good part of the reason was economic. The way the finances were structured, the program could afford only a few episodes that made full use of location shooting.

But as the doctor fad of the late '60s and early '70s unfolded, Hollywood producers sensed that putting a physician in an unusual locale might set their program apart from the competition. Several of the attempts—*Doc Elliot's* rural scenery is an example—forced only a little variance from standard plot lines and characters. Other forays attempted to go further. An early one, "Companions in a Nightmare" (1968) built a whodunit TV movie around a murder in a psychiatrist's therapy group. And "The Incredible Journey of Meg Laural" used rural America during the Depression of the 1930s as a setting for another TV film.

Since the series was where the real money was in television, it made sense for producers to try out nontraditional locations with strong potential for continuing stories. The made-for-TV-movie, instituted by the networks in the 1960s to get around the high cost of renting mediocre theatrical films, became a testing ground for these approaches. One medical area with nontraditional settings that creators initially thought had series potential was the epidemic.

The idea wasn't new. In the early 1960s, David Victor had used *Dr. Kildare* to slip in a pilot program featuring James Caan in a public health unit tracking down the source of a food poisoning epidemic. The show did not go to series, but the idea lived on. In 1967, *Dr. Kildare* again used the search for an epidemic's cause as a major part of the plot. In 1972, the TV movie *Killer by Night* featured a physician (played by Robert Wagner) chasing down the source of a diphtheria scare. In 1975, the TV movie *The Specialists* followed the progress of an agency like the U.S. Center for Disease Control in tracking a number of contagions. And a year later, in the TV movie *Panic in Echo Park*, a different crusading doctor was chasing a disease of mysterious origin in L.A.

The Specialists was definitely a series pilot, and *Panic* was probably one.[7] Like Victor's, though, they never made it past the tryout stage. People connected to both productions suggested a number of reasons for their failure, from the scripting to the acting. But Victor argued flatly that the networks would be correct in turning down all series about epidemic detectives. He had come to feel with network programmers that continuing dramas revolving around the ailments of masses of people would never succeed. "Because it's hard to personalize them," he insisted. "An epidemic is statistical. It lacks the one-on-one."

Whether or not Victor's argument held water was immaterial. Network programmers seemed to believe it, and they were the key gate-keepers. The challenge remained: find a medical idea that could work as a series in an action arena outside a hospital. Looking at the matter very pragmatically, producers and writers tried to splice elements of other popular culture formulas into the doctor show to come up with a hybrid concept that would work.

Emergency! seemed to be one that would. The direct spark for the series was a John Wayne theatrical film called *Hellfighters* that Universal had released in 1969. It was an international adventure tale about men who fight fires on oil rigs. Sid Sheinberg, president of Universal TV, came up with the idea that a variant of that action-packed realism might be just the thing for early-evening TV. He called Jack Webb and asked him if his production company would consider developing a series with Universal about a firefighter rescue team.

Webb certainly appeared to be the right person for that job. He had a reputation dating back to *Dragnet* for scrupulous realism that stressed action. More to the point was the success of *Adam 12*, a police series from Webb's production company. A mainstay of NBC's early-evening lineup since September 1969, *Adam 12* dealt with the day-to-day world of two uniformed policemen assigned to patrol car duty. Each half-hour episode had the two continuing characters encounter a range of cases, some serious, some trivial, some amusing, and some sad. The show was known for its success at garnering child audiences and their parents during the first prime-time hour of the evening, beginning at 8. Network strategists considered this hour a critical "lead-in" period. They felt that when a household chose a channel at the start of prime time, there was a good chance the set would stay on that channel for the entire evening's program flow.

Webb saw the potential for putting the *Adam-12* approach to lucrative use in another early-evening product. He got Robert Cinader, the TV writer who had actually created *Adam 12*, to flesh out the concept. Cinader quickly concluded that Sheinberg's suggestion of worldwide firefighting was too unwieldy and expensive. But on investigating the subject, he discovered that the Los Angeles fire department had recently embarked on a trial program that used paramedics in the field to stabilize people with heart problems and other medical difficulties before they were sent to the hospital. The idea had begun in Ireland, and Seattle had copied it, but the L.A. program was in the vanguard.

Here, Cinader told colleagues, were the elements Sheinberg had wanted, but closer to home. The paramedic branch of firefighting had not been done before on TV. It was exciting, inviting spectacular stunts, and had stories that were as endless as the real-life paramedic runs themselves. The show as conceived by him would have two interacting units. The first would consist of two paramedic regulars and the fire-fighters with which they worked. The second would be the "base" hospital where the paramedics delivered patients. It was a required aspect of the show, but Cinader saw it as secondary to the main drama out in the field.

On this he disagreed vigorously with his boss. Jack Webb, the executive producer, wanted the place where the victims were sent to be central. Webb had cast his former wife, Julie London, and her present husband, Bobby Troup, as an emergency nurse and physician, respectively. Robert Fuller, who was to play the head of Rampart Hospital's emergency division, was considered an up-and-coming actor. Webb wanted those roles highlighted. Cinader, though, felt there was nothing new in situating the program in a hospital and wanted to stress action in the field.

Webb won the first round, the movie-of-the-week pilot, which Cinader worked on with Harold J. Bloom. As aired, it showed the hospital crew thrashing out the correctness of supporting a bill to create the paramedic program. The two paramedics, John Gage (played by Randy Mantooth) and Roy DeSoto (Kevin Tighe) were very much supporting players. The emphasis was Webb's, not Cinader's. After the show went to series, though, the players' importance turned 180 degrees. "Jack had the *Emergency!* pilot re-written [to highlight the hospital]," said one of the program's insiders. "But eventually he lost control of the show."

The program as it evolved celebrated the glories of paramedic action in the field. "Bob's theory was, you can teach through entertainment," said Hannah Shearer, a coproducer. "People don't have to know that they're learning something, to learn." He was particularly gratified to discover that lives were saved because people had picked up safety hints from the program. The crusading spirit also applied to what Cinader would not show. Never in the program's 122 episodes did it depict arson. Cinader worried that if he showed a character starting a mischievous fire, someone in the audience would copy it. He couldn't tolerate even the possibility of that happening.

From the beginning, many organizations and individuals picked up his enthusiasm for the cause, as NBC's press releases pointed out often during the show's five-year run in prime time. The information office of the Tucson Fire Department went on record as saying that rescue procedures depicted in the *Emergency!*'s pilot movie led its members to change the way they went about some rescue work. The California State Senate commended Cinader, Jack Webb, and the cast and crew for helping to spread the word about the importance of paramedics. Similarly, U.S. Senator Alan Cranston from California put out a letter addressed to Jack Webb that drew a direct link between the popularity and accuracy of *Emergency!* and the passage of a Senate bill to promote the training of paramedics around the country.[8]

The series had found success on Saturday evenings at eight. It was considered a killer period, for CBS's *All in the Family*, the nation's number one show at the time, was destroying all comers. Yet by TV logic it had made eminent sense. *Emergency!* was an example of drastic counterprogramming. *All in the Family* was a startling situation comedy, filled with unusual protagonists and caustic references to contemporary issues. Cinader's show, on the other hand, was soothing in its view of humanity, simplistic in its characterizations, and contemporary only in its approach to paramedic technology. NBC's hope was to lure TV watchers who either couldn't stand, or understand, *All in the Family*.

Emergency!'s format was highly predictable. Of utmost importance were the three or four rescue vignettes that made up the bulk of the show. Cinader insisted on a look and feel of utter accuracy. In fact, beyond hiring the requisite medical and firefighting consultants, Cinader made it a routine practice to ride with the L.A. paramedics in search of stories. He suggested that his associate producers and prospective script writers do likewise.

It was impossible to find new rescue ideas for the show every week, particularly since each show needed three or four of them. So, said Hannah Shearer, a coproducer, the way creators got around the problem was by varying the types of people rescued. As in *Dragnet* and *Adam 12*, *Emergency!* thrived on depicting eccentrics.

"We ended up doing heart attacks maybe one hundred times," Shearer recalled. "Bob's favorite was the Greek sailor who had a heart attack while he was humping a hooker. The network said, 'You'll never get this done tastefully.' And he managed, because he did it without dialog. The sailor didn't speak English, and I guess it was Bobby Troup as Dr. Early who asked the hooker, 'What were you doing when it happened?' She looked at him and shrugged her shoulders. So the adults in the audience understood."

Dramatic license played an important role despite Cinader's concern for accuracy. The pragmatic producer and his writers often found themselves stretching what they had seen in ways that emphasized the possible, if not the probable. Shearer remembered arguing about a vignette in which a child ate dough and the dough rose in his stomach. She and Cinader spent hours dickering with the show's medical consultant until they finally convinced him that it could happen.

Weaving around the rescue vignette was a "spine story" that explored personal concerns of one of the continuing paramedic or hospital characters. There was rarely anything serious, just humorous anecdotes designed to give a human touch to characters who were otherwise cardboard-flat, involved only in heroics. "You have these guys going out and performing heroic deeds as part of their everyday life," Shearer explained. "People in the audience might hate them, because they're sitting at home in front of the TV set not doing that. So we made the main characters as vulnerable as possible in their normal lives."

There was general agreement, though, that *Emergency!*'s strength in the ratings lay in its rescue vignettes. As a result, the logic of competitive television dictated their choice and sequence. Not only did each episode's characters and stories have to be balanced for age and type, the stunts had to be distributed in terms of expense. The most expensive rescue had to happen just after 8:30, so that the *All in the Family* audience, switching channels as that show ended, might be lured. The producers often used explosions or other attention-getters. Rescues earlier in the hour were typically not as elaborate.

The show worked well as NBC's counterprogramming bulwark against Archie Bunker. Exploiting its appeal to young children, NBC even bought an animated spinoff for its Saturday morning schedule. Curiously, though, the programming concept *Emergency!* implied came to be judged rather unenthusiastically within the industry.

People pointed out that the show was designed essentially as a program that would lure youngsters and their families to a network at the start of prime time. *Emergency!* may have had the right mix of ingredients for the job, they said, but the two shows that attempted to copy the medical rescue format closely for this purpose during the 1970s (*Code R, Mobile One*) turned out to be unsuccessful.[9] Beyond these failures, though, times had been changing. The preferred program type for lead-in duty during the late 1970s and 1980s had become not the action tale but the family situation comedy (*The Bill Cosby Show, ALF*). Many believed that, from the standpoint of strategic value to a network, the concept of *Emergency!* could ultimately offer little.

Pathologists and Preachers

Built-in barriers to imitation were also judged to accompany the one other successful medical series that left the hospital, *Quincy, M.E.* The particulars were different. *Quincy* was thought to be a problem because much of its appeal, and its drive, were alleged to come from its star, not its concept. That, TV people noted, made it difficult to copy successfully.

Quincy wasn't supposed to be a personality-driven show. When writer Lou Shaw proposed a show about a medical detective to Universal producer Glen Larson, the two saw the concept as a wide-open merging of two popular TV types, the doctor and the private eye. "I was sitting there wondering how I could do some sort of medical show and I [also] wanted to do a detective show," Shaw recalled, "when I came up with the idea of a coroner. Because you always have to have a dead body, don't you? And then to investigate that medically, you have to have a pathologist. So you have a medical detective show. In essence, I created a unique thing."

It was unusual, but not without precedent. Physicians as fictional detectives actually go back to 1907, with the publication of *The Red Thumb Mark,* a novel by physician and mystery writer R. Austin Freeman. The hero, Dr. Thorndike (we never learn his given name) was the first literary creation to use the scientific laboratory in detection.[10] On TV, the forensic physician who preceded Quincy was Dr. Daniel Coffee in a short-lived 1960 summer series called *Diagnosis: Unknown.* The head pathologist at a large metropolitan hospital, Coffee worked closely with police Detective Captain Max Ritter to solve bizarre murders.[11]

In the early 1970s, Canadian television aired *Wojek,* a series about a crusading coroner. The lead character was based on an actual medical examiner who made the public limelight when he mandated that Canadian surgeons count the sponges before and after an operation to ensure that none would be left in a patient. (Medical examiners have actual judicial clout in the Canadian system.)

But even if, as Shaw contends, he and Larson did not have these trailblazers in mind when they set up the Quincy format, it was clear that they were drawing on two time-honored sleuth formulas—the whodunit type (as in Sherlock Holmes and Inspector Poirot) and the hardboiled type (as in Sam Spade and Mike Hammer). As in the case of several previous fictional private eyes, the audience never learned Quincy's first name. Like many fictional detectives, Quincy had a bright but not terribly insightful sidekick (an Asian). And, like many predecessors, Quincy jousted semi-amicably with a police detective (Irish) who was sometimes helpful, sometimes obstructive to the solving of crimes.

Elements of the traditional doctor show were also there. Like many a TV physician, Quincy faced a bureaucratically-minded administrator who tried to keep him from following his fine-tuned medical instincts. It was clear, too, that Quincy was in the line of the hearty hero without personal difficulties to mess up his medical crusades. He was urbane and single, though he had a pretty steady girlfriend. He was well-off; he lived at a marina in his own boat. He was also gregarious. Episodes often ended with the continuing characters adjourning to their favorite bar.

Shaw wrote his pilot script without first trying to learn in detail about what medical examiners do. "Too much research kills stories," he contended. And, in fact, James Moser had done exactly that with a similar idea as a result of research during the late 1950s. He had toyed with writing a series about a forensic physician but discarded the idea when he found out that medical examiners typically do not step out of their laboratories for clues. They leave the footwork to the police.

Shaw didn't realize this fact when he wrote the pilot, and afterwards he didn't care. He knew that medical accuracy was important, but, like many of his doctor show predecessors, he interpreted that narrowly—as meaning the nitty-gritty factual stuff. That, he said, could come after the format was set.

Accordingly, he hired pathologist Victor Rosen to correct his medical errors and, as the series progressed, give writers advice on ingenious ways to kill people so that Quincy (Jack Klugman) could have something to do. Some time later, after the series began to air, the production company also hired Marc Taylor, a scientist at the Los Angeles medical examiner's office, to help with the advanced machinery the TV physician increasingly began to use to solve his cases. Since the creators (especially Klugman) wanted to parade the realism of Quincy's crime-solving procedures on screen, Taylor's chores began to be more important than the pathologist's. Rosen, Taylor explained, "really knows the autopsy end, which we can't show. But [the show needed someone] familiar with the procedures or equipment . . . which we can show."[12]

The pilot plot centered on a straightforward criminal investigation. Circumstances surrounding the murder of a beautiful woman on a beach causes police detective Monahan and his assistants to assume rape was involved. Quincy suspects a very different series of events. Evading police obstructions, he proves that the wounds on the woman (in particular, her broken neck) are part of a pattern of killings in the city that have nothing to do with rape. In the end, it turns out the killings are connected to a scandal in City Hall.

Despite the City Hall connection, Shaw's script had no controversial political overtones. The nearest the writer-producer came to an explicit political statement had to do with giving his character a reason for being a coroner. Shaw felt that Quincy had to have a motive for getting into such a grisly profession, and it took the writer three days to dream it up. Quincy, Shaw let it be known in the pilot, had been a Beverly Hills pathologist before turning to the medical examiner's office. But a rash of murders in the city sickened him, and he decided to do something about it. He was sure that a pathologist specializing in forensics could make a difference.

"Every person who dies before his time is an outrage," he told someone in the pilot and in succeeding episodes. But a pathologist can do something about it, he added. To a pathologist, each person who does die before his time is pointing the finger at the one who caused it.

Quincy's modest crusade, as Shaw and Larson saw it, involved a kind of preventive medicine: discovering where the dead fingers were pointing and, in so doing, discouraging other murderers. Jack Klugman, however, had more grandiose plans for the character. Ironically, the part was not even written for him. Quincy was initially a hip younger man. Shaw and Larson had hoped to get Robert Wagner.

But Wagner turned it down and Universal knew that NBC was trying furiously to find a series for Jack Klugman. The word around Hollywood was that Klugman could be impossible to work with if he didn't get what he wanted. But the middle-aged actor had recently come off TV's smash situation comedy, *The Odd Couple*, and NBC executives saw his presence on their network as sure money in the bank. Klugman couldn't see playing the role as it was written, but when Shaw and Larson rewrote it to fit his persona, he seized on it. Despite the fact that the network's audience tests rated its chances poor, NBC guaranteed the producers five episodes on the strength of the star.

The show was slotted about every fourth Sunday in fall 1976 on a rotating ninety-minute "Mystery Movie" deal Universal had with NBC. It proved so popular that in February 1977 the network shifted it to Friday evening as a regular series. By then, Shaw realized the honeymoon he had early on with the legendarily difficult Klugman was definitely over. Klugman, it became clear, saw his show as an opportunity to make social statements as well as have Quincy catch criminals in a medically authentic manner. Klugman had come into the theater during the Depression with Clifford Odets, through the Federal Theater Project. It was an experience that had shaped his notion of drama.

"Most of us who came out of that era shared the view that socialism—mild socialism—would be the answer," he told a *Washington Post* interviewer. "That an Upton Sinclair socialism would save the world. What Sinclair did with his exposés I want to do with this show. I want to expose things, situations that can be corrected with legislation. And yet, I also want the show to be entertaining."[13]

Klugman conceded that such shows could often fail and that Universal had had experience with them. "The front office is scared of it and they're right. They say, 'Listen, we did shows like *The Senator*. That was a terrific show and it bombed. So they have a point. It's just that I don't want to do shows where the dialogue is 'Move over here, move over there, put up your hands, these are your rights.' "[14]

In fact, he insisted that the show be done his way. He had clout because he was the star and because the show was a hit on a network that sorely needed them. Shouts rang and heads rolled continually as Klugman tried to impose his notion of the program on the producers, story editors, and writers. Shaw left the show because of it, and, years later, Bob Cinader refused to take over the production reigns, though he was offered a lot of money even by industry standards to do it. He told Hannah Shearer it would be an impossible task. It was Klugman's show, and he would brook no true collaborators.

Klugman wanted to merge Quincy's profession of medical detection with his desire to engage in the kind of political controversies which stirred Klugman to anger. There were many, and they were varied: the need to educate emergency room personnel about how to preserve evidence in rape and child abuse cases; the abuse of the insanity plea to protect criminals who should be punished; the legal sale of amphetamine substitutes—"lookalike drugs"—to minors; the need for the government to force pharmaceutical firms to manufacture drugs that can save lives but are not being produced because they are not profitable (called "orphans"). Every such episode gave Klugman, as Quincy, a chance to make an impassioned speech in support of his viewpoint.

To Klugman, this was the core of the show. "Preachments are acceptable by evangelists, if they are good speakers and believe in what they are saying," he argued. "The people who go to see Billy Graham are entertained. They are not bored with it because they believe in what he is saying."[15]

Klugman's "preachments" were controversial ammunition to some. The episodes that evoked the loudest indignation took aim at businesses that saw health care as a profit-and-loss operation. One plot, for example, centered on a private hospital that shunned optimal patient care in pursuit of dividends; the narrative implied that quality treatment and profits could not mix.

The installment drew an angry editorial from *Fortune* magazine. Quincy's pronouncements about the need to exclude monetary efficiency from health care were simplistic and rabble-rousing, the editorial said. *Fortune* added that the show's creators seemed not to understand basic economics.[16]

More generally troubling to *Fortune* and other anti-*Quincy* observers was the idea of an actor using his show as a pulpit and his character as a drawing card to support real-life causes. The issue got its greatest exposure in 1981 when Klugman showed up in Congress to support the orphan drug bill the same week that his program had aired an episode on the subject. A *Fortune* editorial snarled that Klugman was a dilettante with a social conscience who was wrongheaded about getting involved because he didn't understand the issue's realities.[17]

The *Wall Street Journal* saw his congressional testimony as part of a larger issue of the relationship of entertainers to their fictional roles. "Let's try," said an editorial, "to avoid making total fools of ourselves by setting the actors up as authorities on real stuff like public policy and commerce."[18]

Privately, studio and network personnel would have readily agreed that Klugman was a pain, but for different reasons. To them, the trouble with *Quincy* had more to do with personality and style (the star's) than subject matter. From the simple standpoint of dealing with issues, Klugman was not doing anything especially out of the ordinary for doctor shows. True, *Quincy* was unusual in daring to target parts of the medical system for criticism. But this approach was not a weekly staple by any means. Moreover, there was strong evidence that many sides of the medical establishment were in *Quincy's* corner. Network releases gushed with an impressive list of organizations that commended Klugman for his role. The Mount Sinai School of Medicine even asked him to speak to the 1980 graduating class.[19] Besides, even the most potentially volatile *Quincy* scripts did nod to the network requirement of "balance" most of the time. Inevitably one or two characters in the program presented the other side of Quincy's argument, though they weren't nearly as impassioned as the monomaniacal medical examiner.

"Quincy is mostly me," Klugman admitted to a reporter in 1978. "He is my humor. He is my intensity. I built the character from the inside out, and what I didn't have, I found elsewhere."[20]

That, noted a number of observers, may have been just the problem with the *Quincy* concept as it had ultimately become part of the public imagination. Through *Quincy*, the medical detective had taken on the mien of an impassioned public advocate, and it looked like a difficult act to copy without Klugman's zeal. The proof seemed to be that no imitators came to bat despite the show's six years in prime time and its solid success in syndication.

Women in White

At the end of the decade, then, medical storytellers faced the unpleasant verdict that their innovations were striking out often. The consensus was that "epidemic shows" would not work as weekly dramas; that medical series with rural themes had failed; and that *Emergency!* and *Quincy*, while huge successes, were unique programs with little opportunity for fertilizing new groups of series. By that time there had also developed a similar conclusion about women in doctor shows.

On the surface, it seemed that producers and programmers had tried hard when it came to women. There certainly had been a flurry of activity in that direction during the 1970s. Not only did more women physicians appear in guest shots than ever before but a few doctor shows began to include them regularly as central characters. And in 1978 the first medical series aired with a woman as the title character.

The trend stopped rather quickly, though. The same easy generalizing that inhibited TV executives from continuing to explore medicine outside the hospital brought disillusionment regarding women as lead physicians. Industry decisionmakers concluded that the attempts to spark new interest in doctor shows by highlighting women had gone nowhere in the ratings precisely because women were the stars.

The case had a special ideological wrinkle. Looking back, it seems that even the new initiatives toward women were at least partly an exercise in reinforcing old industry prejudices. To understand how, it is first important to recall the traditional prejudice that network programmers felt against women as leads. The relegation of women to the less powerful seats in TV's medical scheme had been a conscious strategy throughout TV's first two decades by the (male) producers and executives who controlled network storytelling. Michael Dann, CBS's chief prime-time strategist during the late 1960s and very early 1970s, had been convinced that this policy was correct.

Dann had told his subordinates that when it came to drama series, only programs revolving around men had a chance of luring the huge numbers of viewers needed to win time periods. Dann had insisted that men were turned off by women as leads in any drama series. His experience with *The Nurses* had reinforced his viewpoint.

Decisionmakers across the networks and within Hollywood production companies continued this reasoning long after Dann left CBS in 1971. According to *Medical Center*'s Don Brinkley, "It was a time that either through the fantasies of the network minds or whatever, the idea was that the male doctor was a fantasy figure for the woman audience. He was a romanticized figure, everything that women wanted to see in a doctor—kind, compassionate, handsome, beautiful, all those things. Plus the fact that he was always available. And there was the intimacy of the medical situation, which made it even more provocative."

There had been a few attempts at distaff physicians prior to 1970. The first one can be tracked to 1956 in the form of a half-hour pilot film called "Kelly." It starred Larraine Day in the title role of Kelly Michaels, M.D., a recent graduate of a top residency program. Day, it may be remembered, had played Dr. Kildare's girlfriend in the MGM film series of the '40s; she was the one who was run over by a truck. In the TV pilot, there were other obvious Kildare connections. The script was written by Harry Ruskin who, with Willis Goldbeck, had penned several of MGM's Kildare and Gillespie films.[21]

The "Kelly" pilot revolves around the fact that its central character is a physician who is female. Ruskin seems to have set up basic conflicts that can dog Kelly through the course of a series, especially prejudice toward woman doctors, their lack of a meaningful love life, and the proper balance between reason and emotion that a woman physician ought to have. But the pilot never aired, and a series was never ordered; it is not clear why.

What is clear is that "Kelly" was years ahead of its time in even suggesting a woman doctor as a title character on TV. In the '50s and '60s *Medic*, *Dr. Kildare*, *The Eleventh Hour*, and *The Breaking Point* were notable for female guest stars playing patients, not physicians. *Dr. Kildare* was especially famous for its procession of dying beauties who fell into the arms of their solicitous, handsome healer.

Probably the most talked about episode was one which starred Yvette Mimieux, portraying an epileptic skier in "Tyger, Tyger." The scantiness of Mimieux's swim suit sparked a fierce argument between the production company and the network. NBC censors finally allowed a bikini, but a more modest suit than the one producer David Victor had originally proposed. On airing, the garment (and Mimieux's filling of it) still caused a sensation and won a spread in *Life* magazine.

Ben Casey's female patients often filled the same romantic purpose. But *Casey* was different because its creator, James Moser, had written a woman anesthesiologist, Maggie Graham, into the continuing cast. Moser had wanted a hospital-based love interest for Casey, and he felt that a nurse would not be strong enough to play off well against the headstrong lead character. Early in the development of the series, though, the producers concluded that any attempt to move the Casey-Graham relationship forward romantically would limit their ability to have him dally with other women. As a result, they alluded to it very lightly, and, after a while, they even had Casey tell another woman character that he and Maggie were "just good friends."

Ben had a much more active love life than Maggie. But occasionally the producers did place her in romantic liaisons with other men. Bettye Ackerman, who played the role, recalled one episode in which the attractive and generous Maggie had a short-lived affair with another doctor. Many viewers picked up the subtle implication that the two had slept together at his house. Ackerman got mail from viewers livid that she had betrayed Casey. She mentioned the reaction to Vince Edwards who, as Ben Casey, had been involved in numerous flings. "You should read my letters when I betray you," he shot back.

The producers would occasionally center an episode around Maggie. But they never probed very far into her professional expertise. On *Ben Casey*, Ben and Dr. Zorba (Ben's boss) were the medical heroes. "The viewer never had a sense of Maggie's duties beyond [her] call for anesthesia," wrote Philip Kalisch, Beatrice Kalisch, and Margaret Scobey after reviewing nearly all the show's episodes. "With the exception of the operating room sequences [where she was shown to be quietly competent], Maggie stood around the nursing station waiting for Ben to say something."[22]

From the storytellers' perspective, the problem seems to be that Maggie needed to be depicted as emotionally stable. During the 1960s and 1970s, a continuing character in a series had to be consistent and upright. A number of episodes revolving around woman physicians as guest stars suggest that when writers introduced women physicians in one-shot appearances, it was to explore what they couldn't with Maggie—romantic insecurity and an unhappy balance between their professional and personal lives.

"Suffer the Little Children," for example, depicts an expert female radiologist who seems not to know how to leave her need for professional power out of her romantic encounters. Out on a date with Casey, she orders him to kiss her. When he refuses, she slaps him. (Thereupon, Ben complies.) Hours later, she apologizes, ruefully admitting that she knows she has spoiled any chance between them. Casey softly agrees with her.

This theme of romantic insecurity tinged with a discomfort over professional power became TV's standard approach to female doctors. It was a theme that came in handy at the turn of the '70s, when producers began to increase the opportunities for distaff doctors on TV. Part of the increase was due to an awareness among writers and producers that women were entering medical school in record numbers. Especially in the new feminist environment, their presence implied highly dramatizable tensions about the role of women in a male world. A critical consideration guiding the use of women doctors in *Medical Center*, Brinkley said, was the production staff's belief that the women in the show's audience wanted to identify every now and then with their own sex as a physician.

As a result, *Marcus Welby, The Bold Ones,* and *Medical Center* began to place female guest stars in physician roles. *Medical Center* even had a woman doctor, Jeanie Bartlett, as a semi-regular for a couple of seasons. A psychiatrist with her own practice, her main role was as Joe Gannon's steady romantic interest when he needed one. A sampling of appearances by other women doctors suggests that the tension between professional concerns and female identities was the major hook. One plot had a female doctor confronting the student health service's policy toward treating women who have had abortions. And a couple of the episodes dealt squarely with what was becoming TV's standard version of the special tension of being a female physician: the frustration of often having to choose between satisfying work and a long-term romantic commitment.

In one story a successful woman surgeon (played, ironically, by Larraine Day) anguishes over her professional commitment when her surgeon husband, who has generally been acting strangely, begins to show interest in a younger woman patient. In another, an intern who is torn between the desire for love and the love of medicine purposely tries to sabotage her own chances for a residency slot in response to the charms of the male resident with whom she is competing for the position.

A variation on this theme also showed up in an episode of *The Interns*. It concerned a quick decision that one of the running characters, Dr. Lydia Thorpe, had to make: accept an offer of marriage and quit her internship, or go on with her hospital appointment and let her boyfriend leave. It is significant that this plot was the only episode of the show in which Lydia Thorpe stood out. Researchers Kalisch, Kalisch, and Scobey report that, of the five interns, the female and black had the fewest opportunities for plots revolving around them alone, as opposed to plots showing them working with the others in a team. Thorpe's only chance in the spotlight hardly dealt with medicine.[23]

But *The Interns* was the only series during the first half of the decade that had a continuing female physician. And despite producers' awareness of the woman's movement and the increase of women in medical schools, the appearance of woman doctors on medical shows was far from routine in minor or major roles. For a 1975 master's thesis at the University of Pennsylvania, James McLaughlin examined tapes of fifteen episodes that included most doctor shows of the early 1970s. Only two (5%) of the 45 physicians who appeared were women.[24]

There is a good chance that McLaughlin would have come across more woman physicians in *Welby*, *Bold Ones*, and *Medical Center* episodes had he included more TV hours in his study. But the percentage of men versus that of women undoubtedly wouldn't have changed much. Women were certainly in the programs, and in large numbers, but mostly as patients and nurses rather than doctors. In his sample, McLaughlin found that all the nurses who appeared were female, as were three out of every five patients.[25]

Prejudices remained, especially at the networks. Matthew Rapf, who produced *Doctors' Hospital* during its four-month run on NBC in 1975, felt that he learned firsthand about network resistance to female doctor leads. The show had started out as an attempt to update *Ben Casey*. Rapf and his co-producer Jack Laird, both *Casey* alumni, had even wanted Vince Edwards for the part of a chief of neurosurgery. Perhaps because of Edwards's reputation as difficult, NBC executives adamantly refused to allow him in the role. As a result, George Peppard was cast as Dr. Jake Goodwin, the rough-hewn but brilliant and fair-minded central character.

A woman doctor, neurosurgeon Norah Purcell, played by Zhora Lampert, was also included. Rapf remembered that putting her in the cast was partly a nostalgic nod to *Casey*'s Maggie Graham, partly a recognition of the increasing number of women in medicine (though he knew they were still exceedingly rare in neurosurgery). Purcell, however, was quite a bit stronger and more self-confident than Graham. Rapf said that Lampert had the ability to project a wide range of emotions expertly, and the producers tried to show her as dedicated, compassionate, and able to maneuver skillfully past anti-female barriers to becoming a successful surgeon.

NBC gave the series a go-ahead for the fall season, with a network option to pick it up for the full year if it succeeded. The ratings turned out to be mediocre. In addition, Peppard and Laird had some unpleasant run-ins. The actor let it be known that even if the network did extend its order for the show into the spring, he probably would not be available for health reasons. Looking for alternative directions for the show without Peppard, Rapf tried without success to convince network programmers that shifting the show's emphasis toward Zhora Lampert was the right way to go. The fact that Lampert was not conventionally beautiful may have been one aspect of their refusal, he suggested. But he added that network executives' fear of risking a time slot by going with a female dramatic lead was undoubtedly a large part of it.

Rapf stressed that few prime-time dramatic series of any sort had women as central characters. During the '70s, the only series to make it in any solid way was *Police Woman*, with Angie Dickinson. In view of the herd mentality common in the television industry, a few failures with women physicians in the continuing cast (*The Interns, Westside Medical, Doctors' Hospital*) might well have spread the caution about female leads better than any executive memos could.

In fact, the one doctor series of the 1970s named after a female character, *Julie Farr, M.D.,* came in through a kind of back door. The show had its beginnings in a 1976 TV movie called *Having Babies.* Executive Producer Jerry Isenberg was energized by the learning experience that he and his wife went through before the birth of their first child. A former administrator of movies of the week for ABC, he succeeded in getting the network's programming executives to fund a film about the birthing experiences of four couples. The idea was to follow a format that resembled the network's popular *Love Boat* series—humorous and romantic tales about ordinary people—with a real delivery as a climax.

The filming, with a script by Peggy Elliott, progressed without major problems, though there was some trouble when network censors insisted that no pubic hair could be shown in the real delivery. The editor managed to eliminate the problem, the ratings were good, and so network programmers asked him and his partner Gerald Abrams to do a second installment. "When we went to do the second one," Isenberg recalled, "we said, 'This is nuts. I mean, we're making another movie. We have to get a pilot out of this. We have to get a hero or heroine that can go on.'"

So Isenberg and Abrams decided to shift the focus of the film from the four patients alone to the patients guided by their physician. It would be a subtle shift, and the new physician would be the continuing feature of the intended series. They decided on a woman obstetrician for reasons of modesty. "I couldn't find a way to handle the intimate stories without being embarrassed for the man," Isenberg recalled. He believed that network programming executives didn't object to the choice of a female because they didn't understand the aims that Isenberg and Abrams had for the new character.

"Basically," he said, "since ABC was much more interested in the 'Having Babies' concept, they were paying little attention to the Julie Farr character. They were paying attention to the people stories. So we . . . slid in a character the way we wanted to do it."

When ratings for *Having Babies, II,* came in a high, network officials agreed to contract for six episodes of a series, preceded by a third TV film. In the third film, Isenberg and Abrams took pains to add some more traditional elements of a doctor series: the lead doctor's stern boss (in this case a slightly older man), the doctor's office nurse, and, in the backdrop, the hospital trustees who sometimes caused trouble for the dedicated lead physician.

In tune with the fashion of the times, the series would also try to humanize its central medical protagonist by injecting subplots about their thirtyish physician's personal life. To Isenberg and Abrams, that meant exploring "the process of women making career choices that put them into a time lock for their own birthing process," in Abrams's phrase. Farr, played by Susan Sullivan, had to face up to "the choices," he said. "I mean, the piper gets paid." So, they encouraged subplots that touched on the self-doubt that they felt had to come with a woman enmeshed in such a demanding profession. "Whether she cheated herself, you know. To make a commitment to an advertising career, for example, is one thing. To make a commitment to the world of medicine and helping others is a far more complex thing."

To stay on track with the anthological medical stories, they hired Joel Rogosin, who had proven his medical show expertise on *The Bold Ones*, to guide the weekly version as producer and executive story editor. Rogosin had a lot to worry about. After a good showing for *Having Babies, III*, the weekly numbers were very soft. One of the first things that he concluded was that Farr's obstetric practice was too limiting a specialty to draw huge audiences on a long-term basis. Farr, he decided, would be better off as head of the hospital's internal medicine department. That would encourage a wider range of life-and-death stories. The shift, welcomed by network officials, dictated a new title. After a few weeks, *Having Babies* was renamed *Julie Farr, M.D.*

It didn't help. The low ratings stayed low, and ABC cancelled the show after its six-installment run. Still, the cycle of experimentation with women doctors hadn't fully run its course. Three more doctor shows with women physicians as continuing characters came on that year and the next. None lasted very long. *The Incredible Journey of Meg Laural*, a pilot on ABC about a Depression-era physician, never got past the TV movie stage. The others, *Doctors' Private Lives* (ABC) and *Women in White* (NBC), were series tryouts that didn't make it beyond four weeks.

In truth, *Doctors' Private Lives* did not really have a continuing female doctor. The closest Peggy Elliot's script came to a distaff physician was a female medical student. On the other hand, *Women in White*, whose characters and setting derived from Frank Slaughter's popular novel, went far to depict women in command. One female physician was a pathologist. Another was the hospital's chief of staff. A third was an eager resident.

But *Women in White*, like *Doctors' Private Lives*, was more concerned with physicians' libidinous peccadillos than with their professional activities. True, there were echoes in the program of a Gillespie/Kildare, Welby/Kiley kind of relationship when the chief of staff played mentor to the resident. (David Victor was, in fact, the executive producer.) Yet their discussions revolved much more around the younger woman's romantic problems than around patients' symptoms.

In general, the program was merely an excuse to bring the predictable conniving and emoting of that newly popular prime-time serial, *Dallas*, to a hospital setting. The pathologist, for example, played a standard miniseries bad guy role. She used her knowledge about the mercy killing of a patient by his daughter/nurse to bargain with the district attorney for an important promotion.

With women physicians around, variations on TV's version of their romantic dilemmas were to be expected. And, in fact, we learn that the middle-aged chief of staff, a cardiovascular surgeon, is in danger of losing her husband out of too much ambition for her own career and some devastating failures in his. As for the young resident, she, hungry for love in the hothouse of tensions, gets involved in an affair with another resident who turns out to be married. The echoes of similar plots in *Medical Center, The Interns, Julie Farr,* and other doctor shows of the '70s are loud and clear. Yet here these issues stand firmly at the core of the programs.

Although both *Women in White* and *Doctors' Private Lives* were initially slated for one-month runs, they could have been renewed had network programmers been happy with the results. They weren't. The fate of these shows along with the abrupt failure of *Julie Farr* reinforced the prevailing industry attitude that medical series with women as title characters were poison.

This postmortem carried over to the few attempts to bring distinctiveness into the doctor form with ethnic and racial diversity. During the 1970s, *Doctors' Hospital* had a Hispanic physician and a Jewish physician. One of the continuing M.D.s in *The Interns* was black, and *The Lazarus Syndrome* even had a black male physician as a lead. But when these series failed, the word was that making the central physician other than an Anglo male hadn't helped the ratings.

Yet these programs did have a cumulative impact. Producers and program executives may not have been disposed much more than before toward accepting women, blacks, or ethnics as central characters. But they would be more likely than before to accept them in supporting roles or as guest stars. The experience with doctor shows of the '70s had shown that no controversy would erupt when non-male, non-Anglo actors played doctor. On a more positive note, that kind of character diversity reflected the kind of liberal pluralism that marketers and programmers liked to see on TV where practical.

At the same time, it certainly didn't look promising for the future of the prime-time doctor drama. With ten series shot down in the ratings, neither network programmers nor program creators could agree on the best ways to propel the form into a successful new cycle. One obvious tack existed, and that was to turn the doctor show upside-down politically, to channel public debate and anger against organized medicine into a program that lambasted the traditional TV icons.

It was a startling idea, but for the first time in network history, network executives, flailing competitively for standout hits, were ready to try it. Knowing it or not, they were picking up the gauntlet to be critical about the medical system that David Rintels, president of the west coast Writers Guild, had thrown at their feet in Congress a few years before.

Yet this go-ahead was really a double-edged sword, and one side was much sharper than the other. Something different might be allowed by nervous network brass, and if it succeeded, as did *Emergency!* and *Quincy*, it *might* spark a trend. Programmers and producers would try to analyze the successes and failures, and unwritten guidelines about the utility of those innovations would result. So, for example, in the absence of solid half-hour comedies, an *Emergency!*-type show might be judged a good vehicle for hooking children and their parents to a network in the early evening. In other words, the industry had given the innovation a niche, if only a small one.

But if an experiment didn't meet ratings expectations, and particularly if the experiment went against Hollywood rules in the first place, the failure would be blamed on "the difference." No matter that there might have been one hundred other reasons for the failure; industry consensus would say that it had to do with the difference. If the unconventional aspect of the show appeared usable in more acceptable ways, the failed program might contribute incrementally to a somewhat different look for the formula. That happened with the presence of women and minorities in doctor roles, and, to a lesser degree, with the portrayal of central physicians as having some continuing personal difficulties in addition to the problems of their patients.

On the other hand, if the unconventional element was felt to clash drastically with basic approaches to the formula, the approach was deemed a dead end. Claims were made that the audience simply would not accept it. And experimentation along similar lines might be closed for years to come.

It was typical television network thinking, and it was being applied with determination on a variety of fronts. Now came the chance to grapple controversially with the most deeply rooted part of the doctor formula, the high esteem it placed on the ever-progressing, apolitical, unlimited nature of modern medicine. Which way would the double-edged sword cut?

10

A Different Spin

The drama immediately plunged the viewer into the chaos of an emergency room.

> A doctor tells an hysterical woman, about to give birth to her fourth child, that she should also agree to sterilization. Cut to a burn patient, the victim of a bomb. Is it worth treating what may be a hopeless case, or should the person be given an overdose of morphine? The more routine cases—the superficial wounds, the broken bones—are lined up, on hold.
>
> Standing in the midst of it all is an idealistic intern, terribly disquieted by what he sees. Later he pours his frustrations out to an older, more experienced nurse with whom he is having an affair. "Don't try to be the world's greatest intern, its righter of wrongs," she advises. "If you do, you become a target for all the doctors to take pot shots at."
>
> But unlike his fellow interns, the young man is unable to contain himself. He soon confronts one of the hospital's most powerful doctors, who wants to perform what the intern considers a needless hysterectomy. The ending is a double whammy: the intern's career in the hospital has been shattered, and the patient dies.

The movie marked the start of *Medical Story*, an anthology series which in its Thursday, 10 p.m. time slot on NBC would skewer many of the comfortable assumptions that had driven TV's images of medicine over the past decades. *Medical Story*'s creators still used the hospital-based world of acute care, and they highlighted the work of surgeons to the virtual exclusion of other specialties. High-pitched life-and-death drama was what they were after. But on this show the formula's rules were clearly changed. Rather than the patient or the guest star physician being the problem, now it was the system.

The show didn't last. Neither did its influence, or the influence of a few other programs that also attempted to build a basic questioning of the medical system into the heart of their plots. They were roads that were explored briefly but afterward felt by programmers and producers to be too dark, too critical, too unfamiliar to draw large audiences. This chapter investigates these medical dead ends and the questions about the portrayal of medical reality that they raised. Their failure forced serious re-evaluations in Hollywood's creative community about the viability of the doctor show. The formula seemed to be caught in a bind between the unacceptable old and the unacceptable new. Where, people began to ask, can the doctor show go from here?

The Biggest Villain

Medical Story was not the first TV story that pivoted around the inadequacies of the medical system. As far back as the turn of the 1960s, a live TV version of Sinclair Lewis's *Arrowsmith*, produced by David Susskind, was aired. It placed a mildly negative light on the medical establishment of decades past. During the 1960s, *The Nurses* sometimes tackled system-wide issues in a tough way, in one episode even underscoring the power of organized physicians to squelch certain kinds of debates about Medicare.

Still, that kind of trenchant criticism was rare. On *Medical Story*, power politics stood out front and center as episodes dissected such problems in U.S. medicine as abortion, unnecessary hysterectomies, malpractice ethics, the right to die, the wholesale sterilization of welfare mothers, and the overcrowded poverty of public hospitals. When these issues had been dealt with previously on TV, the bite, the tone, had been very different. In the *Bold Ones* episode about a patient's right to die, in *Dr. Kildare*'s depiction of malpractice cases, the general spirit toward medicine was generous. Doctors were mostly good. On *Medical Story*, physicians were mostly bad—cynical, overworked. And the system, impersonal and disastrously difficult to change, was the biggest villain of all.

The approach may have been in the Hollywood air. By the mid-1970s, the vigorous criticisms of the medical establishment that had begun in universities and special interest groups at the start of the decade had become familiar throughout much of educated society. In the mid-1970s, some extremist writers were getting popular attention by questioning whether the medical system had done any good at all.

The 1969 theatrical film *M*A*S*H*, which was to lead to a successful TV comedy series in 1970, vibrated an irreverence that implicitly tweaked much in TV's doctor dramas. Also, Paddy Chayevsky's high-pitched, near-surrealistic 1970 theatrical film, *Hospital,* a vicious attack on patient care, had challenged many of the premises of the traditional formula.

Even on TV there were rumblings of change. The spring before *Medical Story*'s fall 1976 debut, a TV movie had aired on ABC that presaged some of that change. *The First Thirty Eight Hours of Doctor Durant* essentially redid the first episode of the *Dr. Kildare* series ("Twenty Four

Hours") from a very different perspective. Dr. Chris Durant, an intern from Hawaii, reports to the surgery department of a major hospital. Quickly, he faces brutalizing hours and severe moral questions.

The writer and executive producer was Sterling Silliphant, a Hollywood veteran with major screenplays to his credit—*The Towering Inferno, In the Heat of the Night, Charley*—and a large number of TV episodes. He had proposed *Durant* as a pilot for a TV series. Although it had not made ABC's fall lineup, Silliphant hoped that the network would consider it as a January replacement or as a series for fall 1976.

Silliphant told TV columnist Kay Gardella that he had written the script two years before but that it had gone nowhere. It had been ahead of its time, he said. The time had now come, he said, because if the medical series did not move toward reality it would perish. And what did "reality" mean? Silliphant spoke about a program that was "the opposite of *Marcus Welby*." While it was not as frantically realistic as *Hospital*, it did convey the raw dialogue and hard-nosed attitude that he thought should be brought out about the people who work in a hospital.[1]

"For instance," said Silliphant, "if you declare a person dead in a hospital, all work on that patient stops. So in our film, when a young female intern asks another doctor for advice when she's faced with this decision, he says to her: 'I'll tell you when he died. When you declared him dead.' "[2]

To Silliphant, showing medical reality also meant confronting medical controversies. Still, he insisted that the program would be pro-medicine and pro-doctor, if only because it would balance all sides of the arguments carefully. The main story line of the pilot dealt with a subject that he noted was touchy to the American Medical Association: ghost surgery. "These are the young doctors who come in after a major operation and put in the final stitches. The AMA has been taken to task for this, but we attempt to show both sides. The doctors' view is that if men are to learn to do advanced surgery they have to come in on a major operation and help out."[3]

The downside of the medical training gauntlet for the patient and the profession was also an element of his new realism. "Breaking the spirit of a young doctor with thirty-six hour shifts is not efficient, as we try to show in the film," he said. He added that if *Durant* went to series he would present it as if it were a book about a doctor's life. The first season would cover Dr. Durant's internship. The second season would propel him to the position of senior resident. And the third season would show him with a practice of his own. By the fourth season he would be caught up in the success syndrome, a syndrome that Silliphant said affects many young doctors.[4]

This sounds like David Victor's scenario for James Kildare, yet with a very different outlook. Viewers never got a chance to follow Chris Durant's progression because ABC never commissioned the series. Silliphant, who considered the pilot a masterful work, was never told why. In the meantime, NBC was going ahead with *Medical Story,* with a first episode even darker than Silliphant's version of health care reality.

Raw Nerve

It is probable that no one was more startled that the series began that way than its originator, David Gerber. Gerber headed a successful independent production company that operated in conjunction with Columbia Pictures Television. He had come up with the idea for an anthology program about medicine after creating one about law enforcement. *Police Story,* begun in 1973, was a solid if not spectacular numbers-getter for NBC. The show was additionally valuable to Gerber and the network because its stand-alone episodes had the potential for sparking series. One, in fact, generated the premise for the long-running *Police Woman* program on NBC. As a result, when Gerber pitched the *Medical Story* idea to the network's programming executives, he was able to get NBC-TV president Herbert Schlosser to guarantee a sale without a pilot.

According to Christopher Morgan, who produced both series, *Police Story* began with the same premise as did its predecessor. Gerber's idea for the cop show had been to show the humanness of policemen. The point was to turn the light on them and their personal and professional conflicts and weaknesses rather than on the victims and the criminals, as was typical in *Dragnet* days. Gerber, he said, felt that a parallel approach to the medical profession would work as well.

The underlying message in *Police Story,* as Morgan saw it, was that the public was lucky to have men and women sacrificing themselves for their profession in order to keep the streets reasonably safe. *Medical Story,* he admitted, turned out to be 180 degrees different. A large part of the reason had to do with the person Gerber chose as the executive producer on the show, Abby Mann.

Mann was highly regarded in the industry for writing such gems of semi-documentary seriousness and popularity as *Judgement at Nuremberg* and *The Marcus-Nelson Murders* (the pilot film for the popular *Kojak* detective series). He was much like Jack Klugman in his commitment to the political possibilities of popular drama as well as in his desire to control the projects in which he was involved. When Gerber approached him he was interested, for Mann was a person with a raw nerve when it came to the medical system.

His wife, actress Harriet Karr, had gone through a harrowing experience several years before. Her gynecologist and a number of others had sternly urged a hysterectomy to alleviate problems she was having. Instinctively wary, Mann refused to take their word and consulted yet another physician who diagnosed his wife's disorder as one not needing surgery. With treatments, she recovered without an operation.

Mann's plan for the entire series was to design an answer to what he regarded as the totally unrealistic portrayals of medicine on TV. His aim in the opening *Medical Story* film, which he wrote, was to dramatize his wife's plight as an example of organized medicine's greedy rush to operate. To bring out the message most powerfully, he altered the ending. In the film, the patient who is told she needs the hysterectomy dies from surgery.

Mann trumpeted his muckraking intentions to the press. Going even further than Silliphant, he told reporters that he was out to repair "the harm" that such series as *Marcus Welby* and *Medical Center* had perpetrated in portraying physicians, especially surgeons, as "demi-gods" and "white knights."[5] To get a feeling for the hospital experience, he noted, he had prowled the halls of L.A. hospitals. He added that the network had not interfered at all during the first episode's filming. (Still, he was careful to conform to network proscriptions against showing too much blood or the body cavity.) He announced proudly that while he used medical advisors, they had no connection to the American Medical Association.

What he came up with—the gritty, shocking scenes in the premiere—showed that he had looked at the hospital with quite a different eye than that of James Moser or E. Jack Neuman, though they, too, claimed a handle on realism. But Mann didn't stay around past the debut, which was a special two-hour TV movie. One reason he gave, a decade later, was that he saw that the network and production company weren't going to allow him to lavish the kind of time and money on the rest of the series installments that he did on the debut. It was also the case that he and Gerber had heated arguments during the course of production, though about what nobody wants to say specifically. It does seem clear that Mann and Gerber were both personalities who needed to be in control; one had to lose in that tug-of-war.

So Christopher Morgan took over the executive production reins. Less hostile toward the medical establishment than Mann, though no less interested in the idea of realism, Morgan built bridges to the AMA. He found his on-site technical consultant, a nurse, through AMA contacts, and he sent the show's scripts to the AMA's Advisory Committee on TV, Radio, and Motion Pictures for additional checks of technical accuracy.[6] Still, most of the episodes looked darkly at the medical profession and its leaders, often using interns or newly practicing M.D.s as their way into the mess.

One episode, "The Quality of Mercy," took aim at public hospitals. As in the pilot, virtually everyone in charge, from the hospital administrator to the hospital board to the city council to the lowly interns, are shown to accept disgraceful mistakes and needless deaths. At one point, when a patient in the crowded wards dies, the house staff cheers:

one fewer patient to take care of. "We're not important," says an over-worked resident, the indignant central character. "The patients aren't important. The bureaucracy—that's what's important."

Here, however, the source of the problem is not as straightforward as in the pilot. While the central character's perspective is given the most attention, other voices stand up for the system, blame the patients, or imply that the indignation the intern expresses is too severe. Morgan had bought Mann's notion that medical realism meant exposing medicine's problems. But he wasn't as concerned as Mann with fixing the blame for the system's ills.

Part of the reason was pragmatic. He found that the network would allow him to deal with explosive issues as long as he structured the dialogue so it appeared he wasn't taking sides. "If you're not vulgar, and you don't take a political position, and if you're dealing with something that's essentially documentary, they can't touch you."

To make sure they couldn't touch him, Morgan and his associates found stimuli for their plots in newspapers and medical magazines. That was not at all difficult, he recalled, for the medical world was bubbling with dramatizable problems. Despite their documentary care, though, they occasionally got into trouble with nervous network officials.

The worst situation resulted from an episode loosely based on a Boston physician who was arrested for performing an illegal abortion. Called "Test Case," the drama concerned a gynecologist (played, ironically, by Vince Edwards) who is trapped in controversy when he performs an emergency abortion on a woman in her sixth month of pregnancy. The episode was certainly not in Abby Mann's spirit of relentless skewering of the medical system. It was more in the *Police Story* vein of showing the professional side behind a complex problem. One reviewer, in fact, wrote that the program was "a defense of doctors like Edelin who are caught up in the furious controversy over abortion, doctors bombarded with rhetoric from both sides while struggling with the realities, the individual cases, at the center of the storm."[7]

NBC's executives, however, saw the whole thing as too volatile, too close to the headlines, too easily raising the ire of too many pressure groups. "[The episode] caused a lot of controversy despite the fact that we didn't take a stand on the doctor's actions," said Morgan. The network pushed back its scheduled air date, and "it was the only show [NBC] ever refused to rerun. I suggested a number of times that they rerun it . . . but the network said no, that they couldn't get any advertisers to sponsor it."

From a network standpoint, *Medical Story*'s ratings were not worth the risk. In late November, two months after the premiere, the series was rated 60th out of 70 rated shows. In January, NBC executives yanked it off. Abby Mann contended that the show failed because its writing lost boldness and energy after its premiere. By and large, however, postmortems blamed viewers for not accepting raw medical reality.

Christopher Morgan contended that *Police Story* worked because viewers could identify with the police in stories where criminals and, occasionally, victims were simply the pawns in officers' personal and professional conflicts. But illness hits too close to home to allow viewers to identify with beleaguered physicians fighting the system, he suggested. As a result, viewers inevitably identified with the patients in *Medical Story*. They didn't like to think of themselves as pawns in struggles within the medical bureaucracy and between doctors and lawyers. So they turned away from the series.

In addition, he lamented, the show was in some ways "too good." The scripts were too literate and filled with philosophical arguments to interest the rank and file in the viewing audience. That in itself boded ill for the series, he suggested, and he recalled the comments of a highly placed NBC programming executive after the show went into production: "I never would have bought the show if I knew it would deal with ideas."

Ambitious Dead Ends

Despite the conviction by many network programmers and producers that *Medical Story* had been too critical of doctors and hospitals, three shows of the late '70s, *Quincy, Seizure,* and *The Lazarus Syndrome,* also aimed severe punches at organized medicine. The people who created those shows didn't remember thinking about *Medical Story* as a precedent, though. It seems likely that they were influenced more by the climate in the TV industry and society at large that had allowed somewhat different versions of medical reality to exist in the most mainstream channel of popular culture.

Both *Seizure* and *The Lazarus Syndrome* had been based on contemporary books that dramatized medicine's shortcomings. The producers were simply trying to walk in step with what they thought was the spirit of the times. After all, medicine, like most American institutions, had come under sharp attack during the late 1960s and early 1970s. The American Medical Association, which heretofore had pounced powerfully on all critics, clearly had lost some of its political and cultural clout. Some TV creators had taken that as an indication that critical themes could be brought out that had not been allowed in earlier years.

The similarity between *Medical Story* and the other three programs shouldn't be stretched too far even from a thematic standpoint, however. As we have seen, *Quincy* had a star who was powerful enough to use the series as a soapbox to rail angrily against a variety of institutional practices, including those of organized medicine. Still, *Quincy* centered around a physician-hero in a first-rate set-up and generally had a view of medicine's capabilities that was a good deal more optimistic than the one in *Medical Story*.

The Lazarus Syndrome and *Seizure* were more based in criticism of the medical system than was *Quincy*. Yet even here one could easily make too much of the comparison with *Medical Story*. It is true that the creators of *Seizure* and *Lazarus* intended very explicitly to challenge television's traditional image of the doctor as a god-like healer. But *Seizure* was a made-for-TV movie, a one-shot never intended as a series, with the leeway that such projects often imply. And *The Lazarus Syndrome* turned out to be a typical doctor series in many ways, tagged "special" by the network more because of its lead character and the critical stance it started out to take than for what it really became.

Seizure claimed to tell the true story of a woman who survived a series of mishaps during brain operations. To the film's director, Jerry Isenberg (who had created *Having Babies* a few years earlier), it was essentially about "a doctor and power." "It's actually a drama about God," he said, "which is how the doctor represents himself to the patient, and, in the end, her lack of willingness to let him continue being God."

The woman's physician is a surgeon with a masterful reputation. However, during two of her operations, as well as afterward, he becomes totally disoriented by the hardly explainable sequence of events relating to her relapse and recovery. Isenberg saw the ending as positive: after a climactic confrontation in which the patient chastises the surgeon for wanting to play God despite his extreme insecurity about performing her impending operation, the surgeon steps away from the procedure, better understanding his limitations.

The Lazarus Syndrome started with a similar premise of the doctor as God, though here it was the patient, not the lead physician, who had to be made aware of the problem. In an interesting inversion of the typical formula, the series pilot shows Dr. MacArthur St. Clair, chief of staff in a large hospital, complaining about how frequently he is drawn into the lives of his patients. For St. Clair (played by black actor Lou Gossett), these extra-curricular patient demands have created a terrible difficulty. They are tearing his marriage apart. He blames this on "the Lazarus Syndrome," the idea people have that doctors are god-like miracle workers.

The show's creator, William Blinn, saw the questioning of that belief as the theme of the program. "[The purpose] was . . . to take the doctor off the pedestal," he recalled. "In humanizing and making more clear his problems and the limitations of medicine, [we would bring] a different understanding of just what a doctor could and couldn't accomplish."

The idea had come to Blinn in the waiting area of a Los Angeles car wash. Glancing through a paperback rack while waiting for his car, he picked up *The Lazarus Syndrome* by surgeon Michael Halberstam. Several years earlier, Blinn had been story editor on *The Interns*. Now he and Jerry Thorpe had a production arrangement with ABC through Viacom.

Attracted by the book's realistic tone as well as by what he saw as its fresh message—that patients should look at physicians and hospitals through critical eyes—Blinn generated the pilot of *The Lazarus Syndrome*: Joe Hamill, a reporter in his late thirties, experiences a heart attack and calls a doctor, who turns out to be St. Clair. While recovering in the hospital, Hamill's journalistic instincts lead him to explore the place and point out its problems to St. Clair. St. Clair agrees with Hamill's observation that the hospital's biggest problem is its chief administrator. He is a martinet who jeopardizes patient care by insisting that the hospital exists primarily not to cure individuals but to support and extend medical research. At the end of the pilot, the administrator leaves, and St. Clair engineer's Hamill's hiring as the replacement. Their mutual goal: to improve care by eliminating bureaucratic nonsense and inefficiency.

Blinn saw this goal as encouraging the dramatic tension between the two characters that was necessary to generate plots and hold viewers. "What we were hoping to set up was a defense and prosecution, ongoing, both of whom respected each other, got along, were friends, but whose interests were a lot of times in conflict." Out of that conflict would come the theme that physicians and hospitals need to be monitored constantly, that even when hospitals are temples of healing, they are also organizations with bureaucratic problems that get in the way of the best approaches to that healing.

ABC programming executives evidently felt they could tout Blinn's idea as a unique approach for TV. The advertising department created an ad for the pilot that called it "a landmark in television drama." "Sparks fly when a brilliant surgeon meets a hot-tempered reformer," said the full-page announcement in *TV Guide*. "But the real fireworks begin when they fight for something bigger—a hospital run to save lives, not to make money. If they can stick together, they just might beat the system."[8]

The "landmark" tag had another meaning, too. *Lazarus* was one of the very few drama series in network history with a black lead. As Bill Blinn and Jerry Thorpe explain the choice of Gossett, it was a simple case of creative casting. The physician in Halberstam's book was Italian, but keeping that wasn't a priority. "We made up a list," recalled Blinn, "and on the list was Lou Gossett. . . . I had worked with Lou on *Roots* [the enormously popular miniseries] and Lou was supposed to do *Brian's Song* [an acclaimed TV movie]. We kicked it around and we asked . . . 'Can it work with a black actor?' And we said, 'Yes it can.' "

Blinn and Thorpe decided that Gossett would play a physician who just happened to be black, and not a slum-bred black, at that. The bio they made up rooted their doctor firmly in the middle class, with his mother a school teacher and his father a postal worker. Ron Hunter as Hamill, on the other hand, got the colorful, street-smart background that, they hoped, would lend bite to arguments between the two.

Bill Blinn recalled that the pilot segment had showed that kind of bite effectively. He admitted, though, that most installments of *Lazarus* weren't nearly as brash or stimulating or as different from run-of-the-mill doctor shows as he would have liked. One story, for example, centered on a young hospital chaplain who makes patients feel worse about their illness rather than better. Another concerned a college superstar in the hospital with a knee injury, who, St. Clair and Hamill learn, was making it through school by cheating. Here, as in the past, was the hospital as a repository of humanity's tales. Here, again, was the physician as the catalyst for making patients (or other guest stars) confront their emotional and physical problems, and for helping to cure them. The main twist in *The Lazarus Syndrome* was that the patient's difficulty often affected the benevolent though crusty hospital administration in a way that led to conflict between Hamill and St. Clair. So, in the case of the athlete, the question was whether hospital personnel had a responsibility to halt academic shoddiness.

Blinn and Thorpe didn't get the chance to move the program up to their expectations. The series didn't last. After a good premiere showing in September 1979, *The Lazarus Syndrome* took a nosedive. A few episodes later, ABC pulled the plug, yanking it off the air for "retooling." But it never returned to the network, even though more episodes had been filmed.

Postmortems in the network and the production company offered five suggestions, none excluding the other, as to why *The Lazarus Syndrome* failed. Three related to the characters and the actors who played them, while two related to the program's basic premises about medical reality. The first character-related explanation was simply that the network audience was not ready for a black dramatic lead. The fact that *Paris*, a black detective series, had failed almost as quickly as *Lazarus* seemed to bolster this argument.

Blinn was not sure that he agreed with this explanation. He did, however, buy the complaint that Gossett's character may have been too bland. In consciously going against the typical black type, Blinn admitted, he "took away from Lou a lot of what Lou does best as an actor." That problem, he noted, may have been compounded by another difficulty: Gossett and Hunter did not jell together well as a team on the tube.

But Blinn was most likely to agree with those who felt the show's biggest problems were thematic. One major difficulty was that the running conflict between St. Clair and Hamill pointed to severe problems, but never to the easy resolution that people in Hollywood insisted was needed in a TV series. That, Blinn said, "was probably why we got taken off the air."

There was a related reason, he added. "I think that we needed to present a more solid hospital, because of the nature of the premise. One of the heroes was at least half of the time saying: 'This institution is fucked; we have to make it better.' Something has to be said of the fact that the audience doesn't want to know about all the doctors who have fears or misgivings or tremors. Do you want that voice of the pilot from the cockpit to be certain, and sure and calm, that we are arriving in New York in two hours? We don't want to hear a tremor. That theory, I suspect, has a lot of currency."

It was an attitude that began to be shared openly throughout the TV industry. To many producers and programmers, *Medical Story* and, to a lesser extent, *The Lazarus Syndrome*, were failed test cases for a new slant on realism about medicine and physicians. Why take a chance on a doctor series whose doctors or hospitals are essentially flawed, they asked, when a good show with those characteristics, *Medical Story*, with a good chance to succeed, bit the dust?

It was really a rhetorical question. The simple answer many gave was that it didn't pay to take a chance. *Washington Post* TV columnist Tom Shales, commenting on *Medical Story* just before it left the air, sympathized with that view. "People are not watching," he agreed, forgetting that while twenty million viewers or more were required to make a network happy in prime time, even the lowest rated network show routinely attracted several million viewers. The low viewership was a pity, Shales opined, because "even if *Medical Story* doesn't blaze a daring trail with every installment, it still seems to be working hard and skillfully at confronting—not just exploiting—subjects that count." To him, the larger implications of the show's failure were clear. "The sadly axiomatic fact of it all," Shales wrote, "is that every time an ambitious series fails, it becomes that much harder to sell the networks on trying another one." [9]

It was particularly tough because *Medical Story* drew a decidedly mixed critical response in addition to poor ratings. Some columnists commended its boldness despite what they admitted was the inconsistent quality of its episodes. Other press observers branded it simplistic and overdone. [10] The tepid reaction and predictions of physicians' discontent gave nervous network officials even less incentive to approve programs along those lines.

Changing Times

Around the TV industry, there began to appear a serious lack of faith in the future of the doctor-show. In the midst of television's medical traffic of the '70s, which included more than a few failed series and stifled concepts, producers and writers were feeling stymied by the doctor show as a dramatic vehicle. Attempts at new directions seemed to have gone nowhere. Some tended to feel, with Jerry Thorpe *(The Healers, Rafferty)*, that the program type had shown it didn't have the resiliency other TV formulas exhibited to express realistically the mood of changing times. The law and detective forms allowed broad license in the attitude toward human life, he suggested. "It's possible on those shows to take life less than seriously," he said, "but on doctor shows you can't do that. So you reach a dead end, a limit beyond which you can't go."

Other creators agreed with Sterling Silliphant, who during the mid-'70s had worked on two medical pilots. After the decade, he began to feel that "beds in hospitals are boring and there are more interesting places to be on TV." Even producers such as Norman Felton, who wanted to use health-related themes to explore the human condition, began to feel that there were better ways to do it than the hackneyed approach of making the physician and hospital central to the situation. Director-producer James Goldstone, who had worked on several doctor-show episodes during the '60s and early'70s, echoed a widespread frustration with what he and others considered the form's basic limitation. "How many times," he asked, "can an audience or a director or actors deal with the same [hospital] paraphernalia?"

The answer for Goldstone and for other people who had worked on doctor shows was that there were more expressive ways to use disease as a realistic catalyst for drama. One alternative that became popular during the 1970s was the coping film. It coincided with the rise of the made-for-TV movie. A revival of an old Hollywood type often classified among "women's films," it centered around the way a person and his or her loved ones cope with health-related adversity; doctors were peripheral to the tale. Coping movies such as *Brian's Song, Eric,* and *Transplant* got good reviews and generally good ratings. It was clear that the potential for profit wasn't as great as in a hit series. But a series was a huge gamble. With the right coping story a producer could make a respectable amount of money through off-network syndication and foreign sales.

So, for example, Norman Felton's final fling at a drama about a young doctor was a 1971 TV movie called *Marriage Year One*. It had many of the requisite trappings of intern stories and it had the requisite new twist: this time, the focus was on the wife's forlorn reaction to her husband's torturous training. After that project, though, Felton found that he got more satisfaction thinking about coping films based on real situations. In 1976 he produced *Babe*, a TV movie about a legendary woman golfer who underwent a colostomy, and in 1982 he coordinated *And Your Name Is Jonah*, a TV film about a boy labeled mentally retarded who turned out, instead, to be deaf.

Not all producers were ready to write off the traditional doctor series. Neither were network programmers. At CBS, especially, executives had always seen the program type as most of all a solid female-oriented vehicle that could be useful if used sparingly in the later hours of prime time. To network strategists, the trick was to find an element that would refresh the form yet not fall into the traps that they felt so many shows of the '70s had stumbled on—the contemporary controversy, the females or ethnics as lead doctors, the attempts at action outside the hospital.

Throughout the '70s, one possible solution loomed large for doctor dramas, though it was never implemented: comedy. *M*A*S*H*, the iconoclastic half-hour series that centered on surgeons in the Korean War by blending comedy and drama, had become an American classic on that network during the 1970s. It had also become a tempting target for imitation. Finding a way to package the essence of *M*A*S*H* became a preoccupation particularly at CBS and Twentieth Century-Fox, the *M*A*S*H* production company. Throughout the '70s, executives tried to repackage the essence of *M*A*S*H* in half-hour sitcoms. By the end of the decade CBS programmers and others also began to hope that infusing a version of *M*A*S*H*'s spirit into an hour-long medical drama might give the form new breathing room.

Trying to use *M*A*S*H* to ignite comedies and dramas brought up a couple of basic difficulties. First, it was not clear what made the series so popular. Second, even when people thought they knew where the source of *M*A*S*H*'s high ratings lay, it was not clear how to transfer it into other programs. The result was that the desire to imitate *M*A*S*H* encouraged sometimes startling—and, by accretion, significant and enduring—departures in TV's depiction of physicians and their patients. At the networks, though, the major way to judge the new approaches was decidedly unphilosophical. What counted was the competitiveness of the programs in a new and uncertain media environment.

From this standpoint, the attempts to distill *M*A*S*H*'s essence proved a mixed blessing. On the one hand, the show's putative aura turned out to be as much a prescription for failure as for ratings-rousing success. On the other hand, the urge to copy the series did send a couple of key doctor dramas on unusual trajectories that gave the formula new strategic significance for the networks. The story of *M*A*S*H*'s curious legacy begins in the next chapter.

11

"Suicide Is Painless"

Larry Gelbart was in London at the turn of the 1970s when Gene Reynolds asked if he would write the pilot for a TV version of *M*A*S*H*. From the standpoint of Reynold's employer, Twentieth Century-Fox Television, there was some urgency to the matter. *M*A*S*H* had done terrifically well as a theatrical film, and the word was that the heads of Fox's film division were considering a sequel. Bill Self, head of Fox's TV operations, had another idea. He wanted to launch a network TV series of *M*A*S*H*. And he wanted to do it fast enough to head off any sequals by the theatrical division that might derail his plans. Reynolds, a successful TV producer for the company, got the assignment.

His first concern was finding someone to write the pilot. Coming up with a good script would be a challenge if the series were to keep the complex flavor that had caused the movie to receive so much attention. *M*A*S*H* was the story of a mobile army surgical hospital (a MASH unit) during the Korean War. Richard Hornberger, a surgeon who had worked in one, had transformed his recollections into a book that attempted to reflect the mixture of pride, amusement, and horror that remained in his memory. Helicopters brought in wounded by the score for emergency surgery. The youthful surgeons, many of them draftees, worked long, hard hours in makeshift operating rooms. The emotional toll on the physicians was severe, and outside the O.R. they blew off a lot of steam.

"Our philosophy was do the job well and after that—do as you please," Hornberger recalled. "We were out there in the middle of nowhere. What could they do, fire us?" [1]

Under Robert Altman's direction, undoubtedly influenced by the rising agony over the contemporary Vietnam conflict, the movie had given Hornberger's tale a startling cinematic spin, alternating between the gore of the operating room and the manic humor of the surgeons needing some relief from the continual agony. The movie's theme song, "Suicide Is Painless," reflected the desperate edge to the comedy. It was the desperate shift between comedy and horror and the curious reason for the shift that Reynolds felt he wanted to bring to the home tube.

The writer who would help him get there, Larry Gelbart, was an old friend. Gelbart was known as a comedy writer in the class of Neil Simon. In fact, he and Simon had been two of the enormously talented team that had worked on the classic *Caesar's Hour* television program during the early 1950s. Reynolds contacted Gelbart in London, where he had settled after the London premiere of the hit musical he had co-authored, *A Funny Thing Happened on the Way to the Forum*.

Gelbart agreed with Reynolds that bringing M*A*S*H to television had intriguing possibilities, but only if they could keep the tone and implications of the original film. He emphatically did not want to be a party to a service gang comedy or a high-jinks war. Underlying the comedy, and alternating with it, had to be an awareness of the seriousness of the physicians' work and the reasons for their antics.

Reynolds and Gelbart both saw that awareness as an irony that would become their central theme in working on the series. "What [the M*A*S*H physicians are] doing is absurd, it's futile," Reynolds said. "They're in the middle of a war where everything is designed to destroy, to tear bodies up, to maim, to kill. They're in the business of putting these bodies back together again, only to have them sent back—sort of like recycling people—which becomes like shoving a rock up a hill only to have it roll down." [2]

Gelbart wrote the pilot while in England. Reynolds and Fox sold it to CBS, whose programmers at the time took pride in their ability to identify successful situation comedies with controversial or unusual angles *(All in the Family, The Mary Tyler Moore Show, The Bob Newhart Show)*. The network scheduled the premiere in September 1973 at 8 p.m. It started off slowly but then gained strong critical acclaim and heavy ratings power, despite the networks' tendency to change its time slot almost every year for the first six seasons.

By 1982, when the M*A*S*H crew ended the show's prime-time life voluntarily with a two-hour finale (the most highly rated series episode in U.S. history), the show had become a TV institution. Its creators had been lionized, its stars (particularly Alan Alda) idolized, its programs discussed in numerous articles and even books. Inside the TV industry, M*A*S*H had become an object for emulation, not just adoration. The cycle of dramatic programs about doctors in the 1970s was matched by a rash of comedy series along medical lines. Hoping to develop a successful sitcom formula that could run parallel to its more serious counterpart, producers, writers, and network executives had to ask a question that had not been asked very often in series TV before Gelbart and Reynolds got to work: How do you make medicine acceptably funny?

Two Acts and a Tag

Two approaches to making medicine funny already had a track record of popularity in American culture. The older one, highlighted in turn-of-the-century vaudeville, showed both physician and patient as wise-cracking fools. The best-known example was the Smith and Dale comedy team's "Doctor Kronkhite" sketch, with lines so sharp that they reverberated across generations (Patient: "It hurts when I do this." Doctor: "Don't do this."). Early silent films, too, used the physician as the butt of humor. There the stress was on visual buffoonery.[3]

To some extent, the vaudeville tack was picked up by TV's variety shows during the 1950s. By that time, though, organized medicine had gained significantly more status, power, and consciousness about its image than in the first years of the century. Maybe for this reason, the doctor as wisecracking incompetent was not a portrayal that took hold in the nation's most shared arena of laughter, the half-hour situation comedy series.

There were no network sitcoms about doctors until the late 1950s. The debut of *The Donna Reed Show* (1958) and *Hennesey* (1959) pointed to a much more acceptable role for the physician in a comedy than vaudeville did. Alex Stone, the pediatrician-husband in the first series, and Chick Hennesey, the young naval medical officer in the other, were central sources of warm humor and generally sane poles around which less decorous hilarity could revolve. Actually, Stone, played by Carl Betz, rarely had anything medical to do. During its eight-year run, *The Donna Reed Show* found its humor in the minor family difficulties of a wife, husband, and their children trying to cope with life in upper-middle-class America. Still, it was clear that Stone was a working doctor. Every now and then he was shown treating children in his office, which was located conveniently in his home. The American Medical Association liked the image so much that it gave Betz an award.

Jackie Cooper, who played Lieutenant Hennesey, also was awarded by the AMA. His program centered more squarely on a doctor and his work. The main character was often shown treating base personnel and their families. Hennesey had an attractive and understanding nurse, Martha Hale (Abby Dalton). Their relationship had an undercurrent of romantic comedy (they married on the final episode). Soft humor also came from Hennesey's work with his boss, the crusty Captain Shafer (Roscoe Karns). Broader comedy came from the young doctor's Bronx-accented assistant, Max (Henry Kulky), and Harvey Spenser Blair III (James Komack), a young naval dentist whose society background and financial independence grated on everyone. Blair followed an established TV type. He was always looking for angles and gimmicks, much in the style of Sergeant Ernie Bilko in a classic '50s sitcom, *The Phil Silvers Show*.

Cooper had created *Hennesey* with writer Don McGuire. It happened that one of McGuire's friends who had been a military physician during World War II regularly regaled people with amusing stories about excuses the men used on doctors to try to get out of work. Cooper, who had recently starred in a successful comedy series, *The People's Choice,* agreed with McGuire that the tales contained the seeds of a successful program. This was still the time when advertisers controlled TV shows. Using their own money, Cooper and McGuire created and filmed a pilot about a physician who reports to the San Diego Naval Base for duty in contemporary peacetime. Then they shopped it around Madison Avenue for sponsors. In time, they persuaded General Food's Jell-O division and later Lorillard's Kent cigarettes to support the show.

Cooper, who produced many of the episodes, and McGuire, who wrote most of them, knew that commercial support from a tobbacco firm was a bit ironic for a program about a doctor. Nevertheless, that was how the TV game was played in those days, and Cooper enjoyed the autonomy that Kent's agency granted his highly rated show. He claimed years later that he always found his relations with sponsors preferable to the bureaucratic meddling of network programmers. To keep the cigarette people happy, he went out of his way to show characters within the program smoking Kent or discreetly tapping a Kent box during a routine conversation. He even added a commercial trailer to the show which featured Cooper dressed as Dr. Hennesey in his dressing room suggesting that the viewer try Kent.

The creators just wanted to turn out a well-crafted, humane program. From the start, they were determined to respect both the military and medicine. They went after accuracy and good will by getting the Navy to assign a doctor to review scripts and suggest medical ideas. Respect for the two institutions was built into the characters. Describing Captain Shafer, for example, Cooper said that he was "a good military man—by that I mean, a man who loves his country and loves what he's doing and is proud of what he's doing both as a surgeon and as a Navy doctor." The qualities had a dramatic purpose. "We gave him all the virtues," Cooper explained, "so that there was somebody from whom Hennesey could learn and who could explain . . . the moral structure of the show and its teachings. You don't like to feel you're teaching, but some of us like to impart some of our moral standards. Not necessarily political beliefs, but at least those things that make us passionate."

Cooper and McGuire saw the messages emerging more through the development of the show's characters than through intricate stories. Hennesey's medical expertise was never questioned. It was a taken-for-granted accompaniment to other themes that came up. A typical example, Cooper recalled, was an episode about a visit by Nurse Hale's father to the base. "One day Abby Dalton was talking about her father and how she loved her real-life father so much. So, one thing led to another and, in the conversation, we said, 'Wouldn't it be nice if someone were to play her father and bring him on the base. He complains of a little chest pain occasionally and Dr. Hennesey says, 'I got the afternoon off and the place is empty. Lay down there. I got a cardiogram. I got all the machinery.'

"He gets a heart attack while having a cardiogram," Cooper continued. "That's just an episode of something that can happen. Now to make a little story out of it: We had the father saying how good a nurse his daughter was and Hennesey said the same and Martha was eating it up and believing in herself. But she panicked during the heart attack when her father was on the table. So in the last twenty percent of the show, the message was, 'Don't be ashamed. You're just as human as anyone else, but you don't always think you're as good as everybody says you are.' That's about all you have to do in a half-hour show. It has two acts and a little tag."

In general, the "messages" in *Hennesey* were purposely moderate—neither very liberal nor very conservative. The "don't rock the boat" perspective reflected Cooper and McGuire's world view as well as the general approach to reality on network TV. Nevertheless, Cooper and McGuire were proud that as the show became popular they veered it into new stylistic territory. They wanted to get away from the typical sitcom tone—a half hour aimed at constant chuckles—toward a more seriocomic style. In tone, Jackie Cooper suggested two decades later, they were forerunners to *M*A*S*H*. The connection was actually quite direct. Gene Reynolds, a friend of Cooper from the days when both were child actors, started working as a TV director on *Hennesey*. It was then that his notion of TV comedy was formed, Cooper suggested.

One example of an unusual episode that went off the beaten track was a half-hour physical exam Hennesey performed on a Navy enlisted man with twenty-five years' experience (played by a very sober Don Rickles). The entire half-hour saw only those two characters. Through a soft-spoken conversation interspersed with Hennesey's basic medical procedures, the viewer got a poignant picture of a recruit who needed renewed faith in his work and his value as a human being. Dr. Hennesey's subtle examination of his emotional state as well as his body leads to a satisfying closure, with the physician helping to renew the soldier's self-esteem and pride in his military career.

Another case of an unusual tone for a sitcom was a gentle script that McGuire wrote on the theme of racial understanding. It has Hennesey in a submarine for eight hours alone with a young black scuba diver (Sammy Davis, Jr.) who had developed the bends. Slowly, they get to know one another. Explicit pleas for racial understanding are avoided, as are overt discussions of discrimination. This, after all, was the time when *Medic* couldn't air a show about a black doctor and Nat King Cole was pushed off the air by indignant station owners in the South. "It was a little story," Cooper recalled, "of confinement and how two people get to know one another and how a young black kid will think at the start that this Navy doctor is probably a snob and maybe not as liberal as he turned out to be."

Black Comedy

It happened that two of the next three situation comedies involving medicine, *Julia* and *Temperatures Rising,* starred blacks. The one that didn't aired two years after *Hennesey* left prime time. Called *Tom, Dick, and Mary,* it lasted for four months during the 1964–65 season. The show revolved around the comedic tensions that arose when an impoverished intern, Tom Gentry, allowed a poor colleague, Dick, to move in with him and his wife, Mary, to help pay the rent. The program came and went with hardly any media coverage.

Julia was a totally different story. Showing up on NBC in fall 1968, it quickly became the subject of public discussion. The series centered on an attractive black widow (played by Diahann Carroll) and her young son. Julia, a nurse, works in the health office of an aerospace firm under the supervision of Dr. Morton Chegley, a middle-aged man whose crusty shell conceals a heart of gold. He was played by Lloyd Nolan, who, in one of those interesting flips in the careers of actors, had been the gangster in *Internes Can't Take Money,* the first Dr. Kildare movie.

The series lasted three years. Articles about it talked less about its plot lines than its racial symbolism. It was the first comedy series to star a black woman in a central prestigious role; that is, as one reviewer commented, "not as a domestic or a second banana."[4] In a national environment crackling with tension after the assassinations of Martin Luther King and Robert Kennedy, *Julia* was part of the message from the network and the sponsor (General Foods's Jell-O) that things were improving for the nation's largest minority group. Pragmatically, too, advertising and network executives were aware that a powerful black middle class was growing out of the struggles of the '50s and '60s. Middle-class blacks bought a lot of products, watched a lot of TV—and could be lured to shows with continuing black characters.

The show really had little to do with the character's blackness or discrimination against it. During the first year, Julia and her son Corey did have a few brushes with prejudice at home and at work, but that theme was eliminated during the rest of the run. Magazine and newspaper articles lambasted the supposed unreality of Julia's solidly integrated, comfortably middle-class station.

Producer Hal Kanter defended his low-keyed approach as an expedient first step in a fragile racial environment. "I . . . feel that if we made social comment within our context our show would have been a failure," he told *TV Times.* "On the other hand, there is a fallout of social comment. Every week [on *Julia*] we see a black child playing with a white child with complete acceptance and without incident."[5]

In what was becoming the style of the late '60s and early '70s situation comedies, the program shifted between the main character's home and office lives, highlighting personal problems and triumphs in both. But *Julia* had little to do with medicine. At work, Julia's on-camera concerns tended to involve activities unrelated to health care, such as coordinating a charity project, dealing with an efficiency expert, and coping with a talkative maintenance man. "Nurse" was more a label designating a middle-class, not "second banana" status than anything else.

In an important sense, though, Julia's designation of nurse did make her a second banana—to her physician-boss at work. William Asher, a white producer with liberal ideas, saw that as a challenge when he pitched *Temperatures Rising* to ABC executives in the early 1970s.

"There were no black people [on TV] at the time who were really professionals," Asher recalled. "And I wanted to show a young black surgeon, and a very skilled one. A hustler and a real street guy and still a competent surgeon. That was my hidden motivation, presenting a young black doctor. I wanted to bury that in the concept."

"The concept" was actually a warmed-over version of a sitcom project called "This Is a Hospital?" that Asher and his partner Harry Ackerman had proposed unsuccessfully in the early 1960s, around the time of the *Kildare/Casey* craze. Written by Sheldon Keller, the pilot starred standup comedian Shecky Green as a mischievous intern. It aimed, Asher recalled, to be "Sgt. Bilko in the hospital." ABC, which financed the pilot, didn't pick it up; Asher and Ackerman never found out why. A decade later, though the pair was hugely successful on that network with a family comedy series about a lovable witch, *Bewitched*. ABC executives were eager for more shows from the pair. Searching for ideas, the two turned to Keller's old script for inspiration.

Asher said that in developing the new pilot he tried to reproduce some of the "Carry On" films that were made in England during the 1960s and 1970s. While the film series was not generally popular in the United States, one, *Carry on Nurse*, did develop a kind of cult popularity after its release about 1970. The roots of the comedy in those films lay in the British music hall tradition of exuberant zaniness, punctuated freely by vulgar dialogue, toilet humor, and visual effects that, one critic noted, "could never be produced in the United States." Thus *Carry on Nurse*, set in the men's wing of a hospital, provides many opportunities for references to male nudity, bedpans, and enemas. For example, as two nurses prepare to remove a patients' underpants, he protests noisily that he would rather do it himself. After the nurses insist on performing the act, one says to him, "What a fuss—about such a little thing." [6]

One wouldn't have expected a U.S. television network to allow that kind of talk, and, in fact, Asher and Ackerman's *Temperatures Rising* had none of it. What it does have is verbal banter and a frantic humor that comes out of a mix of eccentric patients, the mischievous black intern Jerry Nolan (Cleavon Little), and the humorously volatile staff. Nolan, who is Capital General Hospital's chief bookie, is trying to cope with the pressures of internship in his own peculiar style. Intent on putting a lid on the craziness is the no-nonsense chief of surgery, Dr. Campanelli. Campanelli wages a generally losing battle to rein in the intern's Bilko-like impulses.

Unlike Bilko, though, those impulses are typically rooted in generosity. Episode after episode makes clear that Nolan is channeling his gambling instincts into charitable causes—getting stereo equipment for the children's ward, for example, or buying plants for the hospital. This was one way the producers assured that viewers would believe in Nolan as a professional despite the producers' guiding principle for comedic action, what Asher called "high jinks in a hospital."

The producers' intention was not to subvert good medicine comically. Instead, it was to create risible situations in the midst of good medicine. The utility of medicine and the competence of physicians were never at issue. The somber side of hospital life—tragic illness with long-term consequences, or death—was never introduced.

"I didn't want to shake people's confidence in doctors," Asher recalled. "I just wanted to tease them about money and how some of the doctors exploit patients. . . . [But] we really didn't treat them that badly. And our cast and main characters were very responsible. Nolan was a terrific surgeon. Joan van Ark's character was a good nurse. And Campanelli—James Whitmore—was a powerfully dedicated surgeon. They were all dedicated to their patients. It was just the peripheral stuff that we treated in a humorous fashion."

The essence of the approach was reflected in a description that Campanelli gives of Nolan to a nurse who comments on the intern's reputation as a finagler: "He gets things done, in a Disneyland sort of way."

Unlike Julia (or, for that matter, Dr. St. Clair of *The Lazarus Syndrome* a few years later), Jerry Nolan gets things done without ignoring his blackness. References to his race are sprinkled across the programs. Most of the allusions are one-liners. "Guess what, Luther Burbank," a nurse starts a discussion. Another time, eyeing "flesh colored" adhesive strips, Nolan exclaims, "Maybe this is your idea of flesh colored, but it wouldn't make it in my neighborhood." Still another incident has the intern giving cotton to a nurse. "Honey, picking cotton is part of my heritage," he says.

But racial quips were about as far as the show tended to go racially. Special problems of black doctors or black patients were simply beside the point. Asher and Ackerman knew the network was not interested in mixing social issues with their comedy. Some station owners, though, were evidently incensed that a program about a black physician was being carried on ABC's airwaves. A number of affiliates in the South and Midwest refused to carry the show or transferred it to marginal time periods. Nevertheless, the ratings of *Temperatures Rising*, while not great, were decent. It managed a fairly consistent 29 share in an era when a 30 share often guaranteed a show's renewal for the next season.

Network programmers had wanted a blockbuster, though. They concluded that the program had the potential of being a blockbuster if the producers would add the star of another Asher-Ackerman entry of that year, *The Paul Lynde Show*. Lynde had become a household name through his testy, prissy retorts on an ABC daytime game show, *Hollywood Squares*. Nevertheless, his new series was barely holding its own. ABC programmers blamed it on the format, a family situation comedy, not on Lynde. They concluded that by jettisoning *The Paul Lynde Show* and adding Lynde to *Temperatures Rising* for 1973–74 they would give the series the manic lift it needed to grab audiences of all racial and political persuasions.

Asher and Ackerman balked at the idea. For one thing, it didn't fit their initial concept of the show, which they thought was working out pretty well. For another, they had learned that Lynde was extremely difficult to build a show around. The actor insisted that all the funny lines be given to him, even if they didn't fit his character or the particular situation. As a result, the development of other characters was stifled. It also hurt morale on the set.

For Barry Diller, ABC's chief programmer, the proposition was straightforward, however. Either agree to the cast changes or fold *both* shows. "I didn't want to see the show cancelled for the people involved, including Columbia Pictures, my partner," Asher recalled. "So I said, 'You do anything you goddam want. I don't want to have anything to do with it.' I walked away from it, even though I retained ownership." So did Ackerman.

ABC programmers brought in Duke Vincent and Bruce Johnson, two established sitcom producers. Ironically, they had just left a doctor sitcom on NBC called, *The Brian Keith Show* which had started a few days after *Temperatures Rising*. NBC was keeping Keith and the show's soft-comedy tone but changing its format. New producers came on board, and Vincent and Johnson were available.

The tack Johnson and Vincent took toward *Temperatures Rising* was quite drastic by network television standards. Jettisoning the entire cast except for Little, the producers decided that Capital General would be transformed from a public to a private institution. Lynde's persona would come through best, they felt, by making him the insufferable administrator in a hospital owned by him and his mother.

The results, observers in and out of the networks agreed, was a strange black comedy. Scripts for *The New Temperatures Rising* had Lynde and his mother urging physicians to practice unethical medicine, even to the point of covering up malpractice, just to make a buck for their hospital. Ratings started to plummet, and executives blamed the new approach. Strangely, ABC's Barry Diller still hoped to save the project. He got Ackerman and Asher to return and asked them to restore the original flavor of the show. Lynde was dropped, and while Whitmore and most of the original regulars didn't return, an attempt was made to rebuild with the first season in mind.

It was too late. By the time the new episodes were ready to run, the season had ended. The new format was played out in the summer, but by then ABC programmers had no interest in giving it a berth during the regular season. Andy Siegel, then a comedy development executive at ABC, remembers that, to his colleagues at the network, the show's failure meant the public didn't want to see inadequate medical care on the home tube even as a joke. "When people see doctors on television," he stressed, ". . . they really want to feel that they're in good hands. That no matter what happens it is a reassuring experience."

Reluctant Draftees

It was a dictum *M*A*S*H*'s creators sensed from the start, but for different reasons. "There was a real concern [among the writers and producers] that at least technically you had to be beyond reproach," remembered Larry Gelbart. "That unless the doctor behaved in exactly the correct manner we would be open to a considerably loud voice out there, which is the medical population of America."

Gelbart, Gene Reynolds, and associate producer Burt Metcalf also pointed to other reasons for making sure that the continuing doctors on *M*A*S*H* were technically fine surgeons. Logically, the creators claimed, the doctors of the 4077 could get away with their craziness and insubordination only if they were impeccable professionals when it counted. Otherwise, they would have been shipped Stateside and possibly court-martialed. Otherwise, too, in an era when Vietnam servicemen were being treated by medics on the battle lines, portraying bad military medicine might be too painful for viewers to watch week after week.

Gelbart's ultimate justification for this approach to medicine lay in what he and Reynolds found to be the reality of MASH units in Korea. "There wasn't a lot of death on *M*A*S*H* because, reflecting real life, they had a ninety plus percentage rate of recovery," he pointed out. "I mean, they saved people." In addition, Gelbart said, when he and Reynolds took a trip to Korea a few years after the show's TV premiere to see how the medics behaved in that setting still filled with tension, the manic tone they felt was very much what they were already putting on the screen.

"Gene and I saw a lot of *M*A*S*H*-type behavior at the real *M*A*S*H* place," he said. "It was St. Patrick's Day, and somebody was drinking green cocktails and there was a coffin and someone was lying in it. It was like part of a *M*A*S*H* episode." Gelbart admitted that the unit knew he and Reynolds were coming and may have arranged the festivities for their benefit. But he pointed to a novel he had read, a comic French tale of medical students, in which doctors played football with heads in the morgue. That helped to prove *M*A*S*H*'s tone was realistic, he insisted, particularly in a setting of "doctors curing people so they can get up and kill again."

Belief in the realism of this approach was bolstered by a good deal of other research. Early in the history of the show, Reynolds determined to learn as much as he could about the war. He felt that research had served him well in a previous half-hour comedy-drama series he had produced, *Room 222*. For that series, Reynolds had wandered the halls of Los Angeles High School, talking to students and teachers, and watching what was going on.

He was sure *M*A*S*H* would benefit from research, too. Neither he nor Gelbart had ever worked on a doctor show; nor did they have any interest in picking up themes from what they saw on TV. "We wanted to copy from life and not from theater," he said. "So many TV shows and movies are done by people who sit up in the Hollywood hills making movies the research for which is done by going to other movies."

Both read books that dealt with the treatment of casualties in Korea and, more recently, in Vietnam. More important for their scripts, Reynolds and Gelbart spoke to doctors who had been in mobile medical units during the Korean War, and to chopper pilots who had worked with them. They found the physicians had an informal network, that "one guy would lead to another." Whenever they got the name of someone who lived in the L.A. area, they would go out and interview him, have it transcribed, and study the transcriptions. When they ran out of names of MASH physicians who lived in Los Angeles, they phoned others around the United States.

Reynolds had already hired Walter Dishell, the ear, nose, and throat surgeon who consulted on *Medical Center*, as his advisor on medical issues. Dishell was careful to use a 1950 medical text to ensure accuracy in the portrayal of that era's medicine. Reynolds found him very useful for details and eager to help with the scripts.

"So there wasn't a whole lot [the interviews] could give us in the area of 'I then opened the leg and removed the bullet,' and whatever," he noted. "But I learned a lot about what it was like, what kind of speed they had to work under, what kind of conditions, how many people would be waiting. When people broke down, how long they could last, how long they operated at times, what they ate, how they slept, what they wore, what their biggest frustrations were—that kind of stuff."

Their stories became the fodder for the plots Gelbart and Reynolds assembled. Sometimes even stories from Vietnam could be worked into the show. "I talked to one doctor who was in Vietnam," Reynolds remembered. "And he was aboard a carrier and said that those guys would fly over and blow the hell out of the villages and then come back and have a shower and cocktails and steak and look at a movie. So I knew I had something, this idea of commuting to a war, where you live so differently.

"So I developed a story about the pilot commuter, who really was so detached from the war and then went through the M*A*S*H unit and saw what it was really like. What the natives were going through, the people who were subjects of his bombs. And what the foot soldier was going through. . . . One remark like that from the doctor could trigger you."

To Gelbart, Reynolds, and Metcalf, the key to working with serious themes such as these in their comedy format was to ensure that those themes were balanced by less serious ones. "We had to have two acts and a tag," said Reynolds. "I knew every act had to have five story points, five really playable scenes in it in order to make the act full so it wasn't stretched. And the story points related to one another in one way or another. Sometimes they had what I called a harmonic, and other times they wouldn't. You'd do a very heavy story line and a light one. Sometimes we did three stories in one show."

Symbolic of the "heavy" story lines, and central to them, was the operating room. The operating room was where the conflict between healing and hurting clashed most strongly. Gelbart recognized it as crucial to the central dilemma of doctors curing people so they could kill again. It was also crucial to setting a tone that approximated the shifting comedy/drama of the film. In making the pilot, though, neither he nor Reynolds were quite certain "how to mix blood with laughter." Their solution was to start by shooting the O.R. scenes through a red filter. As the episode progressed, the doctors' gowns themselves became bloody, "as our confidence grew that we weren't literally going to have anyone tune out."

But the entire notion of an operating room in a comedy made CBS programming executives nervous, especially when Gelbart and Reynolds insisted the laugh track be halted in the O.R. Reynolds recalled one of the executives saying that when he saw the movie version of *M*A*S*H* he saw women getting up and walking out. CBS program chief Fred Silverman suggested that an hour might be more appropriate for the kind of message *M*A*S*H* was conveying. Reynolds quickly nixed that idea. "I knew it was not an hour show. An hour show is a drama. You've got to bring people back for four acts, so you've got to have strong stories, and strong stories fight the humor."

Another problem for the network people was that the pilot ended with the main characters back in the O.R. The programmers felt that it should finish with a scene relating to the comic turns of the plot, in which a general wanted to reprimand the physicians for being cut-ups. "They were thinking very formula," said Gelbart. "That's how it *should* end. Whereas we simply said that though [the *M*A*S*H* doctors] had gotten into a lot of trouble in the first twenty-two minutes of the episode, it was their skill in operating that got them out of it. And that we wouldn't compromise. And they weren't happy about that, but we prevailed."

Reynolds and Gelbart did agree to de-emphasize the blood-letting and not to show open body cavities. That quieted network nervousness, but not for long. As time went on, the *M*A*S*H* crew insisted on creating programs that stimulated their creative juices and made points about war, explicitly the one in Korea but, by implication, Vietnam too. The plots they cooked up, stimulated by the interviews, used wacky, or at least unusual ways to deal with a range of problems: the hell of operating on a constant stream of wounded bodies; the extra difficulty of doing it with people who were constitutionally different from one another, forced together by dint of military circumstance; and the periodic intrusions of higher authorities—especially "I-Corps," the military command—who constantly tried to bring a bureaucratic version of order to the unit.

To the producers and writers working on *M*A*S*H*, the officers at I-Corps had a palpable reality. They were the network programmers and censors, continually eager to force their concerns on the staff without really understanding the creative process. Perry Lafferty, CBS's West Coast head of programming during the early 1970s, admitted that the programmers under him were constantly clashing with personnel on that show. The arguments had almost nothing to do with medicine, since the network was confident that the physicians were handled well and that advisors were ensuring authenticity. The problems with the programmers tended to revolve around such things as sexual innuendoes in jokes and, more fundamentally, stylistic attempts to break the boundaries between comedy and drama.

An early episode that caused special problems for programmers showed the death of a friend of surgeon Hawkeye Pierce. He was a correspondent who came through the M*A*S*H camp. They had known one another in the States, and they took some time to drink, joke, and reminisce. Then the correspondent went off to the front and was mortally wounded. He died on Pierce's operating table.

"Hawkeye cried and it was some pretty memorable stuff," Burt Metcalf remembered. The point of the script, as he saw it, was that the incident was a watershed in Hawkeye's understanding of the horror of war and the absurdity of his position in it. But the network programmer who read the script didn't want it aired. "What are you doing here?" Metcalf recalls him sputtering. "This is a comedy. You can't have someone die who you've seen earlier on. It's OK to have these thousands of people die if they're just extras. But if you're going to let someone die whom we've gotten to know, it's going to louse up everything."

The producers held firm, and their network counterparts finally relented. "It got on the air and nothing [bad] happened," said Metcalf. So that gave us a kind of encouragement."

So did an episode called "The Interview," in which Reynolds and Gelbart, having run out of ideas with one more show to do at the end of their second season, had their actors respond in character, without a script, to a "reporter" who asked about their feelings regarding their situation. The black and white film the production crew chose and the display of frank emotions regarding injuries and operations and combat irritated the ulcers of several network executives. They tried to discourage it, but the M*A*S*H crew prevailed. The viewers stayed put, and the critics raved.

The show's increasingly strong ratings, the praise it generally received in the press, and the low level of controversy it generated also made high-level network executives relax as time went on. Perry Lafferty sighed when remembering the fuss his lower-level network personnel made about the show. "They were upset whenever the producers tried to play with the form," he said.

"They were upset about the black and white episode because they were afraid viewers would think that something was wrong with their sets. They were upset when an episode only had a few people talking, because they didn't think viewers could take that. They were upset when Henry Blake [the unit's commander] was killed off because they worried that the viewers wouldn't buy his leaving and might want him to come back."

Lafferty, for his part, says he kept trying to calm his staff and divert their attention to other programs. "Why are you trying to take over a hit show?" he would ask. "Leave those guys alone and concentrate on series that really need help."

Everyone agreed that the force driving M*A*S*H popularity despite its unorthodox approach to the half-hour format was its superb etching of characters. Gelbart and Reynolds had an intriguing roster from the movie to start with: Hawkeye Pierce, the wickedly witty chief surgeon, ever ready with a quip and a comeback; Trapper John MacIntire, Pierce's partner-in-wackiness outside the O.R.; Margaret ("Hot Lips") Houlihan, a libidinous nurse deeply involved in a curious affair with Frank Burns; Burns, a rigid, jingoistic surgeon whose operating style betrayed incompetence; Radar O'Reilley, a sardonic and naïve corporal who ran errands for the unit commander, Colonel Henry Blake; and Blake, the boozy, devil-may-care leader who was quite content to let Hawkeye and Trapper run the show.

It was a rich brew that suggested a cascade of rich situations. Still, Gelbart and Reynolds did make a few character changes right from the start. Influenced by the liberal climate of the early '70s, they added to the unit a black doctor dubbed Spearchucker. But the character didn't seem to fit, and he was dropped, with a desire for realism as the excuse. There really weren't any black military doctors in the Korean War, the producers pointed out.

A more long-lasting change that was made at the start of the series concerned Frank Burns. The movie's portrayal of him as an incompetent surgeon had to be toned down, Gelbart and Reynolds decided. "We didn't want to discredit him as a doctor," said Reynolds. "Just as a very foolish, paranoid, and arrogant man. Because you didn't want the audience to feel that kids were going under the knife and were being manhandled. Because if the guy was incompetent he shouldn't be there."

When reminded that inept surgeons certainly exist, Reynolds answered, "But not on half-hour series. We didn't want to say to people week after week, 'Here's an incompetent surgeon.' If you do a series, you get him the hell out of there."

During the first year of the series, its creators pursued their theme of the lunacy of war and the lunatic ways people cope with it by reaching for contrast between the extremes of comedy and drama. Against highly dramatic emergency surgery by skilled physicians was set those same physicians' bizarre extra-curricular antics, their libidinous romps with the nurses, their delight in boozing (often from a still in their tent). Symbolic of the desire for broad humor was the addition of Corporal Klinger as a firmly heterosexual soldier who was trying to leave the army by pretending to enjoy acting like a woman.

Slowly over the next few years, though, the broadness of most of the humor was pushed aside in favor of more subtle comedy that had laced into it the pathos of the wartime experience. Lawrence Marks, who wrote a number of episodes during the first few years, remembers a conscious decision to move away from a high-jinks approach to humor and, instead, to leaven it with ethical substance. When Gelbart left the show after four years, and Reynolds after five, Burt Metcalf and a new group of younger writers—notably Ken Levine, David Isaacs, Larry Balmaggia, and Ronny Graham—preferred to continue reaching for comedy that was quieter than the kind the show displayed in its early days.

Confronting the new generation was a desperate need for material to make the show look fresh. The writers found that one way to do it was to go back to old episodes in search of references or undeveloped actions that suggested plot possibilities. They would then expand those references into central story lines by imagining the reactions of one or more characters to the particular circumstance.

This approach encouraged a deepening sense of the personalities of the 4077's characters. Father Mulcahy, an early addition, proved to be a subtle man whose aura of goodness brought out even more strongly the absurdity of war. With the departure of certain characters (Trapper John, Frank Burns, Henry Blake, Radar) as a result of behind-the scenes politics, the show's creators made decisions that moved the show even

further along a path that would use humor to explore complex personalities. B. J. Hunnicut (Trapper's replacement), Charles Winchester
(Burns's replacement), and the new commander, Colonel Potter, all
proved from the start to be more complex human beings than the relatively unmalleable figures they replaced. Klinger, taking over for Radar as the commander's assistant, toned down his woman act and became a more subtle character, as well.

The clout of actors was sometimes an important factor in a character's change. Partly because of Loretta Swit's desire to see her character
grow, Nurse Houlihan blossomed from a comic authoritarian to a complex woman with a warm heart and caring disposition toward the nurses
she led as well as toward the doctors. At the same time, while Margaret's position was enriched, the role of other nurses in the M*A*S*H
unit did not change much. Out of the O.R., they were sex objects,
butts of jokes for the boozy doctors, Larry Gelbart admitted. The booze
and the sexual innuendo gradually disappeared as the years rolled on,
partly as a reaction to outside criticism. But the corps of nurses still
didn't have much of a role. Insiders on the show attributed this low
profile to Swit's insistence that she have no real female competition
among the *M*A*S*H* crew.

Probably the most important shift of character was that of Hawkeye,
who in many ways became Alan Alda's alter ego. Prodded by Alda
and encouraged by the production team's general desire to explore
characters for story ideas, Hawkeye Pierce evolved into a complex individual. "Hawkeye is a dedicated, talented surgeon, court jester, passionate advocate of justice, instigator of endless mischief, and picture
of pomposity," wrote David Reiss in an "authorized" book about
M*A*S*H written after its eighth year on the air.[7] Reiss continued his
description of Hawkeye, reflecting the creators' aims: "In the midst of
a terrible war, he is forced, complaining and irritated, flailing away
with words and gestures, to change and grow and learn something
about his very own human nature."[8]

Gelbart had started with the notion that Hawkeye Pierce was the
"super doc" of the group, with Henry Blake and Trapper John as
"competent" surgeons, and Frank Burns as "sloppy," though still acceptable. While Pierce never lost his expertise, the emphasis as time
wore on was on the toll war was taking on him. Once he removed the
healthy appendix of a war-happy general who had come to the O.R.
wounded superficially. An appendix removal would force the general
to go Stateside, Hawkeye knew. It was his desperate attempt to stop
the killing. The pressure of seeing the wounded of the war and bureaucracy that caused it came close to breaking him a couple of times.
He did, in fact, ultimately crack, in the final episode, as the war ended
and the M*A*S*H unit folded its tents.

The stress of the war-torn environment and the war-ravaged patients
on Hawkeye showed up among the rest of the unit in a wide variety

of ways. Their reactions to it—their revulsions as well as their comic coping mechanisms—formed a theme that meshed perfectly with the insane situation of healers fixing up people so they could go out and kill or be killed.

It was also, Larry Gelbart recognized, a theme that drastically reversed the traditional approach of doctor shows to their patients and their settings. Previous programs from *Medic* through *Marcus Welby* had focused on the impact (usually positive) of the doctors on their patients and social environment. *M*A*S*H*, by contrast, centered on the impact (usually negative) of the patients and the environment on the physicians.

To Gelbart, the difference came down to a difference in control. The war set up a situation where the doctors weren't the ultimate order givers. "We showed medical men as not being in charge," he said. "It's true that on most shows doctors could suffer frustrations. They're also not in charge of death. But *M*A*S*H* was different in treating them as draftees, and reluctant ones at that."

Bells of Identification

It took a year or two for many TV critics to realize how different *M*A*S*H* was from previous doctor shows, and from TV comedy programs in general. It also took a while for the program to find the consistently huge audience that would make its annual renewal a certainty. One TV writer noted that "nothing in 'audience research' or early ratings or industry wisdom—and nothing obvious in the American consciousness, not even the success of the film from which the series idea was drawn—suggested that *M*A*S*H* would be more than an experiment recalled by cognoscenti." [9] Once the success of the show was clear, though, the attention the press paid it over its long run exceeded even the attention paid to *Marcus Welby* in its heyday.

Not all the comments were favorable. Cleveland Amory, *TV Guide*'s reviewer after the series premiered, found the whole notion of comedy about war distasteful. [10] Richard Hofeldt, in the magazine *Society*, wrote that the series was riddled with cultural biases that reassured viewers about the utility and stability of American values even while it was showing how those values were causing great destruction. [11] Robert Altman, who had directed the film version of *M*A*S*H*, concurred. "The series was done for commerce, not for art," he said. "Having an Asian war in the living rooms for more than a decade is an insidious kind of propaganda filled with easy liberal statements." Altman claimed that the movie "made the audience pay for laughs," whereas the series did not. "We would show crudeness and then we would show the ultimate in bad taste: war." [12]

By and large, people disagreed with him. The program won raves from intellectuals, industry figures, and the general public. Over and over, industry commentators, journalists, and even magazine readers in letters to the editor pointed to the irony of healers involved in war as the wellspring from which the show's creators drew quality inspiration. That irony, opined *Newsweek*, "has steadily gone deeper. Without ever moralizing, *M*A*S*H* is the most moral entertainment on television. It proposes craft against butchery, humor against despair, wit as a defense mechanism against the senseless enormity of the situation."[13]

The strong characterizations that clearly helped bring the audience back week after week led naturally to the appearance of magazine articles about the actors who played those characters. All the major members of the cast had articles written about them, generally following the typical approach of how much or how little the actor resembled the fictional counterpart. Especially in the beginning, the pieces were very positive, about the individuals and their relationship to the cast as a whole.

"I think *M*A*S*H* was very lucky," said Larry Gelbart about the rain of favorable publicity about the cast. He suggested that the program benefited from the absence of a "hunger for conflict" on the part of journalists who wrote about TV performers in the early 1970s. By the time numerous tensions that led to personnel departures and infighting did make the newspaper and magazine columns, the show and its "happy family" aura was already entrenched in the consciousness of viewers, he suggested.

The actor who clearly got the most attention through the years of the series was Alan Alda. Alda, it was said, was the center of the show, a terrific guy with a politically liberal philosophy who was a triple-threat talent—actor, writer, director, and sometimes producer. His writing, acting, and general presence had helped to lift *M*A*S*H* into a class by itself, and to change the program as Alda and the nation changed. Of particular note was his concern with women's issues. That, said a number of articles, helped move *M*A*S*H* away from the sexism that had characterized the early installments.[14]

Some of Alda's comments rankled Larry Gelbart and Gene Reynolds, who felt Alda was taking the credit for a perspective that they had always wanted to bring to the show. But while there may have been a bit of confusion at times about the collaborative responsibility for setting the tone for *M*A*S*H*, there was general agreement in the popular press that the show's approach to medicine was a good deal different from what had preceded it on TV.

"Unshaven, mad-eyed Hawkeye, who is a terrific surgeon," said *Vogue* magazine's TV reviewer ". . . is so raunchy and septic that he couldn't get inside the doors of *Medical Center* where Holy Joe Gannon practices or the Institute where Dr. Kildare is so young and antiseptic." Pointing to the "tented slobbery" of the doctors' quarters and the hillbilly still that fermented whiskey for them amid their belongings, the review invoked Sergeant Bilko, much as the creators of *Temperatures Rising* had. Here, though, the reviewer implied, the intentionally jarring tone of the program helped its characters go beyond a Bilko-like image. "*M*A*S*H* recognizes," *Vogue* said, "that war is dirty, hard, uncomfortable, mean, and, at times, hilarious."[15]

Doctors acting bizarre in a dirty, hard, uncomfortable, and mean environment might not seem like a model for the medical establishment to cherish. Yet many physicians, and organized medicine particularly, seemed to find the program and its stars worthy of praise. Gelbart, Metcalf, Reynolds, and Mike Farrell (who played Hunnicut) all commented on the acclaim medical organizations heaped on their show. The younger generation of doctors seemed particularly enthralled: Alan Alda was asked to give the commencement address at Columbia University's College of Physicians and Surgeons in 1979.[16]

In his address Alda suggested why physicians were actually applauding their image in *M*A*S*H* rather than disdaining it. His character, he recognized, was actually a fine physician caught up in a terrible situation not of his making. And he was a real person, both in the sense that he was modeled after the physicians who gave the interviews and in the sense that he had flaws as well as good points.

"[Hawkeye] has a sense of humor, and yet he's serious," Alda pointed out. "He's impertinent, and yet he has feeling. He's human enough to make mistakes and yet he hates death enough to push himself past his own limits in order to save lives." Alda continued, "[I]n many ways he's the doctor patients want to have and doctors want to be. But he's not an idealization. Finding himself in a war, he's sometimes angry, sometimes cynical, sometimes a little nuts.

"He's not a magician who can come up with an instant cure for a rare disease without sweating and ruining his makeup. He knows he might fail. Not a god, he walks gingerly on the edge of disaster—alive to his own mortality."[17]

This image of the concerned yet harried professional who should be viewed with a combination of awe, concern, and a bit of pity seems exactly the image that many physicians concerned about their public portrayal wanted in the 1970s. It was a time when both the unapproachable demeanor of a Marcus Welby and the reprehensible demeanor of doctors in the movie *Hospital* were creating image problems. *M*A*S*H*'s doctors pointed to a middle-ground image as an attractive yet attainable ideal. They were physicians who certified their humanness by acting strangely to cope with strange circumstances. They were real people who made real mistakes. But, at the same time, they were people who certified their professionalism by living their Hippocratic oath to the utmost in the O.R.

That, in fact, is practically what Drummond Rennie, M.D., wrote in the American Medical Association's general circulation magazine, *To-*

day's Health. Rennie's job was to view the several doctor shows on the air at the time (1973) and report his opinion of their credibility, technical accuracy, educational content, and career motivating power. The chart he came up with listed *Marcus Welby* and *Emergency* as tops in those categories. *M*A*S*H*, he said, really couldn't be compared side by side with the others because of its altogether different style and tone.[18]

Still, he listed *M*A*S*H* together with *Welby* and *Emergency* as television's "best buys" in terms of doctor shows. But even more telling were his comments on those three shows within the body of his article. *Emergency!,* though scrupulously realistic, was clearly for children, he observed. *Welby,* while an adult show and realistic in medical detail, was actually "a perversion of reality." He agreed with a friend who said that "everyone must get the feeling [from *Marcus Welby, M.D.*] that their own doctor can spend all his working (and playing) hours with them."[19]

M*A*S*H, by contrast, rang bells of identification for Rennie. "In terms of acting, of depicting ill patients and harassed doctors, of getting across the true feeling of what being a patient or a doctor is like," he said, *Welby* and *Emergency!* were far less successful than *M*A*S*H*. TV shows, he argued, should teach viewers less about diseases and more about healers. "They should learn that doctors are humans, with their own joys and fears. They should get a feeling for the complexity and uncertainty of medicine, and not merely its diversity. There is too much that is spectacular and irrelevant, and not enough of the blood and the sweat."[20]

"Only *M*A*S*H*, he concluded, "seems to hint at the shifting, tragic, vague, inefficient, catastrophic, funny, no beginning and no end, unheroic nature of medicine."[21]

As he wrote, though, the race was on among producers and networks to prove him wrong.

12

Chasing the Spirit of *M*A*S*H*

Washington Post TV columnist William Henry noted in the late 1970s that executives of all three networks consistently ranked *M*A*S*H* with *All in the Family* as the most respected and craftsmanlike series on the air. They also considered it the most inexplicably successful one, Henry added. That is because simple descriptions of the show's premise, or of individual episodes, wouldn't give anyone the idea that here was a project that was such a solid hit, and an artistic one at that.[1]

That didn't deter television producers or network programmers. With dramatic series about doctors coming on-line incessantly during the first half of the '70s after the success of *Marcus Welby, Medical Center,* and *The Bold Ones,* they saw *M*A*S*H*'s success at mid-decade as an invitation in another direction. The race was on to concoct doctors for comedies. The challenge was to come up with the right combination of elements that would duplicate *M*A*S*H*'s popularity, if not its theme. That proved very hard to do.

"I Want to Get Out"

Five doctor-centered comedy series came through the development gauntlet from 1975 through 1979: *The Bob Crane Show* (NBC), about a middle-aged man making his way through medical school; *The Practice* (NBC), about a dedicated, old-fashioned doctor and his son practicing medicine in New York City; *Doc* (CBS), also about a dedicated, old-fashioned doctor practicing medicine in New York City; *A.E.S. Hudson Street* (ABC), about an emergency room in New York City; and *House Calls* (CBS), about the erratic goings-on in a California hospital.

These series represented more doctor comedies than had hit the air previously in the history of television. None of them was a direct take-off on *M*A*S*H*. In fact, *The Practice* (with popular TV actor Danny Thomas), *Doc* (with experienced stage actor Barnard Hughes), and *The*

Bob Crane Show (whose star had hit it big in a previous sitcom, *Hogan's Heroes*) had the standard approach to situation comedies written all over them. Not long after their debuts, though, network programmers and producers began to insist that the trick to copying M*A*S*H's popularity lay not in simply building shows around physicians but in trying to capture the spirit that made M*A*S*H clearly different from other sitcoms.

The change of tactics is clearest in a comparison of *The Practice* with *Doc* over time. At their inception, the two series were quite similar in tone as well as premise. They mixed gentle humor, one-liners, and put-down repartee among the physicians, the rest of the regular cast, and "visiting" patients. The pace was sometimes vaudevillian (particularly in *The Practice,* with former standup comic Thomas), though the put-down humor was never really at the expense of the physician's dignity or the seriousness of a particular patient's illness. For example:

> JULES BEDFORD [of *The Practice*] to female patient: Take off your shoes.
> PATIENT: I'm not going to have to take anything else off, am I?
> BEDFORD: Why, what else did you have in mind?
> PATIENT: It's just that I have so much better underwear at home.

> DOC BOGART to Mona, who is clearly a prostitute: What is your complaint?
> MONA: Business is terrible.
> DOC: I mean, your medical complaint.
> MONA: My feet. They're killing me. All day long I'm on my feet!
> DOC: How come you're on your feet so much?
> MONA: I told you honey—business is terrible!

The overall mood of the two programs was more like "Marcus Welby meets the TV sitcom" than like M*A*S*H. Doc Joe Bogart and Dr. Jules Bedford were constantly putting their concern for their patients ahead of the almighty dollar. In the classic TV sitcom tradition, each episode saw a storm of conflict rise at the beginning, reach a crescendo toward the middle, and resolve into serenity at the end. Bogart and Bedford both had naysaying companions (a wife and son, respectively) who constantly tried to bring them back to pragmatic realities. But the message across the episodes was that these men were consummate physicians precisely because they went beyond technical considerations and understood the souls of their patients.

In *The Practice,* the sagacity of the traditional, fatherly brand of medicine is contrasted with the scientific aloofness of modern approaches through Jules's son, David, the voice of pragmatism and head of internal medicine at a local hospital. Time and time again, Bedford Senior shows Bedford Junior the usefulness of understanding the whole patient in ways that straightforward medical science can't fathom and only experience can teach.

In one installment of *The Practice* an odd-acting woman contends she will collapse and die on October 14. David dismisses her story as a crazy figment. But Jules is impressed when she reveals an uncanny ability to predict that a chandelier will fall from the ceiling moments before it happens. Undeterred by David's screams about the monetary waste of her hospital admission, he checks the woman into his son's hospital on the fateful day. True to her intuition, she collapses into a coma. Jules, now convinced about her clairvoyant ability, implores her subconscious to predict what is wrong. With a highly skeptical David standing by, she reveals through her coma that her problem is an aneurism. Confirming that she is correct, Bedford takes steps to make her well.

Alongside this portrayal of the superiority of supposedly traditional bedside manners was a display of the supposedly traditional ethic of dedication and inhumanly hard work in the service of patients. "I saw over fifty people today," Jules Bedford says to a black resident. "Just wait, young man, until you start practicing. Then you'll know the true meaning of tired blood."

The healer who works long, tough hours without adequate recompense was also a theme in *The Bob Crane Show*, but it came out in a different way. The show picked up on the idea that aspiring doctors must cope with their share of poverty and hard work. It was, of course, a hoary theme that went back to the Kildare magazine stories. Now, though, a laugh track was added. The poverty of the medical student was turned into a source of standard situation comedy about the way that he and his family tried to cope.

In *Doc's* case, the theme of hard work for little money became the premise that pushed the series on a more *M*A*S*H*-like trajectory. Lawrence Marks, a veteran comedy writer who had worked on several *M*A*S*H* scripts, had a major hand in reshaping the series. "The show was pretty successful in its first year, getting a 28 or 29 share" he recalled. "But it was too quiet for the network powers that be."

Each episode revolved around both office and home, with Doc's wife and son-in-law taking prominent roles. The CBS programmers, he said, were concerned that the shift that the producers kept making between Doc's home life and office life was crowding out a lot of potential comedy in the office. "They liked it but they didn't," Marks said. "They felt it could have more going for it."

To Marks, that meant adding a *M*A*S*H*-like desperation to the life of the central character. The new premise had Doc Bogart as a widower living alone; since the previous season, viewers were told, his wife had died. To further distance the new format from the old, Marks came up with the idea of moving Bogart out of his private practice and into a poverty clinic. The clinic environment, with its wide variety of patients, had great potential for humor, Marks reasoned. His choice of a poverty clinic was made because, as he said, "less wealthy doctors are easier thought of as gods than the wealthy ones." He justified the move to the audience by suggesting that with Bogart's wife dead, "medicine became his next wife, became more important. And that standard thing of wanting to do something to help people."

To kick the humor into still higher gear, the producers gave the clinic an odd bunch of employees who could be the butt of the kind of jokes that the writers couldn't perpetrate on a doctor. They created a Puerto Rican receptionist who yearns to be an actress; a jive-talking black lab technician; and, most prominent, a clinic director who is a stereotyped medical administrator.

As played by David Ogden Stiers, who was later to take the role of the snobbish Charles Winchester on *M*A*S*H*, the administrator isn't the dangerous hospital head that Paul Lynde had portrayed in *The New Temperatures Rising*. He is, rather, the total bureaucrat, concerned to ridiculous extremes that his staff fill out forms, follow petty rules, and perpetuate miles of red tape. Ironically, he himself sometimes makes major errors—forgetting to renew the clinic's lease, for example, which threatens to turn the site into a delicatessen. He is, in other words, the incarnation of I-Corps. He is the force that Doc and his crew often have to get around in order to get good medicine done.

In this environment, the beleaguered Doc Bogart has to find himself wondering why he stayed. In fact, the writers found themselves posing just that question in a number of situations. In one episode, a wealthy private practitioner, an old Bogart friend, urges him to leave the clinic and join his private practice. Earning little at the clinic and spending most of his savings on his eight kids, Doc finds the offer attractive as he contemplates needing money at retirement a few years down the road. At episode's end, though, a medical emergency in the clinic shows Bogart how much the patients and the staff need him. Somewhat resignedly, he falls back into the grips of that slightly insane ambiance and decides to remain, its pole of sanity and good medicine.

This *M*A*S*H*-like theme of a besieged physician locked into an environment so threatening to good medicine that it is funny showed up in another series, *A.E.S. Hudson Street*, that premiered in 1978. The creator was Danny Arnold, who had recently struck Nielsen gold for ABC with *Barney Miller*, a situation comedy about a squad of detectives in a police station. But *Hudson Street*'s humor is more hard-edged than *Barney Miller*'s. *M*A*S*H*'s influence is clear.

Here the embattled facility is an Adult Emergency Service in what the script calls a "deteriorating" New York City hospital. Dr. Tony Menzies (actor Greg Sierra), Chief Resident, is the central, sympathetic character. He is joined by two other physicians—Dr. Mackler, whose comic shtick is to chase women; and Dr. Glick, a slightly eccentric psychiatrist. They are surrounded by an assortment of odder-balls: two constantly bickering ambulance drivers, one a fat woman, the other a skinny man; a sexy, dumb staff nurse; a gay male nurse; a sarcastic, pregnant nurse; and the requisite anal-retentive administrator. ("This joint is broke," he tells Menzies. "So just get 'em in and get 'em out.")

The continuing refrain of the A.E.S. staff is the woeful inadequacy of medical supplies and services that hamper their ability to help patients. In one scene Menzies moans about the need to sterilize and reuse "throwaway" rubber gloves because the hospital has no funds to buy new ones. Another time, a nurse mentions they are out of shaving cream and sharp blades for hernia operations. Terrible frustrations abound. One episode revolves around a surgeon's attempted suicide because he has lost three surgery patients in a row that day. After preventing the act (an injection in the manner of a doctor's attempted suicide in the movie *Hospital*), Menzies sends the surgeon to the psychiatric ward to calm down.

The episodes jump back and forth between the comic and serious in the manner of *M*A*S*H*, but the problems the A.E.S. staff sees come nowhere near the devastating trauma the war-weary 4077 suffers. Even the attempted suicide comes across with a kind of casual humor that pulls away from the darkest implications of the incident. More typical is a storyline about a patient who is brought back from the edge of death, only to rail at the physicians for not allowing him to enter the beautiful afterworld. Another subplot follows a psychiatric patient (a former medic in Korea—shades of *M*A*S*H*) who goes around the hospital acting as if he were a doctor. He even performs a secret, and unsuccessful, vasectomy on a philandering hospital trustee.

Punctuating the action are comic one-liners that emphasize the bizarre nature of what is going on and sometimes lightly zing the healers. (Someone says the counterfeit doctor should have been detected easily—he told one would-be patient that he made house calls.) Menzies, who comes across as an expert physician with a fine bedside manner, despairs of finding happiness amidst all of this craziness. He sends his resume to other hospitals but for a variety of reasons not under his control he keeps missing out on good jobs. Sometimes, though, he thinks he is psychologically drawn to the place.

"I want to get out but I can't," he tells Glick the psychiatrist in a hope the latter can help him rip the binds he feels to the place. "I got this Albert Schweizer complex, except that the city is my jungle. I feel that I've got to help the downtrodden and suffering."

"Even If It Gets Nuts . . ."

Menzies didn't have the chance to play out his angst over an entire season. *A.E.S. Hudson Street* aired only five episodes before ABC programmers pulled the plug. *The Bob Crane Show*, *The Practice*, and *Doc* didn't do terrifically, either. *Crane* and *The Practice* aired for only half a year, and while *Doc* made it to a second year's renewal, the show was yanked by CBS quickly into its sophomore run.

Yet the desire to duplicate the success of *M*A*S*H* was very real on the part of network programmers. That was particularly true at CBS, where executives collaborated with Twentieth Century-Fox to adapt some of the concepts or characters of their hit for new series. Because Gene Reynolds balked at getting involved, Fox assigned another producer to work on *The Nurses*. The idea was to explore life in the MASH unit from the distaff side. The trick, all involved knew, was to capture the essence of what made *M*A*S*H* popular.

"We were looking to do what *M*A*S*H* did," said Andy Siegel, who worked on *The Nurses* pilot from the network end. The participants, he recalled, felt that the core of the hit series lay in alternating between high comedy and medical expertise. "It was the flavor of 'even if it gets nuts, even if you do crazy things, when it comes done to the reality of that operating room, it's the best that money can buy.' "

In general, Siegel claimed, it is very hard to reproduce the flavor of a show without doing a direct spinoff—that is, without using some of the same characters and actors from the original series. *The Nurses*, he felt, suffered from that difficulty, and it didn't stand out to programmers as a viable property. The pilot "just didn't get anyone's imagination" at CBS, and though that segment was aired, the show never went to series.

The basic aim didn't die at the network, though, and the programmers went on to commission "The Fighting Nightingales," a revamped approach to nurses in a field hospital during the Korean War. But that pilot didn't fly either, and network programmers looked elsewhere for medical comedy with series potential that evoked some of the spirit of *M*A*S*H*.

They thought they found it in *House Calls*, a popular 1978 theatrical film. The film itself had its origins in an unsold play crafted by humorist Max Shulman during the 1960s. He wanted to write about a widower who was pursued by many women. He almost made the central character a lawyer, because Shulman's two sons are lawyers. But Shulman remembered a doctor-friend who had a strange incident happen to him that might be worked into the play.

An idealistic surgeon, the friend walked into his hospital one day to see a patient in a head harness. The harness had been put there by the head of dental surgery, a man whom Shulman's friend considered incompetent. Sure that the harness could actually harm the patient, the surgeon ordered it removed. Incredibly, said Shulman, his friend was later brought up on charges in the hospital for interfering with another doctor's care and trying to take a physician's patient. He came out ahead in the proceedings by only one vote.

Shulman tried to blend the widower and medical themes into a stage comedy about a skilled surgeon, his romantic pursuit of the hospital's assistant administrator, and the bizarre activities of an old head of surgery that cause the younger man to resist his power. No one bought it. He did manage, finally, to sell the story to Universal as a film, changing the ending to make the medical satire especially biting: the incompetent old doctor agrees not to press charges if the younger one nominates him to continue as head of surgery.

The studio assigned Shulman to write the screenplay with an old friend, Julius Epstein. Walter Matthau was hired to play the central physician, Charlie Nichols. Glenda Jackson was Anne Anderson, the love interest, and Art Carney took the role of Amos Weatherby, the senile surgical department head.

Translated to television, the pace and themes of the movie had the kind of potential to raise eyebrows week to week that *M*A*S*H* had at its start. Ironically, though, when CBS executives showed interest in adapting *House Calls* for series television, Shulman immediately told himself that the story's focus would have to change. Having worked in TV situation comedy before (he had created the popular *Dobie Gillis* series), Shulman had become adept at the self-censorship he found was required of TV writer-producers. He was sure the network bigwigs would make him de-emphasize the medical satire and stress the semi-sweet relationship between the surgeon and the assistant administrator. "This was not going to be an investigation of American medicine," he emphasized. "CBS would not have wanted us to do that."

The upshot of this assumption was that he and Epstein "hit the love story very hard" when writing the pilot for the *House Calls* series. Weatherby's incompetence did come through in the pilot, but it was not the central point. Moreover, Shulman and Epstein purposefully ignored the film's caustic theme that the clubbiness and irresponsibility of the hospital doctors had perpetuated the existence of a dangerous physician in their midst.

At one point in the pilot, in fact, Charlie (played by Wayne Rogers) staunchly defends modern doctoring to the somewhat too idealistic new assistant administrator (Lynn Redgrave). True to the tradition of American popular arts, their argument is the opening round in their attraction to one another. The program title, which in the movie referred to romantic trysts in the female protagonist's house, now becomes the key term in their exchange about the contemporary relevance of an old-fashioned medical tradition. When Ann says scornfully that modern doctors don't make house calls anymore, Charlie shoots back with great confidence: "Oh, come on. Let's not get romantic about house calls. You know as well as I do that a doctor can treat five patients in his office in the time it takes to make one house call, which means that five people are helped instead of one."

Shulman and Epstein left the show after that first episode, but producer Jerry Davis and subsequent writers followed the lead they had set. Charlie Nichols's dealings with Amos were made much more benign than in the film. To at least one group of reviewers, Charlie came across during the first year as "a very skilled surgeon who, because of his affection for Dr. Weatherby [actor David Wayne], made sure that the older physician did not harm anyone."[2]

Weatherby went through major changes over the first year and a half that the series aired. The producers kept him eccentric, but they rounded out his personality to the point that he became not only more likable but actually a lot more sage than he initially had seemed. Even his supposed difficulty in hearing was attributed in one episode not to a genuine sensory loss but to the old man's desire to play jokes on people. "I don't drink. I don't gamble. I don't chase women," he explains his consistent mispronunciation of someone's name. "I have got to have some fun."

The creators were fully aware that they were making David Wayne's Weatherby more like Lionel Barrymore's version of the blustery but insightful Dr. Gillespie in the MGM Kildare flicks than like Art Carney's mean-spirited version of Weatherby in the original *House Calls* theatrical film. At one point in an episode, in fact, they came close to confessing on-screen their source of inspiration for the rounded character. "Weatherby is to medicine," Amos exclaims proudly, "what Barrymore is to the theater."

With the relationship between Charlie and Amos turning increasingly friendly, the series became what Shulman called much "softer" in its comedy than the movie, or even the pilot, was. Romantic humor centered around the mature, yet often conflictive relationship between Charlie and Ann. Added yucks came from the contingent of pleasant oddballs that was requisite to sitcoms of the day. Here the contingent was comprised of Weatherby; Dr. Norman Solomon, an unmarried Jewish physician whose eye for women was hampered by his obedience to his mother; Mrs. Phipps, the "Gray Lady" who roamed the hospital's halls radiating saccharine optimism and cheer; and an assortment of patients.

Weatherby's development made him a "more likable, more multidimensional character," to quote Shulman. The creators saw this as a problem, however. It took from the show a key element of conflict that had been intended at the start. As a result, by the third year the producers looked for a dislikable character who could incite humorous conflict. They came up with hospital administrator—Conrad Peckler, the skinflint and conniver who became Anne's immediate boss.

The program was a moderate success, a predictably solid ratings-getter for the network. CBS executives could not ignore the possibility that Wayne Rogers was one reason for the show's good ratings. He had been in the national spotlight while playing Trapper John opposite Alan Alda in *M*A*S*H*.

Ironically, Rogers's presence also proved to be a hindrance to the show's longevity. Around the set and off it, stories kept circulating about the star's attempts to control the program, to place his own people in charge, to play down the role of co-star Lynn Redgrave. It was the alienation of Redgrave, his romantic target in the series, that seems particularly to have caused sparks to fly.

The matter came to a head after Rogers refused to work unless he got more money per episode. Universal Television capitulated, whereupon Redgrave demanded more cash as well as the opportunity to breastfeed her newborn daughter on the set. In a furious battle that echoed through the national press, Redgrave and Universal Studios shot back and forth allegations about the breastfeeding demands and possible hidden agendas that related to them. In the end, Redgrave left and Sharon Gless took over her role. It was *House Calls*'s third year by then. CBS officials decided not to renew it, and the series limped toward its final prime-time curtain at the end of the 1981–82 season.

A Logical Extension

But the allure of hitting the jackpot with the spirit of *M*A*S*H* lived on at the network. When Alan Alda and other principals of the show announced that the 1983–84 TV year would be their last, CBS and Twentieth Century-Fox executives renewed their attempts to capture its spirit. They contacted Larry Gelbart, who had written the original *M*A*S*H* episodes for TV.

Gelbart had left the program at the end of its fourth year to write theatrical films *(Tootsie, Movie Movie, Oh, God!)*. He had vowed after a bad experience with an NBC series called *United States* a few years before that he wouldn't do series television again. But when Fox executives approached him abut a sequel to *M*A*S*H*," he felt compelled to accept. "Fox and CBS were more or less determined to continue *M*A*S*H* in some form," he recalled, "and I felt if it was going to go forward, I wanted to have some say in it."

The news that Larry Gelbart was coming back energized the production and writing staff. Burt Metcalf, *M*A*S*H*'s executive producer, who had been with the show from the beginning, agreed to stay with the new program. To solidify writing continually from the old show to the new, Metcalf then hired *M*A*S*H* writers Dennis Koenig, David Isaacs, and Ken Levine as producers and directors. Only three from the cast wanted to transfer to the new show, Harry Morgan (Colonel Potter), William Christopher (Father Mulcahy), and Jamie Farr (Corporal Klinger).

Metcalf and Gelbart decided to build the show around them. They let the word out that any other cast members were invited as guest stars. The trick was now to decide what to do with them all. The creators of *M*A*S*H* were confronting the sixty-four-dollar question: Exactly what did creating a show in the spirit of *M*A*S*H* mean?

Gelbart's idea was to bring the *M*A*S*H* holdovers Stateside to a Veterans Administration hospital. Metcalf and the staff writers quickly agreed. "We said that he didn't have to sell that because that's kind of a notion that we've all had, too," Metcalf recalled. "It seemed like kind of a logical extension. Viewers were identifying with *M*A*S*H* in spite of it being in the Korean War. They were identifying it with the Vietnam experience. And at the time there seemed to be a new kind of awareness of the plight of the veteran."

Gelbart set the approach for the series in the first two episodes. Potter, Klinger, and Mulcahy, having gone their separate ways after the Korean War ended, are reunited three months later at a Veterans Administration hospital in a fictional town near Hannibal, Missouri. Potter becomes chief of staff, Klinger his aide, and Mulcahy a hospital chaplain. Klinger's wife, a Korean woman whom he married in the final episode of *M*A*S*H*, also comes on board. A mean-spirited hospital administrator and his female assistant are added to the brew. And an endless procession of patients, casualties of the war, begin to make their guest appearances.

The creators felt they had a number of interesting plot directions to follow. Their research on V.A. hospitals after Korea had given them what they considered to be a rich fund of interesting ideas for patients. The show's setting would enable Potter, Klinger, and Mulcahy to confront the men they sent home from Korea, with all the humor and pathos it implied. Klinger's wife would provide a way to deal with the acclimation of Asian immigrants to the United States. And the hospital administrator would provide a source of conflict with Potter and the other characters.

Metcalf justified relying on the stock character of a hospital administrator by citing dramatic necessity. "They had to have something to rail against," he insisted. He added, though, that the conflicts between physicians and managers were rooted in the reality of the postwar Veterans Administration. He and Gelbart had come across articles that talked about those kinds of tensions. The administrators, he said, often felt that the doctors worked for them. The doctors, on the other hand, insisted that they worked not for the administrators but for the patients. The conflict was useful dramatically "in the sense of giving us grist for a lot of stories."

Gelbart told a reporter before the series debut that *AfterM*A*S*H*, as it was to be called, would be different from *M*A*S*H*, yet "of a piece with it." [3] Metcalf agreed. "This represented an opportunity to do something that, with the influence of *M*A*S*H*, could aspire to a level of intelligence and sophistication and really strong purpose that you don't often get with a new show," he said in an interview prior to the premiere. He added that they would allow themselves relatively subtle humor. "That's not to say we'll be successful at it, but just to have the opportunity is attractive when you work in episodic television. We don't have to resort to the semi-naked women and pratfalls that we know are so prevalent in television today." [4]

Metcalf's public admission that the show might not be successful in some way reflected severe insecurities the staff of *AfterM*A*S*H* felt about working on the new series. The principal reason had to do with the double-edged sword of living up to the name of what had by then already become a legendary TV series. "We may forever be judged by that yardstick," Metcalf said, acknowledging that it might be an impossible task. [5]

Another worry had to do with an element they sensed from the beginning was missing from their spinoff. The new show did not have the manic war environment that gave the physicians a legitimate excuse to do bizarre things outside the O.R. Making a hospital administrator the source of conflict in a socially marginal medical environment was a *M*A*S*H*-chasing tactic that had been used before, in the second season of *Doc* and in *A.E.S. Hudson Street*. Metcalf and his colleagues may not have realized their setting was fundamentally different from the classic they revered.

"We can't be *M*A*S*H*," actor William Christopher told the press before the show's debut. "We don't have the swamp with those rowdy guys in it and the drinking and the women-chasing. We have to try to find our own way." [6]

But in the absence of the manic hilarity that marked the start of *M*A*S*H*, CBS programmers feared that the writers' *M*A*S*H*-like inclination to deal with the serious as well as the humorous wouldn't work in the hospital setting. According to a number of people involved with the show, the creators' intention of dealing with the aftermath of war—Korea and, by implication, Vietnam—made the network executives particularly nervous. While allowing Gelbart near-total freedom, they nevertheless expressed concern that some of the show's material was too downbeat. Still, they positioned the series Tuesday evenings at eight, as a lead-in to the popular *Newhart* sitcom.

The premiere was a smash, as the Nielsen numbers placed the show near the top of prime time's programs. Soon, however, the ratings started falling drastically. Newspapers and magazines offered various explanations for the downward spiral. Tom Shales of the *Washington Post* suggested bluntly that the sequel suffered under most boring personalities in the 4077.

"If the average *M*A*S*H* fan could pick three characters whose lives would be worth following after the end of the Korean War and the return home," he carped, "most might pick Col. Potter (Harry Morgan). . . . [B]ut does anybody yearn to learn more about the schlemielish Klinger . . . or the insufferably goody-good Father Mulcahy, both of whom join the colonel in the series?" [7]

While perhaps buying this point, CBS officials seemed sure that the main problem with the show was its attempt to mix seriousness with subtle comedy à la the mature *M*A*S*H*. Metcalf said they urged him and his writers to lighten up, to veer away from stories about the war veterans. The hospital environment, they said, was too somber. In *M*A*S*H*, the medical prognosis was generally upbeat for soldiers; they had good physicians and a low mortality rate. The V.A. hospital, though, was the repository of the ones who had barely made it. That was a downer, they argued, and it was chasing viewers away from the show.

What was needed, CBS executives suggested, was a refocusing away from the hospital, toward the lives of the regulars. Metcalf came to agree that a heavy dose of hospital realities was the problem. "They had us pegged pretty well," he admitted. "They said it wasn't funny enough and we were going to need additional characters of considerable importance beyond the three holdovers."

The first new character was the addition of Dr. Boyer, a Hawkeye-type physician who maintained a sardonic wit and expert medical hand despite being literally war-torn: his badges of courage were castration and an artificial leg. Boyer was designed to be the strong core of the show that the producers felt it missed. Still, Boyer's presence mixed sober remembrance with one-line humor. It did not bring the hilarity the network wanted.

With some desperation, the writers looked back to *M*A*S*H*'s approach to the characters for answers. The source of Corporal Klinger's belly-laughable humor in the original, they relearned, was that he was always in a situation he didn't want to be in and would resort to anything outlandish to get out. But his position in *AfterM*A*S*H* didn't lend itself to that kind of comedy. Marriage had brought Klinger bliss but it had gotten him nowhere comedically.

So, for the last episode of the year, they had Klinger hit someone in an argument and go to jail. The idea, borrowed from the hugely popular *Dallas* evening soap opera, was to set up a cliff-hanger that would have viewers wanting to tune in for the resolution if the series were renewed for fall 1984.

"We wrote the episode just as a cliff-hanger for the next year," said Dennis Koenig. "We didn't know where we were going. Then, the network said, 'Look, the ratings are falling. This thing is pretty iffy. What kinds of ideas would you have to get some outrageousness and some fun and some lighter aspects that will take us away from the hospital more?'

"We all knew, we felt it, it wasn't just [the network], that we were getting bogged down. So then with that kind of pressure, an ultimatum in a sense, that sparked us to thinking."

They decided to break Klinger out of jail and have him become a fugitive. "That would place him in a kind of jeopardy that would cause him to do all kinds of outrageous things," Koenig continued. "In the first episode back, he disguised himself as a nurse in order to see his wife and be there for the birth of the baby. That was probably one of the best episodes that we had. It captured the *M*A*S*H* humor."

Another change was to jettison the mean-spirited hospital administrator and replace him with a more comic, bungling one. From the network's standpoint, however, none of this really seemed to matter. Although the CBS programmers had renewed *AfterM*A*S*H* for a second year, their lack of faith in its survival showed in where they placed it: opposite NBC's monster hit, *The A-Team*, an action-adventure series that was then regularly the number 3 or 4 prime-time show on the air.

"Every show that got put in that Tuesday night eight o'clock spot was canned," recalled Dennis Koenig somewhat disconsolately. "It showed that you didn't have the network's faith anymore, like *The Jeffersons* and *Alice*. [which also had that position]. They put those in there because they thought it was a losing battle."

It certainly turned out to be. About a month into the 1984–85 season, the series racked up a pitiful 9.3 rating in the week's Nielsen survey. That placed it number 63 out of 65 shows. *AfterM*A*S*H* had been doing "moderately well" against the baseball playoffs and World Series on NBC during the previous few weeks, Metcalf said. The 9.3 rating came against its regular *A-Team* competition, and that spelled doom. Nine episodes had been taped. CBS allowed them to air, but that was it.[8]

Another medical comedy series had bitten the network dust. But it was not really just another one. This was the series that was to capture the spirit of *M*A*S*H* by using the same people who created that spirit in the first place. That it didn't work probably said more about the serendipitous combination of format, situation, actors, and the spirit of the country at the time of *M*A*S*H*'s debut than it did about some magical quality producers and writers keep chasing.

A Rising Insecurity

There is another point to make about this chasing of *M*A*S*H*'s allegedly chaseable spirit. In a strange, indirect way the creators and programmers of those '70s doctor sitcoms did end up reflecting, as *M*A*S*H* and *The New Temperatures Rising* also did, a rising insecurity many policymakers and members of the general public were feeling about the medical system during the mid- and late 1970s. It was a time, Harvard University health analyst Aaron Wildavsky noted in 1977, when America was "doing better and feeling worse" on the medical front.[9]

Americans, on the whole, were living longer. American hospitals were using some of the best technology in the world. Health care was more evenly distributed among rich and poor than it had ever been. Three-quarters to four-fifths of the population, depending on the survey, said they were getting good medical care. Yet, at the same time, one- to two-thirds of those interviewed thought that the system that was producing those results was in bad shape.

"The system," Wildavsky pointed out, "is an abstract entity," one that people can't see but can only hear about. He suggested that the general population's pessimistic attitude was mostly in imitation "of those interested and vocal elites" who were insisting in the media and elsewhere that the system was in crisis. People did, he admitted, have personal complaints about the medical establishment, usually related to their economic position. "The rich don't like waiting, the poor don't like high prices, and those in the middle don't like both." [10]

But what people didn't understand, he added, was that such complaints were inevitable in view of the scarcity of resources that characterized medical care in any society. In the end, the goal had to be as equitable a distribution of comfort, and discomfort, as possible, since a health care nirvana was simply not possible.

The creators of *M*A*S*H*, *Doc*, *A.E.S. Hudson Street*, and *AfterM*A*S*H* didn't really care much about the problems of late-twentieth-century medicine that Wildavsky described. Nor did they intend to perpetuate an idea of a crisis in the contemporary health care system through their programs. Still, the medical locales they created in the search for popular comedy may have reinforced the insecurity. Certainly, they represented the flaws rather than the flagships of the establishment. Deteriorating facilities and the scarcity of basic supplies were key elements in a storytelling frame which saw doctors bravely flailing against an onslaught of problems that hindered their sanity and their practice of good medicine.

It ought to be stressed, though, that, dark as some of the humor could be, the medical world these shows presented was not a piece with the horrible scenes in *Medical Story*, or even with the sharp criticisms of the social role of hospital-based doctors in the pilot of *The Lazarus Syndrome*. Those shows had implicated system-wide health care issues in the specific problems they were depicting. The comedies, by contrast, plugged into the doctor-show formula's assumption that problems in hospitals were not system problems. Rather, they were caused by the failings of the people involved.

The comedies also picked up another key idea built into the formula—that health care is a social right that can and should be shared to the fullest extent by all because it is essentially an unlimited resource. Blending the two assumptions, it made sense that the comedies conveniently poked fun at what in the formula was invariably the person to blame for threats to equal health care for all, the hospital administrator. Sitcom hospital administrators ran a gamut of types but in general turned out to be inept, sometimes rotten bureaucrats who got in the way of good care. After all, who needs someone to manage a resource that is unlimited? The high way to good care, the logic followed, was naturally for the concerned doctors to find paths around the roadblocks the administrators were constantly setting up.

This pat approach to the problem of scarce medical resources clashed severely with the way insurance company administrators, corporate health care managers, and government overseers of health care who were shaping the medical system during the 1970s preferred to see the world. To many of them, the right to unlimited medical care was no longer to be taken for granted. To most of them, medicine was a genuinely scarce resource. This perception of scarcity led powerful groups in society-private hospitals, public hospitals, physician groups, insurance companies, large employers—to compete over health care dollars.

The upshot was corporate and legislative hardball. Tough decisions were negotiated and legislated about the nature of medical care to be administered, the limits of medical care, the direction of medical research, the direction of medical education, the purchase and use of expensive medical technologies, the cost-effectiveness of saving certain lives over other lives. Health care administrators may have been the incarnation of silliness, evil, or superfluousness in the TV doctor formula. But in the complex political process of the 1970s and 1980s the buck didn't stop there. They were part of a larger decisionmaking process to limit health care that ran from insurance companies and legislative chambers to doctors' offices and employers' board rooms.

None of this really mattered to programmers and producers trying hard to create doctor shows that would have the longevity of a *M*A*S*H*, a *Marcus Welby*, a *Medical Center*. As the '70s turned into the '80s, and as a high proportion of the medical dramas and comedies that hit the air quickly bit the dust, the key questions related not to the medical system's sociopolitical realities but to televisions's: What would it take to get a successful new doctor show on the air?

Previous successes and failures moved producers to think along a subtle, incremental, though, in retrospect, quite clear track. *Welby* and *Medical Center*'s success—along with *Medical Story*'s failure—underscored the importance of portraying a sound health care system commanded by competent physicians. *M*A*S*H* had pointed out the possibility of making physicians attractive to viewers by not portraying them as superdocs. A number of made-for-TV movies and failed pilots had illustrated the possibility of showing the continuing personal problems of physician-heroes as a way of humanizing them. Those shows were also evidence that it was possible to center routine plots around women and minorities as doctors without controversy (if not with high ratings). And the comedies after *M*A*S*H* had come up with an inferior hospital as a Stateside counterpart to *M*A*S*H*'s Korean War.

All these approaches seemed to fit into network executives' and television producers' conception of where the doctor-show formula ought to go within the contemporary social environment. The challenge was to find ways to blend them—guided, most especially, by the spirit of *M*A*S*H*, which the executives saw as incorporating many of those elements—into a successful new whole. By the late 1970s, CBS executives had a new idea. If half-hour comedies weren't necessarily the place where *M*A*S*H*-like jackpots could be found, then perhaps the answer lay in trying to move the show's spirit into dramas.

13

"Our Walls Are Cleaner"

Trapper John, M.D., which began on CBS in 1979, and *St. Elsewhere*, which made its debut on NBC in 1982, were the most successful doctor shows to come after the cauldron of medical comedies and dramas that aired on the home tube during the 1970s. The aims of the shows' creators were so different, however, that they actually disdained each other's work.

"I have to say that there are some things about *St. Elsewhere* that I resent," *Trapper John*'s executive producer, Don Brinkley, said in 1985. "There was an article in *TV Guide* last year or so in which one of the producers [of that show] asked if he wanted to go the *Trapper John* route, and he said, no, that he didn't want to prostitute himself to that extent. I resented the hell out of that."

The differences between the shows were not subtle. San Francisco Memorial, where Trapper John practiced as head of cardiac surgery, was a highly polished environment. Weaving through humorous subplots about the minor difficulties of the main characters were straightforward "patient" story lines that could be wrapped up optimistically within an hour. *Trapper John* also was set in a state-of-the-art hospital.

By contrast, *St. Elsewhere* unfolded consistently meandering and sometimes depressing plots about a struggling Boston teaching hospital in a declining part of town. In St. Eligius (more commonly known to its community as St. Elsewhere), the hospital was as often a place where doctors made mistakes as where they were praised for their prowess. And, unlike Trapper John and his colleagues, many of the professionals in St. Eligius were anything but upstanding, heroic, and cool under real pressure.

Much of that pressure was personal. *St. Elsewhere* went farther than *Trapper John* in turning the focus away from the patients and toward the several physicians and nurses that populated the program. In the space of a few seasons, viewers saw more regular characters with major personal problems than they could have found in the regulars of two previous decades of doctor shows. They saw, for example, Surgeon Ben Samuels give as much time to his libidinous inclinations as to his surgical responsibilities; resident Jack Morrison's marriage fall apart while he was discovered to have misstated his medical background; resident Wayne Fiscus tilt romantically toward a kinky pathology fellow who loved to make love in the morgue; and resident Peter White rape a nurse and, in turn, get shot by her friend.

The look, pacing, and structure of *St. Elsewhere* accentuated the differences between the two shows. *Trapper*, a series with self-contained episodes each week, took a straightforward approach to filming and editing hospital scenes. *St. Elsewhere* was a serial, often with four or more story lines intercutting one another. Hand-held cameras tracked nervous nurses down dingily lit corridors in an emergency. Quick cuts and overlapping dialogue added to the feeling of exhaustion and confusion. Plots and subplots meandered over several episodes instead of being neatly resolved in sixty minutes.

Brinkley understood the differences and was pragmatic about them. "We try to be as accurate medically as we can," he insisted in 1985. "We try to be as impressive dramatically as we can. We aren't kidding ourselves. We are a lighter show than *St. Elsewhere*. We aren't doing the nitty-gritty aspect of it that they're doing. By the same token, we're not quite as florid and lurid as they.

"We don't have rapists being shot in the balls [as *St. Elsewhere* had]. We don't have that sort of thing, we just don't do it. Ours is a more romantic look at the hospital; our walls are cleaner than theirs. We're a little more reassuring to the audience than they are. And we're considerably more popular than they are, and that's why."

The tension in his voice and the conviction in his manner reflected a personal wound. But Brinkley was also mirroring one approach to a question rumbling through the corridors of power at networks and production companies, including the ones where *St. Elsewhere* was filmed.

How far should doctor shows of the 1980s depart from television's traditional look at physicians, hospitals, and patients' life and death? The different answers the creators of *Trapper John* and *St. Elsewhere* came up with reflected a variety of differences: generational differences among the creators, differences in their loyalty to the traditional formula, different degrees of nervousness within NBC and CBS regarding innovation, and different network marketing and audience concerns.

Yet beneath many of the clear dissimilarities in approach between the two shows, there were a number of critical continuities the creators of both series shared with the traditional formula. The continuities reflected much about the way in which elements of a formula are incorporated into new series in response to specific demands from the con-

temporary environment. And they said even more about the intransi-
gence of a longstanding, successful formula in the face of glacial
changes in society at large.

"A Little Bit of *M*A*S*H* . . ."

As Don Brinkley recognized, the basic differences between the two series were rooted in the mandates with which the creators of *Trapper
John* and *St. Elsewhere* had started. In *Trapper John*'s case, almost all the
planning that went into it involved a conscious attempt to plug con-
servatively into the most traditionally successful elements of the formula. That was ironic, since the direct impetus for the program was
TV's most maverick series with a doctor theme, *M*A*S*H*.

When *Medical Center* left CBS's prime-time schedule in 1976 after a
seven-year run, Brinkley and Frank Glicksman, who had worked on it
together from the start, expected with some relief that they were done
with medical series. They were tired of dealing with the same kinds of
plots in the same kind of environment. *Medical Center,* after all, had
come not too long after their collaboration on many *Ben Casey* episodes.
The medical formula had been on their professional minds for about
fifteen years.

But in the television industry the typecasting of producers according
to their successes and failures is about as common as the typecasting
of actors. Glicksman and Brinkley's track record at playing doctor figured in one of the CBS programming department's several schemes to
recreate in other series the spirit and popularity of *M*A*S*H*.

The idea was sparked by the 1975 departure from *M*A*S*H* of Wayne
Rogers, the actor who played Trapper John McIntyre, Hawkeye's sidekick in high jinks and comradeship. The producers felt that since Rogers was identified closely with the character, it ought to be written out
of the show. But Kim LeMasters, the network's chief program developer, saw no reason why Trapper couldn't crop up in another incarnation played by a different actor.

"Fox still owned the character," Brinkley pointed out. "And Kim
LeMasters came to Frank and me and said, 'Hey, you guys know medicine. . . . Here's an irreverent character, a fun character. And we'd
like to see him as a civilian doctor.'"

The near-guarantee of getting a slot in prime time was a carrot
Glicksman and Brinkley found hard to turn down. Still, they approached LeMasters's suggestions cautiously. He originally wanted them
to create a series around Trapper John as a doctor directly after the
Korean War, in the 1950s. Larry Gelbart would later come up with a
similar concept for *AfterM*A*S*H*. But Brinkley and Glicksman balked.
The 1950s, Brinkley averred, "was a dull period. Not particularly inter-

esting cinematically, pictorially, whatever. And to do '50s medicine is very difficult, you know."

So they hit on the idea of placing Trapper almost thirty years into the future, in the late 1970s. The premise had some attractive tensions built into it. "Trapper has middle aged," Don Brinkley explained. "He's become an authority figure, an establishment figure. But his sentiments are still with the maverick. So we have a kid come in who is just like he was back in his youth. And we built the relationship. . . . We had to keep this kid—Gonzo, at the time—a troublemaker. Someone who was a good doctor, but who did things in a very unconventional way.

"Well," Brinkley recalled with satisfaction, "CBS loved that." No wonder: it was the classic formula with a sprinkle of novelty. Here was the traditional older doctor/younger doctor premise that had worked so well going back to *Kildare*. The compelling twist, one that seemed to fit with the times, was that the older doc no longer even tried to wear a sage face and constantly tell his younger colleague the facts of life. To the contrary, the older doctor here was sometimes sparked to unconventional action because of the presence of his younger colleague. Trapper saw in Gonzo's unorthodox attitudes and dwelling a style he had once lived himself. Partly out of nostalgia, partly out of admiration, he was drawn to Gonzo as a buddy. The two ended many episodes on the roof of Gonzo's motor home "Titanic," sipping wine and laughing congenially.

The network brass also liked the rest of the mix Glicksman and Brinkley added to *Trapper John*. Here was a classic television recipe for innovation: a huge helping of the old with a touch of the new. Here was the standard good-looking nurse (the doctors called her "Ripples"), the standard tough nurse ("Starch"), the standard obstructionist administrator, and the standard acute life-and-death drama. All this as made just a bit novel by the comic interplay of the unorthodox doctors as they faced their patients' problems and their own.

The pilot, written by Don Brinkley, clearly aimed to evoke the manic atmosphere of *M*A*S*H* by creating a war-like situation in which to introduce the characters. Gonzo, a jobless *M*A*S*H* veteran of Vietnam, shows up at San Francisco Memorial to apply for work with Trapper, the famous surgeon from the Korean conflagration. He walks in the door to see emergency cases flooding the hospital from a major hotel fire. With the hospital's staff swamped, Gonzo pitches in with scalpel and clamps without going through any formalities of presenting his credentials and getting them approved.

Two subplots revolve around the casualties coming out of the fire. The hectic situation reaches a crisis when a patient in one of the subplots suffers a heart attack at about the same time administrator Stanley Riverside realizes Gonzo has been operating with Trapper illegally.

Stanley makes a fuss, Trapper resolves the situation, Gonzo stays, and the loose plot ends all are tied together by the hour's end.

The subplots, and the episode in general, might have come right out of *Medical Center* were it not for *M*A*S*H*-like comedy that overlaid the crisis atmosphere—the flip jokes the physicians told amid the chaos, the crude references to Nurse "Ripples." Even visually the intent was to evoke connections with *M*A*S*H*. At the opening title, dramatic helicopter photography zeros in on San Francisco Memorial Hospital in a way that is reminiscent of the aerial beginnings of the Korea-based show.

The look was conceived by the episode's director, Jackie Cooper. Cooper had played the title character in *Hennesey*, TV's first medical sitcom. During the 1970s, he had turned increasingly to directing and had directed a number of *M*A*S*H* episodes for his friend, producer Gene Reynolds. It was just the kind of experience Glicksman, Brinkley, and LeMasters wanted in their bid to build an audience for *Trapper John* based on the *M*A*S*H* name.

The bid extended even to subtle actions by the CBS Television Network's publicity office. More often than not, press releases about upcoming *Trapper* episodes were listed on the same page as descriptions of the *M*A*S*H* stories for that week. Network P.R. people were clearly hoping the newspaper columnists who received the releases would see the connection and make the readers aware of it now and again.

From Glicksman and Brinkley's standpoint, though, the *M*A*S*H*-inspired colorations on their new doctor show did not change their feeling that they were essentially doing what they had done for decades. They enlisted Walter Dishell, the surgeon who had started his TV consulting as a script advisor for them on *Medical Center*, and who had worked on *M*A*S*H*, to help out on *Trapper*. They hired some of the same writers, and often used the same basic stories they had used in *Medical Center*. Repeating plots and mixing old and new subplots was a way to work with what was proven and generally uncontroversial. Virtually any idea could be refurbished for the new format.

As in *Medical Center*, the creators' concern was not with the politics of medicine or the specifics of disease. If there were a major departure from the past, it was that, in the manner of *M*A*S*H* and some short-lived medical dramas of the '70s, the running characters were saddled with personal difficulties that often made up the most important plot line.

John Whelpley, the story editor, contended that "for the show to work, [an] emotional dilemma has to land in the lap of our regulars, particularly Trapper and Gonzo." The series, he said, is "about people who work together in a hospital. . . . They have romantic problems, they've got financial problems, they've got stress. They've got emotional things that place a burden on them when they work in a very tough kind of emotional field."

But, Whelpley added, the traditional doctor-patient relationship was there as well; the show tried to keep the old with the new. For example:

—A microsurgery specialist at the hospital accidentally shoots his wife and is too traumatized to operate on a young man who needs surgery or will lose his arm. Trapper must take over the delicate procedure. Meanwhile, he himself is wrestling with an emotional problem of his own involving a burglary and the possible repetition of it.

—Someone is killing patients at San Francisco Memorial, and the investigating detective's prime suspect seems to be Dr. Sarah Franklin, the hospital's new pain therapy specialist. Gonzo also falls under suspicion, while Trapper tries to sort out all of this under the burden of a romantic interest in the new physician.

—A nurses' strike seems ready to hit the hospital. Can Trapper and the hospital somehow continue patient care? Will Gonzo be able to carry on a fulfilling romance with his current flame, a nurse, when she is on the picket line? Can "Starch" weather the painful presence of an old flame, a union negotiator, especially when he is stricken ill and is admitted to the soon-to-be-struck hospital?

"The advantage to a medical show," Don Brinkley observed, making the same comment that was made by Jim Moser about *Ben Casey* and by Al Ward about *Medical Center*, "is that you can go in any direction. You can do a mystery, you can do a plain human emotional drama; you can do comedy, you can do anything."

There had been, he was quick to note, changes across the decades in the kinds of subjects that could be raised. "We can talk about a woman's period today, which we couldn't do then," he offered. "We had a *Trapper* show recently where Nurse Shoop is working temporarily as a school nurse. And one of the high school girls comes in and doesn't want to go swimming. And they talk about her period and how they feel about it.

"We never could have done that in *Casey*. Never. In *Medical Center*, we were beginning to edge up to it. *Medical Center* was not quite as frank as we are in *Trapper John*."

In general, Brinkley suggested, it wasn't so much the kinds of diseases he and his writers would deal with that was different from his earlier hit but the way they could treat them.

"Television has grown up in the last fifteen years," Brinkley said. "There was a time when you couldn't use the word pregnant. Now you can deal a little more honestly and seriously with the aspects of each problem."

Just as important, he added, was the new leeway in approaching continuing physicians of a series. The show had a purposeful air of comedy Brinkley tagged irreverence. Much of *Trapper John, M.D.*, was built around the antics and eccentricities of its running characters.

"We couldn't do some of the irreverence in *Ben Casey* that we do now," he said. He added that the same was true about *Medical Center* and *Trapper John. Medical Center* was "a little more pious, a little more righteous. The doctor was god. . . . The hospital was a citadel, you know."

But Brinkley cautioned, with all the changes, there were still limits to the kind of irreverence that physicians on TV could have and to the way that diseases should be shown. It was a sore point with him, because the creators of the doctor show that was the darling of the press in the 1980s, *St. Elsewhere*, were breaking those rules and tweaking the creators of *Trapper John* while they were doing it.

"Life's Like a Penis"

The difference in approach between the companies producing the shows came down to a difference in philosophy and style. Working under the aegis of the giant Twentieth Century-Fox film factory, Brinkley and Glicksman were admittedly traditional TV creators trying to create the most popular, and profitable, entertainment. By contrast, MTM Enterprises, *St. Elsewhere*'s home, was known in and out of the industry as a firm willing to take chances with "quality" ideas. It cultivated bright, ambitious young production talents, members of the first TV generation, who were consciously trying to work against, rather than with, the grain of many TV traditions.

The two production groups could take the same elements of the doctor-show formula and work with them toward contrasting goals. An example is the very different way *M*A*S*H*'s influence made itself felt in the creation of *St. Elsewhere* compared with the way it was used to develop *Trapper John*. In *St. Elsewhere*'s case the link was not as direct as it was with *Trapper*, but it was clear. It lay in *Elsewhere*'s more obvious connection with *Hill Street Blues*, itself a highly unorthodox series that hit NBC's airwaves in January 1981.

Hill Street Blues had germinated the year before, when Fred Silverman, then president of NBC television, suggested to Brandon Tartikoff, his chief programmer, and Michael Zinberg, the vice president for comedy development, that what the network needed was "a cop show in a neighborhood with a heavy ethnic mix." Tartikoff and Zinberg, in turn, approached two producers from MTM, Michael Kozoll and Steven Bochco. The two had worked on police dramas a few years before. Police dramas had been out of style for a while because of an anti-violence swing against TV, but Silverman was convinced the form was coming back. MTM, with a good reputation among the critics as well as a track record for drawing audiences, might smooth the path.

The NBC executives stressed that Silverman wanted a nervy, rough show from the viewpoint of police on a real-world frontier. Paddy Chayevsky's movie *Hospital* was cited for its ragged, frantic style, its near-surrealistic depiction of the horrors of medical life, its mockery of the conventions of medical shows. David Gerber's *Police Story* TV series was cited because its police had personal lives. Most of all, to Bochco and Kozoll, the NBC executives mentioned *M*A*S*H* and ABC's police sitcom *Barney Miller*. It came down to "a little bit of *M*A*S*H*, a little bit of *Barney Miller*. We'd like you to develop a show that has more to do with cops' personal lives."[1]

Kozoll and Bochco agreed to work on the idea on the condition that "the programming people would genuinely leave us alone to do what we wanted to do."[2] Tartikoff agreed, and the network got a lot more than it bargained for. *Hill Street Blues* was a startling television series, as much for its frenetic, quick-cutting pictorial style, its large ensemble cast, and its many plot tangents, as its gritty view of the world. Although its early ratings were dismal, Silverman and Tartikoff held on to it as a message from the then number-three network that it would support Hollywood creativity. They were rewarded after the first year when the series, after winning a gaggle of Emmy awards, began to climb sharply in popularity.

According to some insiders, that is when Silverman said, "Now we can do Hill Street in a hospital." Brandon Tartikoff remembered that when he arrived at NBC in 1980, he heard about an MTM pilot, *Operating Room*, that had been commissioned by Silverman in 1979. The film was an exceedingly irreverent look at surgeons in a major hospital. Written by Bruce Paltrow and produced by Mark Tinker, the serio-comedy focused on the competitiveness, moneymaking urges, and libidinous drives of a group of surgeons. A good part of the program was taken up with showing the unmarried physicians after hours, relaxing with woman friends in an opulent hot tub.

At the time, Silverman had nixed the program on the grounds that such a degree of irreverence about medicine wouldn't yet be accepted by audiences on a weekly basis. "Let's try it with a cop show first," he said, "and if it works we'll do it with doctors." When *Hill Street* clicked, he began to think again of a medical drama.

The idea must have been in the air, because even a bit before *Hill Street*'s ascendance, a thirty-year-old writer at MTM, Josh Brand, went to Grant Tinker, the head of the company, with the idea of creating the medical series that became *St. Elsewhere*. Brand had been a literature major at City College of New York, and had a master's degree in literature from Columbia under his belt. For the previous two years he had worked on scripts for *The White Shadow*, a moderately successful MTM show series about a high school basketball team. He had become good friends with another young writer on the show, John Falsey. When the series was due to fold after its third year, both went to Tinker individually to discuss the future.

Tinker turned the questioning around. "What do you want to do?" he asked each of them.

"John said he wanted to do a movie or something," Brand recalled.

"But my oldest friend, who I've known since I was ten, was at the time a medical student at the Cleveland Clinic. And I would speak to him all the time. He would say, 'Boy, somebody ought to do something [on TV] about a teaching hospital.'

"So I went up to Grant Tinker and said, 'Well, do a television show about a teaching hospital.' And he said, '*Hill Street* in the hospital. Great!'"

At the time, Brand says, he hadn't even seen *Hill Street Blues*; the show was just in its first season. Tinker, however, guided him toward the idea of creating a medical show with the same serial form, ensemble casting, grittiness, and sense of humor. Thinking he understood, Brand let Falsey in on the idea, and the two expected they would have some time to work on it.

They were wrong. The word spread quickly that Tinker had gone to NBC to pitch a medical show and that the network had ordered a number of episodes. Moving into high gear, Tinker recruited virtually the entire *White Shadow* production team to work on the new series. Bruce Paltrow would be the executive producer; Mark Tinker and John Masius would be line producers, and Brand and Falsey would lead the writing team.

The quick unfolding of events disappointed Brand. He had intended to spend a lot of time with his buddy at the Cleveland Clinic getting a feel for realistic medicine. What he ended up doing, instead, was spending five days there, following the residents around in a manner that harked back to Jim Moser's escapades at L.A. County during the 1950s, escapades that led to *Medic* and *Ben Casey*.

Brand was barely in his teens when those shows were aired, and he hardly remembered them. He suspected, though, that they weren't really reality-based. "I'm not a guy who's familiar with television, and I wasn't familiar with other television medical shows. I mean, I remember vaguely *Ben Casey* and *Kildare*, and though I never watched *Marcus Welby* I knew what kind of a guy he was. And that always seemed to me very silly. And you know, I remember when we first did [*St. Elsewhere*] and were meeting with the press, I said, 'I don't know about you, but I never had a doctor come to my house and knock on the door and ask how I'm feeling today."

Brand's friend at the Cleveland Clinic did his best to try to reinforce the notion that TV's doctor shows from *Kildare* through *Trapper John* simply had the wrong feel for the way physicians behave. He showed him that doctors made jokes in surgery and listened to music; he encouraged the other residents to talk freely and sometimes crudely about patients in Brand's presence. He told him that much of medicine is based on "statistics and luck-of-the-draw and that [often] doctors don't cure anything."

Brand also learned in the Cleveland Clinic about a novel that was popular with residents around the country, *The House of God* by Asher

Shem, a physician. A 1978 satire on medical school and residency, *The House of God* had a ribaldly cynical view of the teaching hospital world, and it revolved around a Boschean array of characters. "Life's like a penis," said the introduction to Part I. "When it's soft you can't beat it; when it's hard you get screwed." And Part II's introduction, intoning the purpose of the residents' frenetic hospital gauntlet, borrowed the words of a Spanish explorer of Mexico, "We came here to serve God, and to get rich."[3]

The book seemed in its own way to reflect for Brand and Falsey the realism their sources at the Cleveland Clinic were trying to impress upon them. Cinematically, they considered the movie *Hospital* inspirational. The next step was creating the setting, plot approach, and characters. Taking a cue from Grant Tinker's suggestion of *Hill Street* in a hospital, they saw their locale as not the *House of God*'s high-profile edifice with a grand reputation, but a marginal teaching hospital in a run-down area. From the residents' standpoint, they argued, the hospital ran an inhumane "hazing process" that wore people down, made them angry at their patients, and often placed people's lives in jeopardy.

Brand and Falsey were focusing on the same aspects of the profession that Frederick Faust had seized on when creating Dr. Kildare in the 1930s. Their approach, though, turned many of Faust's verities upside down. To them, the hard life of the neophyte doctors had little to do with the development of the noblesse oblige life philosophy in which Faust reveled. Rather, it emerged out of the most pragmatic of needs from a hospital standpoint: the need for a cheap labor pool. The mixture of high pressure, competition for position, and lack of sleep was volatile, and it was this volatility that Brand and Falsey wanted to explore. They also wanted to explore what they saw as the most interesting part of medicine, the detective work leading to understanding the cause of a disease.

From the start, and in tune with the *Hill Street* model, they were more interested in the physicians than in the patients. Seen from the perspective of the world-weary residents of the Cleveland Clinic and *The House of God*, the patients became another set of environmental pressures among the constant flow of concerns frazzling the workaday lives of the physicians. Television's traditional doctor-patient relationship was pushed far to the side. "If we are drawing from reality," Brand contended, "then patients' and doctors' interactions are superficial. I mean, people don't go out to lunch with their anesthesiologist."

They drew on a roster of characters based on residents and staff physicians they had met at the Cleveland Clinic. The basic principle was that the older doctors—characters such as Craig, Westphall, Auslander—were very good physicians, though flawed characters in their personal lives. Craig, for example, was a racist. The residents (including a black one) were a decidedly mixed bag in terms of their medical expertise as well as their personalities.

They knew they had to include nurses, and they even inserted a hospital orderly (a black man). "But the heart of the show, and what was most interesting to us," Brand added, "were the residents." "Because they were sort of combinations of doctors and students, and really, they're sort of not doctors yet, and yet they're thrown into life and death situations. And that's interesting."

The next step in the rush toward production was to put some scripts together. The network wanted the pilot written right away so they could put it on that fall. Brand and Falsey traveled to Williamstown, Massachusetts, where Bruce Paltrow was spending the summer, to work on the script themselves. It was then that the tension between their vision and the visions of the other *White Shadow* collaborators began to clash.

Dr. Death and Mr. Depression

Tom Fontana claimed Brand and Falsey really didn't have a coherent dramatic vision. Fontana's experience with the new doctor show was his initiation into the TV business. A struggling New York playwright who had become acquainted with Bruce Paltrow in Williamstown, he was invited by Paltrow to help write the scripts in Los Angeles. "I was so thrilled to be making ten thousand dollars that they could literally have hit me with bricks and I would have said 'Fine, just give me the check.'

"But what happened is that Bruce had said to me in Williamstown, 'I'm really in an advisory capacity. Masius, Mark Tinker, Falsey, and Brand are going to be the four producers of the show.' So I slid [into L.A.] in November of '81 to do my first script, which was the third episode of the first season. And there was—I mean, it was like a battle zone!"

All hell had begun to break loose in Williamstown and it had continued at the MTM offices in Studio City. Masius and Tinker were on one side, Brand and Falsey on the other. "And I was totally naïve about the whole thing," Fontana remembered. "I thought, 'Gee, this must be the way television is done.' Because at the same time that I was learning, I was also realizing that [neither] Falsey [nor] Brand—and really nobody—had a clue [to] what the show was supposed to be. And all we knew is that we were drowning and rather than climbing into the boat and rowing together everybody was trying to knock somebody out."

Masius certainly knew what he didn't like about Brand and Falsey's approach. First, he didn't like their insistence on total control over the creative direction of the show. A thirty-one-year-old Wharton Business School graduate who had gone on to get an MBA from UCLA, Masius carried a zeal for theatrical writing that had impelled him toward the TV business. He had assisted Bruce Paltrow and Mark Tinker on *The White Shadow* and was eager to get in on the ground floor in shaping the new medical series. But Brand and Falsey, he found, wanted no real input into the pilot of the show or its basic direction.

"It was like no one could have an idea," he said. "You weren't allowed to have an idea." He contended that Brand and Falsey acted as if all their ideas came from creative wellsprings within them, when, in reality, they were borrowing rabidly from a number of sources. Even the show's title, he had found out, came from a line in the novel *The House of God* which referred to teaching hospitals that no residents wanted to visit.

Masius and Fontana had become quick allies in resistance. One problem, they contended, was that Brand and Falsey were taking their short experience at the Cleveland Critic too seriously. They had written copious notes and recorded much dialogue from personnel at the hospital. Their aim was to use that in early scripts to lend them a feeling of realism. The difficulty, according to Masius and Fontana, was that Brand and Falsey were insisting on using verbatim hospital exchanges whether they understood them or not. For example, they insisted that when, in a script, one of the orderlies said, "Looks like kings confy to me," it would make a nurse angry. When others on the show asked why and inquired about the meaning of the phrase, Brand simply said to trust him, this was an expression that would make a hospital nurse angry. Instead of trusting them, Fontana suspected they had gotten the phrase from the tapes. He went back to the tapes and heard someone say, "Looks like Kings County [hospital] to me." The phrase had been transcribed incorrectly, Fontana said scornfully, and Brand and Falsey had had used it in the dialogue, even though they didn't understand it.

Incidents such as this made Masius and Fontana fear for the coherence of the show. But they had even more basic problems with Brand and Falsey's notion of realism. The generally cold tone they saw evolving in the scripts was of particular concern. Patients whom the viewer didn't get to know were allowed to die throughout every episode, for no apparent dramatic reason. "It was like Auschwitz," Masius contended. "It really was. It had the same mentality. They would randomly pick people to die. And they thought because that's real, it's OK."

Brand agreed the hospital that he and Falsey were creating was pretty dismal, cynical, dark. "John and I were sort of nicknamed Dr. Death and Mr. Depression,' he admitted, "because a lot of people were dying in this hospital and a lot of people were wheeled out on stretchers." Yet he had no apologies for portraying what he saw as real. "Hospitals are not particularly happy places," he said.

There were other philosophical battles with bottom-line consequences for the scripts. Masius and Fontana found themselves arguing with Brand and Falsey about the way episodes were to be structured, about the need for action and visualness, and about the need for dramatic tension throughout an episode. They complained about a plot on Legionnaire's disease that ran across a number of episodes, only to end with a short phone call from the Centers for Disease Control. It was a nonvisual, anticlimactic way to end an important story line, they agreed. Falsey added that it was simply bad drama. But it wasn't changed.

More broadly, Masius and Fontana argued against Brand's contention that as long as an idea about a character was interesting it was fine to build a scene around it even if the idea had no relation to any other scene in the show. Plotting, Brand felt, was not nearly as important as interesting scenes, even if the scenes went nowhere. "Being a playwright, that was very hard for me to adapt to," said Fontana. "And I was going crazy because I didn't know how to do it. We weren't telling stories."

Beyond these problems lay a problem of program definition that everyone felt. Fred Silverman had bought "*Hill Street* in a hospital." Network publicists began to use that phrase, as well. But the producers and writers were not sure what it meant. "The fact of the matter is," Fontana said, "because police stations are basically blue-collar mentality and men who work in hospitals are basically white-collar, very educated guys, it was never going to be the same. There were never going to be shootouts, there was never going to be much street action. So what we were basically trying to do was *Hill Street Blues* in the hospital without doing it."

NBC programmers didn't get involved in the niceties of trying to resolve that difficulty. They treaded lightly as the show was being developed. The most prominent network suggestion was to make sure that at least one of the physicians involved was a romantic lead, a Kildare type. Brand and Falsey had intended to make one of their characters a charismatic physician, but they were chagrined to be told by the network that a particular actor, David Birney, who had starred in his own series a few years before, should be that person. Brand and Falsey took a kind of revenge by establishing Birney's character clearly as part of the ensemble, not a standout. Moreover, they made him a lecher, a chaser of virtually every woman in the house.

Masius (as a producer) and Fontana (as a story editor) didn't quarrel with that delicious irony. Overall, though, they found the experience of working within Brand and Falsey's dictates depressing. Especially discouraging was the mandate that the production company had to turn out thirteen episodes of the serial before airing. Because of the development difficulties and a writers' strike during the summer of 1981, a fall 1981 start for the series had turned out to be an impossibility. There were network developments that had affected the show, as well. Fred Silverman's regime at NBC had ended. His successor was none other than Grant Tinker, who had sold *St. Elsewhere* to Silverman just two months before assuming his chair. Now Tinker had to judge the scripts his former company was turning out.

According to Masius, Fontana, and Paltrow, the new NBC chairman read the first four scripts and hated them. Still, as the production process was moving ahead and since filming was beginning, it seemed clear that NBC couldn't simply jettison the project. Too much money had been spent. Looking for alternatives, programming executives flirted with the idea of taking the finished episode and editing them into a miniseries. The results were unacceptable. "It looked like *Benny Hill.*" Masius said, referring to a British comedy series that constantly danced with absurdity.

Another problem for NBC at the time was that it didn't have enough strong new series on-line. Nothing had really been commissioned that was plausibly much better than *St. Elsewhere.* The network had little alternative, then, but to schedule it for a fall 1982 start.

John Masius contended that "everyone" at MTM hated the show. For his part, he said, he hoped the series would fold quickly and he would go on to other MTM-supported work. "I was desperate for the show to be cancelled after thirteen weeks," he said.

It wasn't, even though the ratings were horrible opposite a romantic series on ABC called *Hotel.* Part of the reason it was not cancelled was that evaluations in the newspapers and magazines of the plotting, the style, and the acting were glowing. In different words, reviewers around the country echoed Jay Cocks, who, writing in *Time* magazine, said the program "may be the best on the box."[4]

That kind of praise meant a lot to NBC executives who, struggling to get out of the ratings cellar, wanted to keep a quality image in certain selected areas of their schedule while they looked to violent shows like *The A-Team* and insipid sitcoms like *Different Strokes* to ignite large audience numbers. In addition, they hoped the good publicity that was being generated about *St. Elsewhere* would help if find a substantial audience, as had happened with *Hill Street Blues.* Supporting a critically acclaimed show also had a more subtle purpose. It was a message to Hollywood production firms to come first to NBC with good ideas, since the network was willing to be an innovative, forward-looking TV force.

Still, NBC programmers didn't see themselves in the charity business. *St. Elsewhere*'s ratings got no better in the spring, and the show languished near the bottom of the prime-time ratings list. The network stepped in with research that suggested the audience wanted more shows from the patient's point of view. The last point made a lot of sense to Tartikoff because it tied this series firmly into the doctor-show tradition. "Someone watching the show who comes from the *Marcus Welby* school can at least be satisfied that there will be one element of the story that won't be so radical, a patient who needs to be cured and is cured."[5]

Some accommodations in this direction were made, but the show still hovered in the Nielsen cellar. It seemed clear to everyone that *St. Elsewhere* would not get picked up for the following year. Brandon Tartikoff, still head programmer in the Tinker regime, had even told executive producer Bruce Paltrow to expect cancellation. Then came the turnaround: the last episode of *St. Elsewhere*, competing against CBS reruns, attracted respectable ratings. The next day, Tinker, Tartikoff, and other NBC executives agreed not to cancel the series unless a sure-fire hit—"a perfect pilot"—could replace it. "It turned out our pilot development didn't measure up to *St. Elsewhere*," Tartikoff told the press, "so we renewed it."[6]

What really happened quickly became a matter for the gossip mills. Some snickered that Grant Tinker had insisted on keeping the show on the schedule because his son Mark was involved. Others said NBC executives simply wanted to continue their nod to quality with the hope that the show would ultimately make it. Still others, Masius and Fontana among them, insisted the last show of the series was really the beginning of a new *St. Elsewhere* and that the NBC programmers sensed it.

In Masius and Fontana's version, Paltrow, finally fed up with the infighting on the production line, had ordered Brand and Falsey to listen to the others more. Increasingly alienated, the two creators participated less in the process. As a result, Paltrow gave Masius, Fontana, and Tinker the go-ahead to do whatever they wanted for the last episode. "Our hearts were full of revenge and anger," Masius recalled. "So we just basically said, 'Fuck, let's write the show we want to write.'"

That show happened to get higher than normal ratings and happened to become a topic of discussion among the programmers at the very meeting at which Tartikoff was going to announce the show's cancellation. "Why are we going to cancel a show that we all watch?" Tartikoff asked his colleagues. And they made the decision to save it.[7]

But saving it also meant changing it, and this was clear to both the network programmers and the *St. Elsewhere* production staff. In "Addiction," the final show of the 1982–83 season, Masius, Fontana, and Tinker had begun to establish where they wanted to go with their setting and characters, now that Brand and Falsey had left (they were not to return). Their priority was to tell stories that viewers would be able to follow even when the tales went across episodes. "Basically," said Falsey, "we decided to tell five stories. We had a common theme of addiction. It was drug addiction, alcohol addiction, sexual addiction—that kind of thing. In a very subtle way."

Another priority was humor. "We put into that first script a lot of humor," Falsey continued. "A lot of our kind of humor. Like Fiscus going down to the morgue and asking for the results of the Nielsen autopsy. You know, the family that died in front of the TV set."

Humor was to be part of an overall, balanced tone. "Just a lot of elements. We did a thing about the birth of Morrison's child, that was also a thread going through the episode. So there was the celebration of life and there were also the deaths, but the people who died you knew from that episode about who they were."

It was a lighter approach than before, and it was exactly in the direction Tartikoff wanted. He and Tinker told Paltrow that in return for renewing the series they expected a cheerier atmosphere to go with the heavy doses of medical reality. "Grant said it would be nice if it was a lighter, brighter place, with the possibility that more people could leave well," Paltrow recalled. Tartikoff added that NBC's research had determined that the show needed "more simplified storytelling and more upbeat stories," as well as more romance to attract female viewers.[8]

The grateful St. Elsewhere producers were eager to oblige, though at the same time that they wanted to keep the program fresh and not too predictable. Thematically, they decided to stick with the initial idea by Brand and Falsey to focus much more on the hospital staff than on the patients. A few episodes did stress guest star patients such as Alan Arkin and Mabel Mercer, but the producer fell back to focusing on their ensemble for the grist of their plots. "This show," said Fontana, "is ultimately about a bunch of men and women in a very tough situation trying to do the best they can."

In fact, it was the patients who made up a large part of what made life in a St. Elsewhere episode tough for the doctors and nurses. Adopting the hero-as-victim perspective implicit in M*A*S*H and Hill Street Blues, St. Elsewhere went farther than any previous doctor series in portraying patients as part of a threatening, problem-causing environment for doctors. Previous doctor dramas typically had physicians acting as catalysts who helped patients explore (and often resolve) their emotional and physical difficulties. Patients in St. Elsewhere, by contrast, were more often the cause of wide-ranging personal problems for the physicians responsible for dealing with them.

These patients were sometimes serious figures, such as prisoners who raped Morrison while he worked in a prison. More often they were comic figures such as Mrs. Hofnagle, a hypochondriac who used her biting wit to terrorize a fat resident, and John Doe, a psychiatric patient with a mania for adopting new identities who created problems throughout the hospital. Still other times, guest patients were irrelevant to medical plots, as the patients and the would-be healers became one and the same. For example, Dr. Auslander was bedeviled with chronic cancer; Dr. Craig's operating hand became incapacitated; and Dr. Bobby Caldwell contracted AIDS.

An important way St. Elsewhere differed from most previous hospital series was in its tendency to deal with chronic illness that did not necessarily have a sure-fire cure. Since the stories often ran across episodes, the writers had less need than the writers of Trapper John, say, to wrap up the problem within an hour. As a result, plots chose such difficulties as a young girl's liver failure, a couple's infertility problems, and the problems of living with an autistic child.

The actual approach to medicine the creators took varied little from the routines doctor-show producers and writers had established during the past two decades. Throughout the shooting season, they hired an on-site operating room nurse from L.A. County Hospital (first Tia Dankowski, then Barbara Krause) to order relevant equipment for scenes and make sure all actions looked realistic. The producers hired a thirty-three-year-old internist, Dr. Nancy Good, to judge the scripts for accuracy, to add correct jargon to the script (which the writers would often denote by writing "medical bullshit here"), and to answer questions from writers and story editors about how to match plot needs with appropriate diseases.

Typical questions along these lines were very much in the *St. Elsewhere* mode of focusing more on the problems of the residents than on the patients. "If [a certain character] were going to have an existential crisis," a story editor asked, "what would be the medical case that would come in and do this to him?" In one episode, for example, Good helped the writers settle on the death of a homeless man in the emergency room as an event that triggers Dr. Wayne Fiscus's outburst over his frustration with city-hospital medicine.[9]

All involved prided themselves on their attempts to keep the techniques as medically authentic as possible, from the donning of surgical gloves to the performance of CPR. In the press, and on talk shows, members of the cast and crew proudly announced that this was the most realistic doctor show ever. Barbara Krause, the *Washington Post* said, even used videotapes of real operations to coach actors who had to "perform surgery." The writers and story editors tried to be scrupulous in handling diseases, to appease eagle-eyed medical viewers who would write in to complain about every inaccuracy as well as out of a genuine concern that people in the audience learn correct information.[10]

"For instance," said Falsey, "we wanted to do a story about testicular cancer. John [Masius] and I had a conversation about it and realized that we were supposed to be doing self-examinations. We're in the age range when you're most likely to get the disease. So we started to read about it, to talk about it. What were the implications? How would it affect the [college student patient] himself? And that's how the story evolved."

They had already won a fight with NBC's censors over using the word testicle the year before, so it was permissible to use the word again. The producers now argued unsuccessfully, though, to allow the student to use the more colloquial term "balls." More significantly, the censors didn't like the entire premise about a testicular cancer story, since it really hadn't been dealt with in TV fiction before.

But Fontana and Masius had learned to play in the censors' own ballpark. They knew that women having mastectomies had become a common TV theme. "So we said, 'It's alright for us to lop off a woman's breast but not a guy's ball. Isn't that some kind of sexual discrimination?' And they said, 'Oh. Well, OK, you can do it.'"

Much in tune with the history of doctor shows, episodes about particular diseases often were reinforced by the associations that represented those diseases. The American Cancer Society, for example, commended the St. Elsewhere company for portraying Auslander as living a full professional life despite his liver problem. The subplot had begun under the Brand regime and had continued into the second year. One reason they kept Auslander had to do with the producers' respect for actor Norman Lloyd's acting abilities. But another reason for prolonging Auslander's life came from a self-consciousness about the Cancer Society's award.

"We've always intended to kill him off, but whenever we think of it, we get very misty," Fontana said. He added: "Also, the American Cancer Society has practically bronzed him, because it's the first show to have a person who has survived cancer."

They didn't hesitate to knock off other regulars on the show. Part of the creators' attempt to portray the reality of a hospital was to have people come and go for reasons that were mundane or comic or bizarre. Part of their attempt to portray reality, too, was to have the physicians in St. Eligius run the gamut of personality and fallibility. Over and over again, the producers tried to show the fallibility of doctors, strained relations among staff or between doctors and patients, and the ethical dilemmas that were part and parcel of the practice of medicine.

Bruce Paltrow, the executive producer, preferred to be upbeat about the show's message when talking to a Washington Post reporter. St. Elsewhere, he pointed out, is a derogatory hospital nickname sometimes used by real doctors on rounds when presenting the history of a patient newly arrived from another hospital that botched his care. "What we're trying to get across," Paltrow said, "is that there are people working in places that don't have all the patina [of great hospitals], but who do great work and really care."

But, as Fontana and Masius recognized, the message could just as easily be to beware of the St. Elsewheres of this world, which really could be anywhere. That, they admitted, had become part of their purpose. Falsey noted he hadn't watched doctor shows previously because they made him a hypochondriac. Nevertheless, he said he was aware that "they fed into a mythology that we have consciously been trying to shatter."

"We demystify doctors," Masius agreed, though he said it had become much less conscious than it had been at the start of their work. "We put them into a work situation where you understand how they function as human beings, not as gods." And, Fontana piped in, the message to the viewer was that "you've got to be a consumer; it's your fucking body."

A decade earlier, the characterization of occasional grievous errors as predictable results of hospital life might have brought an outcry from organized medicine. Now physicians said that they liked the show's handling of their fictional counterparts. The show seemed to be taking seriously the public appeals by physicians in the mid-1970s to be portrayed not as gods but as human beings who must often cope with the most difficult of circumstances to carry out their mandate.

"I don't know how they manage to do it where other shows don't, but it's really got so much of the tragicomedy of life in a hospital," a psychiatrist told the *Washington Post*. The chief resident at George Washington University Medical Center added: "Some things that happen in a hospital are bizarre, and people on the outside wouldn't believe it. From our point of view, [*St. Elsewhere*] sort of legitimates what goes on."[11]

But, the *Post* noted, the series had its critics as well, not so much because of its depiction of doctors as fallible as because it continued several of the same inaccuracies about hospital life that had plagued previous medical shows. Foremost among them was the presentation of hospital training. The residents seemed to a little bit of everything, and there was no end-point to their experience. They never "graduated."[12]

Masius, Fontana, and Paltrow, for their part, contended they weren't averse to criticism. Some complaints they had thought were particularly legitimate—such as the comments they received from nurses that the show underutilized the nursing profession—had been duly noted and corrected. Others—for example, the cavil that residents should always be assigned to specific specialties—were parried by invoking dramatic license. Confining characters too much to specialties would limit story possibilities, they pointed out.

Some aspects of medical storytelling that *St. Elsewhere* either continued or didn't were ignored by the press. In the category of continuing the doctor-show tradition was the program's failure to concern itself with the changing medical scene outside the hospital. Another was its failure to confront in any but the most superficial ways how the politics of medicine were forcing changes in doctors' approaches to their patients and residents' approaches to their medical futures.

One part of the doctor-show tradition *St. Elsewhere*'s producers chose to ignore were plots where controversial social issues were handled within the framework of a patient's medical problem. The anthological medical dramas of the 1960s and 1970s, especially *Kildare*, *Casey*, *The Nurses*, and *Marcus Welby*, had reveled in using the meeting of doctor and patient as a microcosm to examine the social implications of sub-

jects as diverse as prejudice, malpractice, and child abuse. MTM productions had crafted a well-received "issues show" called *Lou Grant*,
about a journalist, just a few years earlier. *St. Elsewhere*, it was clear,
was not that kind of production.

This is not to say there weren't echos of medical issues. Drs. Westphal and Auslander threw around the phrase "DRGs" every now and
then, a reference to government-mandated cost controls for treating
Medicare patients with particular illnesses. The possible sale of St. Eligius to an HMO became a cliff-hanger at the end of the fifth season.
And, in earlier years, some subplots even dealt with the politics of
medical miracles: Auslander's inability to get a young patient with a
dying liver into an experimental program in Boston General (he tried
his own bold solution, but it failed), and Craig's desire to conduct heart
transplants much to the chagrin of the city's health administrator (he
won). But these were unusual blips in a trajectory that typically avoided
the issues.

Beth Hill Shafer, an associate producer, explained that the creators
had simply made a decision not to go in that direction. Issues, she
said, were not the point of the show. The more private problems of
people were. Defending their decision to avoid the ins and outs of the
current medical world, Masius and Fontana suggested that those developments, and the politics of medicine in general, were "dull." Dull,
they stressed, was certainly not their goal. As a result, they made sure
compelling tales about their continuing characters were at the core of
every episode.

The continuing nature of the drama, while allowing a lot of freedom
for exploring stories, did have its dangers. The creators' biggest fear
was that the serial would turn into a soap opera. "Every so often we
get to the edge of a soap and go 'whoa,'" Fontana admitted to *USA
Today* in 1984. "We step back fast and do something like the 'Dreams'
episode to reestablish where we're coming from."[13]

That hour explored the hospital staff's inner thoughts through music
video and talking-to-the-dead sequences. It, and a near-death experience by Fiscus that involved images out of the show's past, was *St.
Elsewhere*'s equivalent to *M*A*S*H*'s black-and-white "interview" episodes. To keep *St. Elsewhere* fresh, the producers would intertwine
comedy and tragedy in surprising (sometimes even admittedly borderline tasteless) ways. They would make characters go through abrupt
changes, or even leave. And they would change the visual style of the
episodes drastically every now and then.

These aspects of the show garnered by far the most attention of the
newspaper and magazine writers who remarked on the program. They
were also the aspects that the producers and network programmers
figured had raised *St. Elsewhere* out of the very depths of Nielsen's
prime-time roster. Still, it ought to be stressed that ordinarily a series

with the numbers *St. Elsewhere* was getting would be a likely candidate for TV's trivia graveyard. NBC, however, had found a way to sell the show to advertisers that turned many of its eccentricities into gems.

Network researchers had discovered the program was primarily drawing women who were 18 to 49 years old. When judged on those grounds, the series ranked a respectable 24 out of 71 regular evening shows. That was good news because the 18- to 49-year-old female audience was a premium target for some advertisers. So, even though the Wednesday night hospital show ranked 51 out of 71 shows during fall 1984, it commanded ad sales ($105,000 for a thirty-second commercial) consistent with top-25 contenders such as CBS's *Cagney and Lacey* and *Murder, She Wrote.*[14]

Squarely in the middle of that desirable age group were the "baby boomers" of the post-World War II era. A large number of them, in turn, were what was known in the early 1980s as yuppies—intensely ambitious young urban professionals who were just beginning to settle and raise children in frenetic two-career households. From an income and opportunity standpoint, they actually comprised a small chunk of the thirtyish population. But media hype about them had broadcast their alleged "me generation" philosophy widely. These were, it was said, upscale consumers who wanted to have it all, who had transformed their 1960s reformist fervor into 1980s Wall Street fervor. They certainly had their angst and their failings. But even while yuppie had become a somewhat derogatory term, the yuppie's putative lifestyle had become one to identify with and emulate.

It was a lifestyle that increasingly had little time for broadcast television—what with VCRs, compact discs, pay cable, and other forms of indoor and outdoor entertainment. The programming powers at NBC, though, understood that *St. Elsewhere* could turn out to be a supreme yuppie-catcher. That is part of what Brandon Tartikoff, hardly forty, meant when he asked rhetorically at that fateful renewal meeting why he should cancel a show that the programmers sitting in the room— many of them yuppies—liked so much.

The show was created by yuppies (most of the well-paid staff weren't pushing 45). Perhaps more important, it was crafted to reflect the interests and problems of their generation. The focus on the personal (sexual, marital, physical) problems of the St. Eligius staff as opposed to the problems of patients or the politics of medicine certainly fit with the "me generation" approach. In addition, some stories cut straight to the heart of yuppie angst. One was the continuing 1986 tale that focused on a young couple's inability to have children. Another was the one that gave promiscuous Dr. Bobby Caldwell AIDS and had Wayne Fiscus, one of the residents, worriedly questioning his own sexual mores upon hearing about Caldwell's dismal situation.

The show also invoked the collective knowledge of the TV generation with comic allusions to the medium's history peppered throughout various episodes. A few of those references took direct shots at past and present doctor shows. Referring to Kay O'Brien, a physician bound for a surgical residency in a New York hospital (and not coincidentally the title character of a new CBS doctor show), an *Elsewhere* character quips that "she won't last thirteen weeks." In another episode, a resident refers to an anesthesiologist named Steven Kiley—the name of Marcus Welby's partner, who was a family physician, not an anesthesiologist. Perhaps the viewer was invited to conclude that Kiley had, yuppie-like, gotten so burned out on Welby's over-solicitous approach to the world that he had turned to a lucrative area of medicine that required minimal physician-patient interaction.

The producers admitted their yuppie orientation freely. Still, they took pains to emphasize to reporters that they were trying to reach their generation with a self-critical eye. Fontana, Masius, and Paltrow let it be known that they had traveled to see conditions in Ethiopia during spring 1985, with the intention of weaving a world hunger story into their plot scheme. In a manner typical of the show, though, that problem was transformed from a directly political issue to a catalyst for a search by a continuing character (Dr. Westphal) for inner peace and self-worth. Fontana told *USA Today*, in fact, that an underlying theme for many stories of the coming season would be the spiritual quest for a fuller, more generous purpose in life. "There's a certain part of you that wonders is that all there is," he said. "That's what we're trying to do with the infertility story. If anybody's doing the searching, it certainly connects with people our age." [15]

14

Elsewhere and Back

Despite *St. Elsewhere*'s high visibility in the press, a lot of people in the TV industry had problems with its approach. It was generally too odd or dismal, or both, to grab a real mass audience, they argued. Its serial format would be a hindrance to making a profit from syndication rights. They concluded the series was a luxury which could be indulged once or twice by a network trying to lure yuppie-oriented advertisers. It should not, they insisted, be generally imitated.

Even NBC's Brandon Tartikoff, who admitted to personally liking the program, confessed it provided an uncomfortably downbeat view of hospitals. He mentioned the young son of a friend who had an operation scheduled. The son had a very positive attitude toward hospitals and doctors, the friend said, and he attributed it to the images his boy had seen on television. "He surely wasn't watching *St. Elsewhere*," Tartikoff said ruefully. "If he had been, his attitude would be very different."

Trapper John's more optimistic view of hospitals was cited by a number of TV creators as a way that a series was most likely to be successful with huge audiences. Not that *Trapper* exited television in a blaze of ratings glory à la *M*A*S*H*. Rather, its ratings declined slowly, then quickly, beginning in 1984, while the producers tried to find ways to turn the show around. People connected to the series traced its demise to a number of interrelated factors—the death of Frank Glicksman in 1983, a decrease in compelling scripts, bad casting and weak characterization of a few new continuing characters, and the decreasing interest of Gregory Harrison in his key role as Gonzo Gates.

Harrison ultimately decided to leave the show, a move that led to the producers' greatest headaches. They had time to try replacements before he left. Unfortunately, neither the first nor the second actor whom they cast as a handsome, restless doctor worked out. Harrison's final season turned out to be the program's last.

As *Trapper John* limped along toward its last prime-time days during the spring of 1986, the producers and their story editor reached into the history of the doctor formula to hype viewing. The centerpiece attempt was a story in which Gonzo meets a woman, Fran, falls in love, and moves toward a marriage. To make the tale a bit different from the marriages of Steve Kiley, Quincy, and other TV protagonists in trouble with the ratings, they gave the couple the kinds of problems not typically associated with program heroes and heroines.

Fran develops muscular dystrophy. Gonzo, determined to marry her anyway and drive across the continent in the "Titanic," is then felled by a stroke that he must overcome slowly and painfully. In the end, they both hobble into the sunset, determined to make their trip the beginning of a long and wonderful life together.

The episodes had little effect on the trajectory of the show's ratings. Bowing to the inevitable, CBS ended *Trapper John* a bit ignominiously. It played off its final episodes away from the program's traditional Sunday night in a more expendable Monday slot. Still, viewed in perspective, the show had to be considered a solid success. Few prime-time series in the mid-1980s could claim such consistent ratings clout over more than six years.

So it was *Trapper John*'s style, not *St. Elsewhere*'s, that became the clue for producers about the way to go in TV medicine. That was the more traditional one, with the portrayal of medical regulars as idealistic, with a focus on acute care in a hospital where resources were unlimited and the walls were clean, with stories that ended on optimistic notes and presumably made viewers feel good. The one change both *Trapper John* and *St. Elsewhere* encouraged, a change that ironically linked the two with *M*A*S*H*, was a shift of the stories' focus from patients to their caretakers. Whereas in earlier years TV's medical personnel acted primarily as professionals who were dedicated to solving patients' difficulties, now there was greater, even primary, emphasis on the professionals' own problems.

Similar Angst

One of the shows that picked up on this emphasis was *Nurse*, on CBS Thursday at 10 for a year and a half beginning in the spring of 1981. "Mary Benjamin is not only a nurse but a mature, attractive woman alone in a big city after a long and happy marriage," a network press release quoted actress Michael Learned about her starring role. Among the problems faced by her character during the first several weeks, the press release emphasized, would be "the depression of a woman turning 40, the worries of a mother over a college-student son out on his own, her dating for the first time in twenty years, and facing unwelcome news about her past."[1]

Similar angst on the part of the part of a main character was exhibited in another CBS doctor show, *Kay O'Brien*, which premiered in fall 1986, also as a Thursday, 10 p.m. show. About a woman resident trying to make it in the man's world of surgery, a large part of each episode focused on her difficulties in meshing career and home life, particularly love life. Similarly, the CBS 1985–86 situation comedy *E/R*, about the staff of a hospital emergency room, tended to focus on the seriocomic personal problems of the staff. At the center of the goings-on was Dr. Sheinfeld, a cigar-smoking, smart-alecky but expert physician whose former wife and teenage daughter were only two of the many problems in his neurotic life.

Each of these shows did have distinctive attributes. *Nurse*, based on a popular 1978 book, was the first drama series since the early 1960s to focus on the nursing profession. *Kay O'Brien* was the first program since *Julie Farr, M.D.*, in the mid-1970s to revolve around a woman physician (Kay played the younger doctor to two older male surgeons). And *E/R*, based on a theatrical play popular in Chicago, had a clearly Jewish doctor working in an ethnically mixed environment where the Asian receptionist was romantically involved with a black security guard.

But it was clear even to many of the creators that while these novel characteristics tagged the shows as different, they were very much surface changes that tied into the contemporary emphasis on physicians' humanness. At bottom, creators knew, most of the character types and constraints of the old doctor-show formula remained. William Asher, who launched *Kay O'Brien*, said his special concern in the series was to portray a successful woman surgeon, much as his impetus in creating *Temperatures Rising* over a decade earlier had been to portray a successful black surgeon.

Kay O'Brien was a tough sell. In the mid-1980s, network programmers still resisted drama series about women. And after he won, Asher found himself constantly compromising on his approach to medicine in the show.

One compromise was not that difficult for him to accept. Intent on towing what he considered a "realistic" line, Asher wanted O'Brien assigned to a hospital that actually existed. He decided to make her a second-year surgery resident at Manhattan's Bellevue Hospital. Hospital administrators allowed Bellevue's name to be used, but on the condition that they approve the pilot script.

Bellevue had been recently named by the New York Board of Health as one of the six worst hospitals in the city; the place could use a positive TV image. Asher, who defended it as "one of the best teaching hospitals in the world," didn't mind. He knew that he had no ax to grind with respect to hospitals. And he said the Bellevue executives really didn't interfere.

"They had no problem at all with the reality of it," he recalled. "All they said was 'Treat the hospital as it is. Don't make us look bad.' "[2]

It was the network that had a problem with "the reality of it." Asher said he had tried to create a setting that pulsated with the kind of life-and-death tension surgeons confronted daily. To his chagrin, CBS programmers nixed that approach. For example, they vetoed a scene where K.O. (as the main character was called) has to perform an emergency leg amputation on the street after an abortion clinic is bombed. He couldn't get it accepted.

"The network didn't want to do any [stories based on current] headlines at all," Asher complained. "They were very nervous about that. They didn't want to be contemporary. They didn't want to be hard-hitting. They wanted to be more like *Trapper John*." In other words, he explained, they wanted a show where the patients' problems rarely are designed to remind the viewers of real-life medical complications.

The producers of *E/R* ran into the same problem. Actor Elliott Gould, who played Dr. Sheinfeld, recalled that the series was initially pitched to him by officials of Embassy Communications, the production company, as a show that would alternate between the drama and pathos of the emergency room and the comedy of the medical staff who must cope with the tension of it all. Gould, who had been a principal actor in the movie version of *M*A*S*H* (he had played the original Trapper John) understood that CBS officials saw him as a good choice for a show that had *M*A*S*H*-like aspirations.

Early in production, though, Gould continued, it became clear to him and others on the crew that a drastic alternation between stark medical reality and the dark comedy involved in coping would never be achieved, or even allowed. The network, he said, was against it, and the production firm didn't seem to have the clout to do anything about it.

Bernie Orenstein, one of the executive producers on the show, was gentler in his estimation of what had gone wrong. The creators never found the right balance between the comedy and the drama of the E.R., he said. Still, he admitted that CBS programmers had prodded them to take a lighter, more comic, approach to their setting.

Judging from the doctor shows on ABC and NBC during the first half of the 1980s, CBS executives weren't the only ones hesitant to follow *St. Elsewhere*'s lead in aiming for unconventional styles and plots. Imitating the formats and attitudes of successful series was the name of the network game. Thus, *Cutter to Houston* (NBC), about an emergency helicopter team, and *Trauma Center* (ABC), the story of a hospital-based medical team, aped the action-adventure tone of NBC's *Emergency!*. *Ryan's Four* (ABC) and *Chicago Story* (NBC) followed the acute-oriented, respectful approach toward medicine that went back to *Dr. Kildare* and *Marcus Welby*. And three situation comedies, *The Two of Us* (NBC), *Growing Pains* (ABC), and *The Bill Cosby Show* (NBC), used a character's doctor label in a way more in tune with *The Donna Reed Show* and *Julia* of the 1960s than with *E/R*.

Most clearly linked to the past was *The Return of Marcus Welby*. A TV movie on ABC that called on the consulting talents of the now semi-retired David Victor, it brought Robert Young back to television with the aim of restarting the series. The ratings were propitious. But Young, now in his late seventies, couldn't arrange his shooting schedule in a way that would reconcile his desire to rest with his willingness to return to his old persona, and the project was dropped.

The absence of unconventional initiatives in TV's medical arena in the mid-1980s was not the fault of the networks alone. The creators of at least a couple of those projects saw the doctor show more as a clear-cut old formula they could exploit than as a dramatic landscape pregnant with newly planted opportunities. There was little care and less caring. Experienced TV writers spoke offhandedly of recycling uncontroversial doctor-show plots from the 1960s and 1970s into new series by making only cosmetic changes. And one of the developers of *Cutter to Houston,* Gerald Abrams, bluntly compared his work to that of a packaged goods contractor. "If I notice that a network will accept a certain type of show," he said, "I'll supply it—no matter what kind it is."

In the case of *Nurse,* the lead actors felt that the quality of the series episodes the producers had commissioned was unacceptable, leading to a number of angry confrontations. It was a curious situation, since the original made-for-TV movie that turned out to be the series pilot had won rave reviews. The raves came especially from quarters of the nursing profession that had begun to lambast the TV networks for what they considered the lackluster, unrealistic, and even demeaning roles that nurses had played on TV for years. Three commentators on the home tube's image of their profession called the TV movie "the best fictional presentation since the demise of *The Nurses* in 1965."[3]

But as for the series that came from the film, *New York Times* reviewer John J. O'Conner expressed the opinion that the creators had turned a refreshingly realistic portrayal of a nurse into a predictably formularized tear-jerker.[4] To co-star Robert Reed, who played the head doctor to Michael Learned's head nurse, that was an understatement. The experienced TV actor shot off a series of memos to executive producer Robert Halmi that said improbable plots, weak character motivations, and poor working conditions were driving him and star Michael Learned to angry grief. Finally, he refused to continue working.

None of this commotion made it to the popular press. Beyond a few articles about Gregory Harrison, who played Gonzo on *Trapper John,* doctor dramas made little news in the early 1980s. *St. Elsewhere*'s arrival on the scene in 1983 did cause a stir. Over the next few years magazine and newspaper writers expended a fair amount of ink to describe the *Hill Street* style of the series and the determination of the producers to concoct surprising twists in their medical staff's lives. But their interest did not extend to the other doctor dramas on the air.

One reason might be that reviewers and columnists had become more jaded about story lines since the earlier years of TV. The days of *Medic, Kildare, Casey, Marcus Welby, Medical Story,* and *Quincy* were days in which even dealing with certain medical subjects on the home tube was considered a bold act. Every now and then, for prestige and their sense of pride, the creators of those shows had invited scripts on untouched subjects with controversial implications—such as malpractice, abortion, mercy killing, child abuse, and treatment of the mentally retarded. They had done it even though they knew their attempts to deal honestly with the issues would be hobbled by the fears of network programmers, censors, and medical advisors.

By the mid-1980s, virtually every topic had become acceptable to ABC, CBS, and NBC censors. Everyone in the industry understood that it was now not the topic, but its handling, that raised red flags in network offices. So the use of "hot" topics such as artificial hearts and AIDS abounded on TV, if only to draw audiences and prove the programs' currency.

But merely exploiting those subjects through predictable plots didn't ignite the press anymore. To really get press attention, a story line needed not just a controversial subject but a controversial approach. And it was in the area of sparking controversy that producers of most doctor shows of the '80s didn't show the interest or gumption a number of their counterparts had demonstrated in previous decades. *Cutter to Houston, Ryan's Four, Trauma Center, Chicago Story, Kay O'Brien,* and even *Nurse* had no cutting-edge hooks that could grab popular press writers. Those programs handled their issues so appropriately from a network standpoint that the issues became predictable cogs on treadmills of blandness.

Blandness was most widespread when the controversy related to social issues—that is, to stories that connected the physician and the patient to contemporary debates in the society at large. Even *St. Elsewhere's* creators, who could be daring with their show's look and its exploration of personal relationships, said they didn't see social issues as central to their scheme. Other producers pointed out that the networks were calling their tunes, and the networks didn't want their programming to spark angry debate. One story editor added that times had changed and that issue-oriented series were simply out of fashion.

Another reason for the press's lack of interest in most doctor shows of the '80s may have been their tendency to retread plots of the past. The producers and scriptwriters who had worked on previous doctor shows were reworking the same material. Subjects that had merited *TV Guide* closeups and invited pro and con reactions in daily newspapers during the '60s and '70s now elicited implicit yawns.

It was now no longer new for *Chicago Story* to do a episode on its hospital doctor (this time a woman) being accused of malpractice. The same basic story, with the same kind of speech by an older physician defending the honor of accused doctors, had run on *Dr. Kildare* more than two decades earlier. The *Kildare* ending, in fact, was less of a cop-out.

Nor was it new when *Kay O'Brien* wallowed in the difficulties women doctors had in sustaining romantic relationships. The 1970s had seen a number of programs bring up that theme, most notably *Julie Farr, M.D.* Even in the 1980s, *Chicago Story* used that idea to provide some interpersonal angst for its otherwise heroically caring, rational, and dependable trauma surgeon, Judith Bergstrom.

Beyond thematic considerations, it is likely the popular press didn't cover these programs because, simply, they weren't hugely popular. After *Trapper John*, with the exception of *St. Elsewhere*, every new dramatic doctor series expired rather quickly. It was not a trend that encouraged a rash of new programs with medical themes.

In addition, doctor shows were no longer needed as the antidote to anti-violence groups that they had been in the previous decades. During the 1970s, a new substitute for obviously violent shows proved popular. Comedy/adventure series that leavened humor with car crashes and high-speed chases (*The Fall Guy, Simon and Simon, Sheriff Lobo*) seemed to provide audience-grabbing action while they mollified pressure groups that railed against shooting and fist-fighting. Besides, with the rise of a conservative political consciousness and a laissez-faire Federal Communications Commission in the 1980s, traditionally violent programming became acceptable again at the networks. The life-and-death freneticism on shows such as *The Equalizer, Hunter, Hill Street Blues,* and *Miami Vice* must have made a hospital-based doctor show seem, by comparison, tame.

Comedy series with medical overtones were another, more ambiguous story. *The Two of Us*, about a physician and his wife, took a quick dive. *The Bill Cosby Show*, however, became the television hit of the decade, and *Growing Pains*, which followed it by a year, garnered consistently solid ratings.

A number of similarities between *Cosby* and *Growing Pains* were striking. Each was a family program designed for the 8 to 9 hour when children, network officials believe, control a substantial number of household sets. Each involved an upper-middle-class nuclear family with two working parents and more than two children. The physician in each was the father—a psychiatrist in *Growing Pains*, an obstetrician/gynecologist in *Cosby*. And each father—Cliff Huxtable (Bill Cosby) and Jason Seaver (Alan Thicke)—had an office in the home while his wife worked outside.

Cosby's role received by far the most publicity of the two. After the show became successful, the actor/producer told interviewers he had originally envisioned his character as a chauffeur. His wife, he said, insisted he choose a more upscale occupation. According to one of the show's writers, Cosby ended up making his television counterpart, Cliff

Huxtable, an obstetrician because of his strong feelings about the importance of family in people's lives. The medical label, he felt, would give him the opportunity to bring some insight, through comedy, into the process of birth and growth and maturing. One point the entire production staff understood, the writer said, was that race would not be a factor in the patients Huxtable saw. The program had the black doctor talking to and examining white patients as well as black ones.

This black male's practice of gynecology, one of the most intimate kinds of medicine, on women regardless of their color, caused no public stir. In fact, it didn't even become a topic for discussion in the major media outlets. That, in itself, is a remarkable statement on the kind of change the country, and the TV industry, had gone through. In the late 1950s, an episode of *Medic* about a black physician was killed by the network. In the late 1960s, *Julia*, a comedy series about a black nurse, got embroiled in controversy simply because of the central character's race. And in the mid-1970s the failure of *The Lazarus Syndrome* was attributed by many as the color of the lead performer.

It is worth noting that Bill Cosby was someone who already had wide acceptance in American homes because of earlier series and comedy appearances, records, and Jello-O commercials. Also, the show was a situation comedy, a form where black actors had traditionally had an easier time getting a foothold. Dramatic series centering on black leads still remained elusive commodities as TV programmers turned toward the late 1980s. The best that black actors could hope for was co-star or guest-star status—roles such as surgeon Phillip Chandler (Denzel Washington), orderly Luther Hawkins (Eric Laneuville); and woman gynecologist Roxanne Turner (Alfre Woodard) on *St. Elsewhere*.

Actually, both *Cosby* and *Growing Pains* tended to stay away from medical issues. The creators focused on home life, since the cast—his TV family—was most logically situated there. So, very much in the *Donna Reed Show* mold of the '50s and '60s, the Huxtable and Seaver offices became backdrops for a scene only when a practice-related idea seemed too good to pass up, or when some cast members had to be bypassed purposefully in an episode. Hospital scenes were even rarer.

In an important sense, then, *The Bill Cosby Show* marked a turning back toward the earliest use of doctors in situation comedies—as ultimately wise, though slightly befuddled, fathers. The comedy series that tried to tackle medicine more directly had run into a lot of resistance. The trouble *Temperatures Rising*, *A.E.S. Hudson Street*, and, more recently, *E/R* had had with the ratings had given network programmers and industry producers great pause about the viability of weekly comedies that tried to mix humor with the portrayal of medical problems. After the failure of *E/R*, in fact, some TV producers and writers were stating flatly that situation comedies which centered on medicine would not work.

A few went even further to say the entire medical formula was trapped in a logical bind. Viewers, they contended, would no longer accept the standard portrayal of doctor-show medicine, for they clearly perceived it as unrealistic. Yet at the same time, they suggested, the need to satisfy the audience's desire for realism required a level of physical gore and emotional frankness about health which the huge numbers of home viewers network TV required wouldn't accept. The form was near bankruptcy, they concluded.

Others in the industry, particularly those who had worked on doctor shows, shucked off such comments. The key themes doctor shows had always emphasized were still relevant, they said. To their way of thinking, all television works in cycles. Doctor shows were merely hibernating on the down side of a cycle. They would come back sooner or later.

Some were betting it would happen sooner rather than later. As the second half of the 1980s matured, viewers in their thirties, forties, and fifties made up a large, wealthy portion of the target audience for network TV. That population might, the thinking went, be lured to doctor shows with the framework of the old and a touch of the new.

Buck James, new on ABC during fall 1987, and *Heartbeat*, a short-flight ABC series during spring 1988, had just that combination. The first, starring Dennis Weaver, a well-known television actor, was clearly an attempt to pick up *Trapper John*'s gauntlet. The network even scheduled it on Sunday at 10, *Trapper*'s old slot.

The themes of the series were equally reminiscent. Buck is a crack middle-aged surgeon and head of a trauma unit at a university hospital in Texas. As such, he gets to ride a helicopter to where the action is and work with young residents who are struggling toward careers in emergency medicine. In the first episode, in fact, Buck must choose a chief resident from among two candidates, an East Coast Jewish female and a Protestant male from Texas whose wealthy father is leaning strongly on Buck and the hospital administration; he defiantly chooses the woman. But this pressure is child's play compared to Buck's personal problems: a divorced wife who won't let go and a daughter who shows up from Chicago pregnant and unmarried.

Heartbeat, also in the 10 p.m. time slot that has become part of the doctor-show tradition, showed even more of physicians' personal problems than did *Buck James*. Most of its central characters were women, and its closest relative in the history of doctor shows was not *Trapper John* but *Having Babies*.

Like that short-lived ABC series of the late 1970s, the medical backdrop for the physicians in *Heartbeat* is obstetrics. There are some notable differences in professional depiction between *Heartbeat* and previous doctor shows. While most of TV's specialists work in a hospital, the *Heartbeat* physicians (four obstetricians, a psychiatrist, and a pediatrician) practice in a freestanding building that seems to include its own birthing rooms. Too, while nurses in most doctor shows have been vague functionaries, *Heartbeat* has a nurse practitioner with clear lines of authority and autonomy in certain areas.

Perhaps the most emphasized difference, however, relates to the independence of the women physicians. Their TV forebears—from Maggie Graham in *Ben Casey* to Kay O'Brien—were portrayed as the minority gender treading softly through masculine halls. The three women doctors in *Heartbeat* are anything but that. The viewer learns at the start of the series that they had formed their practice, Women's Medical Arts, out of a philosophical conviction that women can practice OB/GYN more expertly than men. They later hired three male colleagues. But the conviction made explicit in the first two episodes is that the practice is better, and different, because it was created by women.

Yet along with the rhetoric of female professional independence runs a theme that has dogged TV's women physicians since their earliest days: their inability to sustain personal relationships with members of the opposite sex. In *Heartbeat*, this theme becomes a central organizing point, though it is applied rather evenhandedly to the men as well as the women. Every episode revolves around attempts by the regulars to cope with their love lives in the face of severe occupational strains. Dr. Joanne Springsteen (Kate Mulgrew), the head of Women's Medical Arts, is particularly plagued by the idea that dedication to her work has not allowed for a mature romantic involvement. She sees her new affair with a colleague as a kind of challenge to that fear; a good deal of the plot is taken up playing out that challenge.

The story lines about the doctors are presented in serialized form. The fact that Esther Shapiro, who helped create *Dallas*, was involved in originating *Heartbeat* suggests an attempt to merge elements of the prime-time soap opera with the most enduring elements of the doctor show. The result is softer than *St. Elsewhere*—or *Women in White* and *Doctors' Private Lives*, the steamy miniseries of the '70s—because although *Heartbeat*'s central characters are flawed, they are all likable, competent, and dedicated. Emphasizing these features, an ad in *TV Guide* for the premiere invoked a familiar doctor-show theme when it announced that here were "young doctors with a crazy new idea—the patient comes first."[5] And, in fact, while the physicians suffer through their personal problems across episodes, they manage to resolve their patients' difficulties, usually happily, within the hour.

Rumors about other doctor series in the works formed along these broadly familiar lines. Two projects even carried names from decades past, Ben Casey and Doctor Kildare. The plot patterns were nearly as well known. In the proposed shows, physicians are undisputed rulers of the hospital, and administrators are their ineffectual foils. Medical attention, in turn, is an unlimited resource. Insurance companies, unions, large private employers, and government policymakers are irrelevant to the illnesses or their treatments. Instead, the diseases are really just apolitical launching pads into the "real" stories: the ones revolving around personal difficulties of both the doctors and patients.

The resonance with shows gone by is remarkable, and troubling. The problem is not merely that medical care can never be unlimited and apolitical. Clearly, that has always been a logical impossibility. Rather, the more significant difficulty is the huge gap that has developed between TV's version of medicine's basic operating principles and the version that policymakers are using.

While medical policymakers in decades past had held firm to an apolitical, resource-rich medical vision both in and out of their professional circles, they now are increasingly acting and talking in ways that argue just the opposite. As a result, the structure of American medicine, and the assumptions of the rulers that shape the structure, have been deeply at odds with the structure and beliefs that bolster prime-time TV's medical realities. To a longtime TV watcher with the optimistic belief that doctor shows have the potential to ignite real cultural discussion about the medical system, this development is disconcerting. It would seem exceedingly difficult to have relevant cultural discussion about an institution when the fundamental images presented on TV about that institution are out of sync with the forces guiding its reality—and when nobody in or out of TV says anything about that. American medicine had changed drastically in three decades, but both TV's storytellers and leaders of the medical community act as if they have hardly noticed. Why?

Tyranny of a Formula

One answer, put briefly, is that there has developed a kind of tyranny in the settings, character types, and patterns of actions that have made up what people in the TV industry see as the basic elements of the doctor show. To begin summarizing what this means and how it works, consider how the traditional structure of medicine and its accompanying belief system have become part of the traditional formula.

Long thought of as the primary action centers of American medicine, the large urban teaching hospital and the small-town private office developed during the 1930s and '40s as the primary locale of hugely popular doctor stories. The heroes of these places were white male physicians. Nurses played purely subsidiary, and often not terribly well-defined roles. The only other medical types to be used consistently were the hospital administrator and the hospital orderly. The many other professional positions that made up the patient's support system in the hospital or elsewhere in the medical world seemed hardly to exist.

From the standpoint of the drama, it didn't matter. The basic stories and themes that were to be woven through doctor series across decades could be built around this limited crew. Over time, a number of broad plot lines became part of the formula's repertoire. The most famous among them, with titles representing their most memorable appearances, have been "Twenty-four Hours" (on the doctor's first day of work); "The Shining Image" (the physician falls in love with his *first* doomed patient); and "Tyger Tyger" (a physician is infatuated with a patient who ends up dying).

Other loosely established scenarios that developed became well trodden from *Kildare* to *St. Elsewhere*. Recall the "continuing romance toward marriage" story; the tale of a "guest star" physician who has broken hospital rules; the guest star physician who tries to hang on when he or she can no longer practice; the relative who is holding back some help that can contribute to a patient's cure; and the patient who, in one way or another, is his or her own worst enemy.

Invariably weaving through these and other plots are the assumptions that guided the policy of the medical establishment when the formula was taking its basic shape. At their core is a belief that unlimited medical care for those needing it is an American right. The belief is built into the plots via a theme that goes back at least as far as *Internes Can't Take Money* in the mid-1930s.

The gist of the theme is that physicians must adopt a noblesse oblige philosophy toward their profession. Recall from Chapter 1 that a central point in this perspective is the physician's mandate to place patients first at all costs. The approach does recognize limits to humankind's ability to circumvent the grim reaper. Medicine can't do everything; patients die. When the illness takes that direction (as in "Tyger, Tyger" and "The Shining Image"), the physician must make sure nothing possible has been overlooked and the patient has reached self-understanding.

Generally, though, the plot's illness remains just inside physicians' boundaries of competence. In such situations, the noblesse oblige theme dictates it is the doctor's duty to ensure that everything medically possible is done to effect the patient's physical and emotional cure. In concert with the traditional settings, characters, and plots, the theme pushes creators toward enacting the traditional vision of unlimited medical care.

Most of the plots stress what is needed from doctors who are up to the required task, or what is missing from physicians who are not. So, for example, the "Twenty Four Hours" plot shows how residents learn that physicians must press themselves and the system to the limits to help the sick, even to the point of sacrificing romance. Stories about doctors who do not perform up to par stress the need for physicians to monitor one another and the importance of ensuring that the best physicians provide the best they have to offer to patients. And stories about patients who are their own worst enemies reflect on the struggle a physician must go through to convince a sick person to accept the medical resources that are unquestionably available.

It is through the continuing prominence of the hospital administrator as a generally unlikable comic character that the doctor-show formula's assumption about resources becomes especially explicit. The hospital administrator is a source of irritation precisely because he acts in a manner needlessly counterproductive to the excellent patient care the physician wants to provide. The administrator is always trying to cut costs, to place limits on patient care. And in a realm where physicians are highly skilled benefactors, where politics is rarely a legitimate factor, and where scarcity is virtually unknown, an administrator becomes an unwelcome intruder. The money manager is a perfect butt of jokes and touchstone for conflict, a person searching for something negative to do and inevitably getting in the way of quality health care.

Writers, producers, and network executives are often quite aware that their shows advocate taking state-of-the art medicine to the limit to save people. Often, in fact, they are proud of it. It ought to be stressed, though, that creators don't have to think about medicine in these terms to believe that unlimited resources ought to be available week after week. Assumptions about the medical system and its resources actually follow naturally from the routines of doctor-show plot creation.

The assumptions are highly accepted by creators as transparent, as commonsense. Consequently, in creating doctor-show episodes the creators merely insist that, like all good TV, the handling of setting, characters, and plot in the doctor show be geared toward enacting a compelling drama of human relations. The stake in this drama is life over death. The medical landscape is the backdrop to what must always be some kind of interpersonal conflict that affects the ultimate stake. Conflicts can be introduced through patients who refuse care, relatives who refuse to help, or doctors who, for myriad reasons, are unable to do what is expected of them. The traditional plot repertoire, quietly threaded with assumptions about medical policy, invites these conflicts. It poses them as challenges to surmount.

Specifically what those challenges are in any particular story, whether they will be surmounted, who will surmount them, and how they will be surmounted become matters that reflect a number of considerations: the ingenuity of the creators, as well as their personal optimism or pessimism; perceptions of the current approach's credibility with the public; the advertiser-chasing strategies of the network; the ways specific aspects of doctor shows have played in the national press; changes in the power and status of physicians in the society at large; and even changes in the approaches other kinds of programs—cop shows, lawyer shows—take in their approaches to the people and concerns of institutions.

These considerations then become the sparks for change in the doctor-show formula across the decades. Spied from the 1980s, it is clear that many aspects of the doctor shows of the 1970s and 1980s would cause surprise, and probably chagrin, among the producers, writers, and medical people who worked the territory during the '30s, '40s, '50s, and even '60s. The innovations that created the changes were mostly incremental. Small alterations in characterization or setting in one show were picked up by other shows that, in turn, borrowed ideas from still other shows. Sometimes, the influences were from programs that had nothing to do with the medical system. Sometimes, too, the influences were the residue of failures.

Nevertheless, over time, the small changes snowballed to make new doctor shows appear increasingly different from their predecessors. The impact of breakthrough shows (*M*A*S*H, Hill Street Blues, St. Elsewhere*) was to bring the incremental changes together under a new storytelling style. Through this combination of many small and a few large innovations, the formula could change significantly with the demands of the TV industry even while its most fundamental elements and assumptions about the institution it depicted remained.

For example, the hospital Dr. Kildare knew went through a number of striking concatenations, from the high-tech setting of *Bold Ones* to the poverty-stricken millieu of *A.E.S. Hudson Street* and *St. Elsewhere*. The modest general practitioner's office that was Dr. Christian's base likewise went through a variety of manifestations. Think of Marcus Welby's comfortable house and the rustic surroundings of Doc Elliot and Meg Laural. And in the '70s and '80s producers paid special attention to the medic's movement outside the hospital, for rescue work (*Emergency!, Matt Lincoln, Code R, Cutter to Houston*) and coroner duty (*Quincy*).

The characteristics of the main characters themselves also changed. By the 1970s, the previously all-white, all-male role of physician had begun to accommodate a few women and minorities. Nurses and even some hospital orderlies began to take up more of the medical stage. Even more substantial, the central doctors had begun to be invested with a greater variety of personalities. The *M*A*S*H* crew and *Hill Street Blues*'s force set the tone for the *St. Elsewhere* ensemble. They were a far cry from the unimpeachable earnestness and honesty of James Kildare, Konrad Styner, Theodore Bassett, and Joe Gannon.

Hand-in-hand with these changes came changes in the older doctor/ younger doctor relationship so common to doctor shows. In the early days the bond was purely one in which a younger man showed careful respect for an older male mentor. In the 1970s, that began to change. The duo began to include female-male and even female-female relationships (as in *Julie Farr, M.D., Women in White*, and *Heartbeat*). The relationship also became more casual and, as in *Trapper John*, less concerned with the younger side of the pair learning professional or moral lessons from the older. Sometimes, the older person learned. Other times, they learned together.

The moral and professional issues that beset them changed over time, too. Gradually, depictions of illnesses became more explicit, and themes relating to personal relationships (especially sexual themes) acquired greater boldness. In turn, these changes were accompanied by a tendency through the 1970s to shift from an anthology-style focus on problems of the patients to a greater concern with the personal and professional difficulties of the medical people themselves.

Together with this shift came perhaps the most striking change in the doctor-show formula: a few shows revealed an unusual pessimism about the ability of physicians to carry out their mandate to provide virtually unlimited resources for medical care. *M*A*S*H, A.E.S. Hudson Street, Medical Story,* and *St. Elsewhere* carried a number of stories about the difficulties of working in a resource-poor medical environment. In *M*A*S*H,* the problem was the war and an inept bureaucracy (I-Corps). In *Medical Story, A.E.S. Hudson Street,* and *St. Elsewhere* the difficulties typically concerned the refusal of government to allocate enough money to the inner-city hospitals.

The episodes of the latter three shows come as close as TV's doctor shows have come to evoking the changed policymaking environment of medicine in the last quarter of the twentieth century. But even these exceptions turn away from the heart of the new medical realities. The theme of resource scarcity is carefully and explicitly limited to hospitals for the least well-off. These places, the protagonist-physicians lament, are the exceptions. In most other hospitals—in fact, hospitals not too far away—the ethos of unlimited medical care prevails.

The point, well intentioned and based solidly in medical practice, is that doctors to the poor aren't given the chance to heal people that doctors in wealthier hospitals have. Politicians and hospital bureaucrats are blamed for iniquities that can be, and ought to be, solved by a re-allocation of funds. And in the shows, the hero-doctor is portrayed as laudable because he decides to stick it out in that hospital and get around the bureaucracy in order to help patients, rather than to take the easy road in "Boston General."

From the standpoint of popular drama, then, the poor-hospital motif is another new way to express how well the hero is following the traditional noblesse oblige philosophy. It does portray the physician as not fully in control of the medical ship, and that is a rare depiction for TV. But it turns away from generalizing that circumstance, and the problem of scarce resources, to the medical system at large. And it ignores the fact that the new assumption of a zero-sum medical game creates tensions about the power of the physician, the role of medical technology, and the arrangements of care that must reverberate from the bowels of *St. Elsewhere* to the state-of-the-art places where Trapper John, Kay O'Brien, and Buck James work.

This, then, is the tyranny of the doctor-show formula: its inability to confront the most important structural changes in medicine of our era. The producers, writers, and network officials who work on medical programs recognize they are working in a TV tradition. But most don't realize they are locked into patterns of setting, characters, and plots even when they are consciously trying to buck the tradition. Most also don't recognize that the assumptions about the medical world which are built into the formula are at odds with the medical environment contemporary policymakers see themselves shaping.

As for the ones who do realize it, there is not much they can, or want, to do. Television, they know, is a high-risk business. People typically get rewarded for telling stories that are "the same, but different." To do that efficiently, the industry has evolved a process for altering the formula that is largely incremental. The process allows, even encourages, the surface of the doctor show to change with the times. At the same time, because the individual changes are typically conservative and small, it virtually ensures that the formula's core characteristics will remain stable.

Breakthrough shows, which people in the industry consider striking deviations from the norm, might be the place where major changes in approach to models of cultural authority would germinate. In the development of doctor shows, that didn't turn out to be the case. *M*A*S*H*, *Hill Street Blues*, and *St. Elsewhere*, the breakthrough programs that counted most here, had their greatest impact on character and plot changes *within* the formula's basic principles rather than outside of them. Even when it came to series that were audaciously different, the creators hesitated to challenge basic assumptions about institutional power and structure. They found it challenging enough to turn less touchy elements of the formula upside down as well as to innovate stylistically. In *St. Elsewhere*'s case, even those changes were unpalatable to many in the industry. Later programs tended to bypass its influence or play it down rather than build on it.

These approaches to innovation have suited the creators in view of the industrial demands on them. But it has prevented them from coming to terms with the new medical environment. The reason is that recognizing the new assumptions of the medical institution would force alterations in the doctor-show form that might be too different. The changes would undermine major storytelling principles.

The changes would, primarily, require moving the physician away from the traditional spot of captain of the medical ship. One thing that developments of the past decade have shown is that individual doctors are no longer the sole arbiters of patient care. Members of review committees, administrators, politicians, insurance executives, and others create layers of control that have tended to place the physician in a much weaker position in making decisions about cutting-edge care. In more and more cases, in fact, the physician is an employee, subject to the pressures of all employees in large organizations. Even a so-called independent practitioner is today subject to cost controls and other outside reviews. All this makes it very difficult to portray the doctor as a rugged individualist angrily breaking established rules with impunity à la Ben Casey or Trapper John.

Coming to terms with the decentering of the physician from the bridge of the medical ship also requires recognizing that the personnel on that ship are quite a bit different today than they were even a decade and a half ago. Osteopaths, chiropractors, optometrists, nurse midwives, psychologists, podiatrists, and dentists are commanding an increasing portion of the medical territory. And in many non-hospital locales, licensed nurse practitioners and physicians' assistants are increasingly brought in by cost-conscious managers to work as near-equals to doctors, but at less pay. To encourage clients to feel comfortable about that situation, managers have begun to give all the medical professionals a new status-breaking title, "provider."

Meet Dr. Welby, your provider. If that has a strange sound for TV, consider the other arrangements a storyteller serious about plugging into the contemporary medical scene would have to understand. One is that independent practitioners, or even two-person practices, are becoming rare among newly graduating doctors as competition and the high costs of entry make it too risky. For them, existing large group practices or multispecialty operations are more viable alternatives. So are the health maintenance organizations, "doc in the box" quick-care centers, and outpatient surgery centers that are increasingly dotting the national landscape.

As for the shape of hospitals, that, too, would require re-evaluation. On TV, intense, emergency-oriented work is typically the hospital's game. But today's competitive hospital executives find that is not enough. The new mandate is to position their organizations in ways that suit the marketplace. That often means paying attention to the certain key demographic groups (such as women of child-bearing age, wealthy people wanting cosmetic surgery, and older Americans with cancer and Alzheimer's disease) that will help support the hospital's inpatient and outpatient facilities. Encouraged by its serial plot structure, *St. Elsewhere* was unusual in showing physicians treating long-term problems on an inpatient and outpatient basis. But this approach only begins to tap into the intricate considerations that are wrenching the American hospital system into a new state.

The medical world is a sobering mosaic that is by no means fully formed. Looking at medicine from the board room of a health care conglomerate, from the strategic planning department of a large private hospital, from the admitting desk of a nursing home, from the presidential suite of an insurance company, from the waiting room of an HMO—or from all of these—could spark a firestorm of new stories about the developing medical world that are poignant and funny. Still, in view of the constraints that always block major innovations in network TV, it isn't surprising that even the producers of contemporary doctor shows who understand the new policy-making environment are not eager to take it on. They fall back on the excuse that the developments are political and that politics on TV is dull.

Television and Institutional Power

Yet why, one might ask, don't representatives of the medical establishment push the networks and the production companies in the direction of greater harmony with the assumptions of the contemporary medical system? The question brings us to the relationship of television's creators to institutional power.

As we have seen, the major considerations that have guided depictions of the medical institution at any point in time have been complex and subtle rather than direct and obvious. It is true, for example, that the Los Angeles County Medical Association and the American Medical Association managed to exercise tight control over scripts from the mid-1950s through the mid-1960s, during the formula's formative TV years. It is also true that physicians' organizations, led by the AMA, managed to make sure the cultural authority of doctors remained paramount when psychologists threatened to move onto their symbolic turf in the early '60s, as a result of *The Eleventh Hour* series.

But that is only part of the story. True to the perspective presented at the start of this book, a clear picture of the relationship between the physicians' organizations and the television industry has to take into account that it has been a two-way street. Sometimes the two sides have had parallel aims, sometimes the aims have conflicted sharply. And organized medicine certainly has not always been in direct control.

Most of the time, the relationship between TV producers and the doctors has been symbiotic, a "you scratch my back, I'll scratch yours" approach that has served the interests of both parties. Physicians have, by and large, received favorable treatment from producers. For their part, program producers have had convenient places to turn for inexpensive advice as well as a patina of credibility regarding accuracy.

Most of the time, too, there has been no need for the AMA, as the recognized representative of organized medicine, to control TV's portrayals. One reason is that the pragmatic producers of doctor shows typically would not risk continually offending one of the most powerful constituencies in American society. Another is that many of the basic beliefs about medicine the Los Angeles County Medical Association and the AMA jealously guarded had actually been built into the doctor formula long before James Moser requested the organization's help in producing *Medic* during 1954. He and others had shaped the prime-time world of TV physicians from building blocks as diverse as *Dragnet*, MGM's Kildare movies, *The Citadel* and *Dr. Christian*. They had shaped it quite self-consciously for dramatic effect, to convince the public of its "realism," and to encourage credibility and support for physician-directed medicine.

Their self-conscious support for physicians and their assumptions were perfectly understandable in the context of the day. They didn't need to be prodded to accept those fundamentals. That is because the 1950s and 1960s represented in many ways the most optimistic medical environment in American history. It was hardly questioned that the physician was the leader of health care in a society where medicine was an infinitely expandable resource.

That having been said, it should also be recognized, as the resource perspective in the Introduction suggests, that the producers' mandate to draw huge audiences with as low a monetary risk as possible did take precedence in their eyes over particular public relations desires of mainstream medical powers. When push came to ratings-point shove, dramatic license won out over the public relations concerns of even the powerful AMA. Even in the days of *Ben Casey*, when the AMA was at the height of its influence over prime-time TV, the Association's advisors couldn't force the program's producers to change what they considered the unacceptable sexual strutting and colloquial language of America's favorite neurosurgeon.

It was during the '70s and '80s that the Medical Association found itself most removed from direct, day-to-day control over its prime-time images. As creators searched for new—sometimes slightly unorthodox—modifications to spruce up the formulas, it became common Hollywood knowledge that AMA interference was sometimes more a pain than an asset. And, as the alternative of independent medical advisors became popular, producers distanced themselves from the main representative of the medical institution.

A major reason they felt secure in doing so had to do with the rising criticisms of the medical profession, especially the AMA, that were becoming increasingly common in society at large. Nevertheless, other links to the medical system remained strong, and have become even stronger. Hospitals have helped provide locations for filming, disease foundations have provided ideas and expertise in plotting, pharmaceutical and medical equipment manufacturers have contributed equipment to enhance "realism," and independent consultants have provided the overall imprimatur the AMA controlled during the formative years of the TV doctor series.

It is noteworthy that no conflicts seem to have arisen between these groups with respect to TV portrayals of the kind that arose between the physicians and psychologists. The reason is certainly not that tensions are nonexistent among physicians' organizations, hospital associations, and pharmaceutical firms. Rather, it appears that, unlike physicians and psychologists, physicians, hospitals, and pharmaceutical firms must work together to approach most profitably the public and private policymakers. As the key groups within the medical institution, they have probably learned to mute their conflicts in favor of an outward show of unity. This approach solidifies their collective power and makes it more difficult for other groups within the institution (such as psychologists, chiropractors, nurse midwives) to get a symbolic foothold.

Through it all, the key participants in storytelling from the medical side have understood clearly that their input has to fit producers' needs and the contours of the formula. True to the two-way nature of their relationship with the TV industry, the producers have succeeded in getting the professionals who give them advice and equipment to recognize the constraints of TV storytelling in the use of what they call dramatic license.

The doctors and nurses who have been consultants for medical programs know they can be important influences on medical programming as long as their suggestions fit the needs of the producers. In addition, the executives of illness foundations and health product companies know they can play important parts in shaping scripts on particular subjects only if their ideas fit producers' needs.

As a result, most of the notable changes in portrayals of doctors, hospitals, and other parts of the medical world on TV have not come from medical people. Nor have they come about as a result of changes in the medical system. Rather, they reflect changes in the TV system. That is, they reflect attempts by network executives and producers to deal with public pressures against TV violence, time period competition, demographic problems, needs of various production companies, images of doctor shows in the press, and other bottom-line considerations.

It is doubtful, then, that actions by organized medicine could break the tyranny of the doctor-show formula even if medical leaders agreed it needed to be done. But there is good reason to believe that, in spite of this, the leaders of organized medicine have no real interest in encouraging television produces to reshape their portrayals of physicians to better match the structure and assumptions guiding contemporary medicine. The consideration comes down, as it usually does, to a question of institutional power.

As things now stand, the American Medical Association, the American Hospital Association, and other representatives of the medical community are struggling furiously to maintain the clout of their constituencies against an onslaught of increasingly formidable foes. These foes include corporations concerned about rising medical insurance costs, insurance companies wanting to keep costs down, government agencies wanting to cap physician fees as they have been capping hospital fees, and others. The issues are as complex as they are important. There are no simple bad guys and good guys here.[6]

The public and private policies over which these struggles are taking place are still emerging, mostly out of view of the general public. It is, in fact, often in the interest of all the parties to keep their contentions out of the mainstream media, because many of the sensitive issues would flare up if exposed to large-scale social inspection and debate. Typically, the contending elites encourage the circulation of their concerns only when acceptable solutions have begun to be worked out, or when issues have gotten to the point where the parties feel comfortable agreeing to disagree in public.

The leaders of organized medicine, then, may feel they have more to lose than to gain by encouraging stories that would explore a medical world with which they don't yet feel comfortable. They may well sense that it is to their benefit for television to continue medical images that, in essence, lead viewers away from where the contemporary action is, under the guise of bringing them behind the scenes.

It should be said that no one in charge of public relations at the major medical organizations has ever admitted to this approach. Whether by design or by default, however, the general approach certainly fits with the medical community's two-track position toward its TV image over the decades. On the one hand, medical leaders have tried to become involved in the creation of images they thought would make doctors look good. On the other hand, they never encouraged any portrayals that would ignite public discussions about the possible contradictions between TV medicine and policymaking.

Every now and then, individual physicians have issued angry denunciations to the press about popular TV physicians, saying their unreality was affecting the business of real-life doctors. But organized medicine—the AMA, especially—tended to take a public stance that not only approved of the programming but lauded its authenticity through a narrow, ambiguous construction of the word "realistic."

From the AMA's standpoint, there was a good political reason for this stance. Since the Association's Advisory Committee had publicized its active participation in the creation of the programs, open criticism of the doctor shows could be taken as a not-so-veiled criticism of the Committee. Today, the official line of the American Medical Association's Advisory Committee on Television, Radio, and Motion Pictures is that its consultants have always gotten involved only in questions of medical accuracy and not in concerns about the portrayals of physicians.[7] This attempt to withdraw from responsibility for public images of medicine at a time when those images are most in need of widespread consideration is irresponsible.

The AMA's posture is not only an attempt to distance organized medicine from a situation in which it has always been intimately involved. It is also a precedent that encourages a pernicious kind of face-saving. For it is only a short step from there to the startling argument some individual physicians set forth publicly when medical costs skyrocketed above 10 percent of U.S. gross national product.[8]

Blame the high cost of medicine on the public, they said. It is the public that has overutilized the most expensive parts of the health care system, the high-tech specialists affiliated with state-of-the-art hospitals. Physicians have only been responding to public demand, they said. When the public is taught, or forced, to make more reasonable demands on the health care system, everyone, including physicians, will be better off.

What this position overlooks, of course, is the great effort organized medicine made over the past decades to boost the expensive approach among Americans. An integral part of that effort involved encouraging fictional images along lines that hyped high-tech, specialty-oriented, high-cost care. To turn around now and disavow any role in this widespread cultural movement—including, by implication, disavowal of a major role in the creation of images—is a classic "blame the victim" strategy.

With respect to TV images, a glimmer of optimism about this sorry situation might lie in the difficulties both sides may begin to see in the tyranny of the doctor formula. Even in the absence of public disenchantment with these images, medical leaders might realize that TV's image of health care is not in their best interests, since it continually reinforces for millions of Americans expectations about their physicians they cannot fulfill. The portrayals may cause an increase in resentment as well as a misunderstanding of the new medical arrangements. For producers and network executives, a motive for changing the contemporary formula may be its apparent decline in popularity. Some may eventually conclude it may take a fundamental re-creation of the formula along the new policymaking lines to reignite strong audience interest in the doctor show.

Speaking about the misconceptions the general public receives about medicine, economist Lester Theroux has said: "To promise to make a system with no limits is to make a phony promise."[9] Out of a power-politics cauldron made of storytelling traditions, production firm needs, and the medical establishment's perceived self-interests, prime-time television has been making a phony promise about medicine for years. What phony promises has the nation's most shared medium of communication been making about other institutions? What considerations have been shaping the views that TV's storytellers have been presenting in enduring formulas about the military, the law, education, the family?

In focusing on medicine's relationship to television, this book has suggested a way to approach these questions. The task is important. Society's images are constantly created, re-created, and shared through the storytelling system we call mass media. If we are to understand our collective selves, how we got there, and why we stay that way, we have to understand how that system works. There is a lot to learn.

Time Line

Prime-Time Network Doctor Series: 1950s

Network		1950	1951	1952	1953	1954	1955	1956	1957	1958	1959
CBS	*City Hospital* (D)			xx							
CBS	*Diagnosis: Unknown* (D)									x	
NBC	*The Doctor* (D)			xxxx							
ABC	*Donna Reed Show* (C)									xxxxxxxxx	
CBS	*Hennesey* (C)										xxxx
ABC	*King's Row* (D)						xx				
NBC	*Medic* (D)					xxxxxxxxx					

Prime-Time Network Doctor Series: 1960s

Network		1960	1961	1962	1963	1964	1965	1966	1967	1968	1969
ABC	*Ben Casey* (D)		xxxxxxxxxxxxxxxxxxxxxxxxxxxx								
NBC	*Bold Ones/The Doctors* (D)									xxxxxxxxx	
ABC	*Breaking Point* (D)				xxxx						
NBC	*Dr. Kildare* (D)		xxxxxxxxxxxxxxxxxxxxxxxxxxxx								
ABC	*Donna Reed Show* (C)	xxxxxxxxxxxxxxxxxxxxxxxxxxxxxxxxxxxx									
NBC	*Eleventh Hour* (D)			xxxxxxxxxx							
ABC	*The Fugitive* (D)				xxxxxxxxxxxxxxxxxxxxxx						
CBS	*Hennessey* (C)	xxxxxxxxxx									
NBC	*Julia* (C)									xxxxxxxxxxxxxxxx	
ABC	*Marcus Welby, M.D.* (D)									xxxxxxxxx	
CBS	*Medical Center* (D)									xxxxxxxxx	
CBS	*The Nurses* (D)			xxxxxxxxxxxxxxx							
NBC	*Tom, Dick, and Mary* (C)				xx						

Note: D = Drama; C = Comedy; MS = Miniseries.

Years stand for TV years (1987 means 1987–88, beginning Fall 87)

xxxx means full year run

xx means one season of that year

x means part of one season

Prime-Time Network Doctor Series: 1970s

Network	Series	1970	1971	1972	1973	1974	1975	1976	1977	1978	1979
ABC	A.E.S. Hudson Street (C)									xxxx	
NBC	Bob Crane Show (C)						xx				
NBC	Bold Ones/The Doctors (D)	xxxxxxxxxxxxxx									
CBS	Code R (D)								x		
CBS	Doc (C)						xxxx				
ABC	Doc Elliot (D)				xxxx						
NBC	Doctors Hospital (D)						xx				
ABC	Doctors' Private Lives (MS)									xx	
NBC	Emergency! (D)			xxxxxxxxxxxxxxxxxxxxxxxxxx							
ABC	Having Babies/Julie Farr, M.D. (D)									xx	
CBS	House Calls (C)										xxxx
CBS	The Interns (D)	xxxx									
NBC	Julia (C)	xxxx									
ABC	Lazarus Syndrome (D)										x
NBC	Little People (C)			xxxxxxxxx							
ABC	Marcus Welby, M.D. (D)	xxxxxxxxxxxxxxxxxxxxxxxxxxxxxxxx									
ABC	Matt Lincoln (D)	xx									
CBS	M*A*S*H (C/D)			xxxxxxxxxxxxxxxxxxxxxxxxxxxxxxxxxxxxxxxxxxxxxxxxxx							
CBS	Medical Center (D)	xxxxxxxxxxxxxxxxxxxxxxxxxxxxxx									
NBC	Medical Story (D)						xx				
NBC	The Practice (C)						xxxxxxxxx				
NBC	The Psychiatrist (D)	xx									
NBC	Quincy, M.E. (D)							xxxxxxxxxxxxxxxxxxxx			
CBS	Rafferty (D)								x		
ABC	Temperatures Rising (C)			xxxxxxxxx							
CBS	Trapper John, M.D. (D)										xxxx
ABC	Westside Medical (D)							xx			

Note: D = Drama; C = Comedy; MS = Miniseries.

Years stand for TVyears (1987 means 1987–88, beginning Fall 87)
XXXX means full year run
XX   means one season of that year
X   means part of one season

Prime-Time Network Doctor Shows: 1980s

Network		1980	1981	1982	1983	1984	1985	1986	1987
CBS	AfterM*A*S*H (C)				xxxxxxxx				
ABC	Buck James (D)								xx
NBC	Chicago Story (D)			xx					
NBC	The Bill Cosby Show (C)					xxxxxxxxxxxxxxxxxxxxxxxx			
CBS	Cutter to Houston (D)				xx				
ABC	Growing Pains (C)						xxxxxxxxxxxxxxx		
ABC	Heartbeat (D)								xx
CBS	House Calls (C)	xxxxxxxxxx							
ABC	It Takes Two (C)			xxxx					
CBS	Kay O'Brien (D)						xx x		
CBS	M*A*S*H (C/D)	xxxxxxxxxxxxxxxx							
CBS	Nurse (D)		xxx						
NBC	Quincy, M.E. (D)	xxxxxxxxxxxxxxx							
ABC	Ryan's Four (D)			x					
NBC	St. Elsewhere (D)					xxxxxxxxxxxxxxxxxxxxxxxxxxxxxxxxxxxxxxxxxx			
CBS	Trapper John, M.D. (D)	xxxxxxxxxxxxxxxxxxxxxxxxxxxxxxxxxxxxxxx							
ABC	Trauma Center (D)				xx				

Note: D = Drama; C = Comedy; MS = Miniseries.

Years stand for TV years (1987 means 1987–88, beginning Fall 87)

XXXX means full year run

XX means one season of that year

X means part of one season

Notes

Introduction

1. For an elaboration on the relationship between resources and power in mass communication, see Joseph Turow, *Media Industries: The Production of News and Entertainment* (New York: Longman, 1984); and Joseph Turow, "Cultural Argumentation in the Mass Media: A Framework for Organization Research," *Communication* 8 (1985), 139–64.

2. Todd Gitlin, "Prime Time Ideology: The Hegemonic Process in Television Entertainment," *Social Problems* 26:3 (February 1979), 251–66.

3. Oscar Gandy, *Beyond Agenda-Setting* (Norwood, N.J.: Ablex, 1980).

4. See, for example, Daniel Katz and Roger Kahn, *The Social Psychology of Organizations* (New York: John Wiley, 1966); and Joseph Turow, "Another View of Citizen Feedback to the Mass Media," *Public Opinion Quarterly* 41 (1977–78), 534–43.

5. See Joseph Turow, "The Influence of Pressure Groups on Television Entertainment," in Rowland and Watkins (eds.), *Interpreting Television*.

6. The classic book on the television industry, now dated, is Les Brown's *Television: The Business behind the Box* (New York: Harcourt Brace Jovanovich, 1972). A more contemporary rendering of the industry's landscape is Todd Gitlin's *Inside Prime Time* (New York: Pantheon, 1984). An overview of sociological approaches to television entertainment can be found in Turow, *Media Industries*. See also Muriel Cantor, *The Politics of TV Entertainment* (Beverly Hills: Sage Publications, 1982); James Ettema and D. Charles Whitney (eds.), *Individuals in Mass Media Organizations* (Beverly Hills, Sage Publications, 1982); and Rowland and Watkins (eds.), *Interpreting Television*.

7. "U.S. Advertising Dollars by Media," *Advertising Age*, Sep. 24, 1987, p. 166.

8. John Cawelti, *The Six-Gun Mystique* (Bowling Green, Ohio: Bowling Green Univ. Press, 1972).

Chapter 1. "Internes Can't Take Money"

Along with other sources that are noted below, this chapter is informed by interviews with Lew Ayres, Joe Cohn, Larraine Day, and Robert Easton.

1. From "A Handbook of General Advance Information on 'Internes Can't Take Money,' " published by Paramount Pictures Advertising and Publicity Department (C.J. Dunphy, Director), 1936, p. 5.

2. Paul Starr, *The Social Transformation of American Medicine* (New York: Basic Books, 1984), 43.

3. Barbara Ehrenreich and Diedre English, *For Their Own Good: 150 Years of Expert Advice to Women* (New York: Anchor, 1978), 42.

4. Starr, *The Social Transformation of American Medicine*, 155.

5. Frank Rowsome, Jr., *They Laughed When I Sat Down: An Informal History of Advertising in Words and Pictures* (New York: Crown, 1959), 48.

6. Starr, *The Social Transformation of American Medicine*, 130.

7. Rosemary Stevens, *American Medicine and the Public Interest* (New Haven: Yale Univ. Press, 1971), 225–31, 238–43.

8. Joanne Trautmann and Carol Pollard, *Literature and Medicine: An Annotated Bibliography*, Revised Ed. (Pittsburgh: Univ. of Pittsburgh Press, 1982); and Jeffrey Meyers, *Disease and the Novel* (New York: St. Martin's Press, 1985).

9. Editorial, "Medicine in the Movies," *Hygeia*, June 1939, pp. 487–89.

10. Ibid., 487.

11. Ibid.

12. Ibid.

13. Ibid., 487–88.

14. Ibid., 488.

15. Hamlin Hall, "Frederick Schiller Faust," in Edward James (ed.), *Dictionary of American Biography*, Supplement Three, 1944–45 (New York: Charles Scribner's Sons, 1973).

16. Robert Easton, "Introduction," in Robert Easton (ed.), *Max Brand's Best Stories* (New York: Dodd, Mead, 1967), p. xii.

17. Robert Easton, *Max Brand: The Big Westerner* (Normal: Univ. of Oklahoma Press, 1970), 31–38. See also Darrell C. Richardson, *Max Brand: The Man and His Work* (Los Angeles: Fantasy Publishing, 1952).

18. Easton, *Max Brand*, 183.

19. Ibid.

20. Paramount Pictures, "A Handbook of General Advance Information on 'Internes Can't Take Money,' " 5.

21. Ibid., 9.

22. Ibid.

23. Ibid., 10.

24. James Robert Parish and Gregory W. Mank, *The Best of MGM: The Golden Years, 1928–59* (Westport, Conn.: Arlington House, 1981), 243.

25. Easton, *Max Brand*, 198.

26. Parish and Mank, *The Best of MGM*, 243; also, interview with Joe Cohn.

27. Easton, *Max Brand*, 212.

28. Ibid.

29. Frank N. Magill (ed.), *Magill's Survey of Cinema*, First Series, Volume 1 (Englewood Cliffs, N.J.: Salem Press, 1980), 651.

30. Easton, *Max Brand*, 213.

31. Parish and Mank, *The Best of MGM*, 244.

32. Ibid., 50.

33. Review of "The Citadel" and "Young Dr. Kildare," *Time*, Nov. 7, 1938, p. 41.

34. Lewis Jacobs, *The Rise of the American Film* (New York: Teachers College Press, 1938), 524.

35. "Medicine in the Movies" Editorial, 488.

36. Easton, *Max Brand*, 217–18.

37. Review of "Doctor Kildare Goes Home," *Time*, Sep. 30, 1940, pp. 74–75.

38. Review of "Doctor Kildare Goes Home," *Commonweal*, Sep. 27, 1940, p. 470.

39. Review of "Young Doctor Kildare," *Time*, Nov. 7, 1938, p. 41.

40. Review of "Dr. Kildare's Wedding Day," *Variety*, Aug. 20, 1941, p. 9.

41. Easton, *Max Brand*, 218.

42. "Happy to be C.O., Ayres Explains," *New York Times*, April 1, 1942, p. 23.

43. "The Case of Lew Ayres," *New York Times*, April 3, 1942, p. 20.

44. "Happy to Be C.O.," 23.

45. Parish and Mank, *The Best of MGM*, 244.

46. Ibid.

47. "Ayres Enrolled in Objectors' Camp; 100 Chicago Theaters Ban Films," *New York Times*, April 2, 1942, p. 23; "Happy to Be C.O.," 23; and "Hollywood Dossier," *New York Times*, April 26, 1942, Section VIII, p. 3.

48. Thomas F. Brady, "A Few Hollywood Aches and Pains," *New York Times*, April 5, 1942, p. 25.

49. "Metro to Continue Lew Ayres Films," *New York Times*, April 3, 1942, p. 25.

50. "Studio Will Remake Lew Ayres Film Play," *New York Times*, April 17, 1942, p. 19.

Chapter 2. "No Compromise With Truth"

Along with other sources that are noted below, this chapter is informed by interviews with Michael Dann, William House, and James Moser.

1. "The Man Behind the 'Medic,' " *Look*, Nov. 30, 1954, p. 100.

2. See, for example, the Dow Chemical ad in *TV Guide*, Sep. 11, 1954, p. 12.

3. "Doctor!" *Newsweek*, Nov. 20, 1955, p. 94.

4. Ibid.

5. "The Man Behind the 'Medic,' " 100.

6. "Strong Medicine," *TV Guide*, Oct. 9, 1954, p. 21.

7. Ibid.

8. Paul Starr, *The Social Transformation of American Medicine* (New York: Basic Books, 1983), 335.

9. Ibid., 335.

10. Ibid., 335–67.

11. Ibid., 285–89.

12. Ibid., 288.

13. Ibid., 336.

14. Ibid., 347.

15. J. Guess, "Medicine's Tragic Failure," *Journal of the South Carolina Medical Association* 48 (1952), 151–53.

16. Ernst Dichter, "Do Your Patients Really Like You?," *New York State Journal of Medicine*, 54:1 (Jan. 1, 1954), 222–26.

17. Ibid.

18. Kyle Chrichton, "Here's the Doctor," *Collier's*, April 4, 1936, pp. 17, 53; "Making Movies with the World's Most Famous Sisters," *Woman's Home Companion*, June 1939, p. 21; Margery Bianco, "Jean Hersholt's Andersen," *The Horn Book*, May 1944, pp. 164–65; Jean Hersholt, "The Two Never Met," *Saturday Review of Literature*, Dec. 21, 1946, pp. 18–19.

19. John Dunning, *Tune in Yesterday* (Englewood Cliffs, N.J.: Prentice-Hall, 1976), 161–62.

20. "Dr. Christian in the House," *Newsweek*, July 7, 1947, pp. 134–35.

21. Ibid.

22. "*Medic*, New NBC Show, Dramatizes Case Histories in Mature Style," *New York Times*, Sep. 15, 1954, p. 48.

23. "Review of *Medic*," *TV Guide*, Oct. 30, 1955, p. 21.

24. "Healer of the Sick," *TV Guide*, Oct. 15, 1955, p. 6.

25. Ibid., 5–6.

26. "Just What the Doctor Ordered," *TV Guide*, April 30, 1955, pp. 20–21.

27. See, for example, "Review of *Medic*" and Jack Gould, "Television in Review," *New York Times*, Friday, Dec. 24, 1954, p. 18.

28. "Review of *Medic*," 21.

29. "TV Show Cancels Childbirth Film," *New York Times*, March 11, 1956, p. 84.

30. "TV's Censored Caesarian," *Variety*, March 15, 1956, p. 24.

31. "Editorial: 'People Lose Faith in Our Program,' " *America*, March 12, 1956, p. 683.

32. "TV's Censored Caesarian," 24.

33. "Editorial: 'People Lose Faith in Our Program,' " 683.

34. Oscar Godbout, "NBC Rift Leads to End of *Medic*," *New York Times*, May 25, 1956, p. 63.

35. Oscar Godbout, "One *Medic* Show Loses Unit's Seal," *New York Times*, April 10, 1965, p. 47.

36. Godbout, "NBC Rift Leads to End of *Medic*," 63.

Chapter 3. The Gentleman and the Bull

Along with other sources that are noted below, this chapter is informed by interviews with George Andros, M.D., John Block, Bert Briller, Calvin Clements, Howard Dimsdale, Vince Edwards, Norman Felton, James Goldstone, Abby Greshler, Eugene Hoffman, M.D., Bettye Ackerman Jaffe, Norman Katkov, James Moser, Marvin Moss, E. Jack Neuman, Matthew Rapf, Elliot Silverstein, David Victor, and Robert Wood.

1. "Ben Casey: TV's Dour Doctor," *Look*, May 8, 1962, pp. 38–49.

2. "Richard Chamberlain: TV's Doctor Kildare," *Look*, Nov. 20, 1962, pp. 137–45.

3. Richard Carter, "What Women Really Think about Their Doctors," *Good Housekeeping*, Aug. 1961, pp. 60–61, 149–53. See also M. F. Cahal, "Nationwide Survey: Family Doctor in High Esteem," *G.P.* 24:145 (1951); "Kalamazoo Sur-

vey Finds Attitudes Toward Doctors, Hospitals," *Journal of the Michigan State Medical Society* 61:1464 (1962); and Elliot Friedson, *Patient's Views of Medical Practice* (New York: Russell Sage Foundation, 1961).

4. Newell Philpott, "Doctors and the Present Challenge," *Journal of Medical Education* 34 (Oct. 1959), 1033–34.

5. Robert W. Wilson, "The Physician's Changing Hospital Role," *Human Organization*, 1959–60, p. 178.

6. Ibid., 182.

7. Melvin Durslug, "Dr. Kildare Is a Doll," *McCall's*, March 30, 1963, p. 15.

8. Muriel Davidson, "Television's Personal Physicians," *McCall's*, Aug. 1962, p. 148.

9. Phyllis Wright, M.D., "I'm Dr. Kildare's Doctor," *Redbook*, Sep. 1963, p. 142.

10. "Report of Board of Trustees," *JAMA* 178:2 (Oct. 14, 1961), p. 159. See also Larry Wolters, "The TV Doctors," *Today's Health*, Oct. 1962, p. 24.

11. Herbert Lawson, Jr., "Drs. Kildare, Casey Get Guidance from Medical Association," *Wall Street Journal*, Dec. 27, 1962, p. 1ff.

12. The quote is from "Report of Board of Trustees," *JAMA*, Oct. 14, 1961, p. 160.

13. Wolters, "The TV Doctors," 24.

14. Wright, "I'm Dr. Kildare's Doctor," 142.

15. Ibid., 140.

Chapter 4. "Oh . . . Doctor!"

Along with other sources that are noted below, this chapter is informed by interviews with George Andros, M.D., Douglas Benton, John Block, Bert Briller, Calvin Clements, Howard Dimsdale, Vince Edwards, Norman Felton, James Goldstone, Abby Greshler, Eugene Hoffman, M.D., Bettye Ackerman Jaffe, Norman Katkov, James Moser, Marvin Moss, E. Jack Neuman, Matthew Rapf, Wilton Schiller, Elliot Silverstein, David Victor, and Robert Wood.

1. "My Son, the Doctor," *TV Guide*, Dec. 16–22, 1961, p. 16.

2. Melvin Durslug, "Dr. Kildare Is a Doll," *McCall's*, March 30, 1963, p. 14.

3. Bill Davidson, "TV's Surly Medico," *Saturday Evening Post*, May 12, 1962, p. 63.

4. Muriel Davidson, "Television's Personal Physicians," *McCall's*, Aug. 1962, pp. 66–67.

5. Durslug, "Dr. Kildare Is a Doll," 14.

6. John Keats, "Rx for an MD on TV," *New York Times Magazine*, May 27, 1962, p. 36.

7. Richard Behman, "Caseyitis: How the Epidemic Started and Why It Spread," *TV Guide*, Sep. 22, 1962, pp. 15–19; and Sep. 5, 1962, pp. 16–19.

8. See, for example, Davidson, "Television's Personal Physicians," 148; "Dr. Kildare Coming to J-A Comic Pages," *New York Journal-American*, Oct. 14, 1962, Section 1, p. 6; and "The Case of Casey (Letter to the Editor)," *New York World Telegram and Sun*, Nov. 27, 1962, p. 26.

9. Durslug, "Dr. Kildare Is a Doll," 15; and "Ben Casey: TV's Dour Doctor," *Look*, May 8, 1962, pp. 38–49. Quote on p. 40.

10. Gehman, "Caseyitis: How the Epidemic Started and Why It Spread," 16; and Durslug, "Dr. Kildare Is a Doll," 15.

11. "Ward Watch," *Newsweek*, March 26, 1962, pp. 82–83.

12. Davidson, "TV's Surly Medico," 64.

13. Durslug, "Dr. Kildare Is a Doll," 15.

14. Davidson, "Television's Personal Physicians," 148.

15. Herbert Lawson, Jr., "Drs. Kildare, Casey Get Guidance from Medical Association," *Wall Street Journal*, Dec. 27, 1962, p. 1.

16. Keats, "Rx for an MD on TV," 36.

17. Jack Gould, "High Ratings of Drs. Casey and Kildare Reveal Public's High Interest in Medicine," *New York Times*, March 12, 1962, p. 55.

18. Lawrence Laurent, "A Second Look at *Ben Casey* Shows Network Feels Impact," *Washington Post*, May 9, 1962, p. C-12.

19. Kay Gardella, "AMA Says *Kildare* Stars Aid Practice of Medicine," *New York Daily News*, June 23, 1964, p. 22.

20. See Val Adams, "News of Television and Radio," *New York Times*, Oct. 13, 1963, Section 2, p. 21; Hal Humphrey, " 'Good Samaritan' Loses Legal Bout," *Los Angeles Times*, June 19, 1964, Part V, p. 14; "VD on TV?," *Time*, Nov. 30, 1964, p. 62; Jessica Mitford, "The Disease That Dr. Kildare Couldn't Cure," *Redbook*, Sep. 1964, pp. 102ff; and "Novak-Kildare VD Two-Parter Axed by NBC-TV," *Variety*, Oct. 7, 1964;

21. Robert Musel, "You Have to Look After Yourself," *TV Guide*, Oct. 26, 1968, pp. 38–40. Quote on page 40.

22. Ibid., 40.

23. "Pep Pills for *Dr. Kildare*," *TV Guide*, Dec. 11–17, 1965, p. 12.

24. "New Prescription for TV Medicine," *Journal American*, Aug. 22, 1965, *TV Magazine*, p. 36.

25. "Pep Pills for *Dr. Kildare*," 12.

26. Barbara G. Meyerhoff and William R. Larson, "The Doctor as Culture Hero: The Routinization of Charisma," *Human Organization* 24 (Fall 1965), 188–91.

27. Davidson, "TV's Surly Medico," 67.

28. Meyerhoff and Larson, "The Doctor as Culture Hero," 189.

29. Paul Starr, *The Social Transformation of American Medicine*, (New York: Basic Books, 1983), 380–405.

Chapter 5. Witchcraft

Along with other sources that are noted below, this chapter is informed by interviews with Michael Dann, Norman Felton, Jack Ging, and Sam Rolfe.

1. "Many Are Filmed but Few Are Chosen," *TV Guide*, April 21, 1962, pp. 24–27.

2. Muriel Davidson, "The 'I Don't Care' Actor Who Cares Too Much," *TV Guide*, June 22, 1963, p. 11.

3. Jack Gould, "Disturbed Television," *New York Times*, Oct. 28, 1962, Section II, p. 21.

4. Ibid.

5. Robert Lewis Shayon, "The Bridge at West Point," *Saturday Review*, May 25, 1963, p. 41.

6. "From the TV Mailbag," *New York Times*, Nov. 11, 1962, Section II, p. 19.

7. Shayon, "The Bridge at West Point," 41. See also Robert Lewis Shayon, "Report from West Point," unpublished manuscript, 1963, in Robert Lewis Shayon Archive at Boston University.

8. Shayon, "The Bridge at West Point," 41.

9. Quote is from an interview with Norman Felton. See also Vernon Scott, "Psychiatry Series Slated for Fall," *World-Telegram & Sun*, July 16, 1962, p. 25.

10. "An Analysis of *The Eleventh Hour*," *TV Guide*, March 2, 1964, p. 18.

11. Ibid.

12. Scott, "Psychiatry Series Slated for Fall," 25.

13. "An Analysis of *The Eleventh Hour*," p. 16.

14. Gabriel Pryor, "Crackup Ahead for TV's Psychos?," *New York Mirror Magazine*, June 2, 1963, p. 10.

15. Richard K. Doan, "Psychologists Hit NBC over 11th Hour Program," *New York Herald Tribune*, Dec. 2, 1962 (no page noted as found in the files of the Television Information Office Library).

16. Emma Harrison, "TV Show Assailed by Psychologists," *New York Times*, Dec. 2, 1962, Section 1, p. 84.

17. Ibid. and Doan, "Psychologists Hit NBC over 11th Hour Program."

18. Davidson, "The 'I Don't Care' Actor Who Cares Too Much," 11.

19. Pryor, "Crackup Ahead for TV's Psychos?," 10.

20. Ibid.

Chapter 6. Narrowed Options

Along with other sources that are noted below, this chapter is informed by interviews with Buzz Berger, Joseph Campanella, Michael Dann, Joel Katz, Arthur Lewis, Eugene Hoffman, M.D., James Moser, and David Victor.

1. Philip Kalisch, Beatrice Kalisch, and Margaret Scobey, *Images of Nurses on Television* (New York: Springer, 1983), 16.

2. Erik Barnouw, *The Golden Web* (New York: Oxford Univ. Press, 1968), 244.

3. Thelma Schorr, "Nursing's TV Image," *American Journal of Nursing* 63:10 (Oct. 1963), 119–21. Quote on p. 120. Quote on p. 120. For a view in the *American Journal of Nursing* on the original *Playhouse 90* program that led to the series, see Patricia Tilton, "Behind the Nurse on TV," *American Journal of Nursing* 59:12 (Dec. 1959), 1715–17.

4. Kalisch, Kalisch, and Scobey, *Images of Nurses on Television*, 29.

5. *Variety*, Oct. 3, 1963, p. 39.

6. Ibid.

7. "Sinking Fast," *Newsweek*, Nov. 26, 1962.

8. Schorr, "Nursing's TV Image," 119–21. For a view that emphasizes the "realism" of the program, see Sally Hammond, "*The Nurse* Plays in a Real Hospital," *New York Post*, July 23, 1962, p. 51; and Bob Lardine, "This Show Needs a Nurse," *Daily News Magazine*, Oct. 14, 1962, pp. 8–9.

9. Schorr, "Nursing's TV Image," 119.

10. Ibid.

11. Ibid., 120–21.

12. Ibid., 121.

13. Ibid., 120.

14. Ibid.

15. Ibid., 121.

16. Ibid.

17. Kalisch, Kalisch, and Scobey, *Images of Nurses on Television,* 31.

18. Ibid., 28.

19. "New Male Stars Will Give *The Nurses* Broader Spectrum of Dramatic Interest," CBS Press Release, Aug. 19, 1964. See also *"The Doctors and the Nurses* New Title for *The Nurses,"* CBS Press Release, Sep. 15, 1964.

20. Kalisch, Kalisch, and Scobey, *Images of Nurses on Television,* 28.

21. Ibid.

22. Ibid.

23. Quoted in *Los Angeles Times,* Dec. 20, 1967, p. 24.

Chapter 7. Doctor Knows Best

Along with other sources that are noted below, this chapter is informed by interviews with James Brolin, Thomas Kurzy, David O'Connell, Clinton Roath, M.D., Martin Starger, Thomas Stern, M.D., Robert Young, M.D., Elena Verdugo, and David Victor.

1. Bob Williams, "On the Air," March 27, 1969, p. 110.

2. Ben Gross, "Want to Become an MD? Just Watch Your Home TV," *New York Daily News,* Sep. 25, 1969, p. 102.

3. "Telepix Review," *Daily Variety,* March 27, 1969, p. 32.

4. Jack Robbins, "Robert Young: Now Doctor Knows Best," *New York Post,* Nov. 1, 1969, p. 29. See also Robert de Rosa, "Life as Father *Really* Leads It," *TV Guide,* Jan. 5, 1962, pp. 22–25.

5. Tom Seligson, "The Private Triumph of Robert Young," *Parade,* Aug. 11, 1985, pp. 4–5.

6. Ibid., 4.

7. Pete Martin, "Marcus Welby, M.D.," *Saturday Evening Post,* Fall 1971, pp. 58ff. Quote is on p. 59.

8. Seligson, "The Private Triumph of Robert Young," 5.

9. Normand Poirer, "Robert Young, Wife in Hospital after Collapse," *New York Post,* Nov. 5, 1966, p. 4; Seligson, "The Private Triumph of Robert Young," 5; and Bob Ellison, "Robert Young's Toughest Role," *Today's Health,* May 1971, p. 27.

10. Gerald Astor, "TV's Dr. Marcus Welby," *Look,* March 23, 1971, pp. 56–59. Quote on pp. 57–58.

11. Seligson, "The Private Triumph of Robert Young," 5.

12. Ibid.

13. Astor, "TV's Dr. Marcus Welby," 58.

14. Seligson, "The Private Triumph of Robert Young," 6.

15. Astor, "TV's Dr. Marcus Welby," 56.

16. Ibid., 59.

17. Carl Schroeder, "Robert Young: TV's Doctor Welby," *Good Housekeeping*, June, 1971, pp. 43–48. Quote on p. 43.

18. Henry Ehrlich, "The Nice Men Cometh," *McCall's*, May 1972, p. 25.

19. Schroeder, "Robert Young: TV's Doctor Welby," 43.

20. Martin, "Marcus Welby, M.D.," 58.

21. Schroeder, "Robert Young: TV's Doctor Welby," 43.

22. Martin, "Marcus Welby, M.D.," 104–5.

23. Ibid.

24. Schroeder, "Robert Young: TV's Doctor Welby," 43.

25. Ibid., 44–48.

26. Martin, "Marcus Welby, M.D.," 58.

27. Arnold Hano, "The Actor Who Looks like a Star but Sounds like a Tax Accountant," *TV Guide*, Sep. 27, 1969, p. 22. See also Melvin Durslug, "Second Stethoscope—For How Long?," *TV Guide*, March 11, 1972, pp. 32–34.

28. Dick Adler, "One Outrage That Ought to Be Aired," *Los Angeles Times*, Nov. 8, 1974.

29. A detailed examination of these activities can be found in Kathryn Montgomery *Target: Prime Time* (New York: Oxford University Press, forthcoming), Chapter 5.

30. Adler, "One Outrage That Ought to Be Aired."

31. Sandra Thompson, "Is Doctor Welby a Menace to Women?," Sunday *Los Angeles Times* article in UCLA Theater Arts Library pamphlet file, from 1976 but not specifically dated.

32. Michael Halberstam, "An M.D. Reviews Dr. Welby of TV," *New York Times Magazine*, Jan. 16, 1962, p. 37, 30.

33. Ibid., 37.

34. Ibid., 34.

35. Ehrlich, "The Nice Men Cometh," 30.

36. *TV Guide*, Central Indiana Edition, Jan. 31, 1976, p. A-33.

37. Schroeder, "Robert Young: TV's Doctor Welby," 44.

38. Halberstam, "An M.D. Reviews Dr. Welby of TV," 37.

Chapter 8. Long Hair, High Tech, and Mod

Along with other sources that are noted below, this chapter is informed by interviews with Marvin Antonowsky, William Blinn, Don Brinkley, Robert Claver, Michael Dann, Walter Dishell, M.D., Vince Edwards, Mike Farrell, John Furia, James Goldstone, Chris Hutson, Norman Katkov, Perry Lafferty, Bernard McEveety, Barry Oringer, Clinton Roath, M.D., Joel Rogosin, Robert Van Scoyk, David Victor, Shimon Wincelberg, and Robert Wood.

1. "Medicine and Long Hair," CBS-TV Press Release, May 5, 1971.

2. Joseph N. Bell, "TV's On-Again Romance with Medicine," *Today's Health* 48:3 (March 1970), 25.

3. Ibid., 27.

4. Erik Barnouw, *The Image Empire* (New York: Oxford Univ. Press), 325; Willard Rowland, *The Politics of TV Violence* (Beverly Hills: Sage Publications, 1982).

5. Les Brown, *Television: The Business Behind the Box* (New York: Harcourt Brace Jovanovich, 1971), passim.

6. Ibid., 61, 79; and Erik Barnouw, *The Sponsor* (New York: Oxford Univ. Press, 1978), 50.

7. Brown, *Television*, 307.

8. Bill Davidson, "Next Week: Periarteritis Nodosa," *TV Guide*, July 16, 1971, pp. 12–13. The pilot movie for *Medical Center* was titled *UMC* (for University Medical Center) and starred Richard Bradford as Joe Gannon. However, audience reactions solicited by CBS found that while people enjoyed the movie, they did not like Bradford. As a result, the network ordered him dropped. Chad Everett was his replacement.

9. Davidson, "Next Week: Periarteritis Nodosa," 16.

10. Bell, "TV's On-Again Romance with Medicine," 27.

11. Ibid., 26.

12. *"The Bold Ones,"* NBC-TV Press Release, July 13, 1970.

13. *"Medical Center,"* CBS-TV Press Release, July 18, 1972.

14. Bell, "TV's On-Again Romance with Medicine," 26–27.

15. Ibid., 23, 83.

16. Ibid., 83.

17. "Are Human Embryo Transplants in the Offing?," NBC-TV Press Release, Oct. 11, 1972.

18. Dick Adler, *"Medical Center,"* Los Angeles Times (found undated and unpaged in the files of the Television Information Office Library).

19. Ibid.

20. Davidson, "Next Week: Periarteritis Nodosa," 14.

21. Ibid.

22. Ibid., 16.

23. Ibid.

24. Ibid.

25. Philip Kalisch, Beatrice Kalisch, and Margaret Scobey, *Images of Nurses on Television* (New York: Springer, 1983), 45.

26. Adler, *"Medical Center."*

27. Tim Brooks and Earle Marsh, *The Complete Directory to Prime Time Network TV Shows, 1946–Present* (New York: Ballantine, 1979), 388.

28. Ray Loyd, "Norman Felton Explodes Past: Says *Playhouse 90* Had to Go," *Hollywood Reporter*, May 21, 1968.

29. "Dial Hot Line," *Daily Variety*, March 9, 1970.

30. "New ABC Television Network Series *Matt Lincoln* Begins Production," ABC-TV Press Release, June 12, 1970; and "New ABC Television Network Series *Dial Hot Line* Gets New Number—Now Called 'Matt Lincoln,' " ABC-TV Press Release, June 8, 1970.

31. Leonard Maltin, *TV Movies 1985–86* (New York: Signet, 1984), 430.

32. Advertising pages to British paperback edition of Richard Frede, *The Interns* (London: Corgi Books, 1962).

33. Brown, *Television*, 264.

34. Ibid., 311.

35. Ibid., 307–8.

36. Ibid., 308.

37. Ibid., 307–8.

38. Paul Starr, *The Social Transformation of American Medicine* (New York: Basic Books, 1983), 379.

39. Ibid., 378–419.

40. Ibid., 405–9.

41. Ibid., 393–408.

42. Ibid., 408–11. See also Ivan Illich, *Medical Nemesis* (New York: Pantheon, 1976); Victor Fuchs, *Who Shall Live* (New York: Basic Books, 1974); Barbara Ehrenreich and Diedre English, *For Their Own Good* (New York: Anchor Books, 1978).

43. Starr, *The Social Transformation of American Medicine*, 383.

44. Daniel Callahan, "Health and Society: Some Ethical Imperatives," *Daedalus* 106:1 (Winter 1977), 23–34. Quote on pp. 32–33.

45. Ibid., 33.

46. Aaron Wildavsky, "Doing Better and Feeling Worse: The Political Pathology of Health Policy," *Daedalus* 106:1 (Winter 1977), 105–25. Quote on p. 105.

47. Joseph Turow, "Coverage of Health Subjects in the Evening News, 1969–71," unpublished research, 1985.

48. Callahan, "Health and Society," 47.

49. David Rintels, "Will Marcus Welby Always Make You Well?," *New York Times*, March 12, 1972, Section 2, p. 1.

50. Dick Hobson, "Tab, Rock, and Now Chad," *TV Guide*, Sep. 19, 1970, p. 26.

51. Richard Warren Lewis, "Thwack: There's Nothing Subtle about Chad Everett's Tennis Game—Or His Life Style," *TV Guide*, March 8, 1975, p. 26.

52. Hobson, "Tab, Rock, and Now Chad," 24.

53. Jeanie Kasindorf, "I Have Three Horses and Three Dogs . . . and a Wife," *TV Guide*, Aug. 19, 1972, p. 15.

54. Muriel Davidson, "Viewer, Heal Thyself," *TV Guide*, July 21, 1973, pp. 21–24.

55. "Look-Listen Opinion Poll Names *Medical Center* as Most Liked Television Program," CBS-TV Press Release, March 23, 1971; and "David Hartman Honored by National Conference on Christians and Jews," NBC-TV Press Release, Oct. 31, 1972.

Chapter 9. Sexism, Stiffs, and Speed

Along with other sources that are noted below, this chapter is informed by interviews with Gerald Abrams, Don Brinkley, Larraine Day, Howard Dimsdale, Norman Felton, John Furia, Lou Gallo, Jerry Isenberg, Bettye Ackerman Jaffe, Michael Kozoll, Randy Mantooth, Mathew Rapf, Clinton Roath, M.D., Victor Rosen, M.D., Victor Shaw, Hannah Shearer, E.W. Swackhamer, David Victor, and Susan Sullivan.

1. Medical consultants had worked in Hollywood since at least the 1930s. They had been overshadowed from the mid-1950s through the late 1960s by the guiding hand of the Los Angeles County Medical Association (LACMA) and the American Medical Association Advisory Panel. As producers backed

away from the AMA as a guarantor of authenticity, and as medical series and TV movies streamed into production around Hollywood, medical consultants came to the forefront.

An article in the *LACMA Physician* referred to the independent consultants as "LACMA doctors," emphasizing their affiliation with the LA County Medical Association. While LACMA's relationship with TV was very different in the 1970s than in the *Medic* days of the mid-1950s, the editors of the magazine, at least, seem to have wanted to give the impression that their organization had some control over TV's images of physicians. See, for example, Charles Witbeck, "Real Live Nursing on TV," *New York Daily Column*, Feb. 27, 1970, Fold-out section; "Our Man in Hollywood," *Advance: The Magazine of the University of Michigan Medical School, Hospitals, and School of Nursing*, Summer 1982, pp. 9–13; Darrell Maddox, "How They Keep TV Medical Shows Honest," *Modern Healthcare*, Nov. 1975, p. 40; and Howard Bender, "The Lacma Doctors Behind the Television Doctors," *LACMA Physician*, Jan. 19, 1981, pp. 35–42.

2. Milford Rouse, M.D., "Joys and Problems of Being a Doctor," *Today's Health*, June 1967, pp. 72, 58; and Stella Neeson, "Mysticism Lost," *JAMA* 232:4 (April 28, 1975), 374–76.

3. "The Superdoctors on TV Do Disservice to Medicine," *National Observer*, Sep. 27, 1975, p. 10.

4. See Joseph N. Bell, "TV's On-Again Romance with Medicine," *Today's Health*, March 1970, p. 23. The AMA continued to act publicly as if it saw an obligation to make sure that its constituency was portrayed well in TV fiction. Its Advisory Committee for TV, Radio, and Motion Pictures continued to check the technical accuracy of scripts voluntarily submitted to it. But the Association's leaders were not as involved in public discussions as they had been during the 1960s. That reflected the organization's decreased role in creating shows and thus its decreased self-interest in comments about them. It also may have reflected a willingness to take a relatively neutral posture and to let the heads of more specialized medical organizations go public with criticisms. That happened increasingly during the 1970s.

Articles in AMA journals displayed mixed feelings about TV's flood of doctors during the 1970s. When the concern was not with the image of physicians (and it wasn't very much), it tended, as in the 1960s, to focus on a narrow notion of learning: on the specific medical facts viewers might pick up from the shows. The articles concluded that doctor shows were interesting and could be informative. However, their diseases were much too exotic for the public to learn medical tips of value. The AMA's leadership seems to have decided that the best way to educate the public about medical care was not through those shows but through the proliferation of local TV information programs specifically about health. See, for example, Norman Mark, "How Television Tries to Close the Health Information Gap," *Today's Health*, Jan. 1976, pp. 31–52; F.J. Ingelfinger, M.D., "Medical Information on Commercial TV" (an editorial), *JAMA* 204:11 (March 11, 1976), 607–8; and Drummond Rennie, M.D., "What You Can Learn About Health from TV," *Today's Health*, Jan. 1973, pp. 22–26.

It might also be added that in 1973, at the height of the '70s doctor cycle, the American Hospital Association set up a Hospital Advisory Council with the goal of cultivating a positive presentations of hospitals and hospital administration and discouraging negative ones. According to an AHA official, what they found, to their dismay, was that many producers and writers were in no mood to get rid of useful stereotypes simply because an organization with a vested interest in the area said that the stereotypes were not realistic. As a result, it did not take long for the Hospital Advisory Council to close shop.

5. Bell, "TV's On-Again Romance with Medicine," 84.

6. "Review of *Medical Center*," *Variety*, Oct. 1971.

7. "Review of 'Panic in Echo Park,' " *Daily Variety*, 1976.

8. The following are titles of representative NBC-TV press releases that deal with the show's impact. The dates of the releases are in parentheses: "*Emergency!* Procedure Adopted by Tucson (Ariz.) Fire Department" (2/7/72); "Young Viewers Benefit from Practical Tips Offered by NBC-TV's *Emergency!*," NBC-TV Press Release (9/4/73); "Popular *Emergency!* Series to Continue on NBC-TV Next Season" (2/19/76); "United States Senator Alan Cranston Lauds *Emergency!*" (no date); "Jack Webb Commended for *Emergency!*" (4/3/72); "*Emergency!* Credited with Spurring Growth of Paramedic Program" (3/15/73); and "Youngsters Benefit from *Emergency!* Series" (3/13/74). For a humorous unfavorable reaction to the series, see Michael J. Arlen's column in *The New Yorker*, Nov. 8. 1976, pp. 160–61.

9. *Code R* concerned a rescue team based on an island off the California coast. It was produced out of Warner Brothers by William Self, who had worked for Webb and Cinader on *Emergency!*. It aired on CBS for only about four months during spring 1977. *Mobile One*, about a mobile medical team—a surgeon, a general practitioner, and a surgical assistant/driver—had no direct connections to the *Emergency!* staff. Bruce Lansbury served as executive producer, with Bob Hamilton as producer and writer of the pilot. It was also for CBS and also for 1977. It never made it past a half-hour pilot stage. The pilot did, however, air during the summer of that year.

10. See Nancy Y. Hoffman, "The Doctor and the Detective Story," *JAMA* 224:1 (April 2, 1973), 74–77; and Julian Symons, *Mortal Consequences: A History from the Detective Story to the Crime Novel* (New York: Harper and Row, 1972), 84–89.

11. For a contemporary evaluation of the series, see "Review of *Diagnosis Unknown*," *TV Guide*, Aug. 13–19, 1960, p. 27. The reviewer (whose name is abbreviated F. DeB.) concluded that "there is nothing really wrong with [the show] except that it's kind of tiresome."

12. Rona Lee Kleiman, "Quincy's Biggest Lab Experiment," *TV Guide* Dec. 5, 1981, pp. 27–30. Quote on p. 28.

13. Sander Vanocur, "The 'Quincy' Statement," *Washington Post*, May 22, 1977, p. L3.

14. Ibid.

15. Ibid.

16. Daniel Seligman, "Operating on Economics," *Fortune*, June 2, 1980, p. 42.

17. Daniel Seligman, "Klugmanism," *Fortune*, April 20, 1981, pp. 97–98. The popular press, however, was on Klugman's side. See Niles Latham, " 'Dr. Quincy' Goes to Bat for Millions," *New York Post*, March 9, 1981, p. 10; and "Jack Klugman Receives Hubert H. Humphrey Humanitarian Award," NBC-TV Press Release (1/24/83). See also Victor Cohn, "TV's *Quincy* Tells Hill About Rare Diseases," *Washington Post*, March 10, 1981, p. A4.

18. "Leave of Reality," *Wall Street Journal*, March 12, 1981, p. 30.

19. Klugman's honors and activities are discussed in, for example, "California State Senate Honors NBC and Jack Klugman for *Quincy* drama about Medical Jurisprudence in Rape Cases," NBC-TV Press Release (6/13/77); "Jack Klugman and *Quincy* honored by Two Organizations of Retirees," NBC-TV Press Release (9/28/78); "*Quincy* Team Honored by Plastic Surgeons' Group," NBC-TV Press Release (1/18/1979); "Jack Klugman Receives First Milton Helpern Award," NBC-TV Press Release (4/9/79); Kay Gardella, "Why Klugman Is a Class Act," *New York Daily News*, July 12, 1979, p. 119; Marilyn Beck, "How Jack Klugman Doctored His Ego," *New York Daily News*, Dec. 28, 1979; and "Jack Klugman Receives Hubert H. Humphrey Humanitarian Award," NBC-TV Press Release (1/24/83). Part of Klugman's speech to the Mt. Sinai Medical School was quoted in the *Wall Street Journal*, Dec. 4, 1980, p. 30.

20. Lou Jacobs, Jr., "Jack Klugman: Television's Medical Examiner says 'Quincy Is Mostly Me,' " *Lab World*, Feb. 1978, pp. 16+.

21. The *Kelly* script can be found in the UCLA Television and Motion Picture Archives. The reader will find many clear and fascinating parallels with the *Kildare* films.

22. Philip Kalisch, Beatrice Kalisch, and Margaret Scobey, *Images of Nursing on Television* (New York: Springer, 1982), 22.

23. Ibid., 62–63.

24. James McLaughlin, "Characteristics and Symbolic Functions of Fictional Television Medical Professionals and Their Effect on Children," Master's Thesis, Annenberg School of Communications, University of Pennsylvania, 1975, pp. 10–13. See also James McLaughlin, "The Doctor Shows," *Journal of Communication*, Summer 1975, pp. 182–84.

25. McLaughlin, "Characteristics and Symbolic Functions of Fictional Television Medical Professionals," 10–13.

Chapter 10. A Different Spin

Along with other sources that are noted below, this chapter is informed by interviews with William Blinn, Walter Dishell, M.D., Norman Felton, James Goldstone, Eugene Hoffman, M.D., Chris Hutson, R.N., Jerry Isenberg, Abby Mann, Christopher Morgan, Clinton Roath, M.D., Victor Rosen, M.D., Sterling Silliphant, Elliot Silverstein, and Jerry Thorpe.

1. Kaye Gardella, "Writer Says Medic Shows Must Be Real or Perish," *New York Daily News*, May 6, 1975, p. 82.

2. Ibid.

3. Ibid.

4. Ibid.

5. Bob Williams, "MD Series Offers a Cure-All," *New York Post*, Sep. 4, 1975, p. 58.

6. Darrell Maddox, "How They Keep TV Medical Shows Honest," *Modern Healthcare*, Nov. 1975, pp. 37–42. Reference is to page 42.

7. Tom Shales, "*Medical Story*: On the Danger List?," *Washington Post*, Sep. 25, 1975, p. E14.

8. Ad for *The Lazarus Syndrome, TV Guide* (New York City edition), Sep. 8, 1979, p. A-89.

9. Shales, *"Medical Story:* On the Danger List?," E14. See also John Carmody, "Reassuring Medicine," *Washington Post,* Aug. 24, 1976, p. B5.

10. For a sample of generally favorable reactions, see Kay Gardella, "Abby Mann to Do Surgery on the Medical Profession," *New York Daily News,* July 14, 1975, p. 63; Val Adams, "Medical Story Premiere Gives Needle to Bad Docs," *New York Daily News,* Sep. 3, 1975, p. 80; John J. O'Conner, "TV: New on NBC, Two Comedies and *Medical Story,*" *New York Times,* Sep. 4, 1975, p. 70; and Bud Gordon, "It's Time TV Showed Doctors as They Really Are," *The National Enquirer,* Sep. 30, 1975, p. 58. For examples of unfavorable reactions in the popular press, see Bob Williams, "MD Series Offers a Cure-All," *New York Post,* Sep. 4, 1975, p. 58; and James Brown, "The Malpractice of *Medical Story,*" Oct. 23, 1975, p. 24. See also *Variety*'s unfavorable review of the premiere episode, Sep. 4, 1975. The same review appeared in *Daily Variety.*

Chapter 11. "Suicide Is Painless"

Along with other sources that are noted below, this chapter is informed by interviews with Harry Ackerman, William Asher, Larry Balmaggia, Jackie Cooper, Walter Dishell, M.D., Mike Farrell, Larry Gelbart, Sheldon Keller, Dennis Koenig, Perry Lafferty, Lawrence Marks, Burt Metcalf, John Mitchell, Gene Reynolds, Andy Siegel, E.W. Swackhamer, Robert Wood, and Perry Grant.

1. Neil Hickey, "It Pays Me an Extra Gall Bladder a Week," *TV Guide,* March 24, 1972, pp. 18–20. Quote is on p. 20.

2. David S. Reiss, *M*A*S*H* (Indianapolis and New York: Bobbs-Merrill, 1980), 110.

3. See Max Alverez, *Index to Motion Pictures Reviewed by Variety, 1907–1980* (Metuchen, N.J: Scarecrow, 1982).

4. Tim Brooks and Earl Marsh, *The Complete Directory to Prime Time Network TV Shows* (New York: Ballantine Books, 1979), 317.

5. Philip Kalisch, Beatrice Kalisch, and Margaret Scobey, *Images of Nurses on Television* (New York: Springer, 1983), 35.

6. Frank N. Magill, *Magill's Survey of Cinema* (Englewood Cliffs, N.J.: Salem, 1980), vol. 1, p. 303.

7. David S. Reiss, *M*A*S*H* (Indianapolis and New York: Bobbs-Merrill, 1980), 16.

8. *Ibid.*

9. William Henry, "M*A*S*H," *Horizon,* Sep. 1978, p. 84.

10. Cleveland Amory, "M*A*S*H," *TV Guide,* Feb. 10, 1973, p. 44.

11. Rogert Hofeldt, "Cultural Bias in *M*A*S*H,*" *Society,* Aug. 1978. pp. 96–99.

12. Lawrence O'Toole, "Farewell to the Gang at the Front, *Maclean's,* Feb. 28, 1980, pp. 46–47. Quote on p. 47.

13. Cyclops, "Mashed Morality," *Newsweek,* Apr. 23, 1973, p. 53. See also Lois Markham, "How to Make Commercial TV Work for You," *Scholastic Teacher,* Nov./Dec. 1974, pp. 8–11; and William Henry III, "M*A*S*H," *Horizon,* Sep. 1978, pp. 84–87.

14. See, for example, "TV's Quadruple Threat," *Newsweek*, Sep. 9, 1974, pp. 52–53; Joseph Bell, "*M*A*S*H*'s Alan Alda: A Real Person in a Make-Believe World," *Good Housekeeping*, Nov. 1974, pp. 96ff; John Rich, "*M*A*S*H*," *TV Guide*, Aug. 30, 1975; Alan Alda, "What Every Woman Should Know About Men," *Ms.*, Oct. 1975, pp. 15–16; Alan Alda, "Why Should Men Care About the E.R.A.?," *Ms.*, July 1976, pp. 48ff; Elizabeth Kaye, "Arlene and Alan Alda: A Love Story," *McCall's*, Jan. 1976, pp. 16ff; Susan Edmiston, "Alan Alda: America's Sweetheart," *Redbook*, July 1976, pp. 88ff; Gloria Emerson, "Alan Alda: What Makes a Woman's Man?," *Vogue*, Jan. 1979, pp. 133ff; George Vecsey, "Alan Alda: Madcap Doctor from *M*A*S*H*," *Reader's Digest*, Aug. 1979, pp. 69–73; and David S. Reiss, "Alan Alda: His Road to Success and Love," *Good Housekeeping*, Nov. 1980, pp. 150ff. The first major article about Alda, in *TV Guide*, took a very different tack. See Dick Lochte, "He Falls Down a Lot," *TV Guide*, Feb. 24, 1973, pp. 20–24.

15. Emerson, "Alan Alda: What Makes a Woman's Man?," 186.

16. See "A *M*A*S*H* Note for Doctors," *Time*, May 28, 1979, p. 68; and "Alan Alda's Prescription for Doctors," *Good Housekeeping*, Oct. 1979, pp. 78ff.

17. "Alan Alda's Prescription for Doctors," 78.

18. Drummond Rennie, M.D., "What You Can Learn About Health from TV," *Today's Health*, Jan. 1973, pp. 22–26.

19. Ibid., 25.

20. Ibid., 26.

21. Ibid.

Chapter 12. Chasing the Spirit of *M*A*S*H*

Along with other sources that are noted below, this chapter is informed by interviews with Larry Gelbart, Jerry Davis, Walter Dishell, M.D., Sheldon Keller, Dennis Koenig, Tom Kurzy, Perry Lafferty, Lawrence Marks, Burt Metcalf, David Newman, Gene Reynolds, Max Shulman, Andy Stein, and E.W. Swackhamer.

1. William Henry III, "*M*A*S*H*," *Horizon*, Sep. 1978, pp. 84–87.

2. Philip Kalisch, Beatrice Kalisch, and Margaret Scobey, *Images of Nurses on Television* (New York: Springer, 1982), 135.

3. Ray Richmond, "An Autopsy on *AfterMASH*," *Los Angeles Times*, Sep. 22, 1983, Life Section, pp. 1ff.

4. Ibid., 1.

5. Ibid.

6. Lee Magulies, "Hoping for Series Life in the AfterMASH," *Los Angeles Times*, Life Section, p. 1 (found undated in the files of the Television Information Office Library, New York).

7. Tom Shales, *Washington Post*, Jan. 28, 1983 (found unpaged in the files of the Television Information Office Library).

8. Richmond, "An Autopsy on *AfterMASH*," 8.

9. Aaron Wildavsky, "Doing Better and Feeling Worse: The Political Pathology of Health Care," *Daedalus* 106:1 (Winter 1977), 105–6.

10. Ibid.

Chapter 13. "Our Walls Are Cleaner"

Along with other sources that are noted below, this chapter is informed by interviews with Ed Begley, Jr., Josh Brand, Don Brinkley, Jackie Cooper, Tia Dankowski, R.N., Walter Dishell, M.D., John Falsey, Tom Fontana, Stephen Furst, Chris Hutson, R.N., Mike Kozoll, Barbara Krause, Norman Lloyd, Howie Mandell, John Masius, Bruce Paltrow, Beth Hill Shafer, Charles Siebert, Brandon Tartikoff, John Whelpley, Shimon Wincelberg, Michael Zinberg, and Randy Zisk.

1. Todd Gitlin, *Inside Prime Time* (New York: Pantheon, 1985), 279.
2. Ibid., 281.
3. Samuel Shem, M.D., *The House of God* (New York: Dell Publishing, 1978), 9, 19.
4. See "Nation's Critics Praise *St. Elsewhere*," NBC Television Publicity Release, Nov. 12, 1982; and "9 More Segments of Acclaimed *St. Elsewhere* Ordered," NBC Television Publicity Release, Dec. 6, 1982.
5. Sally Bedell, "NBC Shapes Strategy to Keep *St. Elsewhere*," *New York Times*, Feb. 2, 1982, p. 19.
6. Fred Rothenberg, "*St. Elsewhere* Deserves Many Happy Returns," a *New York Post* article from the 1983 fall premiere period found, undated, in the files of the Television Information Office Library.
7. Tartikoff quote is based on the recollection of John Masius. See also Rothenberg, "*St. Elsewhere* Deserves Many Happy Returns"; Bedell, "NBC Shapes Strategy to Keep *St. Elsewhere*," 19; "First Aid for *St. Elsewhere*," *Time*, Jan. 17, 1983, p. 63; and Fred Rothenberg, "NBC's *St. Elsewhere*: It's 100 Times Healthier," *New York Post*, Nov. 19, 1986, p. 71.
8. Rothenberg, "*St. Elsewhere* Deserves Many Happy Returns."
9. Susan Oakie, "Art Imitates Life and Death," *Washington Post*, Feb. 5, 1986, Health Section, p. 14.
10. Ibid., 13.
11. Ibid., 14.
12. Ibid., 12.
13. Jefferson Graham, "*St. Elsewhere* Carves Its Niche," *USA Today*, Dec. 18, 1984, p. 5D.
14. Ibid.
15. Monica Collins, "*St. Elsewhere*: Healthy Dose of Fresh Ideas," *USA Today*, July 23, 1985, p. 3D.

Chapter 14. Elsewhere and Back

Along with other sources that are noted below, this chapter is informed by interviews with Gerald Abrams, William Asher, Don Brinkley, Tom Fontana, Elliot Gould, Robert Halmi, Chris Hutson, Jay Kahn, M.D., John Masius, Jerry McNeely, Bernie Orenstein, Bruce Paltrow, Robert Reed, Charles Siebert, and David Victor.

1. "Michael Learned Gets Inside New Character," CBS Television Network Press Release, March 13, 1981.

2. "New Hospital Series," *New York Daily News*, June 25, 1986, p. 71. Bellevue's citation as one of the city's worst hospitals is also in this article.

3. Philip Kalisch, Beatrice Kalisch, and Margaret Scobey, *Images of Nurses of Television* (New York: Springer, 1983), 153.

4. John J. O'Conner, "TV: *Nurse* Back as 6-Part Series with same Stars," *New York Times*, April 2, 1981, p. C-20.

5. *TV Guide* (Philadelphia edition), March 23, 1988, p. A-130.

6. See, for example, the weekly issues of the *American Medical News*, published by the American Medical Association, for these and other developments.

7. By the early 1980s, the American Medical Association, in a cost-saving move, closed the Advisory Committee office in Los Angeles and carried on the operation from Chicago. Panel members such as Eugene Hoffman objected that the distance would weaken the ability of the Association to influence Hollywood, but their argument wasn't persuasive.

8. See, for example, William Hunter, M.D., "How to Boost the Cost of Health Care," *American Medical News*, Feb. 17, 1984, p. 4; Malcolm Watts, "The U.S. Way of Doing Things," *American Medical News*, March 16, 1984, p. 4; Timothy Flaherty, "AMA Membership a Necessity," *American Medical News*, Feb. 1, 1985, p. 4; Ellis Moffitt, "What's Ahead for Physicians," *American Medical News*, Oct. 12, 1984, p. 4; Maurice Albin, "Public Needs Information on Trends, M.D. Warns" (Letter to Editor), *American Medical News*, July 27, 1984, p. 6; David Gray, "The Perception of M.D. Fees," *American Medical News*, March 8, 1985, p. 4; and Paul Honan, "M.D. Asks: Can U.S. Afford Best Medical Care?" (Letter to Editor), *American Medical News*, June 7, 1985, p. 5.

9. The comment was made on the PBS program *Managing Our Miracles*.

Bibliography

Adams, Val. "Medical Story Premiere Gives Needle to Bad Docs." *New York Daily News*, Sep. 3, 1975, p. 80.

Adams, Val. "News of Television and Radio." *New York Times*, Oct. 13, 1963, Section 2, p. 21.

Adler, Dick. *"Medical Center."* *Los Angeles Times* (found undated and unpaged in the files of the Television Information Office Library).

Adler, Dick. "One Outrage That Ought to Be Aired." *Los Angeles Times*, Nov. 8, 1974.

"Alan Alda's Prescription for Doctors." *Good Housekeeping*, Oct. 1979, pp. 78ff.

Albin, Maurice. "Public Needs Information on Trends, MD Warns." (Letter to Editor), *American Medical News*, July 27, 1984, p. 6.

Alda, Alan. "What Every Woman Should Know About Men." *Ms.*, Oct. 1975, pp. 15–16.

Alda, Alan. "Why Should Men Care About the E.R.A?" *Ms.*, July 1976, pp. 48ff.

"Alfred Schneider Points Out That the Treatments of Doctors and Lawyers on Television Have Evolved into 'Better Rounded Portraits' Than in the Past." ABC-TV Press Release, Oct. 18, 1979.

Alverez, Max. *Index to Motion Pictures Reviewed by Variety 1907–1980.* Metuchen, N.J.: Scarecrow, 1982.

Amory, Cleveland. *"M*A*S*H."* *TV Guide*, Feb. 10, 1973, p. 44.

"An Analysis of *The Eleventh Hour.*" *TV Guide*, March 2, 1964, pp. 18–21.

"Are Human Embryo Transplants in the Offing?" NBC-TV Press Release, Oct. 11, 1972.

Arlen, Michael. Column in *The New Yorker*, Nov. 8, 1976, pp. 160–61.

Astor, Gerald. "TV's Dr. Marcus Welby." *Look*, March 23, 1971, pp. 56–59.

"Ayres Enrolled in Objectors' Camp: Chicago Theatres Ban Films." *New York Times*, April 2, 1942, p. 23.

Barnouw, Erik. *The Golden Web.* New York: Oxford Univ. Press, 1968.

Barnouw, Erik. *The Image Empire.* New York: Oxford Univ. Press, 1972.

Barnouw, Erik. *The Sponsor.* New York: Oxford Univ. Press, 1978.

Beck, Marilyn. "How Jack Klugman Doctored His Ego." *New York Daily News*, Dec. 28, 1979.

Bedell, Sally. "NBC Shapes Strategy to Keep *St. Elsewhere.*" *New York Times*, Feb. 2, 1982, p. 19.

Bell, Joseph N. "TV's On-Again Romance with Medicine." *Today's Health* 48:3 (March 1970), 23–84.

Bell, Joseph. "*M*A*S*H*'s Alan Alda: A Real Person in a Make-Believe World." *Good Housekeeping*, Nov. 1974, pp. 96ff.

"Ben Casey: TV's Dour Doctor." *Look*, May 8, 1962, pp. 38–49.

Bender, Howard. "The LACMA Doctors Behind the Television Doctors." *LACMA Physician*, Jan. 19, 1981, pp. 35–42.

Bianco, Margery. "Jean Hersholt's Andersen." *The Horn Book*, May 1944, pp. 164–65.

"The Bold Ones." NBC-TV Press Release, July 13, 1970.

Brooks, Tim, and Earle Marsh. *The Complete Directory to Prime Time Network TV Shows*. New York: Ballantine, 1979.

Brown, James, "The Malpractice of *Medical Story.*" *New York Post*, Oct. 23, 1975, p. 24.

Brown, Les. *Television: The Business Behind the Box*. New York: Harcourt Brace Jovanovich, 1972.

Cahal, M.F. "Nationwide Survey: Family Doctor in High Esteem." *G.P.* 24:145 (1951).

"California State Senate Honors NBC and Jack Klugman for *Quincy* Drama About Medical Jurisprudence in Rape Cases." NBC-TV Press Release, June 13, 1977.

Callahan, Daniel. "Health and Society: Some Ethical Imperatives." *Daedalus* 106:1 (Winter 1977), 23–34, 47.

Cantor, Muriel. *The Politics of TV Entertainment*. Beverly Hills: Sage Publications, 1982.

Cantor, John. "Reassuring Medicine." *Washington Post*, Aug. 24, 1976, p. B5.

Carter, Richard. "What Women Really Think About Their Doctors." *Good Housekeeping*, Aug. 1961, pp. 60–61, 149–53.

"The Case of Casey." (Letter to the Editor), *New York World Telegram and Sun*, Nov. 27, 1962, p. 26.

"The Case of Lew Ayres." *New York Times*, April 3, 1942, p. 20.

Cawelti, John. *The Six-Gun Mystique*. Bowling Green, Ohio: Bowling Green Univ. Press, 1972.

Chrichton, Kyle. "Here's the Doctor." *Collier's*, April 4, 1936, pp. 17, 53.

Cohn, Victor. "TV's *Quincy* Tells Hill About Rare Diseases." *Washington Post*, March 10, 1981, p. A4.

Collins, Monica. "*Elsewhere:* Healthy Dose of Fresh Ideas." *USA Today*, July 23, 1985, p. 3D.

Cyclops, "Mashed Morality," *Newsweek*, Apr. 23, 1973, p. 53.

"David Hartman Honored by National Conference on Christians and Jews." NBC-TV Press Release, Oct. 31, 1972.

Davidson, Bill. "Next Week: Periarteritis Nodosa." *TV Guide*, July 16, 1971, pp. 12–14, 16.

Davidson, Bill. "TV's Surly Medico." *Saturday Evening Post*, May 12, 1962, pp. 62–67.

Davidson, Muriel. "Television's Personal Physicians." *McCall's*, Aug. 1962, p. 148.

Davidson, Muriel. "The 'I Don't Care' Actor Who Cares Too Much." *TV Guide*, June 22, 1963, pp. 10–13.

Davidson, Muriel. "Viewer, Heal Thyself." *TV Guide*, July 21, 1973, pp. 21–24.

de Rosa, Robert. "Life as Father *Really* Leads It." *TV Guide*, Jan. 5, 1962, pp. 22–25.

"Dial Hot Line." *Daily Variety*, March 9, 1970.

Dichter, Ernst. "Do Your Patients Really Like You?" *New York State Journal of Medicine* 54:1 (Jan. 1, 1954), 222–26.

Doan, Richard K. "Psychologists Hit NBC over 11th Hour Program." *New York Herald Tribune*, Dec. 2, 1962 (no page noted as found in the files of the Television Information Office Library).

"Doctor!" *Newsweek*, Nov. 20, 1955, p. 94.

"The Doctors and the Nurses New Title for *The Nurses."* CBS Press Release, Sep. 15, 1964.

"Dr. Christian in the House." *Newsweek*, July 7, 1947, pp. 134–35.

"Dr. Kildare Coming to J-A Comic Pages." *New York Journal-American*, Oct. 14, 1962, section 1, p. 6.

Dunning, John. *Tune in Yesterday.* Englewood Cliffs, N.J.: Prentice-Hall, 1976.

Durslug, Melvin. "Dr. Kildare Is a Doll." *McCall's*, March 30, 1963, p. 15.

Durslug, Melvin. "Second Stethoscope—For How Long?" *TV Guide*, March 11, 1972, pp. 32–34.

Dwight Whitney. "The Courtship of Sam Jaffe." *TV Guide*, Jan. 5, 1963, pp. 19–21.

Easton, Robert (Ed.). *Max Brand's Best Stories.* New York: Dodd, Mead, 1967.

Easton, Robert. *Max Brand: The Big Westerner.* Norman, Okla.: Univ. of Oklahoma Press, 1970.

Edmiston, Susan. "Alan Alda: America's Sweetheart." *Redbook*, July 1976, pp. 88ff.

Edwards, Vincent. "My Battle with Ben Casey." *Seventeen*, Feb. 1964, p. 194.

Ehrenreich, Barbara, and Diedre English. *For Their Own Good: 150 Years of Expert Advice to Women.* New York: Anchor, 1978.

Ehrlich, Henry. "The Nice Men Cometh." *McCall's*, May 1972, p. 25.

Ellison, Bob. "Robert Young's Toughest Role." *Today's Health*, May 1971, pp. 25ff.

"Emergency! Procedure Adopted by Tucson (Ariz.) Fire Department." NBC-TV Press Release, Feb. 7, 1972,

"Emergency! Credited With Spurring Growth of Paramedic Program." NBC-TV Press Release, March 15, 1973.

Emerson, Gloria. "Alan Alda: What Makes a Woman's Man?" *Vogue*, Jan. 1979, pp. 133ff, 186.

Ettema, James, and D. Charles Whitney (Eds.). *Individuals in Mass Media Organizations.* Beverly Hills: Sage Publications, 1982.

"First Aid for *St. Elsewhere."* *Time*, Jan. 17, 1983, p. 63.

Flaherty, Timothy. "AMA Membership a Necessity." *American Medical News*, Feb. 1, 1985, p. 4.

Frede, Richard. *The Interns.* London: Corgi Books, 1962 (advertising pages to British paperback edition).

Friedson, Elliot. *Patient's Views of Medical Practice.* New York: Russel Sage Foundation, 1961.

"From the TV Mailbag." New York Times, Nov. 11, 1962, Section II, p. 19.

Fuchs, Victor. Who Shall Live. New York: Basic Books, 1974.

Gandy, Oscar. Beyond Agenda-Setting. Norwood, N.J.: Ablex, 1980.

Gardella, Kaye. "AMA Says Kildare Stars Aid Practice of Medicine." New York Daily News, June 23, 1964, p. 22.

Gardella, Kaye. "Why Klugman Is a Class Act." New York Daily News, July 12, 1979, p. 119.

Gardella, Kaye. "Abby Mann to Do Surgery on the Medical Profession." New York Daily News, July 14, 1975, p. 63.

Gardella, Kaye. "Writer Says Medic Shows Must Be Real or Perish." New York Daily News, May 6,, 1975, p. 82.

Gehman, Richard. "Caseyitis: How the Epidemic Started and Why It Spread." TV Guide, Sep. 22, 1962, pp. 15–19.

Gehman, Richard. "TV's Surly Surgeon Softens." TV Guide, April 3–9, 1964, pp. 20–22.

Gitlin, Todd. Inside Prime Time. New York: Pantheon, 1985.

Gitlin, Todd. "Prime Time Ideology: The Hegemonic Process in Television Entertainment." Social Problems 26:3, pp. 251–86.

Godbout, Oscar. "NBC Rift Leads to End of Medic." New York Times, May 25, 1956, p. 63.

Godbout, Oscar. "One Medic Show Loses Unit's Seal." New York Times, April 10, 1956, 47.

Gordon, Bud. "It's Time TV Showed Doctors as They Really Are." The National Enquirer, Sep. 30, 1975, p. 58.

Gould, Jack. "Disturbed Television." New York Times, Oct. 28, 1962, Section II, p. 211.

Gould, Jack. "High Ratings of Drs. Casey and Kildare Reveal Public's High Interest in Medicine." New York Times, March 12, 1962, p. 55.

Gould, Jack. "Television in Review." New York Times, March 11, 1956, p. 84.

Graham, Jefferson. "St. Elsewhere Carves Its Niche." USA Today, Dec. 18, 1984, p. 5D.

Gray, David. "The Perception of MD Fees." American Medical News, March 8, 1985, p. 4.

Gross, Ben. "Want to Become an MD? Just Watch Your Home TV?" New York Daily News, Sep. 25, 1969, p. 102.

Guess, J. "Medicine's Tragic Failure." Journal of the South Carolina Medical Association 48 (1952), pp. 151–53.

Halberstam, Michael. "An M.D. Reviews Dr. Welby of TV." New York Times Magazine, Jan. 16, 1962, pp. 34ff.

Hall, Hamlin. "Frederick Schiller Faust." In Edward James (ed.), Dictionary of American Biography, Supplement Three, 1944–45. New York: Charles Scribners' Sons, 1973.

Hammond, Sally. "The Nurse Plays in a Real Hospital." New York Post, July 23, 1962, p. 51.

A Handbook of General Advance Information on "Internes Can't Take Money." Paramount Pictures Advertising and Publicity Department, 1936.

Hano, Arnold. "The Actor Who Looks like a Star but Sounds like a Tax Accountant." TV Guide, Sep. 27, 1969, p. 22.

"Happy to Be C.O., Ayres Explains." New York Times, April 1, 1942, p. 23.

Harrison, Emma. "TV Show Assailed by Psychologists." *New York Times*, Dec. 1962, Section 1, p. 84.

"Healer of the Sick." *TV Guide*, Oct. 15, 1955, pp. 5–6.

Henry, William III. "*M*A*S*H*." *Horizon*, Sep. 1978, pp. 84–87.

Hersholt, Jean. "The Two Never Met." *Saturday Review of Literature*, Dec. 21, 1946, pp. 18–19.

Hickey, Neil. "It Pays Me an Extra Gall Bladder a Week." *TV Guide*, March 24, 1972, pp. 18–20.

Hobson, Dick. "Tab, Rock, and Now Chad." *TV Guide*, Sep. 19, 1970, pp. 24, 26.

Hofeldt, Roger. "Cultural Bias in *M*A*S*H*." *Society*, Aug. 1978, pp. 96–99.

Hoffman, Nancy Y. "The Doctor and the Detective Story." *JAMA* 224:1 (April 2, 1973), 74–77.

"Hollywood Dossier." *New York Times*, April 26, 1942, Section VIII, p. 3.

Honan, Paul. "MD Asks: Can US Afford Best Medical Care?" (Letter to Editor), *American Medical News*, June 7, 1985, p. 5.

Humphrey, Hal. " 'Good Samaritan' Loses Legal Bout." *Los Angeles Times*, June 19, 1964, Part V, p. 14.

Hunter, William, M.D. "How to Boost the Cost of Health Care." *American Medical News*, Feb. 17, 1984, p. 4.

Illich, Ivan. *Medical Nemesis*. New York: Pantheon, 1976.

"The Images of Doctors and Lawyers: Recommendations for Actions." University of Pennsylvania News Bureau, week of Oct. 19, 1979, p. 1.

Ingelfinger, F. J., M.D. "Medical Information on Commercial TV." (Editorial), *JAMA* 204:11 (March 11, 1976), 607ff.

"Jack Klugman and *Quincy* Honored by Two Organizations of Retirees." NBC-TV Press Release, Sep. 28, 1978.

"Jack Klugman Receives First Milton Helpern Award." NBC-TV Press Release, April 9, 1979.

"Jack Klugman Receives Hubert H. Humphrey Humanitarian Award." NBC-TV Press Release, Jan. 24, 1983.

"Jack Webb Commended for *Emergency!*" NBC-TV Press Release, April 3, 1972.

Jacobs, Lewis. *The Rise of the American Film*. New York: Teachers College Press, 1938.

Jacobs, Lou, Jr., "Jack Klugman: Television's Medical Examiner Says 'Quincy Is Mostly Me.' " *Lab World*, Feb. 1978, pp. 16ff.

"Just What the Doctor Ordered." *TV Guide*, April 30, 1955, pp. 20–21.

"Kalamazoo Survey Finds Attitudes Toward Doctors, Hospitals." *Journal of the Michigan State Medical Society* 61 (1962), 1464.

Kalisch, Philip, Beatrice Kalisch, and Margaret Scobey. *Images of Nurses on Television*. New York: Springer, 1982.

Kasindorf, Jeanie. "I Have Three Horses and Three Dogs . . . and a Wife." *TV Guide*, Aug. 19, 1972, p. 15.

Katz, Daniel, and Roger Kahn. *The Social Psychology of Organizations*. New York: John Wiley, 1966.

Kaye, Elizabeth. "Arlene and Alan Alda: A Love Story." *McCall's*, Jan. 1976, pp. 16ff.

Keats, John. "Rx for an MD on TV." *New York Times Magazine*, May 27, 1962, pp. 33–38.

Kilgallen, Dorothy. "Broadway Graprvine." *New York Journal American*, April 20, 1962, p. 11.

Kleiman, Rona Lee. "Quincy's Biggest Lab Experiment." *TV Guide*, Dec. 5, 1981, pp. 27–30.

Lardine, Bob. "This Show Needs a Nurse." *Daily News Magazine*, Oct. 14, 1962, pp. 8–9.

Latham, Niles. " 'Dr. Quincy' Goes to Bat for Millions." *New York Post*, March 9, 1981, p. 10.

Laurent, Lawrence. "A Second Look at Ben Casey Shows Network Feels Impact." *Washington Post*, May 9, 1962, p. C-12.

Lawson, Herbert, Jr. "Drs. Kildare, Casey Get Guidance from Medical Association." *Wall Street Journal*, Dec. 27, 1962, 1 ff.

"Leave of Reality." *Wall Street Journal*, March 12, 1981, p. 30.

Lewis, Richard Warren. "Thwack: There's Nothing Subtle About Chad Everett's Tennis Game—Or His Life Style." *TV Guide*, March 8, 1975, p. 26.

Lochte, Dick. "He Falls Down a Lot." *TV Guide*, Feb. 24, 1973, pp. 20–24.

"Look-Listen Opinion Poll Names *Medical Center* as Most Liked Television Program." CBS-TV Press Release, March 23, 1971.

Loyd, Ray. "Norman Felton Explodes Past; Says *Playhouse 90* Had to go." *Hollywood Reporter*, May 21, 1968.

"*M*A*S*H* Note for Doctors." *Time*, May 28, 1979, p. 68.

Maddox, Darrell. "How They Keep TV Medical Shows Honest." *Modern Healthcare*, Nov. 1975, pp. 37–42.

Magill, Frank N. *Magill's Survey of Cinema*. Vol. 1, Englewood Cliffs, N.J.: Salem Press, 1980.

Magulies, Lee. "Hoping for Series Life in the *AfterMASH*." *Los Angeles Times*, Life section, pp. 1ff (found undated in the files of the Television Information Office Library).

"Making Movies with the World's Most Famous Sisters." *Woman's Home Companion*, June 1939, p. 21.

Maltin, Leonard. *TV Movies*. New York: New American Library, 1980.

"The Man behind the *Medic*." *Look*, Nov. 30, 1954, p. 100.

"Many Are Filmed but Few Are Chosen." *TV Guide*, April 21, 1962, pp. 24–27.

"Mark, Norman. "How Television Tries to Close the Health Information Gap." *Today's Health*, Jan. 1976, pp. 31–52.

Markham, Lois. "How to Make Commercial TV Work for You." *Scholastic Teacher*, Nov./Dec. 1974, pp. 8–11.

Martin, Pete. "*Marcus Welby, M.D.*" *Saturday Evening Post*, (Fall 1971), 58 ff.

McLaughlin, James. "Characteristics and Symbolic Functions of Fictional Television Medical Professionals and Their Effect on Children." Master's Thesis, Annenberg School of Communications, University of Pennsylvania, 1975.

McLaughlin, James. "The Doctor Shows." *Journal of Communication*, Summer 1975, pp. 182–84.

"*Medic*, New NBC Show, Dramatizes Case Histories in Mature Style." *New York Times*, Sep. 15, 1954, p. 48.

"*Medical Center*." CBS-TV Press Release, July 18, 1972.

"Medicine and Long Hair." CBS-TV Press Release, May 5, 1971.

"Medicine in the Movies. *Hygeia*, June 1939, pp. 487–89.

"Metro to Continue Lew Ayres Films." *New York Times*, April 3, 1942, p. 3.

Meyerhoff, Barbara, and William R. Larson. "The Doctor Culture Hero: The Routinization of Charisma." *Human Organization* 24 (Fall 1965), 188–91.

Meyers, Jeffrey. *Disease and the Novel.* New York: St. Martin's Press, 1985.

"Michael Learned Gets Inside New Character." CBS Television Network Press Release, March 13, 1981.

Mitford, Jessica. "The Disease That Dr. Kildare Couldn't Cure." *Redbook* (Sep. 1965), pp. 102ff.

Moffitt, Ellis. "What's Ahead for Physicians." *American Medical News,* Oct. 12, 1984, p. 4.

Montgomery, Kathryn. *Target: Prime Time.* New York: Oxford University Press, forthcoming.

Musel, Robert. "You Have to Look After Yourself." *TV Guide,* April 21, 1962, pp. 24–27.

"My Son, the Doctor." *TV Guide,* Dec. 16–22, 1961, p. 16.

"Nation's Critics Praise *St. Elsewhere.*" NBC Television Publicity Release, Nov. 12, 1982.

Neeson, Stella. "Mysticism Lost." *JAMA* 232:4 (April 28, 1975), 374–76.

"New ABC Television Network Series *Dial Hot Line* Gets New Number—Now Called 'Matt Lincoln.' " ABC-TV Press Release, June 8, 1970.

"New ABC Television Series *Matt Lincoln* Begins Production." ABC-TV Press Release, June 12, 1970.

"New Hospital Series." *New York Daily News,* June 25, 1986, p. 71.

"New Male Stars Will Give *The Nurses* Broader Spectrum of Dramatic Interest." CBS Press Release, Aug. 19, 1964.

"New Prescription for TV Magazine." *Journal America,* Aug. 22, 1965, TV Magazine, p. 36.

Newcomb, Horace, and Paul Hirsch. "Television as a Cultural Forum," in W. Rowland and B. Watkins (eds.), *Interpreting Television.* Beverly Hills: Sage Publications, 1985.

"Nine More Segments of Acclaimed *St. Elsewhere* Ordered." NBC Television Publicity Release, Dec. 6, 1982.

"*Novak-Kildare* VD Two-Partner Axed by NBC-TV." *Variety,* Oct. 7, 1964.

O'Connor, John J. "TV: *Nurse* Back as 6-Part Series with Same Stars." *New York Times,* April 2, 1981, p. C-20.

O'Connor, John. "TV: New on NBC, Two Comedies and *Medical Story.*" *New York Times,* Sep. 4, 1975, p. 70.

O'Toole, Lawrence. "Farewell to the Gang at the Front." *Maclean's,* Feb. 28, 1980, pp. 46–47.

Oakie, Susan. "Art Imitates Life and Death." *Washington Post,* Feb. 5, 1986, Health section, pp. 12–14.

"Our Man in Hollywood." *Advance: The Magazine of the University of Michigan Medical School, Hospitals, and School of Nursing,* Summer 1982, pp. 9–13.

Parish, Robert, and Gregory W. Mank. *The Best of MGM: The Golden Years, 1928–59.* Westport, Conn.: Arlington House, 1981.

"People Lose Faith in Our Program." *America,* March 12, 1956, p. 683.

"Pep Pills for *Dr. Kildare.*" *TV Guide,* Dec. 11–17, 1965, pp. 10–12.

Philpott, Newel. "Doctors and the Present Challenge." *Journal of Medical Education* 34 (Oct. 1959), 1033–34.

Poirer, Normand. "Robert Young, Wife in Hospital After Collapse." *New York Post,* Nov. 5, 1966, p. 4.

"Popular *Emergency!* Series to Continue on NBC-TV Next Season." NBC-TV Press Release, Feb. 19, 1976.

Pryor, Gabriel. "Crackup Ahead for TV's Psychos?" *New York Mirror Magazine,* June 2, 1963, p. 10.

"*Quincy* Team Honored by Plastic Surgeons' Group." NBC-TV Press Release, Jan. 18, 1979.

Reiss, David S. "Alan Alda: His Road to Success and Love." *Good Housekeeping,* Nov. 1980, pp. 150ff.

Reiss, David S. *M*A*S*H.* Indianapolis and New York: Bobbs-Merrill, 1980.

Rennie, Drummond, M.D. "What You Can Learn About Health from TV." *Today's Health,* Jan. 1973, pp. 22–26.

"Report of Board of Trustees." *JAMA* 178:2 (Oct. 14, 1961), 159–60.

"Review of 'Panic in Echo Park.' " *Daily Variety,* 1976.

"Review of *Diagnosis Unknown.*" *TV Guide,* Aug. 13–19, 1960, p. 27.

"Review of *Doctor Kildare Goes Home.*" *Commonweal,* Sep. 27, 1940, p. 470.

"Review of *Doctor Kildare Goes Home.*" *Time,* Sep. 30, 1940, pp. 74–75.

"Review of *Dr. Kildare's Wedding Day.*" *Variety,* Aug 20, 1941, p. 9.

"Review of *Medic.*" *TV Guide,* April 30, 1955, p. 21.

"Review of *Medical Center.*" *Variety,* Oct. 1971, p.

"Review of *The Citadel* and *Young Dr. Kildare.*" *Time,* Nov. 7, 1938, p. 41.

"Review of *The Nurses.*" *Variety,* Oct. 2, 1963, p. 39.

"Review of *Young Doctor Kildare.*" *Time,* Nov. 7, 1938, p. 41.

Rich, John. "*M*A*S*H.*" *TV Guide,* Aug. 30, 1975, p. 28.

"Richard Chamberlain: TV's Doctor Kildare." *Look,* Nov. 20, 1962, pp. 137–45.

Richardson, Darrell, C. *Max Brand: The Man and His Work.* Los Angeles: Fantasy Publishing, 1952.

Richmond, Ray. "An Autopsy on *AfterMASH.*" *Los Angeles Times,* Sep. 22, 1983, Life Section, pp. 1ff, 8.

Rintels, David. "Will Marcus Welby Always Make You Well?" *New York Times,* March 12, 1972, Section 2, p. 1.

Robbins, Jack. "Robert Young: Now Doctor Knows Best." *New York Post,* Nov. 1, 1969, p. 29.

Rothenberg, Fred. "NBC's *St. Elsewhere:* It's 100 Times Healthier," *New York Post,* Nov. 19, p. 71.

Rotherberg, Fred. "*St. Elsewhere* Deserves Many Happy Returns." (*New York Post* article from the 1983 fall premiere period found, undated, in the files of the Television Information Office Library).

Rouse, Milford, M.D. "Joys and Problems of Being a Doctor," *Today's Health,* June 1967, pp. 58, 72.

Rowland, Willard. *The Politics of TV Violence.* Beverly Hills: Sage Publications, 1982.

Rowland, Williard, Jr., and Bruce Watkins (eds.). *Interpreting Television.* Beverly Hills: Sage Publications, 1984.

Rowsome, Frank, Jr. *They Laughed When I Sat Down: An Informal History of Advertising in Words and Pictures.* New York: Crown, 1959.

Schorr, Thelma. "Nursing's TV Image." *American Journal of Nursing* 63, No. 10 (Oct. 1963), 119–21.

Schroeder, Carl. "Robert Young: TV's Doctor Welby." *Good Housekeeping* (June 1971), 43–48.

Schudson, Michael. "The Politics of Lou Grant." *Society*, Jan./Feb. 1980, pp. 83–85.

Scott, Vernon. "Psychiatry Series Slated for Fall." *World-Telegram & Sun*, July 16, 1962, p. 25.

Seligman, Daniel. "Klugmanism." *Fortune*, April 20, 1981, pp. 97–98.

Seligman, Daniel. "Operating on Economics." *Fortune*, June 2, 1980, p. 42.

Seligson, Tom. "The Private Triumph of Robert Young." *Parade*, Aug. 11, 1985, pp. 4–5.

Shales, Tom. "Medical Story: On the Danger List?" *Washington Post*, Sep. 25, 1975, p. E14.

Shayon, Robert Lewis. "Report from West Point." Unpublished manuscript, 1963, in Robert Lewis Shayon Archive at Boston University.

Shayon, Robert Lewis. "The Bridge at West Point." *Saturday Review*, May 25, 1963, p. 41.

Shem, Samuel, M.D. *The House of God*. New York: Dell Publishing, 1978, pp. 9, 19.

"Sinking Fast." *Newsweek*, Nov. 26, 1962, p. 56.

Starr, Paul. *The Social Transformation of American Medicine*. New York: Basic Books, 1983.

Stevens, Rosemary. *American Medicine and the Public Interest*. New Haven: Yale Univ. Press, 1971.

"Strong Medicine." *TV Guide*, Oct. 9, 1954, p. 21.

"Studio Will Remake Lew Ayres Film Play." *New York Times*, April 17, 1942, p. 19.

"The Superdoctors on TV Do Disservice to Medicine." *National Observer*, Sep. 27, 1975, p. 10.

Symons, Julian. *Mortal Consequences: A History from the Detective Story to the Crime Novel*. New York: Harper and Row, 1972.

"Telepix Review." *Daily Variety*, March 27, 1969, p. 32.

Thompson, Sandra. "Is Doctor Welby a Menace to Women?" *Sunday Los Angeles Times* (found undated in UCLA Theater Arts Library pamphlet file).

Tilton, Patricia. "Behind the Nurse on TV." *American Journal of Nursing* 59, No. 12 (Dec. 1959), 1715–17.

"The Top 100 National Advertisers." *Advertising Age*, Sep. 4, 1986, p. 1.

Trautman, Joanne, and Carol Pollard. *Literature and Medicine: An Annotated Bibliography*. Revised Edition. Pittsburgh: Univ. of Pittsburgh Press, 1982.

Turow, Joseph. "Another View of Citizen Feedback to the Mass Media." *Public Opinion Quarterly* 41 (1977–78), 534–43.

Turow, Joseph. "Coverage of Health Subjects in the Evening News, 1969–71." Unpublished research, 1985.

Turow, Joseph. "Cultural Argumentation in the Mass Media: A Framework for Organization Research," *Communication* 8 (1985), 139–64.

Turow, Joseph. "The Influence of Pressure Groups on Television Entertainments," in W. Rowland and B. Watkins (eds.), *Interpreting Television*. Beverly Hills: Sage Publications, 1985.

Turow, Joseph. *Media Industries: The Production of News and Entertainment*. New York: Longman, 1984.

"TV Show Cancels Childbirth Film." *New York Times*, March 11, 1956, p. 84.

"TV's Censored Caesarian." *Variety*, March 14, 1956, p. 24.

"TV's Quadruple Threat." *Newsweek,* Sep. 9, 1974, pp. 52–53.

"United States Senator Alan Cranston Lauds *Emergency!*" NBC-TV Press Release (no date).

"U.S. Advertising Dollars by Media." *Advertising Age,* Sep. 24, 1987, p. 166.

Vanocur, Sander. "The 'Quincy' Statement." *Washington Post,* May 22, 1977, p. L3.

"VD on TV?" *Time,* Nov. 30, 1964, p. 62.

Vecsey, George. "Alan Alda: Madcap Doctor from *M*A*S*H.*" *Reader's Digest,* Aug. 1979, pp. 69–73.

"Ward Watch." *Newsweek,* Mar. 26, 1962, pp. 82–83.

Watts, Malcolm. "The US Way of Doing Things." *American Medical News,* March 16, 1984, p. 4.

Whitney, Dwight. "Vince Baby Plays It Cool." *TV Guide,* Feb. 18–24, 1967, pp. 6–9.

Wildavsky, Aaron. "Doing Better and Feeling Worse: The Political Pathology of Health Policy." *Daedalus* 106:1 (Winter 1977), 105–25.

Williams, Bob. "MD Series Offers a Cure-All." *New York Post,* Sep. 4, 1975, p. 58.

Williams, Bob. "On the Air." *New York Post,* March 27, 1969 (found unpaged in the files of the Television Information Office Library).

Wilson, Robert W. "The Physician's Changing Hospital Role." *Human Organization,* 1959–60, p. 178.

Witbeck, Charles. "Real Live Nursing on TV." *New York Daily Column,* Feb. 27, 1970, Fold-out section.

Wolters, Larry. "The TV Doctors." *Today's Health,* Oct. 1962, p. 24.

Wright, Phyllis, M.D. "I'm Dr. Kildare's Doctor." *Redbook,* Sep. 1963, p. 142.

"Young Viewers Benefit from Practical Tips Offered by NBC-TV's *Emergency!*" NBC-TV Press Release, Sep. 4, 1973.

"Youngsters Benefit from *Emergency!* Series." NBC-TV Press Release, March 13, 1974.

Index